INDIA, PAKISTAN, *and the* KASHMIR DISPUTE

Also by Robert G. Wirsing

INTERNATIONAL RELATIONS AND THE FUTURE OF OCEAN SPACE (*editor*)

PAKISTAN'S SECURITY UNDER ZIA, 1977–1988

PROTECTION OF ETHNIC MINORITIES: Comparative Perspectives (*editor*)

SOCIALIST SOCIETY AND FREE ENTERPRISE POLITICS: A Study of Voluntary Associations in Urban India

R

INDIA, PAKISTAN, *and the* KASHMIR DISPUTE

On Regional Conflict and Its Resolution

ROBERT G. WIRSING

ST. MARTIN'S PRESS
NEW YORK

INDIA, PAKISTAN, AND THE KASHMIR DISPUTE:
ON REGIONAL CONFLICT AND ITS RESOLUTION

ISBN 0–312–17562–0 paperback

Library of Congress Cataloging-in-Publication Data

Wirsing, Robert.
India, Pakistan, and the Kashmir dispute : on regional conflict and its resolution / Robert G. Wirsing.
p. cm.
Includes index.
ISBN 0–312–08442–0 (cloth) 0–312–17562–0 (pbk.)
1. Jammu and Kashmir (India) — Politics and government. 2. India — Foreign relations — Pakistan. 3. Pakistan — Foreign relations — India. I. Title.
DS485.K27W57 1994
327.5405491—dc20 94–25862
CIP

Interior design by Harry Katz

First published in hardcover in the United States of America in 1994
First St. Martin's paperback edition: February 1998
10 9 8 7 6 5 4 3 2 1

For Nancy

Contents

List of Maps

List of Tables

ACKNOWLEDGMENTS

Research for this book was supported by timely and generous grants from the United States Institute of Peace (1990), the Office of Research of the U.S. Department of State (1991, 1993), and the Department of Government and International Studies, University of South Carolina (summer 1991). To all three of these organizations, I wish to express my sincere thanks. The opinions, findings, and conclusions or recommendations expressed in this book are, of course, those of the author alone and do not necessarily reflect the views of the grantor agencies.

For their meticulous care and skill in the preparation of maps, I owe special thanks to Jerald S. Ulrey, Staff Cartographer, Department of Geography, University of South Carolina, and William W. Bain, a talented and amazingly resourceful undergraduate student in the Department of Government and International Studies. I thank also Roger Moore, a graduate student in the same department, for his invaluable assistance with research at a key point in the book's writing.

I owe a substantial debt of gratitude too to Alastair Lamb, who generously and perceptively commented on the final draft of the manuscript.

I am grateful to the librarians and staffs of the following institutions: the India Office Library and Records in London; the Geography and Map Reading Room of the Library of Congress in Washington, D.C.; the Institute for Defence Studies and Analyses in New Delhi; and the Institute of Regional Studies in Islamabad. As so often in the past, I benefitted greatly during recent research visits to India from the facilities and hospitality of the India International Centre in New Delhi.

I wish to express appreciation to Westview Press and to the editor of *Indian Defence Review* for granting me permission to draw from writings of mine published earlier by them.

Simon Winder, my editor for a second time at St. Martin's Press, I thank for his patience, encouragement, and invariably good advice at all stages of the book's progress.

Warmest thanks of all go to the scores of people—military officers, politicians, government officials, academics, diplomats, and others—who, in interviews, briefings, and informal conversations during my research visits to India and Pakistan over a period of several years, enriched my knowledge and understanding of the Kashmir conflict. I could not possibly have drawn conclusions about this conflict that would satisfy Pakistanis, Indians, and

Kashmiris alike. I can only hope that my effort to be fair to their views is apparent. The names of those formally interviewed are listed in an appendix. My debt to all of them is incalculable.

My wife, Nancy, who completed a book of her own while I finished this one and who knows all too well the agonies and the ecstasies of authorship, I thank in the most heartfelt way for her constant support, lively mind, and loving companionship. I dedicate this book to her with deep affection.

Columbia, S.C., January 1994
R.G.W.

INDIA, PAKISTAN,
and the
KASHMIR DISPUTE

INTRODUCTION

Modern European imperialism compelled a fundamental redrafting of the political map of the Asian and African lands that had been brought under colonial rule piecemeal from the seventeenth century onward. By the start of the twentieth century, this redrafting had succeeded in superimposing on this vast area boundaries that had been decided in large part in European capitals, in accord with knowledge derived from European explorers and cartographic surveys, on the basis of European criteria of territorial possession, and in deference to the balance of political and military power prevailing among European states. These new boundaries were relatively unmindful of the customary notions of territorial possession that had stood for centuries in this area before the arrival of the Europeans; and the physical scale of the territories they encompassed took little account of the ethnic loyalties of the people included within them.

Map 1

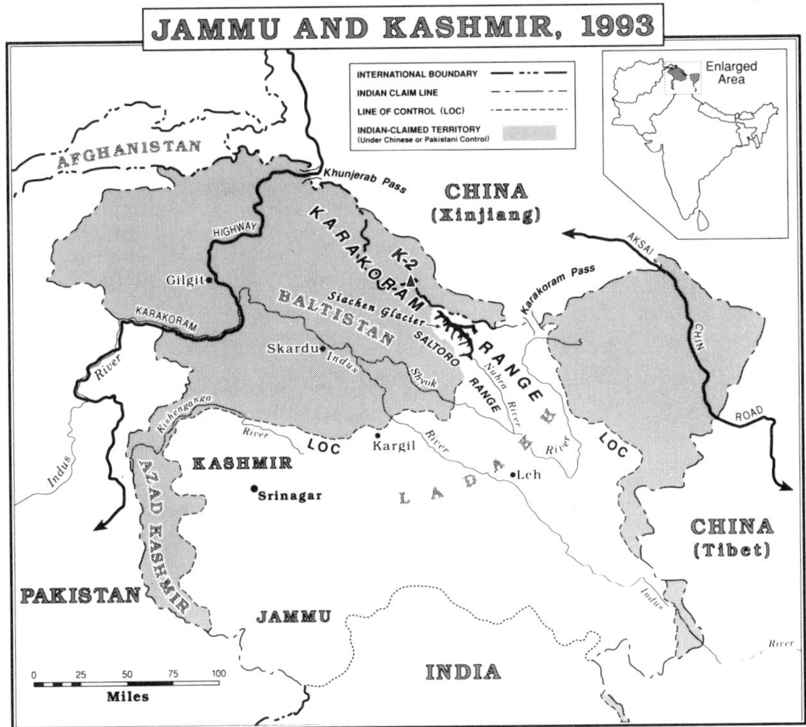

With imperialism's retreat in the second half of the twentieth century, the map of this part of the world was once again substantially redrawn. The redrawing took place with the myriad pressures and contradictions of decolonization weighing heavily upon it and more often than not under circumstances that precluded consistent observance of rational rules of territorial delimitation. Happily, this reallocation of territorial sovereignty, even when it seemed to tear cohesive and long-standing cultures in two and to place them—permanently—on two sides of an international border, was in most places accepted without major complaint by the indigenous inheritors of power. In a number of cases, however, the end of colonial rule left in its wake serious disputes over the placement of the new boundaries. These disputes had differing roots, were of differing types, and were far from uniform in the degree of resistance they put up against negotiated settlement. Of those that have persisted as major sources of international conflict into the last decade of the twentieth century, none was more complicated, more multifaceted, or more pregnant with potent material consequences for the contending successor states than the dispute over Kashmir between India and Pakistan. None, furthermore, has stimulated a greater flood of documentation or a larger (or intellectually more compelling) literature, or prompted more heated argument than this one. And none, it can safely be said, has better embodied the chilling truth of a geographer's observation, made on the eve of World War II, that "the study of boundaries is dangerous . . . because it is thoroughly charged with political passions and entirely encumbered with afterthoughts. The people are too interested in the issues when they speak of boundaries to speak with detachment: the failing is permanent!"[1]

The Kashmir dispute was born amid circumstances that were uniquely well tailored to stir up bitter controversy. Within the jurisdictionally complex framework of the British Indian empire, Kashmir had retained quasi-autonomous status in a feudal arrangement that placed a Hindu maharaja in control of an overwhelmingly Muslim principality. British authority (or "paramountcy") over Kashmir and the other princely states of the subcontinent lapsed at independence in August 1947. The decision on whether Kashmir would opt for Hindu-majority India or Muslim-majority Pakistan, in line with the rules for partitioning British India agreed upon by the British and the two successor governments, thus fell to the then ruling prince—Maharaja Hari Singh. Preferring Kashmir's independence over accession to either India or Pakistan, he delayed making a decision until after Britain's withdrawal. His procrastination was fateful: It offered a tempting opportunity to each of the newly empowered governments of India and Pakistan to endeavor, by whatever means were available, to subvert the maharaja's ability to make an unfettered choice. Neither government resisted the temptation. The maharaja came under heavy pressure from both. Consequently, when a decision favoring India finally came in late October 1947, it was instantly rejected as unfair, fraudulent, and nonbinding by the losing Pakistani side. The Pakistanis have never relented from this position. Neither have the Indians been willing to abandon their own.

The resulting standoff over Kashmir has continued for over 46 years. This standoff has borne a heavy share of responsibility for two wars between India and Pakistan, for the massive arming of both sides, and for the entanglement of both in Cold War alliances. It has inflicted immeasurable costs on their social, economic, and political systems; and it has been an enormous impediment to the normalization of relations between them. With the passage of time, moreover, it does not seem to have lost any of its capacity to generate the most intense distrust and hatred between them. Serious students of international boundary conflict will understand, then, that I undertake a study of the Kashmir dispute with a strong sense of the necessity for treating the controversies imbedded in it with about the same amount of precaution exercised by those in the unquestionably hazardous profession of disarming live explosives.

This book departs from most previous studies of the Kashmir dispute in two ways. One is its fairly heavy emphasis on *current* developments (the last decade or so) in this dispute. This does not imply a deliberate downgrading by the author of the importance of developments occurring in the first years of the dispute's history. On the contrary, knowledge of those developments remains acutely relevant to a contemporary understanding of the dispute. They are examined in this book, necessarily, in some detail. What it does signify, however, is the author's strong conviction that the Kashmir dispute, in the past decade or so, has entered a fundamentally new phase in its history, that it has undergone a number of fundamental mutations in this new phase, and that this phase therefore merits particularly careful examination in its own right.[2]

This new phase is distinguished by three profoundly important sets of changes in the geopolitical context of the Kashmir dispute. The first consists of changes in the *internal* political and military environment of Kashmir itself. By this is meant, on the one hand, the emergence and spread since 1989 of a powerful separatist movement among India's Kashmiri Muslims, and, on the other, India's massive military response to it. Together these two developments have brought violence and popular alienation from government on a scale hitherto unknown in Kashmir. They have focused attention as never before on the issue of Kashmiri political rights, including the right of Kashmiri Muslims either to assert their full independence or to identify themselves politically with Pakistan. They have, moreover, made India more vulnerable to embarrassing international criticism of its human rights record at the same time as they have vastly magnified opportunities for Pakistan's crossborder intervention on behalf of its Kashmiri coreligionists. They have forcefully injected into the political equation of Kashmir a new, Kashmiri, actor; and they have made of the Kashmir dispute a domestic as much as an international conflict.

The second set consists of changes in the *regional* political and military environment of India-Pakistan relations. These include the transformation of India and Pakistan into nuclear or near-nuclear weapon states; the acquisition by both countries of advanced ballistic missile capabilities; the Indian army's successful deployment of mountain-trained troops in spring 1984 onto the Siachen Glacier at the northern edge of Kashmir and the waging since then of an extremely costly, high-altitude, and prolonged miniwar between India and Pakistan; Pakistan's conversion to civilian rule; the rise of Hindu nationalism in India; and India's conversion to an unstable multiparty system. These developments do not point inexorably in any single direction. They present opportunities for a more peaceful and cooperative subcontinent alongside those for a more conflicted one. On the whole, however, they do not describe an increasingly secure and stable environment, nor one whose immediate political or military future lends itself to prediction. They may well increase the prospects of war.

The third set consists of changes in the *extraregional* or *global* political and military environment of India-Pakistan relations. These include Moscow's retreat from Afghanistan and the end of the Cold War; the breakup of the Soviet Union and the emergence of a new tier of independent Islamic states in Central Asia; the virtual collapse of Moscow's defense relationship with India; China's conversion to a market economy and its swift transformation into a regional superpower; the emergence of new global norms in regard to the protection of ethnic minorities and the observance of human rights; and the cutoff of American military assistance to Pakistan. As with the preceding set, this third set of changes does not point fixedly in any one direction. On the contrary, it is notable mainly for the volatility of the political and military circumstances to which it has given birth. It has endowed Kashmir's neighborhood with a whole new cast of international actors, given new meaning to China's military occupation of part of Kashmir, raised disturbing questions about American intentions in Kashmir, and in general produced uncertainties in regard to Kashmir's Asian neighborhood that are matched in their scope and intensity by no other region on the planet.

Taken together, these three sets of changes have given the Kashmir dispute a dramatically new character. Appreciation of these changes is vital to an understanding of the Kashmir dispute in the present decade. This book seeks to meet this need.

A second way in which this book departs from most previous studies of the Kashmir dispute is in the systematic attention it gives to the problem of *resolving* it—especially to the *current* problem of resolving it. This approach guided research, and it fundamentally shaped the book's structure and content. Only so much of the historical record is included, for instance, as is required to respond to the questions: What are the basic issues in this dispute, and how did they develop? How do the rivals in this dispute view these issues? What is their negotiability? Why have they for so long resisted settlement? And what are potentially more fruitful ways to deal with them? A conscious effort is made to keep the perspective current and analytical. By the same token, full recognition is given to the dispute's multiple dimensions: It is a separatist as much as a boundary problem; it poses questions of human rights no less than of border security; and its resolution must take account of domestic politics and policy every bit as much as of international politics and diplomacy. Motivating the book is the author's judgment that most previous discussions of the Kashmir dispute have been content merely to chronicle the record of international mediation efforts and bilateral negotiations, or have dealt with resolution in abstract, often utopian terms, or have bypassed the subject altogether. Obviously, the problem of resolution has been an integral part of this dispute from its beginnings; and whatever may be the immediate or long-term prospects for settlement, this problem, this author is convinced, needs to be understood.

This book is organized in four parts. Part I is focused specifically on the boundary problem. Three aspects of this problem are analyzed: Chapters 1 and 2 focus, respectively, on entitlement and delimitation issues stemming from the rival territorial claims in Kashmir of India and Pakistan; Chapter 3 moves the discussion to consider strategic questions arising from rival Chinese and Indian boundary claims in the Aksai Chin area of Ladakh. Part II focuses on the ethnic separatist problem in the Indian state of Jammu and Kashmir. Chapter 4 examines the Kashmiri Muslim uprising that began in earnest late in 1989; Chapter 5, the counterinsurgency operations undertaken in response to the uprising by India's security forces; and Chapter 6, the struggle by New Delhi to formulate an appropriate domestic policy for Kashmir.

In Part III the discussion turns fully to the problem of settlement. Alternative approaches (multilateral, third-party, and bilateral) are explored in Chapter 7; alternative solutions (partition, modification of sovereignty, autonomy, independence) are compared and evaluated in Chapter 8.

Part IV concludes the book with two sets of recommendations. The first set, aimed at U.S. policymakers, is set forth in Chapter 9. The second set, aimed at Indian and Pakistani policymakers, is presented in Chapter 10. These two chapters will make clear that the author takes a very conservative view of the potential of India and Pakistan for resolving the conflict over Kashmir, at least in the near term. From the restrained language used in considering an appropriate American role, they should also make clear that he harbors no grandiose expectations about Washington's potential for ending it.

These final chapters do clearly affirm, however, that the possibility exists for making at least partial or incremental progress in the direction of a fair and peaceful settlement of the Kashmir dispute. This possibility can be considerably expanded, the author believes, if the principal disputants—the governments of India and Pakistan—can be persuaded to launch their countries' most able, independent, and imaginative intellectuals upon a fresh and unfettered reexamination of this dispute—in particular of ways in which these governments can extricate themselves from the present deadlock without excessive injury either to the national interests of India and Pakistan or to the right of self-determination of the peoples of Kashmir. This book is meant to contribute to such a project.

Part I

The Boundary Problem

In Part I, our task is, first, to identify and define the fundamental boundary-related issues that are in contention today over Kashmir; and second, to present clearly and to evaluate as fairly as we can the arguments advanced on various sides in regard to these issues. The purpose is diagnostic. If we succeed at this, we will have laid part of the foundation for later discussion focusing on the problem of designing a peaceful settlement of the dispute.

The issues themselves are grouped under three headings: those relating more or less specifically to questions of territorial entitlement are dealt with in Chapter 1; those relating more directly to boundary delimitation are taken up in Chapter 2; and those relating primarily to the strategic context of the dispute are addressed in Chapter 3. Our method is analytical rather than historical: Only as much of the historical background and record is included as is essential for grasping these issues and for judging the quality of the debate that has been carried on in regard to them. Throughout the discussion the primary focus is on the arguments and counterarguments in this debate and on the ways in which they have shaped and complicated the search for settlement over time.

CHAPTER

·1·

ENTITLEMENT ISSUES

The Kashmir dispute is obviously not just about the positioning of a line on a map. Even at its outset in 1947 it held meanings that went well beyond that; and since then it has helped to shape, and in turn been shaped by, practically all aspects of the relationship between India and Pakistan. It has had a profound effect not only on the development of their foreign policies, in both bilateral and multilateral settings, but on their domestic political evolution as well. Its symbolic impact (on the content of their respective national ideologies, for instance) has certainly been considerable, and its substantive impact—whether in terms, for example, of demography, economic development, the conduct of national politics, defense expenditure, or the framing of military strategy—has doubtless been enormous. Nevertheless, it *is* a boundary dispute, and at its core are the same sorts of questions in regard to the allocation of territories and location of boundaries as have conventionally been addressed by geographers and others specializing in boundary problems.[1] We thus begin our study of the Kashmir dispute by taking a close look at its boundary dimension.

This dimension of the dispute is itself highly complex. More than most boundary disputes around the world, this one is entangled with other major boundary disputes, involving China and Afghanistan, and—at least in the case of the Sino-Indian border problem—these other disputes present serious problems in their own right. Claims and counterclaims in regard to the location of the boundary present a bewildering cartographic problem, made all the more confusing by the area's complicated ethnography and equally complicated political history. Kashmir's boundaries have been fought over, violently and with little pause, ever since independence. Practically everything about them is in dispute, not just their location but their legality, their naming, their functions, and whether they even exist.

Our examination of the boundary dimension of the Kashmir dispute is divided into two parts. In this chapter, the focus is on problems arising from differences between India and Pakistan over *territorial entitlement,* that is, over original rights to territory. In the following chapter, we examine problems arising from differences over *the delimitation of boundaries.*

State claims to disputed territory have historically been grounded in a diverse array of factors, including territorial contiguity and proximity, natural geographic barriers, preservation of territorial integrity, economic linkages, military conquest, physical presence (past or current), strategic requirements, compensation for past injury, treaty obligations, ethnic similarity, and popular preference.[2] Nearly all of these have been introduced into the Kashmir dispute at one time or another by advocates of either the Indian or Pakistani side since the dispute's inception in 1947. Those making the case for Pakistan, for instance, have placed great emphasis on the predominantly Muslim composition of Kashmir, on the area's physical contiguity with Pakistan, and on the moral and legal right of the Kashmiri people to self-determination. But they have also built the case in terms of natural geographic features, traditional trade patterns, Pakistan's strategic vulnerabilities, and—pointing, for example, to the alleged failure of Maharaja Hari Singh of Jammu and Kashmir, in agreeing to Indian military intervention in the state in October 1947, to fulfill obligations under the standstill agreement executed between his government and Pakistan on Independence Day in the preceding August—the sanctity of treaty obligations.[3] Those making the case for India, on the other hand, while giving particular emphasis to the presumed legality of Kashmir's accession to India, have also pointed to the preferences of the Kashmiri people, India's inherited strategic role as guardian of the subcontinent's northern frontiers, and—turning Pakistani arguments upon themselves—Pakistan's abrogation of its own treaty obligations under the standstill agreement executed between itself and the state of Jammu and Kashmir.[4]

More than has usually been the case in territorial disputes, arguments over Kashmir coming from both sides have focused with particular consistency on specifically legal issues—on the question of to which country Kashmir *should* belong (by right of law), in other words, rather than on the question of which country's claims were more *appropriate* (by virtue of geography, ethnicity, economy, and so on).[5] This may be attributed in part to the fact that India and Pakistan's founding fathers were mainly men thoroughly steeped in the law; but it more likely resulted from the unique character of the process by which Great Britain transferred power to the successor states of the British Indian Empire. That process, in contrast with the experience of many other colonized areas, was determined down to the minutest detail through peaceful negotiation between the departing British and those inheriting power from them; and it was driven to an extraordinary extent by concern for constitutional propriety. Moreover, it was played out immediately after a disastrous world war that had left in its wake an understandable global preoccupation with the need for orderly change. That the process of transferring power was barely finished when the issue of Kashmir landed in the lap of the Security Council in the newly fashioned United Nations organization surely helped to reinforce the legalistic tendencies that were already strongly evident in the argumentation over Kashmir.

In spite of the dispute's oversized legal underpinnings, no effort has ever been made by the international community formally to fix responsibility for its emergence. No agency representing the international community has ever conducted an open independent investigation of it; and the dispute has never been submitted to an international tribunal of any kind for arbitration. The Security Council, on whose agenda the Kashmir dispute has remained ever since being lodged there in January 1948, has functioned formally in regard to it exclusively in a mediatory and not arbitral capacity. Never did it pronounce final judgment on any of the fundamental questions arising from this dispute. Hence, none of the issues relating to territorial entitlement has ever been formally adjudicated; and in regard to the details of these issues, no single rendering can be considered authoritative. This, of course, does not mean that systematic exposition of the territorial entitlement problem has been neglected. On the contrary, there now exists a very large corpus of published official documentation (Indian, Pakistani, British, United Nations, and others) in addition to numerous unofficial accounts (including memoirs, biographies, diaries, correspondence, journalistic reportage, and scholarly examinations) in which entitlement issues are treated from many angles and in extraordinary detail. It does mean, however, that when it comes to assessing the reliability and accuracy of these materials, we are left largely on our own to sift through accounts that are often incomplete, inconsistent, and in the production of which fidelity to the truth has not infrequently been sacrificed to partisan causes. We thus venture forth to consider the problem of territorial entitlement fully aware that practically every inch of the way is mined with controversy and that in regard to practically no issue does a certifiably neutral and generally accepted juridical opinion now exist.

We focus our inquiry on three issues that have been at the heart of the controversy over entitlement from the outset: (1) the *conspiracy* issue stemming from allegations that Kashmir's absorption by India was aided by secret understandings and collusive arrangements involving Indian political leaders, representatives of Great Britain, and officials of the state of Jammu and Kashmir in the period immediately preceding partition; (2) the *aggression* issue stemming from allegations that official Pakistani support of Pashtun tribal invasions of Kashmir in the months following partition constituted an act of aggression, both precipitating and justifying Kashmir's accession to India as well as India's subsequent military intervention; and (3) the *plebiscite* issue stemming from allegations that Kashmir's accession to India was legally invalid and incomplete pending conduct of a popular plebiscite as promised by Indian leaders at the time of accession and as formally agreed to by them on repeated occasions thereafter.

PARTITION PHASE: THE CONSPIRACY ISSUE

On 30 December 1947, Pakistan's prime minister, Liaquat Ali Khan, addressed a lengthy letter to the Indian prime minister, Jawaharlal Nehru, in which he rebutted Indian charges, which were to be formally placed before the UN Security Council two days later, that the Pakistan government, in supplying assistance to tribal invaders of Kashmir, had committed an act of aggression against India. "The Pakistan Government," said Liaquat Ali Khan, "has not accepted and cannot accept the so-called 'accession' of the Jammu and Kashmir State to India. We have said it before and repeat that the 'accession' was fraudulent inasmuch as it was achieved by deliberately creating certain conditions, with the object of finding an excuse to stage the 'accession.'"[6]

Elsewhere in the letter the Pakistani prime minister complained that "large tracts of Muslim majority areas which under the Boundary Award had been most unjustly included in East Punjab were depopulated."[7] The inclusion of Muslim majority areas in East Punjab (within India, in other words) at the time of partition was not, in this letter, explicitly identified as one of the "certain conditions" created by India to ease the way to accession. But by the time the letter was written that connection had already become an article of faith, and it was thereafter to remain among the primary grounds offered by Pakistanis to explain their contention that they had been the victims of a carefully planned conspiracy to deprive Pakistan of its just entitlements under the partition agreements.

The award referred to in the letter was, of course, the report of the Punjab Boundary Commission, one of two commissions set up by Britain's last viceroy in India, Lord Louis Mountbatten, to determine the new boundaries of the two provinces, Punjab in the northwest and Bengal in the northeast, which were to be partitioned between India and Pakistan.[8] The necessity for their partitioning followed acceptance by the top leadership of both the Congress and Muslim League organizations of the so-called Mountbatten

Plan of 3 June 1947. This plan, which came after months of fruitless endeavors by the departing British to leave behind them a united India, outlined the procedures to be observed in the transfer of power. It also conceded, for the first time, the establishment of a fully separate and independent Muslim state of Pakistan. Incorporated in the Indian Independence Act approved by the British Parliament in mid-July, the plan called upon the two boundary commissions to partition Punjab and Bengal "on the basis of ascertaining the contiguous majority areas of Muslims and non-Muslims." In ascertaining the new boundaries, they were also instructed to take other—but unspecified—factors into account as well.[9] Until the report was finished, provisional boundaries based on existing and undivided districts of the two provinces and allocated on the criterion of contiguous Muslim numerical majority were to be used. These so-called notional boundaries were indicated in a 1941 census-based list of Muslim-majority districts of Punjab and Bengal contained in an appendix to the plan.[10] In the Indian Independence Act, these same Muslim-majority districts were identified once again, but this time even more explicitly as provisionally forming parts of the new provinces of West Punjab and East Bengal.[11] This allocation was explicitly said to be temporary, pending the outcome of the boundary commissions' deliberations. But publicized in the way they were, these provisional boundaries unquestionably helped to shape popular expectations of what that outcome would or should be.

Composition of the two commissions, which were to operate under the general chairmanship of the British jurist Sir Cyril Radcliffe, was announced on 30 June. There were two nominees of the Congress and two of the Muslim League on each of them. Radcliffe, who had never been in India before taking up this assignment, arrived in New Delhi on 8 July. The final decisions on the boundaries were necessarily to be his alone, since the party-nominated commissioners, as expected, failed entirely to reach agreement over the relevance of "other factors" in determining the boundaries. Faced with Mountbatten's last-minute decision to speed up the timetable for Britain's departure from India, Radcliffe moved swiftly and against the odds to complete his complicated and obviously delicate mission before the appointed 15 August deadline for the transfer of power. The final boundary awards were placed in the hands of Mountbatten's staff on 12 or 13 August—about 36 days after Radcliffe had begun his work. Radcliffe himself departed India on 15 August, never to return.

Mountbatten had wrung in advance from Nehru, Mohammad Ali Jinnah, and other political leaders a pledge to accept the award whatever their feelings might be about particular aspects of it. Its details were revealed to them on 16 August, the day following the transfer of power. Inevitably, it was coolly received and bitterly criticized. All sides, however, honored their commitment to Mountbatten. Jinnah, in a radio broadcast made on 31 August, soon after taking up his duties as governor-general of Pakistan, mirrored the disappointment in regard to the award that must have been shared by many on the Pakistan side at the time:

> The division of India is now finally and irrevocably effected. No doubt we feel that the carving out of this great independent Muslim State has suffered injustices. We have been squeezed in as much as it was possible, and the latest blow that we have received was the Award of the Boundary Commission. It is an unjust, incomprehensible and even perverse award. It may be wrong, unjust and perverse; and it may not be a judicial but a political award, but we have agreed to abide by it and it is binding upon us. As honourable people we must abide by it. It may be our misfortune but we must bear up this one more blow with fortitude, courage and hope.[12]

The Punjab Boundary Commission's writ did not extend to the state of Jammu and Kashmir, which was one of 565 semiautonomous princely states whose future following the departure of the British was to be decided separately through a process that allowed the princely leaders, at least in principle, the right to accede to either India or Pakistan, or even—though this was the focus of considerable controversy—to choose independence.[13] In practice, tremendous pressure was brought to bear on them to limit their choice to that of accession to one or other of the two successor states; and in all but a handful of cases their choices were duly made prior to the transfer of power and in conformity with the compulsions of their geographic location and demographic composition. Maharaja Sir Hari Singh, fourth in the line of Hindu Dogra rulers that had been granted title to the vast territories of Jammu and Kashmir by the British in 1846, ruled an area that was contiguous to both India and Pakistan but whose population was predominantly Muslim. Fatefully, he let Independence Day come and go without announcing his decision. And when he finally did decide, 72 days later, to accede to India, his decision seemed to Pakistanis not only to be a brutal betrayal of the contiguous communal majority principle underlying the entire project of partition, but also to confirm their already substantial doubts in regard to the motives underlying the boundary awards made by the chairman of the two boundary commissions. While the connection between the boundary award in the Punjab and the Maharaja's decision was thus obviously indirect, it fed controversy over the impartiality of that award that continues unabated to this day.

A main focus of that controversy has been the manner in which Radcliffe chose to dispose of Gurdaspur district, a Muslim-majority district in Punjab that adjoins the southern border of the state of Jammu and Kashmir. Gurdaspur, which reported a total population of about 1.14 million in the census of 1941 (slightly over 50 percent of it Muslim),[14] was among those districts listed in the Indian Independence Act provisionally in Pakistan's West Punjab. Radcliffe's award, released on 16 August, had based the new international boundary in large part on the line of the river Ravi running *through* Gurdaspur district, placing three of its four *tehsils* (subdistricts)—two of them (Batala and Gurdaspur) with substantial Muslim majorities—in India's East Punjab. Hindu-majority Pathankot *tehsil* went to India, Muslim-majority Shakargarh to Pakistan. Together with additional encroachments on the notional boundary in the territory southward from Gurdaspur, this meant that Radcliffe's award handed India a total of seven Muslim-majority *tehsils* (Gurdaspur, Batala, Ajnala, Jullundur, Nakodar, Ferozepur, and Zira) and part of another (Kasur). No non-Muslim-majority (Hindu or Sikh) *tehsil,* in contrast, was awarded to Pakistan in the Punjab.[15]

Neither in the boundary award itself nor later in his life did Radcliffe supply a full accounting of the reasoning that underlay his departure in Punjab from the principal of contiguous communal majority. In his award, he conceded that "the truly debatable ground in the end proved to lie in and around the area between the Beas and the Sutlej rivers on the one hand and the river Ravi on the other." He referred to a number of factors—among them the existence of canal, road, and rail systems and of "the stubborn geographical fact of the respective situations of Lahore and Amritsar, and the claims to each or both of those cities which each side vigorously maintained," the latter an oblique reference to rival claims by Sikhs and Muslims to these major urban centers—that had complicated the process of delimiting boundaries in these areas. He confessed that he had

> hesitated long over those not inconsiderable areas East of the Sutlej River and in the angle of the Beas and Sutlej Rivers in which Muslim majorities are found. But on the whole [he had] come to the conclusion that it would be in the true interests of neither State to extend the territories of the West Punjab to a strip on the far side of the Sutlej and that there are factors such as the disruption of railway communications and water systems that ought in this instance to displace the primary claims of contiguous majorities.[16]

With regard, in particular, to Gurdaspur district, Radcliffe explained the award of all but one *tehsil* to India exclusively in terms of the need to protect the integrity of the area's irrigation system. In this, he admitted, he was only partially successful; he had "not found it possible to preserve undivided the irrigation system of the Upper Bari Doab Canal, . . . although [he had] made small adjustments of the Lahore-Amritsar district boundary to mitigate some of the consequences of this severance."[17] The Madhopur headworks of the canals irrigating Amritsar district, a non–Muslim-majority area (and headquarters of the Sikh religious community) allotted to India, were in Gurdaspur district. Within days of his return to London, Radcliffe reaffirmed that his reason for dividing Gurdaspur district in the way he did was to ensure that "as much as possible of these canals [was kept] under one administration."[18]

Since Radcliffe upon his departure from India apparently destroyed his personal records of his deliberations, the field for speculation in regard to the actual influence of "other factors" on the allotment of territories was quite wide open. Pakistanis inevitably questioned the motivation for the particular decision in regard to Gurdaspur, since it seemed to them to create conditions on the border between now independent India and the coveted state of Jammu and Kashmir—whose future affiliation was yet to be decided—that favored or at least facilitated Kashmir's accession to India a few months after the boundary award was announced. Aside from containing the headwaters of the Upper Bari Doab Canal (UBDC) system, Gurdaspur district held a railhead and the only serviceable fair-weather road connection with Jammu and Kashmir then available on the Indian side. The ability of Indian military forces to defend the state, with access from the northern plains otherwise blocked by high mountains, would thus have been handicapped without it, at least until alternative routes had been developed.

Defense of the impartiality of the Gurdaspur decision has relied to a large extent on two main arguments.

The first of these is that the boundary decision was a practical response to compelling circumstances in the Punjab province itself, in anticipation of which the allowance for factors other than communal majority had been included in the instructions given to the boundary commissions. This argument Radcliffe had made in a general way, as pointed out, when he remarked in the award on the importance of protecting the integrity of rail and irrigation systems. No doubt, the threat to their integrity was a major problem in all of the districts of Punjab, including Gurdaspur, faced with partition. There were other and at least as compelling circumstances within the province, however, which Radcliffe also alluded to but which may have had an equal or even greater bearing than irrigation problems on the Gurdaspur decision. One of the Muslim members of the Punjab Boundary Commission, for instance, apparently believed that Radcliffe was primarily driven by his concern to avoid the geographic isolation of Amritsar district, which lay adjacent to Gurdaspur district on the south and which would be threatened, were district-level communal majority to govern the boundary decision, with being surrounded on three sides by a potentially hostile Muslim Pakistan.[19] The threat of massive communal violence was clearly developing in the Punjab while the Boundary Commission deliberated its fate. Widespread killing of Sikhs in the western part of Punjab had begun in January 1947, months before the Boundary Commission had even been formed; and Sikhs were being systematically mobilized into armed groups for purposes of revenge weeks before its final report was finished. A welter of utterly incompatible territorial demands affecting the Sikh homelands had been set before the Boundary Commission by the Congress, Muslim League, and Sikh leaders themselves.[20] No one involved in dividing that province could possibly have avoided reflecting on the implications of the division for the further spread of lawlessness. The Muslim numerical edge in Gurdaspur district was far from overwhelming; and the Sikh presence there—far larger in some *tehsils* than their overall percentage of the provincial population (14.3 percent)—could well have tempted appeasement. The Boundary Commission was under no obligation to adhere strictly to district (or even *tehsil*) boundaries, any more than to contiguous communal majority, in making the allocations. It is virtually inconceivable, therefore, that Radcliffe would ignore local circumstances in Punjab—the predicament of the Sikh community among them—in coming to his decision; and it certainly cannot be ruled out that they had a significant part in determining the content of his decision.

The second argument is that the alleged partisan political motivation for the boundary awards and for the Gurdaspur decision, in particular, was a fabrication, that the alleged connections between this decision and the later decision of Maharaja Hari Singh to accede to India were spurious, and that, in any event, credible documentary evidence to support a conspiracy theory in regard to the determination of the boundary awards has never come to light.

Some of those who have tended toward the Indian side of this issue have acknowledged that there was considerable direct strategic gain to India implicit in the Gurdaspur decision. Lord Birdwood, for example, a British army officer who served in British India, observed in a 1953 volume that "had the Gurdaspur District not been awarded to India, India could certainly never have fought a war in Kashmir."[21] Others, however, have held that the strategic gain was nothing to boast of. H. V. Hodson, a British author with close ties to Lord Mountbatten, has argued, for example, that

> the two main routes into Kashmir, via Rawalpindi and Murree and via Sialkot and the Banihal Pass, would in any case have gone to Pakistan. The Pathankot tahsil, which on any showing would have

> gone to India, had at that time no good road into Kashmir and Jammu, nor had the Gurdaspur tahsil, which, if it had gone to Pakistan, could have been bypassed by India in developing a new route into the State via Pathankot. The decisive action at the opening of the Kashmir warfare was accomplished by India with an airlift without over-flying any territory that could have been seriously disputed between India and Pakistan.[22]

Common to virtually all of India's supporters in the matter of the Gurdaspur decision, however, has been the contention that whatever strategic gain to India there may have been was strictly fortuitous, not the product of premeditated design. Any suggestion that Lord Mountbatten may have used his personal influence to pressure Radcliffe into modifying the Punjab boundary award in India's favor has been vehemently rejected. Cited as evidence by many in this connection was the assurance given by Alan Campbell-Johnson, Mountbatten's press secretary for his ten-month stay in India, that the viceroy "from the outset had given his staff the most explicit directions that they were to have no contact whatever with Radcliffe while he was engaged on his difficult and delicate arbitral task and has himself kept clear of him after the first welcome. We had accordingly no firm knowledge how far or by what route he had proceeded [in making the boundary awards]."[23]

It was freely admitted by the defenders of India's point of view that the proceedings of the boundary commissions had not been entirely secret and that some leakage in regard to the final awards had occurred prior to their official release. Michael Brecher, in an early and highly sympathetic biography of Nehru, conceded, for instance, that there clearly had been improprieties committed in the last stages of the Punjab Boundary Commission's work. The most notorious of these had to do with a sketch map, showing the probable boundary line in the Punjab award, that was sent in early August by the viceroy's private secretary, Sir George Abell, to Sir Evan Jenkins, who was then the governor of the undivided Punjab. As Brecher tells it, Jenkins sought information from Abell about the probable location of the new international boundary so that local civil authorities could be alerted and troops and police properly deployed in the Punjab's border districts prior to publication of the boundary award. Abell, writes Brecher,

> got in touch with the Secretary of the Radcliffe Commission and, on the basis of a telephone conversation, drew a sketch-map which was sent to Jenkins—along with the comment that the final, official Punjab Award would not be ready for a few days. The sketch-map showed the sub-districts of Ferozepur and Zira on the Pakistani side

of the line. In the official Radcliffe Award, however, these two areas were included in India.[24]

Jenkins left the map in his safe, where his successor later discovered it and turned it over to Pakistani authorities. The map, as Brecher describes it, was crudely drawn, and the areas shown on it were located well to the south of Gurdaspur district. But the Pakistanis assumed both that it was official and that it was the product of direct collusion between Radcliffe and the viceroy. From that point it was an easy logical step for them "to conclude that the Viceroy's influence was responsible for the decision to allocate Gurdaspur as well to India, thereby giving it a direct connection with Kashmir." Deriding all this as "The Sketch-Map Story," Brecher put the incident down to administrative bungling. He stoutly defended the integrity of both Radcliffe and Mountbatten, and insisted that the Pakistani complaint over Gurdaspur was "only an inference from an unproved allegation."[25]

In the first two decades or so of published works on the Kashmir dispute, Brecher's interpretation was shared not only by legions of Indian authors but by many of the most respected foreign (especially British) writers on Kashmir. Birdwood (1953), for example, declared that the "suspicion, even conviction, of Pakistanis that Radcliffe, with Lord Mountbatten, was guilty of a plot to deprive Pakistan of Kashmir, is most unfortunate. . . . Accusations of collaboration [were] certainly not to be accepted";[26] Hodson (1969) maintained that the sketch map was "not important" and that "no evidence of the influence or pressure which Lord Mountbatten is alleged to have brought on the Chairman of the Commission in those last days has yet been produced";[27] and Ian Stephens (1963), editor of *The Statesman* in India at the time of partition and often inclined to sympathize with Pakistan, confessed that when it came to the belief that "Lord Mountbatten or his entourage somehow influenced Sir Cyril Radcliffe towards finalising his Punjab Boundary Award detrimentally to Pakistan," the Pakistanis were wrong.[28] Even the British historian Alastair Lamb, whose recent work, as we shall see, provides the most convincing support yet for the conspiracy thesis, in his first work on Kashmir (1966) maintained (citing Brecher's biography of Nehru as his source) that "it is now clear that the Radcliffe award here [Gurdaspur district] was in no way related to the Kashmir question; rather, it was based on considerations arising from the division of the waters from certain canals."[29]

The "impartial partition" thesis, though very widely supported, naturally did not go unchallenged. Pakistani leaders had expressed serious reservations about the independence and neutrality of the Radcliffe boundary commissions even before the awards were made; and announcement of the awards inevitably turned these reservations into accusations. Chaudhri Muhammad Ali, who represented Pakistan on a key committee working under Mountbatten's Partition Council and who served as prime minister of Pakistan from 1955 to 1956, revealed in a book published in 1967, for instance, that Muslim League leader Mohammad Ali Jinnah a week prior to release of the boundary award "had received very disturbing reports about the likely decision on the Punjab boundary, particularly in the Gurdaspur district." Jinnah had asked Ali, on his return to Delhi, "to see Lord Ismay [chief of the viceroy's staff] and convey to him, . . . that if the boundary actually turned out to be what these reports foreshadowed, this would have a most serious impact on the relations between Pakistan and the United Kingdom, whose good faith and honor were involved in this question." According to Ali, when he arrived at Delhi, he "went straight from the airport to the viceroy's house where Lord Ismay was working. I was told," he wrote,

> that Lord Ismay was closeted with Sir Cyril Radcliffe. I decided to wait until he was free. When, after about an hour, I saw him, I conveyed to him the Quaid-i-Azam's [Jinnah's] message. In reply, Ismay professed complete ignorance of Radcliffe's ideas about the boundary and stated categorically that neither Mountbatten nor he himself had ever discussed the question with him. It was entirely for Radcliffe to decide; and no suggestion of any kind had been or would ever be made to him. When I plied Ismay with details of what had been reported to us, he said he could not follow me. There was a map hanging in the room and I beckoned him to the map so that I could explain the position to him with its help. There was a pencil line drawn across the map of the Punjab. The line followed the boundary that had been reported to the Quaid-i-Azam [showing most of Gurdaspur in East Punjab]. I said that it was unnecessary for me to explain further since the line, already drawn on the map, indicated the boundary I had been talking about. Ismay turned pale and asked in confusion who had been fooling with his map. This line differed from the final boundary in only one respect—the Muslim majority tahsils of Ferozepore and Zira in the Ferozepore district were still on the side of Pakistan as in the sketch-map.[30]

Aside from the sketch map (which, as pointed out, was provided to the governor of the Punjab, Sir Evan Jenkins, by George Abell, Mountbatten's private secretary, a few days prior to Radcliffe's submission of his final award) and the penciled-in line on Lord Ismay's office wall map, Chaudhri Muhammad Ali had very little solid evidence to fortify his argument. In his chapter discussing Radcliffe's boundary awards, he noted that Radcliffe and his staff were lodged in a wing of the viceroy's house, where discreet contact between them and Mountbatten's aides could easily have been arranged. He pointed out that Mountbatten, in response to a question raised at his 4 June press conference about the mutability of the notional boundaries set out in the partition plan of 3 June, had revealed unusual familiarity with the demographic details of Gurdaspur district. He implied, moreover, that Mountbatten used the occasion of his visit to Kashmir later in June to urge the maharaja to consider accession to India. But the conclusion he drew from all of this—that Mountbatten had very likely "reached an understanding with Congress leaders in respect of Gurdaspur district"[31]—was obviously speculative and far exceeded the evidence presented in its support.

Of the first generation of books dealing with the onset of the Kashmir dispute, there was only one, by the American geographer Aloys Michel, that attempted a thorough examination of Radcliffe's explicit—irrigation-based—rationale for the decision he took on Gurdaspur. Michel's study, published in 1967 (based on field research conducted in 1963–64), cast grave doubt on Radcliffe's public explanation of his decision without, however, necessarily lending any weight to allegations of political impropriety. According to Michel, the logic of irrigation considerations in the affected districts of Punjab actually reinforced the argument, which had underlain the assignment of the notional boundaries, based on the principle of contiguous communal majority. Lands that were allocated by Radcliffe to Pakistan, he said, were in fact more heavily dependent on the water supplied by the UBDC system, control over whose headworks had been passed to India, than were lands allocated to India; and the award of the whole of Gurdaspur district to Pakistan, he said, would actually have unified the administration of that water system. "[I]f irrigation considerations were to take precedence," he asked,

> why not give the Madhopur headworks to Pakistan, since the area served was mainly in the Lahore District, since Pakistan could not supply Lahore without supplying Amritsar on the way, and since—if Pakistan were to interfere with supplies on the two southern branches [of the UBDC system]—India could retaliate by cutting off supplies from the Ferozepore headworks to the Dipalpur Canal?[32]

What he found especially puzzling, said Michel, was that Radcliffe, in making up his mind over the Ferozepore and Gurdaspur awards, had applied no consistent principle at all. Both communal majority and irrigation considerations had, in fact, been overruled. "If the irrigation factor," he pointed out,

> was strong enough at Gurdaspur to vitiate the communal majority principle to the extent of partitioning a Muslim-majority district and awarding not only the non-Muslim Pathankot tahsil but two Muslim-majority tahsils to India, then the irrigation consideration should have prevailed at Ferozepore at least to the extent of giving Pakistan control of the right-hand portion of the headworks with the intake of the Dipalpur Canal. In other words, if the Ravi was the logical boundary in the Gurdaspur District, then the Sutlej was the logical boundary in Ferozepore.[33]

There was the possibility, he suggested, that Radcliffe had chosen to give more importance to land communication between India and the state of Jammu and Kashmir than to either of these other factors; but for this, he said, there was insufficient evidence.

More recent decades have witnessed a torrent of publications containing new evidence in regard to these developments at the onset of the Kashmir dispute. Landmark events in this connection were the publication in 1971 of the private correspondence of Congress leader Sardar Vallabhbhai Patel, who in the immediate prepartition period had charge of the vital States Department and who at independence became India's first deputy prime minister, and the opening up to scholars at the end of the 1970s of Mountbatten's papers (Broadlands Archives).[34] Of greatest importance, however, was the decision in 1966 by British prime minister Harold Wilson to reduce the closed period for official records from 50 to 30 years and the decision a year later that the first materials to be published under the new plan would be documents from the India Office Records relating to the transfer of power. The first volume in this project was published in 1970. The final four volumes, which contained documents pertaining most directly to Kashmir, appeared between 1980 and 1983.[35]

Publication of these materials has impacted strongly on subsequent scholarly examination of the Kashmir dispute: It reopened discussion of some unsettled historical issues, stimulated a number of important reinterpretations of the major events and personalities associated with this dispute,[36] and supplied a fund of information for a new round of debate over Kashmir among Indian and Pakistani scholars.[37] It did not result, however, in an immediate or wholesale abandonment of long-held views on the origins of the dispute. There was a notable reluctance, in particular, to concede the Pakistani contention that the partition process had been fouled from the start by underhanded dealings between Congress leaders and the departing British. British historian Hugh Tinker, for instance, reviewing newly released documents held by the India Office Library and Records relating specifically to the Radcliffe awards, concluded in an essay published in 1977 that these documents did not support the

Pakistani charge that India's occupation of Kashmir had been made possible by collusion between Mountbatten and Radcliffe over the dividing line between India and Pakistan in Punjab. He argued that the charge was ex post facto, that Radcliffe's decision to award most of Gurdaspur district to India was adequately explained by the "para-political" requirement that the boundary settlement not result in geographic isolation of the beleaguered Sikhs, and that, in any event, there still was no evidence to contradict Radcliffe's assertion that the award was "his own unfettered judgment."[38]

In a book published a decade later, R. J. Moore, the renowned historian of the British Commonwealth, clearly evinced somewhat greater skepticism in regard to the impartiality of the boundary settlement than had Tinker. Citing Michel, he dismissed as running contrary to the facts Radcliffe's claim that the Gurdaspur decision was based on the need to protect the integrity of the area's irrigation system.[39] He allowed that Mountbatten knew very well that Congress party leaders considered the award of Gurdaspur district to India crucial to their campaign to win Kashmir for India, and, moreover, that Radcliffe must have "realized that a district-wise observance of the contiguous-majority principle in Gurdaspur . . . would have closed off the Maharaja of Kashmir's option of adhering to India."[40] He conceded, further, that the possibility of viceregal influence on the decision—and of an actual meeting between Mountbatten and Radcliffe in that regard—had to be considered. For the most part, however, Moore's rendering of events did not depart significantly from the standard versions we have already examined, and, in its stout defense of Radcliffe's integrity and in its emphasis on the importance to Radcliffe of placating the Sikhs, it was largely consistent with Tinker's.[41]

The Pakistani position did not receive much encouragement, either, from publication in 1985 of Philip Ziegler's monumental biography of Mountbatten. In this work, the official biography of the British statesman, Ziegler found little reason to question Mountbatten's claim that Radcliffe had acted free from official pressures, and in most respects he, too, simply echoes Tinker's arguments. Radcliffe himself he describes as "a lawyer of great intelligence, probity and an intellectual toughness that was to enable him to withstand almost intolerable pressures."[42] About the decision to award most of Gurdaspur district to India, he says that Radcliffe had ample justification in the need to avoid isolating Sikh strongholds in Amritsar district. He points out, moreover, that at the time the Gurdaspur decision was announced, the Pakistanis did not appear overly surprised or upset by it. The allegation "that Mountbatten had awarded Gurdaspur to India so as to make possible land communications with Kashmir," Ziegler observes, "is ingenious, but suggests remarkable prescience on the part of the Viceroy, who anyway at the time was still engaged in trying to ensure that the Maharaja of Kashmir acceded to Pakistan."[43] There was "some tenuous support" for allegations that Mountbatten had met with Radcliffe in regard to the allocation of Ferozepore district. But

> to argue that Mountbatten tampered with the awards is to suggest that Radcliffe, a man of monumental integrity and independence of mind, meekly allowed his recommendations to be set aside by somebody who had no official standing in the matter. . . . It would suggest too that Mountbatten risked his reputation and all he had achieved in India for little advantage. . . . It is easy to believe that Nehru pressed him to amend the awards, far harder to find any reason why he should have succumbed to the pressure.[44]

Ziegler conceded that in regard to Mountbatten's innocence of any tampering with the awards, "a nugget of uncertainty" remained. There was good evidence, he noted, that Mountbatten at least *contemplated* asking Radcliffe to amend his awards; and he may in addition have openly considered this alternative with his close associates.[45] Ziegler concluded, however, that "commonsense and the counsels of Ismay must have convinced him that the risks were too great; the game was not worth even a small part of the candle. He may have been guilty of indiscretion, but not of the arrant folly as well as dishonesty of which his enemies accused him."[46]

Ziegler's defense of Mountbatten's integrity and common sense was clearly dealt a setback in February 1992 by revelations of the viceroy's behind-the-scenes manipulation of the Punjab award made public by Christopher Beaumont, secretary to Radcliffe in India and the last to survive of those British officials with intimate personal knowledge of the partitioning process. In a written statement he had originally deposited in 1989 at All Souls College, Oxford, with the instruction that its contents not be disclosed until after his death but which he had subsequently decided to make public, Beaumont said that Radcliffe had, in fact, allotted Ferozepore and Zira *tehsils* to Pakistan in the completed Punjab boundary award.[47] Learning of the allocation, Mountbatten arranged a luncheon meeting with Radcliffe, from which Beaumont himself "was deftly excluded." At this luncheon, held a day or two before the Punjab award was completed on 12 August, Radcliffe, according to Beaumont, was apparently persuaded to alter his decision in favor of India, and by evening of the same day he had made the change. Beaumont speculated that Mountbatten was under tremendous pressure from Nehru to make the change and that Radcliffe may have succumbed to the argument that failure to alter the line might lead to war between the two newly independent countries.[48] Nevertheless, in Beaumont's view changing the award cast "grave discredit" on both Radcliffe and Mountbatten.[49]

Beaumont's disclosure on its own obviously warrants at least some revision in our appreciation of Mountbatten's role in the transfer of power. Confronted with Beaumont's statement, Ziegler himself reportedly confessed that the nugget of doubt over Mountbatten's impartiality had now become a boulder. The disclosure proved nothing, of course, about Gurdaspur and the Punjab's northern border with Kashmir, even less about Kashmir proper. It clearly pointed to the possibility, however, that in regard to those cases, too, partisanship may have been present to govern Mountbatten's decisions. At a minimum, it suggested that a fresh reexamination be conducted in regard to Pakistani allegations that collusion between the departing British and the leadership of the Congress had deprived Pakistan of Kashmir.

Even before Beaumont spoke, just such reexamination had already been performed by Alastair Lamb. Lamb's comprehensive rewrite of his 1966 study of the Kashmir dispute, taking advantage of the massive documentation that had surfaced in the intervening years, appeared in late 1991.[50] It aroused immediate controversy and clearly established him as the dispute's foremost revisionist interpreter. The book takes the view that the origins of the Kashmir dispute have to be sought in the strategic outlook that the British acquired in regard to India's vulnerable northern frontier during the colonial period. And it argues that the accession of Kashmir to India on 27 October 1947 was the end result of deliberate planning, begun well before independence was achieved, and that it was orchestrated to a considerable extent by Lord Mountbatten.

In the chapter entitled "Partition 1947," where evidence relating to the Radcliffe awards is reviewed, Lamb raises two questions: first, whether Mountbatten had a Kashmir policy of his own in which India's future access to the state via Gurdaspur would have figured (and, as part of this question, did he actually appreciate Gurdaspur's importance in that respect); and second, whether Mountbatten's policy and appreciation significantly influenced Radcliffe's final decision in regard to Gurdaspur. Insofar as the second part of the first question was concerned, there was, according to Lamb, absolutely no doubt that Mountbatten fully appreciated the importance of Gurdaspur's geographic placement to India's future access.[51] As to whether Mountbatten had a Kashmir policy of his own, however, Lamb is a bit more equivocal. The British Indian government, he says, had not spent the previous century building a policy to guard against Russian-Soviet penetration of the subcontinent only to see it trashed overnight by inattention to the problem of political succession on the northern frontier. Mountbatten made it perfectly clear that he opposed Kashmir's independence; and, says Lamb, it is most likely that the

British strategists then advising Mountbatten would have considered India a better choice than Pakistan as new guardian of the northern frontier. As proof that the viceroy himself leaned in this direction, Lamb points to the fact that Mountbatten, hardly a month after taking up his post in India in March 1947, urged the British government to restore the area of the Gilgit Lease to the state of Jammu and Kashmir in advance of the transfer of power. Mountbatten's motive, Lamb argues, was to prevent the leased areas from ever becoming a part of Pakistan. If kept legally *separated* from the maharaja's realm, he says, they would, according to the rules of partition, very likely have gone to Pakistan: They were not geographically contiguous with India, and they were almost wholly Muslim in population. Lamb argues that, had Mountbatten not cared one way or the other about Kashmir's accession decision, then "he could perfectly well have left the Gilgit Lease alone."[52]

Reinforcing his argument, Lamb suggests that Mountbatten could hardly have avoided being influenced in regard to Kashmir by the strong arguments put to him about India's interest in that state by the Congress leadership. He points in particular to an emotional private letter sent to the viceroy by Nehru's close friend and political ally, Krishna Menon, on 14 June and a lengthy note on Kashmir, dated 17 June, prepared at Mountbatten's own request by Nehru himself. Both were received just prior to Mountbatten's departure on his first and only official visit to Kashmir as viceroy. Menon's letter, on the one hand, warned Mountbatten that British interests in the region might well be put at risk were Kashmir to go to Pakistan. Nehru's note, on the other hand, sought to persuade Mountbatten that Jinnah's Muslim League had very little influence in Kashmir and that the state's political future really lay in the hands of Nehru's political allies there, Sheikh Abdullah and the National Conference. Like Menon, Nehru stressed the strategic significance of the state to India, and he too warned of dire consequences were Kashmir not to join India.[53]

One further piece of evidence offered by Lamb was the wording in Mountbatten's report, dated 22 June, of his interview in Srinagar with Pandit Ramchandra Kak, prime minister of the state of Jammu and Kashmir and the target of especially venomous Congress criticisms. In it, Mountbatten recorded that he had made plain both to Kak and to the maharaja that the choice of joining either India or Pakistan was for Kashmir to make. If the choice were Pakistan, "presumably," he said, "Mr. Jinnah would protect [the maharaja and his government] against pressure from the Congress." If, on the other hand, the choice were India, then, he said, "it would be inevitable that they would be treated with consideration by Hindustan." For Lamb,

> the *certainty* of a Congress welcome contrasted with the *probability* of Mr. Jinnah's ability to "protect" against some danger unspecified. It would not be too difficult to interpret these words as implying that the Maharaja of Jammu and Kashmir would be well advised to join India if he entertained any hope of retaining his own position in the State. The Congress would keep him on his throne: Mr. Jinnah and his Muslim League would make sure that his Muslim subjects brought about his overthrow.[54]

On the basis of these speculations, Lamb answers the question about Mountbatten's having his own Kashmir policy with necessarily less than a ringing affirmative. The evidence, he says, does

> rather suggest that he [Mountbatten] personally favoured a solution where the Maharaja left the decision to Sheikh Abdullah's National Conference which appeared to him to be representative of the people of the State as a whole; and, as Nehru's Note suggested, Sheikh Abdullah would surely opt for India. This outcome would in his view not only be politically just but also geopolitically desirable in that it ensured that the Gilgit Agency and the defence of the Northern Frontier would remain in Indian hands. We can never be absolutely certain; but that is what the balance of probabilities would indicate.[55]

Moving to consider his second question—whether Mountbatten's outlook on Kashmir actually influenced Radcliffe's decision in regard to Gurdaspur, Lamb uncovers no new evidence. He concedes, quite in keeping with the judgments of Moore, Tinker, and others, that the Sikh problem alone could provide political reason enough for the inclusion of part of Gurdaspur district in India.[56] His argument in regard to the partition process differs substantially from those just reviewed, however, in its basic premise that there surely was conspiracy afoot, that Mountbatten (and/or his associates) were at the heart of it, and that it had as its objective the accession of Jammu and Kashmir to India.

Lamb's argument in this connection is essentially threefold: (1) There was nothing very secret about Radcliffe's deliberations over the boundary. Leaks were plentiful. Final modifications to the award took "place in anything but total secrecy and isolation from politically interested parties." Mountbatten and his staff had every reason to keep a close watch over Radcliffe and they had plenty of opportunities to intervene discreetly. (2) About Gurdaspur, Mountbatten and his staff would certainly do what they could to bring about a decision favorable to India "if only to present the Maharaja of Jammu and Kashmir with a genuine choice." Accordingly, Radcliffe's initial award of Ferozepore and Zira *tehsils* to Pakistan was primarily intended to compensate Pakistan for the loss of the three eastern *tehsils* of Gurdaspur district to India—a virtually unavoidable loss if there was to be a land link between India and Kashmir. The device failed, in part owing to the explosiveness of the Sikh problem. (3) The Radcliffe Commission's vaunted independence "was something of a charade." Mountbatten had to appear "impartial, neutral and above party in all his actions during the birth process of the two Dominions. Here the Radcliffe Commission, seeming to act in total independence, was an extremely useful scapegoat."[57]

As was noted earlier, Lamb's own views in regard to the relationship between the boundary settlement and the accession of Kashmir to India have evolved considerably in the quarter century or so that has passed since his earlier study was written. He had said then, we may recall, that the Radcliffe award "was in no way related to the Kashmir question."[58] The interpretation he now gives to these events, while obviously pitting him against the bulk of Western scholarship addressed to these matters, is naturally strongly welcomed in Pakistan, whose scholars have long been engaged in the rather lonely effort to build a case against Mountbatten.[59] Strangely enough, however, some of the strongest support for Lamb's point of view came from an Indian writer, a Muslim but with impeccably pro-Indian (and pro-Congress) credentials. In a biography of Nehru published in 1988, M. J. Akbar, an acclaimed journalist and a successful Congress (I) party candidate for the ninth parliament, narrates the events leading up to partition in words scarcely distinguishable from Lamb's. V. P. Menon, Reforms Secretary (and, after 5 July, the secretary of the pivotal States Commission), the only Indian in a senior advisory capacity on the viceroy's staff and the man entrusted with crafting the detailed partition plan announced on 3 June, is described as a Congress "mole," the man who kept Sardar Vallabhbhai Patel secretly informed by telephone of the goings-on at Viceroy's House.[60] Nehru, he says, very early in the game planted in Mountbatten's mind the absolute necessity that Gurdaspur district be denied to Pakistan in order to make possible the accession of Kashmir to India.[61] According to Akbar, Mountbatten tailored his entire policy on Kashmir to fit Nehru's unhesitating ambitions in regard to the state. "Not only was Nehru's mind extremely clear about Kashmir," Akbar wrote approvingly, "but he had the foresight to plan far ahead. This foresight kept Kashmir in India."[62]

At this point, we need to pause for a moment to summarize our findings so far in regard to the entitlement issue. First, there can now be no reasonable doubt that Pakistan's suspicions in regard to the fairness and impartiality of the Punjab boundary settlement were justified. These suspicions arose in the first place because Pakistan, judged in terms of the award's deviation from the notional boundaries given in the 3 June plan, clearly fared less well than

India in the settlement. That much can't seriously be questioned. What Pakistanis have always alleged, however, was that this lopsided outcome was in some way preplanned, the result of behind-the-scenes manipulation by the viceroy (or his staff) and the Congress leadership. This accusation can no longer be dismissed heedlessly. Admittedly, most of the evidence of direct political interference in the making of the boundary remains circumstantial; but over the years the circumstantial evidence has been accumulating at a rate and of a quality far in excess of anyone's ability to explain it away. Obviously, we are never going to possess evidence sufficient to convince everyone that a bona fide conspiracy in fact took place. Flawless evidence of that sort, however, is rarely made available to students of international relations, and there is no good reason why it should be insisted upon in the present case. There may not be enough evidence to convict, in other words, but there is clearly enough to reconsider the question of innocence. What most catches one's eye in the controversy over the Punjab boundary settlement, in fact, has been the tremendous reluctance on the part of so many scholars to concede that certain key British figures involved in the transfer of power may have been lying and that the Pakistanis were not merely being poor sports when they cried foul over the settlement.

Second, evidence available to us today does not lend unambiguous support to that part of the conspiracy thesis alleging that Gurdaspur district was divided as it was solely or primarily to satisfy the Indian wish for convenient and strategically important land communications between India and Kashmir. Indeed, the evidence does not rule out the possibility that the Gurdaspur decision would have been the same had there been no question at all of India's access to Kashmir. Gurdaspur's Pathankot *tehsil,* in which the bridge across the Ravi into Jammu was located, was overwhelmingly non-Muslim in population and could have been assigned to India, assuming that the principle of contiguous communal majority was being applied at the *tehsil* level, on that ground alone. Maintaining the integrity of the UBDC irrigation system, especially if done on a tit-for-tat basis with the Ferozepore headworks to the south, was clearly a reasonable objective. There is no question, moreover, that Gurdaspur district was part of the area that "represented the heart of the Sikh community"[63] and that assuring that community of a secure homeland in East Punjab may have been a dominant consideration. The Sikhs' future after partition had not been directly addressed in the partition plan; and Radcliffe would have had to possess extraordinarily steely nerves to have ignored their demands. Credible evidence of any kind that Mountbatten himself gave the factor of India's access via Gurdaspur exceptionally high priority, or that he actually sought to bring pressure to bear directly on Radcliffe in order to assure that the Indian wish in that regard was satisfied, simply does not exist. Citing Mountbatten's explicit naming of Gurdaspur district when exemplifying the mutability of the notional boundaries in Punjab is not conclusive evidence that he was then busily engaged in a collusive operation to deprive Pakistan of it. As Michel pointed out, "there was only one district (Gurdaspur) in all of the British Punjab where either the Muslim or the non-Muslim majority was less than 3.5 per cent above or below 50 per cent."[64] It was, therefore, the best possible example of the point Mountbatten was trying to make.

The stubborn fact remains that Radcliffe's award is readily explicable in terms that do not include Kashmir. The contention, therefore, of the government of Pakistan that the Gurdaspur decision "was clearly designed to provide India with a link to Jammu and Kashmir and thus to enable the feudal ruler of the States [*sic*] to arrange its accession to India," and that Radcliffe's award in this respect was the product of a "premeditated plan" hatched by Lord Mountbatten before the Boundary Commission was established, cannot be accepted at face value.[65]

Nevertheless, the evidence now available, as Lamb observes, does unquestionably "leave room for a degree of reasonable doubt."[66] Indeed, the doubt looms even larger, with Beaumont's disclosure, than it did when Lamb was writing his book. We now have much better reason than before to suspect that the curious inconsistency in Radcliffe's award illuminated long ago by Michel—that is, the absence of a common principle underlying his decisions in regard to the irrigation systems of Gurdaspur and Ferozepore districts—was forced upon Radcliffe at the last moment by Mountbatten, that the initial award of the Ferozepore salient to Pakistan was indeed meant to compensate it for the loss of Gurdaspur, and also that Radcliffe's independence of mind was something of a myth. British strategists on Mountbatten's staff, as Lamb pointed out, very likely did prefer vastly larger and probably more durable India over Pakistan as guardian of the northern frontier. Mountbatten was, we have already observed, fully aware of the common belief that Kashmir's accession to India was impractical unless India acquired land access to Kashmir via Gurdaspur district; and India's leaders, Nehru above all others, had never been shy about making their preferences known in this regard. That all of this had come very quickly—and forcefully—to the attention of Radcliffe is virtually certain.

But, when all is said and done, was Radcliffe really part of a carefully planned Kashmir plot? Lamb's account comes very close to saying that he was—that Mountbatten in large part adopted as his own Nehru's vision of India's postindependence political and strategic requirements; that he, together with his advisers, consciously designed a complex and multiphased politico-strategic plan (including, presumably, appointment of a suitably pliable chairman of the boundary commissions) to achieve that vision; and that, in executing the plan, he not only prudently arranged well in advance to restore the Gilgit Lease to the maharaja's domain to preclude its absorption by Pakistan, but also saw to it that Pakistan's acquiescence in the plan was purchased with a militarily and economically attractive salient in Ferozepore district, and then, at the last moment, when the compensatory package of the Ferozepore *tehsils* stirred up too much resistance from Congress, that he caused Radcliffe to redraft the award. Implicit in Lamb's account, too, is the belief that Mountbatten was audacious enough to think that he could control the unfolding of events according to this plan and, moreover, that he could see to its execution in association with a mixed band of coconspirators without fear of ultimate disclosure.

Lamb's argument is very compelling and, in large measure, plausible. From all accounts, Mountbatten was a bold and decisive man, given to strong opinions, and certainly not above guile in achieving his objectives. He was open in his preference for Indian unity and made no real effort to conceal his hostility for the idea of Pakistan. Surely one must be skeptical—in the face of his extraordinarily close friendship with Nehru—that he could have maintained throughout the partition phase the complete impartiality between India and Pakistan that he went on claiming for himself right up until his death in 1979.[67] Still, there is a world of difference between a display of partiality in one's attitudes and verbal utterances and the masterminding of a conspiracy on the scale implied by Lamb. In the effort to make the latter seem more plausible, Lamb's argument necessarily puts some strain on existing facts.

His argument, for one thing, clearly hinges on the assumption that Nehru exerted unusually powerful influence over Mountbatten—that the viceroy, in fact, "unhesitatingly trusted what Nehru had to say." According to Lamb, Nehru's views about Kashmiri politics were accepted by the viceroy and his staff without question. Contrary opinions about the Muslim dimension of Kashmiri politics weren't sought. The viceroy "got on well with Jawaharlal Nehru, whom he both admired and trusted." Jinnah, on the other hand, wasn't taken seriously. Mountbatten, says Lamb, "was presented with but a single view, that Sheikh Abdullah and his National Conference represented the overwhelming majority of the people of the State of Jammu and Kashmir."[68]

For evidence of Nehru's persuasive logic on the subject of Kashmir, Lamb relies very heavily on Nehru's note of 17 June, which, he says, "cannot have failed to impress Mountbatten." The note, which fills about six pages in the *Transfer of Power,* is indeed well written and its arguments, especially those hinting strongly at violent upheaval in Kashmir if Nehru failed to get his way, would certainly have been given close scrutiny by Mountbatten and his advisers. But what they also could not have failed to notice was Nehru's transparently self-serving, subjective, and simplistic political analysis. Sheikh Abdullah's Kashmir National Conference, according to Nehru, "was by far the most widespread and popular" party. It had "demonstrated its hold on the masses and there is no doubt that Sheikh Abdullah himself is by far the most outstanding leader in Kashmir." Abdullah "was amazingly popular among the masses and numerous songs and legends grew up about him." On the other hand, "certain reactionary Hindu and Muslim groups opposed him and his movement." These groups were the allies of Jinnah's Muslim League, but, Nehru assured Mountbatten, "they had little influence in the State." The maharaja had been frightened into indecision and inaction by his wily, conniving, and ruthlessly ambitious prime minister, Pandit Kak, who had "succeeded in antagonising every decent element in Kashmir and in India as a whole." The maharaja "obviously" wanted to join the Constituent Assembly of India; only Mr. Kak, by threatening communal riots that he would himself create, stood in the way. "The normal and obvious course," Nehru reassuringly concluded, "appears to be for Kashmir to join the Constituent Assembly of India. This will satisfy both the popular demand and the Maharaja's wishes. It is absurd to think that Pakistan would create trouble if this happens."[69]

According to his admiring biographer, Philip Ziegler, Mountbatten was "predisposed to like everyone he met."[70] Jinnah seems to have defeated this predisposition, however, and there is little question in Ziegler's mind that Mountbatten much preferred the warm-hearted and charming Nehru over what may have seemed to him the coldly analytical, suspicious, and distant leader of the Muslim League.[71] Insofar as friendship counted in Mountbatten's policymaking, Nehru does seem to have held the advantage over Jinnah. Obviously, this may have led Mountbatten himself, if not his advisers, to accept somewhat uncritically Nehru's arguments in regard both to the strategic necessity and the political feasibility of Kashmir's accession to India—especially if Mountbatten was already inclined in this direction. Mountbatten's vanity and capacity for self-deception were legendary; but Ziegler's biography does not leave the impression that Mountbatten was politically naive, much less a fool. On the contrary, Ziegler describes him as possessing "a powerful, analytical mind of crystalline clarity."[72] If so, he would certainly have recognized Nehru's note for what it was—rather heavy-handed political propaganda—and have appropriately discounted it to that extent.

Lamb's comment that Mountbatten was getting from his advisers "but a single view" on Kashmir must also be questioned. On the face of it, it is difficult to believe that no one among Mountbatten's senior advisers would have pointed out to him—assuming that he was not competent to make this judgment himself—that Congress claims in regard to the political loyalties of Kashmir's Muslim masses had to be taken with a pinch of salt. In fact, there is quite unambiguous evidence in the documentary record that at least some of them did precisely that. Included among the documents in *The Transfer of Power* is a telegram, dated 13 August, dispatched to George Abell, Mountbatten's secretary, from the British resident in Srinagar, Lieutenant-Colonel Webb. Webb, responding directly to a request by Mountbatten himself for amplification of information reported in a telegram sent a day earlier, explained the reasons for Prime Minister Kak's sudden resignation on 11 August. In the course of his comments, he made it very clear—in matter-of-fact language—that neither he nor either the outgoing or incoming Hindu prime ministers of the state of Jammu and Kashmir had a sense of the political culture of the state even remotely like that of Mr. Nehru. The break between Kak and the maharaja, suggested Webb,

> came because of indecision of His Highness to make up his mind either to join one or other Dominion, or in peculiar circumstances for Kashmir to come into the open and ask for agreements with both. His Highness, Dogras and Hindu communities incline towards India *but bulk of population are Moslem and if consulted would probably favour Pakistan especially Mirpur, Poonch and Muzaffarabad area.* Kak although Hindu clearly saw implication and felt that if Kashmir joined either Dominion *especially India* it would mean serious trouble.

Webb went on to say that he had met with Kak's replacement, Major-General Janak Singh. The new prime minister, he said, "although inclining towards India as a Hindu, *realises bulk of Moslems will not accept decision.* He therefore wishes for agreements with both [India and Pakistan]."[73] This telegram obviously does not rule out the possibility that Mountbatten and his advisers considered the accession of Kashmir to India of sufficient importance to warrant taking a risk with the political inclinations of the Kashmiri people. It does suggest, however, that in building the case for conspiracy, one must not rely too heavily on Mountbatten's ignorance.

Third, even though the question of a link between Kashmir's accession to India and Radcliffe's disposition of Gurdaspur district in the Punjab boundary settlement must remain a tantalizing proposition, the fundamental revision in historical interpretation that we have observed in regard to the *pre*partition period, in particular the emergence of virtually incontrovertible evidence that the boundary settlement *as a whole* was not impartially decided, clearly compels us to take a fresh look as well at the principal entitlement controversies that arose in the immediate *post*partition period—the 72 days that passed between the transfer of power and the accession of Jammu and Kashmir to India. These controversies we consider now.

ACCESSION PHASE

The controversies we examine in this section pertain to events in the immediate postindependence or accession phase of the Kashmir dispute's origins. While discussion of the territorial entitlement problem in this phase focuses more directly on Kashmir itself, the shift in focus won't make the task of unraveling these controversies any less perplexing. One reason for this is that public access to official Indian, Pakistani, and Kashmiri archival materials relating to this phase has been largely choked off by the governments of India and Pakistan.[74] Not yet has either government felt the compulsion for public disclosure that moved Britain, in the 1960s, to the wholesale release of classified foreign affairs records. In this phase, major decisions about Kashmir were firmly in Indian and Pakistani hands; hence, the British documentary record for this period, while instructive, is much less revealing. True, Mountbatten, in his capacity as governor-general, continued to play an important role in government on the Indian side until his final departure from India in June 1948; and British military officers and civil servants continued to serve in both India and Pakistan, albeit in rapidly diminishing numbers, for some time thereafter.[75] But all of them, including Mountbatten, wielded sharply reduced power, and all of them played far less central roles in the making of high policy in this phase of the dispute.[76] Publication of the memoirs or private papers of some key Indian and Pakistani officials—of the correspondence, for instance, of Sardar Patel—has helped to fill the knowledge vacuum. But there is nothing available on the official side covering developments in this period, one of simply extraordinary political turmoil and confusion, that corresponds even faintly to the India Office records.

Another and far more important reason why the analytical task will remain perplexing is that, with the transfer of power, a profound change occurred in the nature of the legal standard against which entitlement questions were to be judged. The rules of partition and for the integration of princely states had been specially drawn up for the specific purpose of dividing British India and for assuring a smooth transfer of power; and both sides had accepted the British to act as impartial referee in regard to those rules. With the passing of the British raj, however, the authority of the British to act in this capacity was abruptly swept aside, and the rules themselves, though not discarded, no longer commanded uniform definition. The question of Kashmir's accession became overnight a matter of India-Pakistan relations, subject—in addition to the rules carried over from British India—to the infinitely less specific and more contentious rules pertaining to the acts of independent states in international relations. Unless India and Pakistan chose to invite one, there no longer was an impartial referee at hand.[77] Fairness would be more difficult than ever either to achieve or to judge.

Maharaja Hari Singh's decision to let the transfer of power pass without having acceded to either dominion thus placed the problem of accession in a very different light. India and Pakistan would now compete for title to Kashmir as separate nations, deploying state resources and employing diplomatic and other techniques, both overt and covert, as would any other pair of independent nations engaged in a fight over territory. However, the leaders of India and Pakistan would continue to make selective use of British-sanctioned preindependence rules, not only because these rules supplied a coating of legality to their own actions in regard to Kashmir but also because they could be used expediently to condemn the actions of their adversary.

The rules were well suited to just such use. The partition plan of 3 June, as we have seen, did not apply to the princely states. It mentioned them only to reassert that the decisions announced in the plan applied strictly to British India and not toward the Indian states, which, it said, continued to be governed by the policies contained in the Cabinet Mission memorandum of 12 May 1946.[78] That memorandum, the result of negotiations carried out between the princes and a British government team led by Sir Stafford Cripps, outlined basic rules for the severance at the time of the transfer of power of the princely states' formal political dependence on the British Indian government. As V. P. Menon summarized it, the memorandum affirmed that when a new government or governments came into being in British India, the British

> would cease to exercise the powers of paramountcy. This meant that the rights of the States which flowed from their relationship to the Crown would no longer exist, and that all the rights surrendered by the States to the paramount power would return to them. Political arrangements between the States on the one side and the British Crown and British India on the other would thus be brought to an end. The void would have to be filled by the States entering into a federal relationship with the successor government or governments in British India, or by entering into particular political arrangements.[79]

At the time, Congress and the Muslim League took very different positions on this formula. Congress leaders fiercely resisted it, preferring that British paramountcy over the princely states pass automatically, with the transfer of power, to the successor state or states. Muslim League leaders, in contrast, took the side of the princes, holding out for the princely right to choose not only between India and Pakistan, but between accession and retention of independence. Since all but a few of the states were obviously destined to associate themselves with India, the difference in the positions taken by Congress and Muslim League leaders was hardly mysterious.[80] The British viceroy's formal position was ambiguous, since it affirmed, on the one hand, that the princely states should recover full independence, and yet maintained, on the other, that the princes' freedom to exercise that independence would be tacitly restricted. Mountbatten, in fact, personally inclined strongly to the Congress's position and went to extraordinary lengths to convince the princes both that they should make up their minds in regard to accession before 15 August and that, however vague formal British policy may have been in this regard, their only *practical* choice lay in accession to either one or the other of the two new dominions. Mountbatten appears to have given no serious thought to the option of *permanent* independence for the princely states.[81]

For the most part, Mountbatten was successful in the effort to coax the princes into making timely accession decisions: Prior to the appointed date for the transfer of power, 552 of the 565 princely states had acceded to India, and of the remainder only three—Hyderabad, Junagadh, and Kashmir—posed serious problems.[82] These three were more than enough, however, to expose the deficiencies in the existing rules.

The first two of these holdouts, neither of which was contiguous with Pakistan and both of which had non-Muslim (Hindu) majorities, India was ultimately able to absorb on its own terms. The Muslim nawab of Junagadh, a small maritime state located in what is now India's Gujarat state, acceded to Pakistan on 15 August. India promptly protested, pointing out that the action obviously violated the facts of Junagadh's geographic situation. An economic blockade was organized, rebellion broke out, and both Junagadh state forces and troops of the Indian army took to the field. In the face of increasing disorder and the threat of overwhelming force, the nawab fled and the prime minister of the state requested that India take charge of its administration. Accounts of the exact unfolding of events naturally differ widely; but the upshot was that Junagadh's accession to Pakistan was overturned by the Indians in November, and, following an Indian-organized referendum on 20 February 1948, the state acceded to India. Pakistan declared the accession to India a fraud and to this day claims Junagadh as part of its own territory.[83]

Hyderabad, like Junagadh ruled by a Muslim, was a much larger state, and the refusal of its ruler (the nizam) to accede to India before the transfer of power seemed to many Indians, as Menon put it, to create "a Pakistan island within

India."[84] Without a seaport and surrounded by India, its assertion of independence appeared even more than Junagadh's to violate the compulsions of geography. The nizam declined to accede to either India or Pakistan, but expressed willingness to enter into a treaty relationship with India. A standstill agreement was concluded between India and Hyderabad in November 1947; but prolonged negotiations over a more permanent settlement, in which Mountbatten played a key role up until his departure from India, ultimately broke down in June 1948. Indian forces subsequently were sent into the state in September 1948 to break the stalemate. Following a brief resistance, the nizam's forces surrendered, ending the confrontation. Hyderabad was eventually dismembered and its territories parceled out among adjoining provinces.[85]

The Hyderabad and Junagadh cases developed side by side with the Kashmir crisis; and, though they were in many respects quite dissimilar from the case of Kashmir, they inevitably held precedential importance for the latter. Pakistan's material role in Hyderabad's confrontation with India was very modest; it did, however, express support both for the nizam's right to remain independent *and* for his right to make the decision without formal reference to the mainly Hindu (over 85 percent) population.[86] In the case of Junagadh, as we saw, Pakistan had also upheld the right of a minority ruler, in that case also a Muslim, to decide upon accession without recourse to a plebiscite. Pakistan's positions in these cases, which seemed in certain respects to contradict its postindependence position on Kashmir, obviously would return at a later point to haunt its leaders.[87] As far as setting precedents was concerned, however, India was no better off. In both the Hyderabad and Junagadh cases, it had refused to accept as legally valid the minority rulers' decisions in regard to accession. In both it had supported insurgent groups against the ruling princes. In Junagadh's case, it had overturned by force the nawab's legally executed accession to Pakistan; and in Junagadh's case also, it had maintained, as it did in Kashmir, that that state's final accession to India had to be confirmed by a popular plebiscite. "The Pakistanis," observed Ziegler, "argued that Junagadh, having legally acceded, was now part of their country, and India had committed aggression. Though the referendum . . . showed an overwhelming majority for accession to India, legally Pakistan was in the right."[88] It was not wholly in the right, however; and, in any event, for neither India nor Pakistan did being right in these other cases translate readily into being right in the case of Kashmir.

Kashmir was ruled by a Hindu; but it was home to a very substantial Muslim majority (77.11 percent according to the 1941 Census) and was contiguous with Pakistan as well as with India. It thus stood in a category all of its own. According to the pure principle of contiguous communal majority, it naturally belonged to Pakistan. Purity of principle, as we have seen, was deliberately diluted in the rules governing partition, however, by the agreed allowance for "other factors" in the determination of territorial affiliation. In the rules laid down for the termination of British paramountcy over the Indian states, in contrast, the choice of affiliation, in principle, belonged to the princes. Here, too, however, it was not *exclusively* their choice, for the princes' freedom to decide between India and Pakistan, like their freedom to decide whether to accede at all, had itself in practice been substantially diluted by the strong and explicit recommendation that they take geographic realities into account. When Mountbatten addressed a special session of the Chamber of Princes on 25 July, "he made it clear," according to V. P. Menon, "that though the rulers were technically at liberty to link with either of the Dominions, there were certain geographical compulsions which could not be evaded." Mountbatten reminded them that the vast majority of the 565 states were "'irretrievably linked geographically with the Dominion of India.'"[89]

What should now be obvious is that the preindependence rules pertaining to postindependence legal entitlement to Kashmir were riddled with ambiguity. They had worked well enough so long as the British were on hand to settle differences that arose in regard to them; and India and Pakistan, long after the British had left, had perforce to refer to them in establishing their own claims. As the showdown over Kashmir neared in the autumn of 1947, however, the weaknesses of these preindependence rules grew steadily more apparent and India and Pakistan showed less and less inclination to rely on them. The manner in which the accession of the state of Jammu and Kashmir to India actually occurred reflected, then, not only the fundamentally changed political circumstances in which India and Pakistan found themselves but also the equally fundamental erosion of rules governing the relations between them that had gone on since the transfer of power.

With this as background, we can now more easily appreciate the major controversies that were set in motion by the specific events surrounding accession in October 1947. One that we consider has come down to us in countless discussions of the accession crisis as "the tribal invasion." We will call it the aggression issue. The other is the matter of plebiscite, a commitment to which of some sort formed part of the accession agreement. These controversies, at bottom, are really two sides of the same coin: They are both intimately concerned with the justness of the act of accession—the one (the tribal invasion) essentially with the question of responsibility for the events that precipitated it, the other (the commitment to a plebiscite) with the question of the legal validity of the act of accession itself. We consider first the tribal invasion and the question of responsibility.

The Aggression Issue

The tribal invasion refers, of course, to the crossing of Kashmir's border with Pakistan in the latter part of October 1947 by Pashtun (Pathan) tribesmen coming from the semiautonomous tribal belt that lines the border between Pakistan's North West Frontier Province (NWFP) and Afghanistan. Most Indian accounts of their action would include at least the following: After making their way across Pakistan in hundreds of vehicles, the tribesmen, numbering in the thousands, crossed into Kashmir near Muzaffarabad, a small district headquarters town on the river Jhelum, on 22 October. Following their capture of Muzaffarabad two days later, they advanced in the direction of Srinagar, the summer capital of the state and the maharaja's chief residence at the time, about 100 miles away by road. The tribesmen were in no great hurry; and alarming reports were broadcast of their indiscriminate killing, looting, and rape along the way. State forces, weakened by heavy defections and already bogged down in an attempt to quell an internal antigovernment uprising that had been under way in Poonch, in the western sector of Jammu, since the preceding August, were no match for the tribesmen. Alarmed that his state was about to be overrun, the maharaja appealed for military assistance to New Delhi. A decision to intervene was quickly taken, and with Mountbatten, now governor-general, taking overall charge of military operations, combat forces were soon on their way. On 27 October, the first airborne troops landed at Srinagar airport just in time to mount a successful defense against the oncoming tribal raiders. Stipulated by the Indian government as a condition of the military aid granted was the state's accession to India. That, too, was very rapidly consummated. On the same day that the troops landed at Srinagar, Mountbatten officially accepted the state's accession to India.

About these and other events that took place in that brief period of a week or so leading up to the accession of the state to India, there is nothing today even remotely resembling a consensus. There is dispute about the number of tribesmen involved, about who supported them, certainly about their motives, about the things they did, and about the dates on which they supposedly did them. And as for the government of India's reactions to the tribesmen, the range of things disputed—indeed, whether India was simply *reacting*—is even greater.

New Delhi's own official interpretation of the events of October was laid out in a carefully compiled and documented *White Paper on Jammu and Kashmir* produced not long after the events occurred. In it the Indians pursued two fundamental themes—one aimed at establishing India's innocence of any premeditated plan to seize upon the tribal invasion as an excuse to secure Kashmir for itself, and the other at establishing Pakistan's guilt of active complicity in the tribesmen's acts of aggression against Kashmir. In line with the first theme, the *White Paper* argued (1) that the government of India's military intervention in Kashmir was undertaken entirely as a *reaction* to the tribal invasion of the state on 22 October and, specifically, that the first request for military aid from the maharaja's government was received on 24 October, that not until then had the government of India considered any plans for sending troops to Kashmir, that orders for the preparation of plans for the sending of troops to Kashmir by air and road were not given to the Indian armed forces until 25 October, and that Indian troops were not sent to Kashmir until after the maharaja had signed an Instrument of Accession on 26 October; and (2) that the objective of India's military intervention in Kashmir, corresponding to its reactive role in the first place, was exclusively to clear the raiders from the state so that a plebiscite or referendum could be held "by the people of Kashmir to decide finally as to which dominion they will accede."[90]

Protagonists of the Indian point of view, reinforcing the theme of "reactive intervention," have suggested over the years that the government of India was, in fact, largely caught off guard by the tribal invasion; that it was preoccupied at the time with other matters; that official contacts with the state were actually fairly modest and certainly did not involve military considerations; that Mountbatten's only role prior to the tribal invasion had been to secure for the maharaja an unfettered decision; that Nehru was more interested in the release from prison of his friend, Sheikh Abdullah, and in fostering democracy and the people's welfare in Kashmir than in the state's accession to India; and, in any event, that there was no coercion at all from the Indian side in producing an accession decision favorable to India. Commenting on Pakistan's standstill agreement with Kashmir, reached on 15 August, V. P. Menon, for instance, expressed the view that India, in contrast with Pakistan, had

> left the State alone. We did not ask the Maharajah to accede, though, at that time, as a result of the Radcliffe Award, the State had become connected by road with India. Owing to the composition of the population, the State had its own peculiar problems. Moreover, our hands were already full and, if truth be told, I for one had simply no time to think of Kashmir.[91]

Menon allowed that, once the tribal invasion had occurred, the security and integrity of India took precedence over all other considerations. "Srinagar today," he said, recalling Muslim conquests of past ages, "Delhi tomorrow." He stoutly maintained, nevertheless, that India even then had entertained no territorial ambitions in Kashmir whatsoever.[92]

Echoing Menon, Hodson spoke of the "comparative detachment" that characterized Delhi's view of Kashmir's future up to the end of October 1947. Contrary to Pakistan's claims, he said, the Indian government displayed strikingly little interest in the accession matter. "After independence," he observed by way of illustration,

> a representative of the Kashmir Government who sought a lead from the States Ministry on the choice between India and Pakistan was told by the Secretary (Mr. V. P. Menon) that the Government of India could give no guidance in the matter, and that if a formal proposal for accession was received it would be considered in the light of all the relevant factors. The Kashmir Government was also rebuffed when it sought to discuss the terms of a standstill agreement with India.

Whatever Nehru and other Indian leaders may have been saying to the Kashmiris in private, Hodson said, "it is significant, and indeed astonishing in the light of subsequent events, and of allegations that the accession of Kashmir was a deep-laid Indian plot, that even after the organised incursion of tribesmen into Kashmir powerful men in the Indian Cabinet still hesitated to seek or accept the Maharajah's accession."[93]

In regard to the second main theme—the one holding Pakistan to be an active accomplice to the tribesmen's aggression, the *White Paper* had argued that (1) threats of invasion and other forms of provocation from the Pakistan side of the border had actually been made against the government of Jammu and Kashmir as early as August 1947, soon after the transfer of power, and there had been, in fact, a steady buildup in organized raids from Pakistan against the state in the months thereafter; and (2) there was "abundant circumstantial evidence"[94] that the government of Pakistan was behind the invasion, that it had given massive material assistance to the raiders, including military equipment and training, and that personnel of the Pakistan army were directly involved in the fighting.

Writers taking India's side in these matters have generally been as quick to agree with the *White Paper*'s position and to declare Pakistan guilty of complicity in the tribal invasion as they had been to declare India's innocence of any territorial ambitions in Kashmir. Menon observed, for instance, that "to contend that the tribal invasion of Kashmir was wholly a spontaneous affair would be too huge a strain on human credulity. That it was a pre-planned and well-arranged affair can today admit of no doubt."[95] "[T]he preponderant evidence," said the historian Russell Brines, "is that Pakistan permitted the tribal incursions of 1947 and probably instigated them."[96]

Even those observers of a more neutral inclination, however, have found Pakistan's official expressions of complete innocence difficult to swallow; and many have accepted Lord Birdwood's judgment that "while there was no plan of control by the Pakistan Government at the highest level, there was knowledge and tacit consent."[97] In fact, some evidence has accumulated over the years, including the testimony of retired Pakistani military and civil officials, that Birdwood's characterization of the government of Pakistan's role in Kashmir in the few months' interval between partition and accession may itself have been a bit too gracious.

In the account, for instance, of the development of events in this period given by retired Major General Akbar Khan, details of the government of Pakistan's postpartition authorization of clandestine efforts to force the issue of accession are candidly related. According to the author, a near-legendary figure who informally took charge of organizing Pakistan's military operations in Kashmir during the first week of November 1947 and who was later charged with plotting against the government in the Rawalpindi Conspiracy case, Pakistan's covert involvement in Kashmir in support of the internal rebellion in Poonch had clearly proceeded beyond the talking stage some time before the tribesmen came into the picture. Only a few weeks after independence had come, Akbar, who was then director of the Weapons and Equipment Division at army headquarters in Rawalpindi, was himself contacted on behalf of the prime minister by a senior Muslim League leader, who enlisted him in an "unofficial" scheme "to help the Kashmiri Muslims and to prevent the State's accession to India."[98] Akbar was charged with developing a plan of action. The plan was not to involve Pakistani troops or officers, who were still commanded by the British. It was hoped that some ex-officers of the defunct Indian National Army could be coaxed to join in. "The [Pakistani] authorities needed a lot of assistance from the Army," said Akbar, "in the shape of plans, advice, weapons, ammunition, communications and volunteers. They did not ask for it, because the whole thing had to be kept secret from the Commander-In-Chief and other senior officers who were British."[99] According to Akbar, there were many senior Pakistani officers, as well, from whom the plans had to be kept secret.

Akbar's own plan, he says, focused on the arming of rebels within Kashmir and on the development of tactics to prevent reinforcement of the maharaja's forces by India. There is no mention that his plan in any way envisioned use of tribal warriors. He calculated that he could lay his hands on about 4,000 rifles and some old stocks of ammunition. He was soon summoned to Lahore, where he participated in a number of meetings where his and other plans were discussed with Prime Minister Liaquat Ali Khan,

Finance Minister (and later Governor-General) Ghulam Mohammad, and other civilian political leaders.

Akbar does not say when or by whom the decision was taken to organize a direct tribal attack on Kashmir. However, he indicates foreknowledge of the tribesmen's recruitment by one Khurshid Anwar, a commander of the Muslim League National Guards, who had already been designated by the prime minister's group to head up covert operations along the sector of the Kashmir border north of Rawalpindi.[100] This information obviously does not qualify as incontrovertible evidence that the central government in Karachi "instigated" the tribal invasion; it does suggest, however, that, along with the undoubted involvement of the NWFP provincial government, the central government was itself at least indirectly involved in the organization of the tribal invasion and also that its involvement may have gone somewhat beyond the level suggested by Birdwood—that of mere "knowledge and tacit consent."[101]

Whatever we may decide in regard to that issue, we need to take a look at another of Birdwood's conclusions, namely "that both from the military and political points of view the tribal invasion proved a disaster for Pakistan."[102] This judgment, on its face, doesn't appear to be in any need of amendment. After all, if the object of the attack was to keep Kashmir from falling into India's hands—and it certainly must have been that at least in part—it was incontestably a failure. And along with that failure, the rather unexalted behavior of at least some of the tribesmen clearly eased the way for India to describe its takeover of Kashmir as a mission of mercy and, while doing that, to hand Pakistan a major public relations defeat besides. While there is thus no obvious reason to differ with Birdwood on this point, there can be no doubt that it is subject to widely varying interpretation.

Pakistanis themselves have certainly been quick to join with Birdwood's bleak assessment of the tribal invasion's consequences. In particular, they haven't really tried to conceal their bitterness over the failure of the tribal raiders to capitalize on their early victories and to capture Srinagar in time to interdict the arrival in Kashmir of airborne Indian troops. In *The Kashmir Saga,* for example, Sardar Mohammad Ibrahim Khan, a leader in the Poonch uprising against the maharaja in western Jammu and the first president of Azad (Free) Jammu and Kashmir (hereinafter designated alternatively as Azad Kashmir), made it painfully apparent that the tribesmen had not exhibited model behavior while in Kashmir. Not only had they "committed certain excesses" against the Kashmiri people, but they had turned out to be undependable warriors and very doubtful military assets.[103]

Akbar Khan's depiction of the disaster that befell Pakistan in Kashmir is far more vivid and extensive than Ibrahim Khan's. For him, however, the deficiencies of the tribal raiders accounted far less for the disaster than those of the Pakistani civil and military officials entrusted with supporting them. The planning and organization of Pakistan's covert operations in Kashmir struck Akbar from the moment of their inception in the weeks following partition as utterly chaotic. Of one of the conferences in which he participated at that time, at which a number of high level officials (including the prime minister) were present, Akbar wrote that "the unpleasant truth, as I now see it, was that there was complete ignorance about the business of anything in the nature of military operations."[104]

Akbar Khan, like Ibrahim Khan, confessed some disappointment with the tribesmen's shortcomings, in particular with their failure to live up to the requirements of modern warfare; but his most acid comments were clearly directed against the intrigues and frequent bungling by the civilian officials in his own government. Among other things, he criticized their tendency to indulge the wildest fantasies of well-intentioned, but badly misguided, individuals. Among these fantasies was the outlandish proposal for a glider-borne invasion of India requiring 2,000 (nonexistent) gliders; another was a project for the building of a long-range rocket that culminated, after six weeks of effort, in "a twenty-foot long bullet shaped solid piece of wood painted green, with a white crescent and star at the base!"[105]

Equally unsparing of Pakistan's own political leadership in regard to the responsibility for Pakistan's failure in Kashmir is A. H. Suharwardy's book, *Tragedy in Kashmir.* Suharwardy, a retired Pakistani civil servant who once served as chief secretary of the Azad Kashmir government, based his account to an important extent, he claims, on interviews with some of the principals in the fight for Kashmir. Consistent with most Pakistani versions, he denies that the Pakistan government inspired, organized, conducted, or supervised the initial tribal raids in late October. He maintains, on the contrary, that, in the face of tremendous suffering among Muslim coreligionists in East Punjab, what was most surprising at the time was that "the attitude of the entire spectrum of opinion in government was opposed to tribal intervention."[106] He extols the tribal raiders as a brave force; and, while acknowledging that they perpetrated some excesses against the Kashmiri population, he acquits them of most of the vandalism and destruction of which they have been charged. Indian estimates of their numbers, he says, were vastly inflated; and Indian allegations that they were commanded by professional Pakistan army officers and that they were well equipped with modern weapons, he insists, were utterly false. The truth, he says, is that they "were nothing more than a few thousand undisciplined tribesmen," rapidly outnumbered and wholly outgunned by the Indians, overwhelmed with logistical problems, and very poorly led. He does not deny that regular Pakistani troops soon joined with the tribals in Kashmir; but "the few regular soldiers who accompanied the tribesmen," he points out, "were not even of platoon strength and must have suffered some casualties in the course of the march to, and attack on Srinagar."[107] He admits that "a few sympathetic army officers" diverted some condemned ammunition for the use of the tribal raiders; but what was most apparent is that "they were getting no pay, no uniforms, not even arms from the Pakistan Government *in an adequate or open manner.*"[108]

In his summing up, Suharwardy describes the tribal invasion of Kashmir Valley in the most dire terms as "another fatal mistake . . . unfortunate."[109] The tribesmen, he says, invaded at the wrong place—the Muslim-inhabited portion of the state—"and it was largely the Muslims who suffered." Once the tribal invasion was launched, moreover, "whether they liked it or not, the Pakistan Government did get involved. . . . The story of tribal invasion was not one merely of bad planning but of no planning at all." Volunteers "met discouragement almost at every step from the Pakistan Army as well as [from] many high-placed Muslim civil officers. . . . [T]he attitude of many senior Pakistani officers was not only unhelpful but also enigmatic." The attitude of the defense secretary at the time, Iskandar Mirza, "was one of active opposition to any interference in the Kashmir State. . . . Many senior officers of the Pakistan Army . . . neither bothered nor helped in the least." And what about Pakistan's "clumsy attempt to double-cross India"—its disingenuous denial, in other words, of any involvement at all in Kashmir? "How," he asked sardonically, "could any man with common sense believe that without the Pakistan Government's help, however meagre, untimely and grudging, the Azad troops and the Pathan tribesmen could liberate two-thirds of the entire Jammu and Kashmir State [in the period from October 1947] up to about May 1948?"[110]

These reflections of former Pakistani officials should certainly provoke some skepticism in regard to Menon's statement, quoted earlier, that the tribal invasion was a "pre-planned and well-arranged affair." Such praise, viewed from almost any angle, doesn't really seem to have been earned. The government of Pakistan, at the time, was clearly being swept along by events as much as it was deliberately contriving them. Faced with tremendous social and political dislocation, encumbered with huge resource scarcities (including a shortage of trained foreign affairs specialists), and preoccupied with the task of consolidating its control over the country, it simply didn't have the ability to orchestrate an operation as slick as Menon implied. On the contrary, its Kashmir policy in the months following independence often appeared both erratic and amateurish. The dispatch to Srinagar in early October of a fairly junior diplomat to negotiate the delicate matter of assuring shipments to Kashmir of needed supplies under the standstill agreement signed on 15 August was only one of many signs that the government of Pakistan, at that critical moment, may neither have grasped the full seriousness of Srinagar's complaints nor have been prepared to take effective action to counter them.[111]

To return to the central issue: Did the actions of the government of Pakistan at that time merit the accusation that Pakistan was itself primarily responsible for the maharaja's accession to India?[112] Did Pakistan, as could well be inferred from the remark of Lord Birdwood quoted earlier, bring upon itself India's military intervention on 27 October?

That accusation, we should recall, lay at the heart of the first theme of India's *White Paper,* discussed earlier, which maintained that India's intervention in Kashmir was undertaken strictly in reaction to the Pakistan-supported tribal invasion, that it was not premeditated, and that India, in fact, had no territorial ambitions in Kashmir whatsoever. Obviously, if it had no such ambitions, then Pakistan's actions in regard to Kashmir would indeed appear to have been foolishly provocative. Wiser, seemingly, would have been the more energetic pursuit by Pakistan of peaceful diplomacy aimed at exploiting to Pakistan's advantage the maharaja's apparent inclination to avoid accession to either of Kashmir's neighbors. By assuming the worst about Indian intentions toward Kashmir, in other words, Pakistan guaranteed the worst possible outcome for itself. But were these assumptions about Indian intentions that far off the mark? When it came to Kashmir's future, were Indian leaders as indifferent, and were their policies as innocent, as they and so many of their supporters claimed?

The answer to this question, though it must be qualified, is certainly no. There is much evidence to indicate that the reality of Indian attitudes about Kashmir at that time was a great deal more complicated—and far less altruistic—than the *White Paper* let on and, moreover, that had Pakistani leaders been less suspicious of New Delhi's motives, the eventual outcome in Kashmir might have been even less in Pakistan's interest than what actually occurred. By and large, the actions that Pakistan took in regard to Kashmir weren't very helpful; but to put all, or even most, of the blame for what happened on the Pakistanis is clearly not warranted by the available facts. There were a number of good reasons for them to do the things they did, even if they did them poorly.

First, as we have already observed at a number of points in our discussion, the manner in which partition and the transfer of power were carried out left ample grounds for suspecting that impartial application of preindependence rules for integrating the princely states into the successor dominions could not realistically be expected. Many years would pass before the Pakistanis would possess convincing documentary evidence of deceit in the dividing up of Punjab; but they certainly had enough evidence available to them in August 1947 to fuel their skepticism. In other words, even if the Indian government had done *nothing* to arouse suspicion in regard specifically to Kashmir itself in the months immediately before and after independence, Pakistanis would have been well advised to exercise considerable caution anyway.

Second, the truth, however, is that the Indian government did many things in that period to corroborate Pakistani suspicions that Kashmir itself was not something about which the Indian government was indifferent. A great deal of evidence has come to light, in fact, that Indian leaders had given much thought to Kashmir and had implemented plans—including military plans—to secure its accession to India that were at least as broad in conception and as sophisticated as anything produced in Pakistan. No less than this conclusion can be drawn from recent reviews of the evidence in regard to accession done by such scholars as Alastair Lamb and R. J. Moore.[113]

Among the evidence that these authors point to was the rapid changeover in the political coloration of key officials in the maharaja's government that occurred in the three months or so before accession. These changes included the forced resignation from the maharaja's government on 11 August of Prime Minister Kak, whose known opposition to accession to India we noticed above had very early drawn fire from Nehru, and his replacement by General Janak Singh. Kak himself was promptly thrown in jail on charges of corruption, which took him entirely out of the picture. Proof that Kak's downfall was engineered, or even prompted, by New Delhi does not exist, and it could perhaps be explained simply as India's extraordinary good luck. Viewed in the broad context of developments in Kashmir at that time, however, only a very credulous person would not suspect that there were factors other than luck at work.

Only ten days before Kak's dismissal, Mahatma Gandhi had paid a visit to Srinagar, a visit that had generated an unusual amount of correspondence between Mountbatten and both Nehru and Gandhi. The correspondence gave no hint at all that Gandhi would use the visit to bring about Kak's exit. It gave ample hint, however, that the Indians were extremely perturbed over the political direction in which the Kashmir state government seemed to be moving.[114] A few days after Kak's dismissal, the maharaja's government had requested from India the loan of Janak Singh's son, Lieutenant Colonel Kashmir Singh Katoch, to serve as commander-in-chief of Kashmir armed forces. The loan of Katoch was approved by New Delhi in September, apparently on the urging of Sardar Patel, and in early October, in what must be viewed as a most timely installation, he took over as chief of Kashmiri forces.[115] Janak Singh was himself soon replaced by Justice Mehr Chand Mahajan, who was formally offered the prime ministership on 18 September and who took up his position in Srinagar in mid-October, in what appears to be, once again, a most timely installation. According to Lamb, Mahajan was the nominee of Patel, "who had brought his name to the notice of the Maharaja in the first place, and [whose] appointed task was to see through accession to India."[116] Mahajan, who had very recently served as a Congress nominee on the Punjab Boundary Commission and who was, therefore, exceptionally familiar with the territorial issues then developing between India and Pakistan, left abundant testimony in his autobiography not only of where his own sympathies lay but of the lengths to which Indian leaders went to impress upon him prior to his taking up responsibilities in Srinagar the urgency of Kashmir's accession to India.[117]

A related development of particular importance was the release from jail in mid-September of the National Conference leader and Congress ally Sheikh Abdullah. Soon after his release, which Nehru had been urging upon Srinagar strenuously for months, other National Conference detainees were released in a general amnesty (which, curiously, was not general enough to cover imprisoned members of the Pakistan-backed Muslim Conference). That Abdullah and his associates had "decided for the Indian Union" was promptly (albeit quietly) communicated to New Delhi.[118]

These developments are certainly strongly suggestive that India was exerting influence on the appointment of top officials in Kashmir and, also, that it was moving to put Kashmir's political house in more congenial order as well. However, India's ministration of Kashmir's needs did not stop with personnel. Sardar Patel's official papers are well stocked with indications that India had concerned itself throughout September and October with the improvement of Kashmir's transport, road, and communication systems, and that, by early October, it was engaging in serious discussions with Srinagar over the supply of military stores.[119] Contingency planning for emergency military aid to Srinagar was on Patel's mind at least as early as 7 October. To Defense Minister Baldev Singh, he wrote:

> I think the question of military assistance in time of emergency must claim the attention of our Defence Council as soon as possible. There is no time to lose if the reports which we hear of similar preparation for intervention on the part of the Pakistan Government are correct. It appears that the [Pakistan] intervention is going to be true to Nazi pattern.[120]

That an emergency requiring Indian military aid was also on Nehru's mind, along with much else indicative of the very close watch India was keeping on Kashmir, was perfectly clear from a much-cited letter he addressed to Patel on 27 September. In this letter, Nehru warned Patel of the deterioration of the political situation in Kashmir, of the approach of winter, of the likelihood that Pakistan would take military advantage of the state's inaccessibility from the Indian side in coming months, and that, therefore, Patel should "take some action in this matter to force the pace and to turn events in the right direction . . . so as to bring about the accession of Kashmir to the Indian Union as rapidly as possible with the co-operation of Sheikh Abdullah."[121]

This secret letter of Nehru's to Patel, it is important to observe, was not the kind of letter one might expect from a cunning coconspirator, confident of his plans and eagerly awaiting the denouement of certain victory. On the contrary, its eleven paragraphs are mainly devoted to expressing Nehru's fears and doubts about the developing situation in Kashmir and, in particular, to calling Patel's attention to the urgent need for shoring up the maharaja's wavering willpower and even that of the far-from-hostile prime minister–designate Mahajan. It was written exactly one month before accession took place. The Indian leadership was then obviously banking on bringing off accession by arranging somehow for Sheikh Abdullah's inclusion in the Kashmir government, which would then, speaking presumably on behalf of the Kashmiri people (including the Muslim communal majority), request accession to India. Yet Sheikh Abdullah, who was the pivotal figure in these plans, was still in jail. Rebellion, led by Pakistani sympathizers, was in progress in western Jammu. There were reports (not wholly inaccurate) of clandestine Pakistani operations under way in Kashmir. The maharaja's government, it seemed, was nearing collapse. Meanwhile, the Junagadh and Hyderabad cases continued to fester. On top of all this, Nehru could not have been fully confident of all the members of his own government, some of whom undoubtedly gave to Kashmir lower priority than he did and would not have approved the aggressive strategies he seems to have thought necessary to secure its accession. Nehru, after all, was scarcely being subtle when he urged Patel to "force the pace" a bit, a suggestion that Patel, for long an archrival of Nehru's, may well have considered a criticism of himself. In short, Nehru had plenty of reasons for the anxieties that crowd his letter.

While it can thus no longer be disputed that the Indian government was far from indifferent to Kashmir's fate in the period before accession and that it had taken numerous concrete steps to secure its interest in Kashmir, it seems equally clear that the Indians, like the Pakistanis, were also reacting to events, including reports of their rivals' plans. Circumstances were undoubtedly confusing for both sides; and both governments appear to have had much difficulty shaping events to their liking. To say this, let us be clear, is not to contradict Lamb's view

> that both Sardar Vallabhbhai Patel and [Defense Minister] Baldev Singh were heavily engaged in the planning of some kind of Indian military intervention in the State of Jammu and Kashmir, if only on a contingency basis, by at least 13 September 1947; and that by the third week of October a substantial foundation for such an operation had been laid.[122]

However, with the caveat that the government of Pakistan had perforce to work its plans indirectly through rebellious Kashmiris or tribal invaders, control of whom was inherently problematic, these words could just as well be applied to Pakistan. One could argue, of course, that the initiative here lay *primarily* with India, that it was more often acting than reacting, and that, in general, India should bear the greater part of responsibility for the evolution of the accession issue into a military confrontation. Viewed in this way, the tribal invasion more than anything else was just a convenient excuse—a streetcar, so to speak, like the Viet Cong attack on the American military installation at Pleiku in February 1965 was said to have been in the Indo-China war—for which the Indian army had been waiting for some time.[123]

Lamb's narrative of India's move to direct military intervention in the last days before accession leaves one in no doubt that he inclines strongly toward this view—that the Indian government had, in fact, made up its mind weeks in advance that direct Indian military aid would soon be required and that it must have given discreet orders then to appropriate individuals to begin making preparations. According to Lamb, the true nature and extent of these preparations force us to rethink the question of who was the aggressor in Kashmir. His explicit answer to this question is not unequivocal, but his discussion implies strongly that a very good case for aggression—better, seemingly, than the one made about Pakistan—can be made about India.

One of the most arresting bits of evidence Lamb considers in this connection was the presence in the state of Jammu and Kashmir since the early part of October (well *before* the tribal invasion was launched, in other words) of a battalion of infantry and a battery of mountain artillery loaned to Maharaja Hari Singh by the Sikh maharaja of Patiala, one of the largest and most influential of the princely states of the Punjab. Patiala gunners, says Lamb, had taken up positions at the Srinagar airfield at least by 17 October, and they were there when the Indian troops landed on 27 October. There has never been any secret about their presence in Kashmir at that time. In fact, the very first document shown in the Indian *White Paper,* a report about the tribal invasion taken from a December 1947 edition of the Pakistani newspaper *Dawn,* speaks of the Pashtun tribesmen's encounter at Uri in the early days of the invasion with "the first Sikh Regiment of Patiala State."[124] Lamb suggests, however, that while the presence of the Patiala men was commented upon often enough, very few of the commentators appear to have wondered at its implications. These, according to Lamb, included not only the fact that troops "in theory subordinate to the Commander-in-Chief of the Indian Army"—Indian troops, in other words—were deployed in Kashmir and engaged in fighting well *before* accession, but the great likelihood that, since the Patiala men were in Kashmir also *before* the Pashtun tribal advance of 22 October, "the presence of the tribesmen was a direct response to the arrival of the Patiala troops."[125]

Lamb is on somewhat shaky ground here. In a lengthy footnote questioning the legal position of the Patiala troops in Kashmir, he states that Patiala, in acceding to India,

> had handed over to the Government of India all powers over defence and foreign relations: this was a standard condition of accession. It meant that at the moment of the Transfer of Power the State Armed Forces were taken under the command of the Armed Forces of India; and their deployment beyond the Indian external borders (as the State of Jammu and Kashmir was situated prior to joining India) was without doubt from that time a matter of foreign policy which could only be authorised by the Government of India at the highest level. It would seem to follow, therefore, that either the Patiala men were in Kashmir in blatant violation of the *de facto* Indian Constitution or that their presence was approved by New Delhi. If the former, then their status on the most charitable interpretation was very similar to that of the Pathan tribesmen: if the latter, then the Government of India was sponsoring direct military involvement in the State of Jammu and Kashmir before the tribal "aggression", let alone the Maharaja's accession.[126]

Now there is little doubt that the Patiala matter deserves inclusion among those military developments preceding accession that seem to link New Delhi with a more aggressive posture toward Kashmir than the Indian government itself has normally conceded. After all, who could believe that the dispatch of these troops to Kashmir, following Patiala's accession to India and at a singularly critical moment in the subcontinent's history, would have been done without the full knowledge, approval, and cooperation of the government of India? The actual legal implications of this matter, however, are a great deal less straightforward than Lamb says; and the interpretation he places upon it seems to force his point.

Upon acceding to India, Patiala clearly had not in a strictly legal sense "handed over to the Government of India all powers over defence and foreign relations," and such action was definitely not "a standard condition of accession." Accession, in fact, had been designed very carefully to *appear* to preserve at least the semblance of the rulers' sovereignty. A schedule attached to the instruments of accession signed by the rulers specified the matters over which the Indian government would exercise supreme authority. These were limited to the three subjects of defense, external affairs, and communications. New Delhi's explicit legal authority, so far as defense was concerned, was defined mainly in terms of India's right to intervene with its *own* forces within the acceded state. According to Menon, "the States Forces were excluded from the scope of 'defence' and therefore, except when they were attached to or operating with any of the armed forces of the Dominion [not the case with Patiala], the authority over them vested exclusively in the rulers or in the State governments, as the case might be."[127] Assertion of full control over these forces by the government of India, Menon stated, "should be a gradual rather than a precipitate process."[128]

One may contend, of course, that all of this was mere pretense, very soon to be overturned. After all, the 1950 Constitution contained a number of provisions bringing the armed forces of the princely states more directly under New Delhi's control; and, as Menon concedes, their full integration into the Indian army took effect on 1 April 1951.[129] But the issue here pertains to October 1947 and, moreover, is one of technical legality, not political reality.

Another body of evidence that Lamb focuses on is that relating to the massive Indian airlift of troops to Srinagar on 27 August. He scoffs at the notion, "argued by Indian apologists and by British officials," that the airlift, involving the assembly at New Delhi and its vicinity of 100 transport aircraft and two infantry battalions, all in the space of 24 hours, "was the result of a triumph of improvisation." He reminds us that the Indian army at the time, unlike its Pakistani counterpart, "was essentially the old Indian Army of the British period; and it did not lack for able, experienced and senior Indian staff officers." He suggests that Mountbatten himself had become by that time wholly Indian in his strategic outlook and, like the Indians, saw Pakistan as the enemy. Lamb implies that the "unorthodox" issuance later on by the three British commanders of the Indian services denying any knowledge or involvement by their headquarters in any planning for the Indian airlift before 25 October, if not a product of deliberate deception, certainly did not give a full picture.[130]

About this particular event, the documentary record can offer only a glimpse of what happened, and well-informed observers have yet to come to a consensus about it. Ian Stephens, for instance, a renowned journalist with pronounced pro-Pakistan sympathies, arrived at a judgment of the Indian airlift wholly different from Lamb's and says that he did so only after "exhaustive" inquiries. Stephens, who was in New Delhi at the time of accession and whose newspaper, *The Statesman,* editorially criticized the decision to send Indian troops into Kashmir, wrote that the scale and effectiveness of the airborne operation implied

> that there must have been careful military planning as well as political intrigue by India beforehand. That was this writer's view at the time; he could not believe that so effective an airborne operation had been improvised. Yet exhaustive later inquiries have disclosed that on this point he was wrong. No evidence in support had been got; and specific written assurances are on record from senior British officers of the Indian Forces—which some Pakistani officers, then still in Delhi awaiting transfer, tend to confirm—that the airlift actually was an impromptu affair, enough aircraft happening to be on the spot or quickly obtainable: an instance, perhaps, just of "Mountbatten's luck."[131]

Whatever role luck may have played in this case, neither side could possibly have been greatly surprised by the events at the end of October 1947. India's activities in Kashmir in the period leading up to those events could not have failed to alarm the Pakistanis; and Pakistani activities in the same period likewise could not have failed to alarm the Indians. Together these activities led to accession—and then to war. Establishing which side's activities were *most* responsible for the outcome is not possible without much more information than is presently available. It is clear, nonetheless, that the contention that India's intervention in Kashmir at the end of October was entirely reactive, unpremeditated, and entailed no territorial ambitions whatsoever—that it was, as implied in the *White Paper,* essentially an afterthought—is not worth a moment's consideration. Neither, however, is the contention that Pakistan was an innocent bystander, the unfortunate victim of an Indian plot.[132] Key leaders in both countries, we now know without question, harbored unambiguous territorial ambitions about Kashmir; and in neither of them was there more than the flimsiest regard for the maharaja's right to make up his own mind—uncoerced—about the future of his then putatively independent state. By 27 October nothing of substance, in fact, remained of the fig leaf of independence that had been put up by the British to cover the shame of the princes' utter defeat and humiliation at the hands of Indian and Pakistani nation-building in the subcontinent. Under these circumstances, pinpointing the side guiltiest of aggression in the buildup to accession seems almost pointless. But if aggression was committed against Kashmir in the weeks or months prior to accession, it most likely was committed by both sides.

Accession, we said earlier, had prompted debate not only over responsibility for the events that precipitated it—the extent, in other words, to which the maharaja's decision had been coerced, or at least conspired at, by one side or the other—but over the legal validity of the act of accession itself. Its legal validity is also at issue because Pakistan has never accepted the Indian contention either that the maharaja, at the time the instrument of accession was executed, was legally entitled to make the decision in regard to accession or that the decision itself was legally binding. The implications of Pakistan's challenge are obvious at once. If, in fact, accession was legally invalid, then the argument that the territory of Jammu and Kashmir had, by virtue of accession, become a part of India and that aggression against that territory thereafter was thus aggression upon Indian soil would obviously be seriously weakened. If, on the other hand, the accession decision was legally valid, then Pakistan's official acknowledgment in early July 1948 that its regular troops had been fighting in Kashmir alongside tribesmen and rebels ever since the preceding May would likely appear in a rather unfavorable light.

Had this issue been settled one way or another on the battlefield, the world would probably have forgotten it rather quickly. But it was not settled on the battlefield; instead, it was placed on the agenda of the United Nations. Much of the discussion about Kashmir that was to go on there in the first five months of 1948 and, intermittently, for a decade thereafter was focused, to the great chagrin of Indians, directly on this issue—that is, on the validity of the maharaja's accession to India. Ironically, India itself bore heaviest responsibility for putting the focus there. This brings us to the last of the entitlement issues that we consider—that of plebiscite.

The Plebiscite Issue

The government of India's 1948 *White Paper,* we observed earlier, described the objective of India's military intervention in Kashmir as that of clearing the raiders from the state so that a plebiscite or referendum could be held to settle the matter of accession. Elaborating on this objective, the *White Paper* went on to say that

> [i]n Kashmir, as in other similar cases, the view of the Government of India has been that in the matter of disputed accession the will of the people must prevail. It was for this reason that they accepted only on a provisional basis the offer of the Ruler to accede to India, backed though it was by the most important political organization in the State [Sheikh Abdullah's National Conference]. . . . The question of accession is to be decided finally in a free plebiscite; on this point

> there is no dispute. It is, however, impossible to hold a plebiscite so long as the State is infested by freebooters from outside. The only purpose for which Indian troops are operating in Kashmir is to ensure that the vote of the people will not be subject to coercion by tribesmen and others from across the border who have no right to be in Kashmir. Since the State is now part of India, these troops have a legal and a moral obligation to defend it.[133]

The commitment to a plebiscite or referendum expressed here stemmed directly from the reply of Governor-General Mountbatten, dated 27 October, to Maharaja Hari Singh's letter, dated 26 October, which contained the signed instrument of accession of the state to India. In his reply, Mountbatten said that the government of India had decided to accept the accession of Kashmir to India. He then said:

> Consistently with their policy that, in the case of any State where the issue of accession has been the subject of dispute, the question of accession should be decided in accordance with the wishes of the people of the State, it is my Government's wish that, as soon as law and order have been restored in Kashmir and her soil cleared of the invader, the question of the State's accession should be settled by a reference to the people.[134]

This wish of the Indian government, like so many other good intentions, might simply have been dropped and forgotten had New Delhi not decided, less than two months after accession and while the fighting in Kashmir still raged, to bring the issue of Kashmir before the Security Council of the United Nations. In doing so, the government of India itself took the first step to internationalize the conflict and, more than that, to create an attentive international audience for the Pakistani contention that the maharaja's accession of the state to India had not been legal and that Kashmir, in fact, was disputed territory and not a part of India at all.

There can be little question that M. J. Akbar spoke for a great many Indians when he wrote, in his 1988 biography of Nehru, that in spite of Nehru's "extremely clear understanding of the Kashmir issue," he had, in choosing to take the issue to the United Nations, committed a colossal blunder. Said Akbar:

> By referring to the United Nations, Nehru allowed what was legally a domestic Indian problem to become an international issue. If there was any argument over the ratification of the accession by Hari Singh, then the only parties to the argument could be Nehru and [Sheikh] Abdullah; how did Pakistan have any *locus standi?* The

> reference to the UN gave Pakistan a place in the argument. It was perhaps the most serious error of judgment which Nehru made, and he had no one to blame but himself.[135]

Nehru's blunder, if that is what it was, was certainly not made all at once (or all alone). Well before Nehru's cabinet endorsed the decision on 20 December to submit the issue of Kashmir to the Security Council, India's commitment to a plebiscite under UN auspices and, by virtue of that, to a conditional accession had already been emphatically and repeatedly made—and apparently without much resistance from within the government. At a meeting in Lahore on 1 November, just days after Kashmir's accession to India, Mountbatten proposed to Jinnah that there be a plebiscite to settle the matter and, mentioning it for the first time publicly, that it be held under UN auspices.[136] Then, on 2 November, Nehru in a broadcast from New Delhi remarkable for its candor declared that his government, having decided to accept accession and to send troops to Kashmir, had

> made a condition that the accession would have to be considered by the people of Kashmir later when peace and order were established. We were anxious not to finalise anything in a moment of crisis, and without the fullest opportunity to the people of Kashmir to have their say. It was for them ultimately to decide. . . . [I]t has been our policy all along that where there is a dispute about the accession of a State to either Dominion, the decision must be made by the people of that State. It was in accordance with this policy that we added a proviso to the Instrument of Accession of Kashmir. . . . We have declared that the fate of Kashmir is ultimately to be decided by the people. . . . We will not, and cannot back out of [that pledge]. We are prepared when peace and law and order have been established to have a referendum held under international auspices like the United Nations.[137]

On 25 November, Nehru informed the Indian parliament that "in order to establish our *bona fides* we have suggested that when the people [of Kashmir] are given the chance to decide their future this should be done under the supervision of an impartial tribunal such as the United Nations Organisation."[138] Furthermore, when Nehru, Mountbatten, and Pakistani Prime Minister Liaquat Ali Khan gathered in Delhi early in December, the matter of a UN-supervised plebiscite was again raised by the Indian side.[139] And when India formally lodged its complaint against Pakistan with the Security Council on 31 December, these various sentiments were all contained in it.[140]

Presentation of India's case to the Security Council in the early months of 1948 did nothing to dilute New Delhi's public position up to that point on the conditionality of accession or to undo its embrace of the plebiscite proposal. On the contrary, the leader of the Indian delegation, Gopalaswami Ayyengar, seemed to go out of his way to reinforce them. Brecher, only one of many who have complained bitterly over Ayyengar's performance, lists among the errors in his opening statement (1) his failure or unwillingness "to condemn Pakistan as a *de facto* aggressor"; (2) overemphasis of the fact "that India accepted the principle of a plebiscite as the ultimate determinant of Kashmir's status"; and (3) underemphasis of "the legality of the Accession" to such extent that "he made it appear as if the Accession was absolutely conditional upon the results of a plebiscite."[141]

Presentation of the Pakistani case, in contrast, appears to have been ably handled by Foreign Minister Sir Mohammad Zafrullah Khan. He successfully sidelined the tribal invasion, making it appear as the inevitable by-product of a much larger communal holocaust in which India bore heavy responsibility. When he was through, emphasis in the Security Council discussions had shifted from aggression to plebiscite, and even the title of the complaint before the UN body was changed from "The Jammu and Kashmir Question" to "The Indo-Pakistan Question." Notice here that an ironic conversion had occurred at about this point in the dispute: The Pakistan government, which had shown very little interest in the idea of plebiscite when it had first been suggested,[142] suddenly became its strongest advocate; the Indian government, which was both the first to propose a plebiscite for Kashmir and the first to refer the matter to the international community, now began to regret its decisions. These transposed attitudes gradually hardened into the formal, fixed positions of the two governments.

To be sure, India's initial espousal of conditional accession was far from unqualified. It had, in fact, been clothed in virtually impenetrable ambiguity from the very outset. India's complaint to the Security Council, which on the one hand seemed to leave no reasonable doubt of India's commitment to a plebiscite to settle Kashmir's future political affiliation, stated flatly, on the other, that the state of Jammu and Kashmir had "acceded to the Dominion of India and is part of India."[143] From Mountbatten's reply to the maharaja onward, moreover, the conditionality attached to accession was anchored to an equivalent conditionality attached to Pakistan's alleged aggression, Pakistan's "vacation" of which was a prerequisite of the plebiscite. This seemed to enmesh the Pakistani position in a circular logic from which there was no obvious escape. There has thus been no shortage of arguments for those wishing to defend the Indian point of view; and, over the years, they have certainly demonstrated resourcefulness in exploiting these ambiguities for all that they were worth.[144]

At no point since accession, in other words, has India found it difficult to marshal creditable arguments in support of its position; and one might even argue, on grounds both that Pakistan has obstructed creation of the conditions prerequisite to a plebiscite and that Kashmir's circumstances today bear little resemblance to those of 1947, that its arguments have improved with age. On balance, however, India's case for entitlement to Kashmir, to the extent that it rests specifically on the legality of the instrument of accession, seems permanently impaired.

The impairment was made explicit, of course, with passage of UN resolutions calling for conduct of a UN-supervised plebiscite to determine the political will of the Kashmiri people. There were three major resolutions bearing on plebiscite: Security Council Resolution 726 of 21 April 1948, an enabling resolution that authorized formation of the UN Commission on India and Pakistan (UNCIP) as well as spelling out in detail the conditions for plebiscite; UNCIP Resolution 995 of 13 August 1948, which only very briefly and vaguely endorsed the idea of Kashmiri self-determination; and UNCIP Resolution 1196 of 5 January 1949, which again spelled out the conditions for plebiscite in detail. These resolutions vary in important respects; and the governments of India and Pakistan both expressed strong reservations about some of the conditions specified in them. Both countries, however, formally signified their acceptance of the proposal for a plebiscite made in the final 5 January 1949 resolution. And that resolution, in its first operative paragraph, stated that "the question of the accession of the State of Jammu and Kashmir to India or Pakistan will be decided through the democratic method of a free and impartial plebiscite."[145]

India's supporters have crafted ingenious arguments, of course, to mitigate the harm done to the legality of accession by the UN resolutions. These include, for instance, the argument that Mountbatten's letter containing the initial commitment to "a reference to the people," since it was a strictly *political* undertaking *separate* from the formal acceptance of accession, is not binding on India; that the will of the people could be ascertained, in any event, in ways other than through a formal plebiscite; that the UN resolutions pertaining to plebiscite are themselves riddled with ambiguity; and that the people of Jammu and Kashmir, having already had plentiful opportunities for the exercise of "their right of self-determination in a free and democratic manner, as distinguished from its suppression in Pakistan and Pakistan-occupied Kashmir," would not benefit anyway from a plebiscite.[146] These arguments stand firm, however, only so long as one unrelentingly excludes from consideration evidence of their inconsistency, exiguity, and casuistry.

Observe, however, that the vitiation of India's case for entitlement to Kashmir has not yielded an inversely proportional benefit to Pakistan's own case. This stems from the fact that Pakistan's arguments in relation to plebiscite are vulnerable to precisely the same sorts of criticism as India's. This is clearly the case when it comes to the use of historical analogies. It has been pointed out, for instance, that the Junagadh affair, in which the Indian government held that that state's accession to Pakistan was invalid because its Muslim ruler did not have the right to decide the fate of his mainly Hindu subjects, "was the mirror image of [and] clearly a precedent for the State of Jammu and Kashmir."[147] True enough, but the precedent in this case, as we observed earlier in this chapter, cuts both ways. What served the purposes of Pakistan's argument (India's denial of the Muslim maharaja's right to decide), when inverted (Pakistan's denial of the Hindu majority's right to decide) equally well served India's. The vulnerability of Pakistani arguments to criticism is plainly apparent also when we inspect Pakistan's claim that Maharaja Hari Singh had not the right to decide his people's future not only because he belonged to an alien minority community but also because he represented a cruel and despotic dynasty that had been imposed on the people by a colonial ruler in 1846.[148] One need not question the accuracy of this claim to note that, with some allowance for differences in their histories, it could just as well be applied to the Muslim ruler of Junagadh.

In one respect, at least, the Indian and Pakistani cases for entitlement to Kashmir both seem over the years to have increased their vulnerability to criticism in regard to plebiscite. The government of Pakistan, for its part, once having embraced the notion of plebiscite, never officially abandoned it. By the same token, however, neither did it ever concede officially that Kashmiri self-determination might involve more than the choice between accession to India or Pakistan. The government of India, for its part, first embraced the idea of plebiscite, then abandoned it. There are indications, in fact, that at an early stage in the Kashmir conflict India's leaders did reflect on the possibility that the plebiscite might even include a third option—the independence of Kashmir. Mountbatten is said to have proposed this option at a meeting of the Defense Committee of the government of India gathered to consider the maharaja's appeal for military aid;[149] and Nehru, in drafting India's appeal for UN intervention in the dispute in December 1947, seems to have given at least fleeting thought to it as well.[150] The independence option never got very far in India, however, and soon the whole idea of plebiscite, even if limited to two options, began losing ground. With ratification early in 1954 of the accession of Jammu and Kashmir to India by the Kashmiri Constituent Assembly, India, in fact, moved close to the position—which it soon adopted formally—that the accession to India was irrevocable and that there would be no plebiscite. The demand for Kashmiri self-determination that has erupted with vehemence in recent years is not easily contained in either the Indian or Pakistani formula. But that is the topic of a later chapter.

CHAPTER

·2·

DELIMITATION ISSUES

Entitlement issues, as we defined them in Chapter 1, are concerned with the principles or rules governing the allocation of rights to territory. They *affect* boundaries, of course, in particular their legitimacy; but they are not *about* them. What we shall now identify as delimitation issues obviously overlap with entitlement issues. Nevertheless, they are distinct from them. Delimitation issues relate directly to the establishment of boundaries—to their delineation or marking, whether on maps or physically on the ground, in or around the disputed territory[1]—and to their management. They are explicitly *about* boundaries, in other words, about their location, design, purpose, transit, policing, fortification, fencing, permanence, even naming. Issues of this kind were only faintly visible in the immediate postaccession phase of the Kashmir dispute; but with the division of Kashmir during this phase into two separate and deeply hostile sectors, they were brought sharply into focus. Over time, political upheavals in Kashmir's vicinity (the Communist takeover in China in 1949, for instance, and China's subsequent absorption of Tibet), military encounters involving one or both of the two adversaries in Kashmir (the Sino-Indian war of 1961, the Indo-Pakistan war ten years later), and the spread of ethnic separatism in Kashmir itself in the present decade have vastly magnified their importance.

Our discussion in this chapter is focused on Kashmir's inner boundary,* by which is meant the cease-fire line (CFL)—renamed the line of control (LOC) or line of actual control in 1972†—that divides Indian- from Pakistani-held

---

* Issues pertaining to Kashmir's *outer* (or international) boundary with China are dealt with in Chapter 3.

† Some confusion is bound to arise from the change in the name of the CFL. For clarity's sake, we will use the compound CFL/LOC when speaking of this boundary except when reference is solely either to the *pre*-1972 period, in which case we will use CFL, or to the *post*-1972 period, in which case we will use LOC.

sectors of the state of Jammu and Kashmir. This boundary was established following the suspension of armed hostilities that took effect between India and Pakistan on 1 January 1949. It was delimited in general terms in the so-called Karachi Agreement, which was signed on 27 July 1949 by military representatives of the two countries meeting under the auspices of the Truce Sub-Committee of the United Nations Commission for India and Pakistan (UNCIP).[2] Mutual verification of this line, carried out on the ground with the aid of UN military observers, was completed on 3 November.[3] It is doubtful that anyone at the time even remotely expected that the boundary thus created would last as long as it has—or that longevity itself would be the source of so much confusion.

The CFL possessed very few of the attributes of a permanent boundary. It was wholly military in its conception; and, drawn on the basis of positions held by the combatants at the time fighting between them ended, it was clearly designed for temporary use. Over most of its length, it followed no natural geographic barrier or traditional political boundary; and it was viewed officially by both countries as a temporary line, limited in function and, in principle, subject at some future date to a more rational and permanent division. Provisions of the agreement creating it related exclusively to the military situation, specifically to the maintenance of the cease-fire. Nothing relating to the ultimate political status either of the line or of the territories adjacent to it was addressed. Granted, the delimitation exercise carried out in autumn 1949 yielded a minutely detailed description of the line. It was not formally marked on the ground, however, since that might have implied a more permanent status than either side was then willing to accept.

In spite of its original limited purpose, the "temporary" boundary separating Indian from Pakistani forces in Kashmir is today well into its fifth decade of existence. Long life has no doubt hardened it somewhat, certainly in terms of the military fortifications lining each side; and some would argue that it has already become, appearances aside, the de facto international boundary between India and Pakistan. Just such an argument has undoubtedly animated the many proposals for resolving the dispute that have urged the CFL/LOC's formal conversion into the de jure international boundary; and, in fact, official support from within the region for a solution of this kind has been far from negligible. The Indian government, in particular, has from time to time given fairly explicit indications that it would be willing to settle for a permanent division of Kashmir on the basis of the present line.[4] So far, however, this suggestion has not been welcomed—at the official level, anyway—by Pakistan. The result is that the CFL/LOC continues yet today to radiate impermanence.

The impermanence of the inner boundary places Pakistan's territorial claims in Kashmir in an especially disadvantageous position relative to India's. To understand this, we need to go back for a moment to the discussion of entitlement in Chapter 1. As we saw there, the two countries do not, in fact, agree that the territory of Kashmir is even in dispute. India, for its part, has argued ever since accession took place in October 1947 that Kashmir is not disputed territory, that the CFL/LOC is located in *Indian* territory, and that the problem in Kashmir is simply of Pakistani aggression against a neighboring country. This problem required Pakistan's military withdrawal from Kashmir, its "vacation of aggression," not a territorial redivision. In the early stages of the dispute, New Delhi did, of course, concede that the accession was provisional pending conduct of a popular plebiscite. It maintained from the start, however, that its relationship with Kashmir was proprietary, even if *conditionally* proprietary. Long before the boundary was redrawn and renamed in 1972, moreover, India had moved to declare the state's accession final and irrevocable, discarding the conditions and, insofar as New Delhi was concerned, rendering its sovereignty over Kashmir complete. That part of Kashmir yet under Pakistan's control the Indians dubbed Pakistan Occupied Kashmir (POK), underscoring what they insisted was the illegality of Pakistan's claim—in other words, of the nonexistence of a *legitimate* territorial dispute. When the 1972 Simla Agreement gave summons to the signatories to continue the search for durable peace in the region, its Indian-inspired phrases referred only to "a final settlement of Jammu and Kashmir"—not of the Jammu and Kashmir *dispute*.[5]

Pakistan, in contrast, has argued virtually from the outset of the conflict that Kashmir is disputed territory, that it belongs to neither India nor Pakistan, and that the question of permanent possession of the territory could be resolved only by reference to the Kashmiri people, that is, by allowing them to exercise the right of political self-determination through plebiscite. This right, as seen from Pakistan, was formally guaranteed by UN resolutions passed in the early stages of the conflict and repeatedly acknowledged by the leaders of both India and Pakistan in the years thereafter. True, it was never expressed as an unfettered right: Kashmiris were to be held to a bifold choice of accession to either India or Pakistan; the choice of independence was ruled out. Neither, however, was Pakistan's own right to Kashmir held to be unfettered: Pakistan's leaders did not then nor did they ever claim for Pakistan unconditional ownership of the whole of Kashmir. That part of the state controlled by India they called "held" Kashmir. That part under Pakistan's control they spoke of as "liberated" and used it to shelter the client government of Azad Kashmir, a political entity of uncertain standing that had been established in the days immediately before accession.[6] With this government Pakistan's relationship was said to be temporary and custodial. The government of Pakistan eventually conferred upon it many of the formal (albeit not the substantive) trappings of independent statehood, including its own constitution, flag, president, prime minister, and supreme court. In theory, it is the extension of this "independence" to the rest of Kashmir, not the arbitrary joining of Kashmir to Pakistan, which Pakistan seeks pending conduct of a UN-supervised plebiscite. Understood in these terms, the CFL/LOC obviously is not located either in Pakistan or on its border.

The difference we see here in the description of territories *adjacent* to the CFL/LOC makes the line itself a rather unusual boundary: Depending on one's perspective, it can readily be said to divide a territory belonging to India, to divide the disputed territory of Jammu and Kashmir, or to do both these things simultaneously. Judged entirely in terms of *formal* territorial claims, however, it cannot be said—on this the two countries are agreed—to divide India from Pakistan.

Concretely, this means that there exists a wedge of territory between the CFL/LOC on the east and the recognized border of Pakistan on the west that is occupied by Pakistan but is claimed outright only by India. This anomaly would not have come into existence in the first place—and the Kashmir dispute might have been somewhat simpler—had Pakistan's forces fallen back to the Pakistani border by the time the cease-fire was arranged. It would end, of course, on the day that either Pakistan or India was able to extend its control to the whole of the state of Jammu and Kashmir. As things turned out, however, the cease-fire left Pakistan in physical possession of a large part of the disputed territory, lands to which it gave the names Azad Kashmir and the Northern Areas. India's title to this territory the Pakistanis, of course, have always fiercely contested; but they have been quite reluctant, at the same time, to assert their own title in its place. This practice has inevitably attached to Pakistan's territorial claim in Jammu and Kashmir, even in that part under its control, a contingent character that India's claim explicitly denies.

This calculated ambiguity in Pakistan's claim was not without some benefit to Pakistan. It obviously strengthened Pakistan's case for a plebiscite to settle the question of a permanent boundary between India and Pakistan; and it meant that in the meantime, Pakistan would have at its disposal, in Azad Kashmir, an ostensibly independent entity that could act as its political and even military surrogate in Jammu and Kashmir. From the very beginning, however, the arrangement clearly gave to the Indian side, which unequivocally claimed all of Jammu and Kashmir as an integral part, a considerable psychological advantage. After all, if Pakistani armed forces were to move east across the CFL/LOC, they could not defend their action as the recovery of *Pakistani* territory. Very likely, in fact, their action would be understood by the international community—it would certainly be presented as such by India—as an act of aggression upon the territory of India. If, on the other hand, Indian armed forces were to move west across the CFL/LOC, that too might be understood by the international community as an act of aggression—but it could not easily be presented by Pakistan, which has argued so strenuously for the *disputed* status of Kashmir and the *temporary* character of the CFL/LOC, as an act of aggression upon itself. Unlike their Indian rivals, in other words, Pakistanis have been forced by circumstances to expose to risk the part of Jammu and Kashmir now in their possession in order to safeguard their claim to the part that isn't.

Not unexpectedly, Pakistani policymakers have sought to reduce the risk to the part of Jammu and Kashmir under Pakistan's control by removing at least some of the ambiguity in its territorial claims. One possibility was to reach agreement with China over delimitation of the outer boundary of northern Kashmir. No move was made in this direction during the first decade or so following independence, since in that period Pakistan, like India, rejected China's territorial claims on Kashmir. The 1963 Border Agreement, as we will observe later on, changed all that; Pakistan clearly lost ground on the map in that agreement, but in real terms it gained not only territory but a firm and formally demarcated northern boundary.

Pakistan's defeat at the hands of India in the Bangladesh war of 1971 gave impetus to yet another possibility. This was to compensate for the manifestly dangerous impermanence of the CFL/LOC by hardening Pakistan's legal, administrative, and political relationships with that part of the disputed territory occupied by Pakistani forces. Rearranging these relationships with this territory to achieve a kind of quasi-integration with Pakistan was difficult to finesse, of course, without doing irreparable damage to Pakistan's claim to the whole of Kashmir. In the early 1970s, for instance, Prime Minister Zulfikar Ali Bhutto was apparently forced to back down from a proposal to absorb Azad Kashmir as a fifth province of Pakistan when Kashmiri leaders in Pakistan objected that it would imply recognition of the CFL/LOC as a permanent international boundary.[7] Bhutto went ahead with a plan, however, to create the quasi-federal Kashmir Council, chaired by the prime minister of Pakistan and consisting of elected representatives of the Azad Kashmir Assembly, the Pakistan National Assembly, and members of both the Azad Kashmir and central cabinets, making explicit the *federal* presence in the governance of Azad Kashmir and, in the opinion of a senior minister in Bhutto's cabinet at the time, taking a clear step toward the integration into Pakistan of Azad Kashmir.[8]

Bhutto's successor, President General Mohammad Zia ul-Haq, carried integration—especially in regard to the Northern Areas—several steps further.

When martial law was promulgated in July 1977, it was formally extended for the first time in Pakistan's history to the Northern Areas (albeit not to Azad Kashmir). In April 1982, three men from the Northern Areas (but, again, none from Azad Kashmir) were granted observer status in the Federal Advisory Council (Majlis-i-Shura), the nominated, quasi-legislative body introduced under martial law. In November 1983, in a largely symbolic gesture, Zia hosted a much-publicized state dinner in Gilgit, the principal town and administrative hub of the Northern Areas, to which over 40 foreign envoys based in Islamabad had been invited. And in July 1986, Zia was reported to have announced that the federal government was giving serious consideration to the matter of political representation of the Northern Areas in the National Assembly.[9]

Long before these political and administrative initiatives had taken place, however, there was already evident on official Pakistani maps signs of the government's desire in some way to "shrink" the size of the territory in dispute. This desire was most conspicuous in the depiction on these maps of the western half of the Northern Areas, the so-called Gilgit Agency, as an integral part of Pakistan, or at least as *not* part of the disputed territory. In regard to Gilgit Agency, there is no doubt that Pakistani practice in the first years after independence had been to picture it on official maps *within* the territory displayed as in dispute.[10] Precisely when the change took place is difficult to document. According to one author it was in the mid-1950s.[11] This practice ultimately prevailed, in any event, and by the 1980s Pakistani-made maps—such as the official *Atlas of Pakistan* published by the Survey of Pakistan in 1985—generally excluded Gilgit Agency from the area marked "disputed territory."[12]

Pakistan's justification for truncating the disputed territory in this manner had its genesis in events surrounding accession. The area of the Gilgit Lease, we may recall, although forming part of the state of Jammu and Kashmir, had been directly administered by the British Indian government since 1935 through a political agent. Following announcement by the British viceroy Mountbatten of the 3 June 1947 plan for independence, the leased area was retroceded to the Dogra ruler. The governor appointed by the maharaja to take over from the British in Gilgit arrived there late in July only to find the Gilgit Scouts, an almost exclusively Muslim paramilitary force (all of whose British officers had opted for service in Pakistan), in a state of near rebellion. The maharaja's accession of the state to India a few months later prompted a full rebellion. During the night of 31 October, the governor was taken into custody by the Gilgit Scouts. A provisional government was promptly formed. It made a decision to join Pakistan; and on 14 November a representative of the government of Pakistan arrived in Gilgit to take charge of administering the area. In the complete failure of the maharaja to reassert his authority over the territory of Gilgit lay the grounds, obviously, for the Pakistani contention that Gilgit Agency—via a popular political upheaval—had gotten "outside the arena of conflict in Kashmir."[13]

From the Indian point of view, of course, Gilgit Agency had done no such thing: Even less than the rebellion in Poonch, the Gilgit rebellion, coming *after* the maharaja's accession of the state had been formally accepted by India and involving primarily military troops, did not deserve recognition as a popular revolution.[14]

Pakistani leaders clearly had reservations of their own over the political implications of the Gilgit rebellion. According to the former diplomat and chairman of UNCIP Josef Korbel, the fledgling Pakistan government in Karachi "refrained from accepting the act of accession [of the provisional government of Gilgit], possibly because it feared that such acceptance might imply their approval of a division of the state."[15] Pakistan has never entirely overcome this fear, which inhibited it from taking any steps toward the disputed territory that might weaken its case before the United Nations. Azad Kashmiri leaders, in particular, have resisted the assertion that Gilgit Agency, having won its independence in a successful local revolution against the maharaja, could no longer be considered a part of the disputed area.[16] And Pakistani cartographers even today appear unprepared to commit themselves flatly one way or the other in regard to the finality of Gilgit Agency's present territorial status. The 1985 *Atlas* did not include Gilgit Agency in its list of Pakistan's administrative divisions. Instead, in a gesture that left the question of the Northern Areas' territorial status about as murky as ever, it listed Gilgit by itself *beneath* the list—separate, that is, both from Pakistan *and* from the disputed territory of Jammu and Kashmir.[17]

Fear that Pakistan's failure to nurture the contested status of Jammu and Kashmir might one day lead to the hardening of the CFL/LOC into a permanent international border has never displaced the larger fear, however, that failure to integrate formally into Pakistan proper the disputed territory under its control may one day provide India with justification for helping itself to that territory. India's leaders, after all, remain committed to a definition of the physical scale of the state of Jammu and Kashmir that is far larger than either its Chinese or Pakistani neighbors would allow. Included in the Indian definition is all of the state now held by India (the Valley of Kashmir, most of Jammu and part of Ladakh), the Aksai Chin region of Ladakh presently under Chinese control, those territories to the immediate north and west of the CFL/LOC now under Pakistan's control (Azad Kashmir and the Northern Areas, including both Gilgit Agency and Baltistan), those territories north of the present

Sino-Pakistani border that India claims were illegally ceded to China in 1963, and—in some formulations—even Chitral district in Pakistan's present North West Frontier Province.[18] Included in the standard Pakistani definition, on the other hand, are only those parts of the state now in Indian hands, Pakistan-controlled Azad Kashmir, and part of the Northern Areas (Baltistan). (See Map 1.) The difference here does not necessarily imply that Indian intentions in regard to Kashmir are any more aggressive or expansionist than Pakistan's.[19] It does mean, however, that the "permanent impermanence" of Kashmir's inner boundary has had far-reaching consequences for the evolution of the Kashmir dispute; it means, also, that the delimitation issues arising over that boundary are matters of enormous importance to both sides.[20]

These propositions are vividly illustrated in the two cases we now review. The first concerns the status of the United Nations Military Observer Group in India and Pakistan (UNMOGIP), the organization assigned to monitor or police the cease-fire agreement reached in 1949. The second concerns an armed confrontation that developed in 1984 between India and Pakistan over the whereabouts of the inner boundary in a stretch of uninhabited terrain in the Karakoram Mountains at the northern edge of Jammu and Kashmir.

UNMOGIP: THE PEACEKEEPING ISSUE

The CFL/LOC draws for legal sanction on two different treaties—the Karachi Agreement of 27 July 1949 and the Simla Agreement of 2 July 1972. These agreements are separated chronologically by little more than two decades; the substantive gap between them, however, is sizable. They were made under fundamentally different circumstances—the former following a prolonged but relatively small-scale armed confrontation that ended in military stalemate,[21] the latter following a very brief but major armed confrontation that ended in Pakistan's defeat and humiliation; and they reflect not only a basic change in the power equation between India and Pakistan that occurred in the intervening years, but an equally basic change in the legal standing of the international community in the Kashmir dispute. In particular, they symbolize the progressive and not-so-subtle downgrading over time of the role of the United Nations in this dispute—from one of direct aid in mediating the settlement in 1949 to one of deliberate exclusion from it in 1972—and a corresponding upgrading of the role of the regional actors. If, in other words, the former settlement symbolizes *multilateralism* in the debate over Kashmir, Simla symbolizes *bilateralism.*

Strictly speaking, there is, of course, no question that the LOC was the direct legal offspring of the Simla Agreement—a wholly bilateral accord, without international participation, guarantees, or content of any kind, signed by the prime ministers of India and Pakistan at the close of the Bangladesh war. This agreement, over whose terms India was obviously positioned to exercise disproportionate influence, called not for a new cease-fire line but for a "line of control" based on the positions held by the armed forces of the two sides at the time of the cease-fire of 17 December 1971. Physical modifications to the original CFL were, in fact, kept to a minimum; but in its name and formal design, and certainly in the minds of its Indian makers, the new line obviously replaced the CFL constructed in 1949 under UN auspices. It did not fully replace the CFL, however, since at least part of the legal and institutional apparatus of the earlier line remained more or less intact.

The Karachi Agreement, like the Simla Agreement, was a direct bilateral accord. Nevertheless, it had a substantial multilateral foundation in the UN resolutions that had preceded it. The Security Council's enabling resolution of 21 April 1948, in what was the first formal reference to a cease-fire, called upon India and Pakistan to "do their utmost to bring about cessation of all fighting." Paragraph 17 of the same resolution granted initial legal authority for the posting of UN military observers in Kashmir. It called upon UNCIP, which it had created the preceding January, to "establish in Jammu and Kashmir such observers as it may require of any of the proceedings in pursuance of the measures" outlined in the resolution.[22] The UNCIP resolution of 13 August 1948 went considerably further: It called upon the warring parties, which by now were explicitly acknowledged to be India and Pakistan,[23] to issue cease-fire orders to their forces in Kashmir; and it advised that the commission could "appoint military observers who, under the authority of the Commission and with the cooperation of both Commands, will supervise the observance of the cease-fire order."[24] The first contingent of military observers arrived in the subcontinent on 24 January 1949, a few weeks following implementation of the cease-fire. India and Pakistan explicitly sanctioned their presence in Kashmir in the Karachi Agreement of 27 July 1949. This agreement, which was formulated under direct UNCIP supervision, provided both for verification on the ground of the cease-fire line "with the assistance of the United Nations Military Observers" and for the stationing of these observers in Kashmir.[25]

In sharp contrast to the 1949 Karachi Agreement, the Simla Agreement was devoid of any reference to the UN's mediation and peacekeeping roles in Kashmir. It said nothing of the UN resolutions that had enabled the original cease-fire; and there was no mention of the role that UNMOGIP—by that time, in existence for more than 20 years—might play in delimiting the new line or in policing it. These omissions, in keeping with India's long-standing reservations about the international community's role in the Kashmir dispute, clearly placed in some jeopardy the legal underpinnings of Pakistan's territorial claim, dependent as it is on international guarantees, not to mention those of the military observer teams operating in Kashmir under UNMOGIP auspices. However, the Simla Agreement did not explicitly disestablish UNMOGIP, and neither did it constitute a formal repudiation of the UN resolutions that, apart from spelling out the conditions for demilitarization and the conduct of a plebiscite, had brought UNMOGIP into being in the first place. On the contrary, Indira Gandhi's apparent reluctance at the time of the Simla negotiations to force Pakistani prime minister Bhutto's hand in regard to Kashmir left that issue about as beclouded as ever. In the final hours of the talks, Bhutto managed to obtain Indira Gandhi's consent to wording that substantially diluted the agreement's bilateralism as well as its intended break with the past. The new LOC, said the final draft, was to be respected by both sides but "without prejudice to the recognised position of either side." This formulation left Pakistan's right to invoke the UN resolutions in defense of its territorial claims in Kashmir—and, more than that, the legality of continuing UN involvement in regard to the CFL/LOC—still under protective wrap.[26] Pakistan could continue to say that the Karachi Agreement was still valid, "and that the new line is but the old one with some changes."[27] The wrap was a lot thinner than it had been, however; and, insofar as the UN peacekeeping operation on the CFL/LOC was concerned, it seemed nearly threadbare.

Even before Simla, UNMOGIP's ability to perform its declared mission—"to observe and report on developments pertaining to the observance of the cease-fire and to provide its good offices when appropriate to assist both sides in keeping the peace,"[28] in brief, to supervise the implementation of the cease-fire agreement—suffered from a number of severe limitations. Some of these were inherent simply in its size. Except during the 1965 war, when its ranks were temporarily augmented, the number of military observers attached to UNMOGIP has generally ranged between 29 and 44 officers.[29] In recent years, the number has hovered just under 40. Divided between two countries and manning a dozen or so field stations scattered along the entire length of the CFL/LOC, these observers obviously could not begin to "observe" very much of the line, even less to keep track of the activities of the huge military forces arrayed on both sides of it. Size alone, of course, could not assure effectiveness; and UNMOGIP's reputation for fairness and impartiality at times undoubtedly helped to compensate for the small number of observers.[30] Nevertheless, in comparison with other peacekeeping missions mounted over the years by the United Nations, UNMOGIP stands out as by far one of the smallest.[31]

More of UNMOGIP's limitations, one suspects, were inherent in its original mandate. Admittedly, that mandate, which included a number of investigative, adjudicative, and reporting functions, was fairly broad. Almost alone among UN peacekeeping missions, for example, its duties included the extremely sensitive function of gathering military intelligence data from the two sides.[32] Nonetheless, as its name indicated, UNMOGIP was in Kashmir to observe, not to enforce, the cease-fire. This fact clearly dominated its day-to-day operations. For instance, upon receiving a complaint of violation from either India or Pakistan, it was authorized to mount a full investigation. But upon reaching a decision in regard to the complaint, it could do little more than announce what it called an "award"—the finding, in other words, that a violation of the cease-fire had or had not occurred, or that there could be no determination one way or the other. Responsibility for the violation (who shot first, in other words, or with least provocation) was not declared; and UNMOGIP itself was empowered to take no disciplinary action in regard to it. Full reports of the investigations—classified "top secret"—were sent directly to the UN secretary-general in New York. Ordinarily, neither these reports nor whatever action the secretary-general took in regard to them was made public.[33] It is clear, nevertheless, that *reporting* the violations exerted little, if any, impact on their *frequency.* Observe that the annual rate of reported incidents grew from two dozen in 1954 to 2,000 by 1961; and, while the rate has varied considerably in the years since then, never again were the placid days of the early 1950s to be seen on the CFL/LOC.[34]

The most fundamental limitation in UNMOGIP's original mandate, of course, was the fact that authorization for it, once the Security Council–authorized UNCIP was dismantled in 1950, lay almost entirely with the Karachi Agreement. That agreement, as we noted earlier, was a bilateral accord between India and Pakistan. Hence, UNMOGIP's writ in Kashmir, in a strict legal sense, could extend no further than Indian and Pakistani tolerance of it. Pakistan's tolerance has almost always been greater than India's; but India's, at least since the Simla Agreement was signed in 1972, has been very meager indeed.

The Simla Agreement, it will be recalled, had nothing at all to say about the UN's peacekeeping mission. On the contrary, it emphasized the bilateral settlement of all disputes between India and Pakistan. The multilateral machinery remained in place: Since 1972 India has taken no formal steps to shut down the UNMOGIP operation entirely; and India continues yet today to supply UNMOGIP headquarters and field stations with logistical and administrative support. Nevertheless, the impact of the Simla Agreement on UNMOGIP's ability to police the cease-fire has been devastating. For over two decades, in fact, UNMOGIP has been operating essentially—and dishearteningly—on one leg in Kashmir.

The Simla-induced limitations on UNMOGIP's peacekeeping duties are multiple. First, on the Indian side, the military observers are totally barred from access to the CFL/LOC except at three crossing points.[35] Second, the Indians no longer bring complaints of cease-fire violations to the attention of the UN observers; hence, UNMOGIP's awards, which now unavoidably favor Pakistan, are entirely lopsided and of even less value than before.[36] And third, the definition of what constituted a "violation" of the cease-fire has been significantly abbreviated, if not wholly discarded. The definition of a breach of the cease-fire had been agreed upon by the two sides in 1949. As modified in 1965, six categories of activity were prohibited:

1. crossing of the CFL, or infringement of the prohibition on troop movements within 500 yards of the line;
2. firing and use of explosives within 5 miles of the CFL without advance warning of the UN observers;
3. new wiring or mining of any positions;
4. reinforcing of forward defended localities with men or warlike stores, or strengthening of defenses in areas where no major adjustments were permitted by the agreement;
5. forward movement into Kashmir of any warlike stores, equipment and personnel, other than for relief and maintenance; and
6. flying aircraft over the other side's territory.[37]

The fifth element of the definition had never been even remotely enforceable; and at no time in the history of the CFL/LOC was any of them fully or consistently enforced. They were unceremoniously set aside, of course, when India and Pakistan went to war in 1965; and with execution of the Simla accords in 1972 they seemed largely irrelevant. The Karachi Agreement had specifically barred positioning of troops in the cease-fire zone—a 500-yard-wide strip on either side of the line over most of its length. Prior to 1972, the UN observers customarily visited both Pakistani and Indian forward pickets to confirm visually that no alterations in defenses or deployments had been made in this zone. With the CFL's conversion to the LOC in 1972, this zone effectively disappeared. The whole basis of the Karachi Agreement, a senior UNMOGIP officer told the author, was simply "not there." At the end of the 1971 conflict, troops were not withdrawn to their old positions. As a result, the UN observers had no choice but to fall back on the new cease-fire line of 17 December 1971. This line had no cease-fire zone; hence, the ban on reinforcement of positions in it could not be applied.[38] The result is that Indian and Pakistani forces, as another UNMOGIP officer put it to the author, stand today practically "eyeball-to-eyeball," at some points with scarcely 50 yards to separate them, over as much as 50 percent of the line's length.[39] Forward pickets on both sides often overlook the adversary's defensive installations, a situation that invites retaliation for either real or imagined encroachments on the other's territory.

After 1971, the Pakistanis insisted that UNMOGIP carry on according to the Karachi Agreement. The United Nations apparently continues to view that agreement as valid; and UNMOGIP does continue to monitor deployments and fortifications—but strictly on the Pakistani side and, even there, less fully than before.[40] On the Indian side, it maintains a presence, but little more than that. Said an UNMOGIP observer: "We regularly visit Pakistani headquarters units and pickets along the line of control [to monitor military activity]." Hence, "we know a great deal about Pakistani troop deployments; we know *nothing* about Indian deployments because we are not allowed to move about in their forward areas."[41]

The cumulative impact of all these limitations became glaringly apparent in the early 1980s when the dispute first arose between India and Pakistan over the Siachen Glacier. The glacier, as we will observe later in this chapter, lies beyond the northern terminal point of the CFL/LOC. Nevertheless, when the Pakistan army discovered in August 1983 that an Indian army reconnaissance patrol had penetrated midway onto the Siachen and had established a camp, with a hut and helipad, on one of its branches, it brought the matter to the attention of UNMOGIP authorities, declaring that the Indians had violated Pakistani territory. UNMOGIP conveyed the Pakistani protest to the Indians, who rejected it, apparently on grounds that it was the Pakistanis, and not the Indians, who were violating the other's territory. A month or so later, a UN observer was flown over the glacier in a Pakistan air force helicopter and was shown debris that the Pakistanis alleged had been left behind by the departing Indian patrol. The Indians, learning of the flight, protested that it was a violation of Indian territory and that representatives of UNMOGIP should not fly over the glacier without Indian approval. Thereafter, neither side brought any complaints of violations stemming from the Siachen dispute to UNMOGIP, at least up until 1986; and UNMOGIP's peacekeeping function, in spite of the heavy fighting over the Siachen area, has not been extended in any way to there.[42]

The steady erosion of UNMOGIP's mission became even more evident, of course, with the outbreak of severe unrest in Kashmir in 1990. Accompanying the unrest were blatant and routine breaches of the cease-fire by both sides along the entire CFL/LOC. On the Indian side, UNMOGIP was unable to fill any peacekeeping role whatsoever; and on the Pakistani side, it was little more than a spectator, its resources—and now shrunken mandate—wholly inadequate to the scale of violations that were occurring.

Bearing witness to UNMOGIP's declining fortunes, scholarly assessments of the second half of its existence are remarkably more somber than those of the first half. Pre-Simla commentaries described UNMOGIP as "highly successful in keeping a rather precarious ceasefire from deteriorating into open conflict,"[43] as having "very effectively carried out" its peacekeeping tasks,[44] as "fairly successful,"[45] and as "one of the most commendable and admirable activities carried on by the United Nations."[46]

Post-Simla commentaries, in contrast, exude considerable pessimism. The British scholar of peacekeeping Alan James, for instance, while conceding that in the period 1949 to 1972 "Unmogip gave notable assistance in the maintenance of relative calm in Kashmir," suggests that the UN body even then was largely dependent for its success on a favorable political context: If the two sides wanted peace, things went well for the UN observers; if they wanted war, then things did not go well at all for them. In the first instance, "there is a question as to whether Unmogip was necessary for the maintenance of peace." And in the second instance, when war threatened, "there was virtually nothing which Unmogip could do, or could be expected to do, to avert it."[47] When it comes to the post-Simla phase, James maintains that arguments for UNMOGIP's survival are growing thin. He admits that from 1972 until the end of 1989 the CFL/LOC was fairly quiet, disturbed mainly by incidents that were "routine" in nature. But since India during this period was not cooperating with the observers, "this stability can hardly be attributed to the UN's peacekeeping role."[48] James suggests that "the strongest argument" for UNMOGIP's retention is that to dismantle it "would give the clear appearance of submitting to India's unilateral claim that Kashmir is over and done with as an international issue." But even that function, he notes, "could perfectly well be served by a much scaled-down Unmogip."[49]

The present turmoil in Kashmir has probably given UNMOGIP a breather; under present circumstances shutting it down, or even just scaling it down, would probably not strike many as desirable. There is no question, however, that the UN peacekeeping operation in Kashmir—and the responsibility of the world community in regard to Kashmir that it represents—is in considerable jeopardy. One reason for this is the obvious fact that the Indians, stung by what they consider to be Pakistan's betrayal of the commitment to bilateralism made at Simla in 1972, were most unlikely to be found in the vanguard of any effort to restore UNMOGIP to its meatier pre-Simla role. (On this, see Chapter 7.) No major Indian leader or political party was on record in favor of that. Much more common in India, in fact, were efforts to discredit UNMOGIP as corrupt or as a den of spies.[50] There was a report in July 1990 that India's Ministry of External Affairs was considering a demand for the recall of the observers from Kashmir, a move that, were it ever actually taken, would confine UNMOGIP to its headquarters in New Delhi.[51] From the Indian point of view, UNMOGIP was an unwanted reminder of India's originally conditional claim to the state of Jammu and Kashmir, of its initial acceptance of the Kashmiris' right to a plebiscite, and of its deference to international opinion. It was, in other words, an irritation that New Delhi tolerated, perhaps by necessity, but whose final departure from the region was ultimately desirable. Pakistanis, for their part, had no illusions about the peacekeeping capacities of the UN observers; and one could not be certain how far even they would be prepared to go in authorizing a rejuvenated UN policing role on the CFL/LOC. Nevertheless, UNMOGIP remained the most tangible evidence available to Pakistanis that Kashmir, in the judgment of the international community, was still *disputed territory.*[52] Pakistan's direct military benefit from UNMOGIP's presence was not very great, in other words, but the political costs to Pakistan of its absence could well be enormous.

We come now to the Siachen Glacier dispute. An offspring of the Kashmir dispute, it is as deeply colored by the impermanence of the CFL/LOC as its parent. Unlike the parent dispute, however, this one concerns the *absence* of the CFL/LOC in an area adjoining China's Xinjiang province in northern Kashmir. We will consider the diplomacy generated by this dispute later on in Chapter 7. Here we examine the issue of unilateral territorial annexation—or "mountain poaching"—that came into public view in 1984.

SIACHEN GLACIER: THE "MOUNTAIN-POACHING" ISSUE[53]

The original CFL in Kashmir was drawn between the positions held by the Indian and Pakistani armies at the time hostilities ended in 1949. It extended from a point just west of the Chenab River near Chhamb in Jammu in a rough arc running a bit under 500 miles (497.12 miles) north and then northeastward to a point (map coordinate NJ 9842) about 12 miles north of the Shyok River in the Saltoro Range of the Karakoram Mountains. Its southern terminus near Chhamb fell on the traditional boundary between the preindependence state of Jammu and Kashmir and what is now Pakistan's Punjab province. From there to the recognized international border between India and Pakistan beginning just west of the Ravi River was a distance of about 124 miles. That stretch of boundary, included neither within the CFL nor within the international border dividing East from West Punjab that resulted from the Punjab Boundary Commission award of 1947, retained an odd status. Pakistanis have always resisted any reference to it as "the border between India and Pakistan," insisting that it is simply the border dividing Indian-occupied *Jammu* from

Pakistan.[54] They currently speak of this stretch of border simply as "the border," while the Indians prefer to call it "the working border."

At the northern end of the CFL lay an even more unusual situation, for there no clear traditional boundary existed and none had been delimited in 1949. The UNCIP-supervised Indian and Pakistani military teams that had undertaken the delimitation exercise at that time had stopped their work well short of the international border with China—about 40 miles short, to be more exact, if measured against the boundary line agreed to by China and Pakistan in the Border Agreement of 1963. From that point on lay some of the highest, most rugged, glaciated, remote, and unpopulated portions of the Karakoram Mountains—seemingly inaccessible terrain in which neither side's troops had ever been deployed.

From the beginning, the Indians and Pakistanis thus had three distinct types of boundary situations to contend with in Kashmir: no boundary at all for about 40 miles in the far north, about 500 miles of delimited (but formally undemarcated) cease-fire line cutting through most of the state, and about 124 miles of traditional, quasi-recognized "border" or "working border" at the southern end. Conversion of the CFL to the LOC in 1972 involved some modest territorial exchanges along the line and a full redelimitation exercise as well, this time without benefit of any UN supervision. But since there were again no troops in contact in the area north of map coordinate NJ 9842, and because at the time neither India's nor Pakistan's armed forces had the technological capability to imagine a serious contest for possession of this area, there was no compelling reason to extend the new line beyond its existing terminus. Neither was there any change made to what had been the CFL's southern terminal point. Thus Kashmir entered the post-Simla period with the trinary boundary system erected in 1949 essentially intact and with no part of it yet qualifying as international border.

For a decade or so following the signing of the Simla Agreement, the Kashmir issue occupied a noticeably less conspicuous position on the public agenda of India-Pakistan relations than had been characteristic up to that point. True, neither side showed much interest during this period in advancing further the cooperative spirit briefly displayed at Simla; and neither did either side show any unambiguous signs of retreat from positions adopted in the dispute's first decade. Provocative public verbal exchanges over Kashmir were commonplace. So were firing incidents along the LOC. From a strictly military perspective, in fact, Kashmir had clearly lost none of its importance. Nevertheless, it was quite apparent in these years that the two adversaries—their agendas already overflowing with other domestic and international problems—preferred to keep the issue of the contested border in Kashmir securely on a back burner.

That circumstance came to an abrupt end in 1984. On 13 April in that year, special units of the Indian army were airlifted to preselected mountain outposts in the undelimited sector of Jammu and Kashmir immediately north of map coordinate NJ 9842. The daring maneuver, codenamed Operation Meghdoot, planted the Indians astride three key passes (Sia La, Bilafond La, Gyong La) in the Saltoro Range dominating traditional approaches onto the massive Siachen Glacier. Holding the high ground, they were able to resist repeated efforts by Pakistani commandos to dislodge them. The two armies, equally unwilling to yield and faced with extraordinary hazards of altitude and climate, committed substantial military assets to the struggle. Neither side seemed willing or able to break the resulting deadlock. Costs and casualties mounted; and progress in India-Pakistan relations was undermined. In the meantime, the whole issue of boundary delimitation in Kashmir was reopened. Its reopening exposed another glaring delimitation problem.[55]

This problem arose, of course, from the decision of the LOC's designers, like the designers of the CFL before them, to leave the northern terminal point of the line untouched. While this decision was certainly understandable, it was, nevertheless, unfortunate. India's unresolved border dispute with China over the Aksai Chin region of northeastern Ladakh already assured a high level of strategic tension in northern Kashmir; and the signing of the Sino-Pakistan Border Treaty in March 1963, within four months of the disastrous rout of India's forces by China in the 1962 border conflict, had long since made plain that between India and Pakistan, too, there existed serious differences in regard to the location of China's border with Kashmir. That treaty scrapped India's territorial claims reaching north into China's Xinjiang province well beyond the main Karakoram range. It replaced them with an international boundary that ran about 200 miles from the trijunction of Afghanistan, Pakistan, and China eastward to the Karakoram Pass, along the way passing just north of the Siachen Glacier. Obviously, the status of Indian, Pakistani, and Chinese territorial claims in the eastern Karakorams had materially changed between the drawing up of the CFL and the LOC. This seems to have been ignored in the 1972 delimitation exercise, however, which was guided by the same rule of thumb as in 1949: that the LOC was a temporary arrangement, a marking off of forces-in-place on a stilled battlefield, not a permanent international boundary.

The CFL/LOC's incompleteness had not gone entirely unnoticed, however, and well before the end of the 1970s it was already giving signs of emerging as a potentially troublesome problem. One of these signs was Pakistan's rapidly increasing access to the eastern Karakorams, in which the Siachen Glacier is located. Largely responsible for the dramatic gain in access was Pakistan's construction, with massive Chinese assistance, of a network of strategic highways linking hitherto remote corners of Pakistan's Northern Areas with China's adjacent Xinjiang province. The network's centerpiece was the 500-mile Karakoram Highway, a nominally all-weather road that connected these two closely allied countries through the 15,430-foot Khunjerab Pass. Begun in 1969, the highway was completed in 1978.[56] It clearly did not live up to its all-weather billing; and its dozens of bridges were obvious candidates for precision bombing. Nonetheless, it immediately enhanced the maneuverability of the Pakistan army and, with expansion of secondary roads, promised eventually to give the Pakistanis far superior access to the northernmost stretch of the CFL/LOC (and to the Siachen area) than the Indians possessed.

Adding measurably to Indian anxieties in this regard was the international community's gradual acceptance during the 1970s of Pakistan's administrative jurisdiction over that part of the eastern Karakoram Mountains containing the Siachen Glacier. One indication of this acceptance was the general practice of international mountaineering groups in this period to seek authorization for expeditions to the vicinity of the Siachen Glacier from Pakistani—and not Indian—authorities. Foreign climbing expeditions to the eastern Karakorams, which contain numerous lofty peaks prized among mountaineers, had been banned by Pakistan from 1961 to 1974. When the ban was lifted in 1974, foreign expeditions, their way eased not only by the expanding network of roads in the Northern Areas but by Pakistan's waiver of royalties on some peaks, returned to the area in larger numbers than ever. Word of Pakistan's seeming control of the area was spread throughout the world by widely circulated international alpine journals and trekking guides. A leading American journal, for instance, footnoted a report from India of an Indian army team's 1980 traverse of the Siachen Glacier and successful ascent of Apsarasas peak with the remark that it was "surprising that an Indian Army force should have crossed the Cease-Fire Line and entered into what is generally held to be Pakistan, although the Indians would dispute this."[57]

A second and perhaps more telling indication of the world's growing acceptance in these years of Pakistan's jurisdiction over the Siachen area came in the changed depiction of the CFL/LOC in widely sold commercial international atlases. By the early 1980s, practically all of the most respected of such atlases—including the National Geographic Society's *Atlas of the World* (1981), the University of Chicago's *A Historical Atlas of South Asia* (1978), and *The Times Atlas of the World* (1980)—were showing the CFL/LOC extending beyond grid reference point NJ 9842 about 55 miles in a clear northeasterly direction all the way to the Karakoram Pass on the Chinese border.[58] The extension was a distinct departure from past cartographic practice.

UN maps of Kashmir produced in the early years of the dispute all terminated the CFL at map coordinate NJ 9842.[59] In India and Pakistan, display of the CFL or LOC on publicly sold maps has been officially discouraged at least since the 1965 war; but among the scores of pre-1965 official or officially approved Indian and Pakistani maps surveyed by this author in the Library of Congress, not a single one showed any extension beyond NJ 9842.[60]

The international mapmakers' change in depiction of the CFL/LOC did not come all at once, and in some cases, at least, it came rather clumsily. The 1977 edition of *The Times Atlas of the World,* for example, like the 1980 edition, represented the CFL/LOC (still labeling it simply the CFL) running all the way to the border with China. In the earlier edition, however, the extended CFL/LOC was shown running *westward* of the Siachen Glacier, reaching China about 60 miles west of the terminal point shown in the 1980 edition of the same atlas.[61] Surprisingly, an even earlier edition of this atlas (1959) depicted the CFL running to the Karakoram Pass![62] Despite these detours, a nearly universal shift by mapmakers to an extended and *eastward*-running CFL/LOC was eventually achieved. And it seems to have resulted from a new and conscious consensus in regard to the line's terminal point.[63]

Precisely what motivated this new (and, at least from the Indian point of view, disturbing) consensus is not clear. Unquestionably contributing to it, however, were erroneous depictions of the CFL/LOC on some official maps produced by agencies of the U.S. Government.

As early as 1964, at least one commercial U.S. mapmaker, presumably influenced by the Sino-Pakistani Border Treaty of the preceding year, depicted the CFL extended to the Karakoram Pass.[64] This was very likely the product of sloppy cartography, however, since official U.S. maps of Kashmir distributed by the Department of State and Central Intelligence Agency at least through 1968 consistently depicted the CFL's northern terminus at NJ 9842. Near the end of the 1960s, however, U.S. maps of the South Asian region produced under the auspices of the Department of Defense began to depict the CFL (after 1972, the LOC) in a fundamentally new way. In at least one such case, the change amounted simply to an extension of the CFL to the Karakoram Pass on the Chinese border.[65] By far the more curious change, however, was in the delineation shown in the widely distributed aeronautical maps prepared by the Defense Mapping Agency (DMA), the successor to the Army Map Service (AMS). On these maps, the extension depicted, surprisingly, is not an extension of the CFL/LOC at all. On the contrary, these maps depict the east–west running Sino-Pakistan border established by treaty in 1963 *extending unbroken from the Karakoram Pass southeastward to map coordinate NJ 9842.* These maps unambiguously depict the approximately

55-mile stretch that separates the terminal point of the Sino-Pakistan boundary near the Karakoram Pass from the terminal point of the CFL/LOC south of the Siachen Glacier as an *international* boundary; in other words, *not* simply as an extension through disputed territory of the CFL/LOC. An Air Defense Information Zone (ADIZ) band, standard on all U.S. air force Operational Navigation Charts, overlies the boundary line, with the words "Pakistan North ADIZ" clearly alerting pilots that they are entering Pakistani airspace when they cross over the line from the Indian side.[66] Unlike the CFL/LOC, this line follows a perfectly straight course that passes about five miles *east* of Dzingrulma, a point directly at the eastern snout of the Siachen Glacier, where a major base for Indian military operations on the glacier now lies. The line places the entire Siachen area securely within Pakistan. One can hardly escape the conclusion that the U.S. Defense Mapping Agency, one of the largest and probably the most influential of international mapmakers, played a far from inconsequential role in the world's cartographic "award" of the Siachen to Pakistan.

On 31 May 1991, this author addressed a large gathering of active and retired Indian military officers at the Ministry of Defense in New Delhi on the subject of the Siachen dispute. At the end of the presentation, one of the officers present—retired Lieutenant General M. N. Kaul, who commanded Northern Command (including Jammu and Kashmir) toward the end of the 1970s—commented that the Indian army had taken keen interest at that time in trying to determine how, when, and why the U.S. DMA had taken upon itself the task of completing the unfinished business of boundary delimitation in the eastern Karakorams. Repeated official written inquiries to Washington, he said, had turned up the information that the DMA had begun in 1967 to display on its maps an India-Pakistan international border to the east of Siachen. That, however, was all that India was able to discover. U.S. officials, he complained, had eventually written that no records remained with DMA to explain why that decision had been taken.[67]

This author's inquiries with the Defense Mapping Agency and with the Office of the Geographer of the Department of State elicited the straightforward reply that representation of the CFL/LOC in northern Kashmir on aeronautical maps of the DMA was indeed erroneous, that the choice of Karakoram Pass as the northern terminal point of the closing line from NJ 9842 "undoubtedly" originated in the Sino-Pakistan Border Agreement of 1963, and—most important—that it had "never been US policy to show a boundary of any type closing the gap between NJ 9842 and the China border."[68] According to a guidance sent to producers of official U.S. maps by the Office of the Geographer on 12 March 1987, an official review of the cartographic depiction of the Kashmir boundary on U.S. government products had "evidenced an inconsistency in the depiction and the categorization of the boundary by the various producing agencies." It supplied specific instructions for future depiction that would assure that the CFL/LOC would "not be extended to the Karakoram pass as has been previous cartographic practice."[69]

In the years since the outbreak of fighting on the Siachen in 1984, Indians and Pakistanis have engaged in relentless controversy over where (or whether) the "real" border exists in the Siachen sector of Kashmir. Indians have accused the government of Pakistan of "mountain poaching"—of the unilateral extension of the CFL/LOC northeastward to the Karakoram Pass. Pakistanis, in turn, have accused the government of India of violating its commitment in the Simla Agreement to the peaceful settlement of all disputes. Both sides have dredged up arguments resting not only on the evidence of international maps and mountaineering expeditions, but also on the history of British colonialism and the Indian independence movement, on the placement of ethnographic boundaries, on the records of district and subdistrict administration, on past patterns of military deployment, on the transcripts of parliamentary debates, and—by no means least—on the language of formal treaties. In regard to the latter, for example, much has been made of wording in the 1949 Karachi Agreement, specifically the statement that the CFL, from the last-named location (Khor) given in the summary verbal description of it, moved "thence north to the glaciers."[70] Numerous Indian commentators have claimed that the agreement's authors meant by this that the CFL continued beyond map coordinate NJ 9842 more or less directly north through glacial terrain all the way to the Chinese border.[71] Since this reading appeared to put most of the Siachen Glacier legally in Indian hands, Pakistanis naturally rejected it.

Fairly close scrutiny of the evidence marshaled by both sides in the Siachen dispute in regard to the alleged whereabouts of the CFL/LOC north of map coordinate NJ 9842 has led this author to conclude that the line simply doesn't run there. Western-produced atlases, like the 1990 edition of the National Geographic Society's *Atlas of the World,* may continue to say that it does.[72] But the facts of the matter are these: The CFL/LOC ends at NJ 9842, and there does not exist today any known international agreement that would warrant delineating any sort of boundary between the Karakoram Pass and map coordinate NJ 9842. Specifically, there is nothing in the wording of the 1949 Karachi Agreement that would lend serious support to the Indian contention that the authors of that accord intended the CFL to extend beyond map coordinate NJ 9842. Indeed, no such coordinate is named in the Karachi Agreement; neither are the glaciers (of which there are many) in which the CFL was said to terminate. Like it or not, the cease-fire agreement signed by

India and Pakistan in July 1949 is vague on the subject of the CFL's terminal point. The formal and months-long joint delimitation exercises that *followed* the signings of both the 1949 and 1972 agreements, on the other hand, produced detailed, step-by-step descriptions of the line between the opposing forces; and, in both cases, these descriptions, together with the jointly initialed maps that accompanied them, show the CFL/LOC ending abruptly and absolutely at NJ 9842. It is only in these very bulky documents, in fact, that map coordinate NJ 9842 is mentioned at all; and, judging from the best evidence available, nothing is said in either of them about any extension beyond this coordinate.[73]

Neither is there anything in the 1963 Sino-Pakistani Border Agreement that would lend substance to the common Pakistani contention that that treaty, since it established a common border extending to the Karakoram Pass, at least indirectly sanctioned extension of the CFL/LOC up to that point. The treaty's preamble does refer to the territory lying south of the newly established boundary as "the contiguous areas the defence of which is under the actual control of Pakistan."[74] Nowhere, however, does the treaty describe this territory as *Pakistani* territory. And, in expressly conceding the provisional status of the agreement pending Pakistan's final settlement of the Kashmir dispute with India, the treaty hardly warranted the unilateral extension by Pakistan of the CFL/LOC. India, after all, rejected the border settlement.

Accurate and impartial maps of the northern frontier between India and Pakistan were an early casualty of the Kashmir conflict. More often than not, representation of boundaries on maps produced in India and Pakistan was dictated by political rather than cartographic norms. In both countries, confusion in regard to proper boundaries has been widespread, even among specialists;[75] and the deliberate, sometimes ludicrous, distortion of cartographic facts has been common practice. One of the more conspicuously Procrustean treatments of the Siachen issue, for example, was an essay published in 1989 by the Ministry of Defence–supported Institute of Defence Studies and Analyses in New Delhi. Written by retired Air Commodore Jasjit Singh, director of the institute, the article managed to squeeze more India-friendly inferences from the spare wording of the Karachi Agreement than had almost any of its predecessors. According to Jasjit Singh's analysis, the agreement's four words "north to the glaciers" left very little doubt not only that its authors intended that the CFL run *due* north but that, in employing the plural form of glaciers, they wanted it to run in "a more north-northwesterly direction" along the Saltoro ridge—that is, *between* the "two main groups of glaciers—the Siachen glacier system and the Baltoro glacier system . . . separated by the crests of the Saltoro range." Therefore, he observed, "the extension of the old CFL . . .

can only be along the Saltoro ridge."[76] It is this ridgeline, of course, that commands the access routes to the Siachen Glacier and in which the Indian army's forward positions are now located.

Western cartographers, whether official or commercial, have scarcely been guiltless themselves. In one way or another, their mistaken representations of the "missing piece" north of map coordinate NJ 9842 materially contributed to the problem. The truth is that the inner boundary between Indian- and Pakistani-held parts of Kashmir is today unquestionably incomplete. Its northernmost sector awaits delimitation.

CHAPTER

The Strategic Context

It should be clear by this point that boundary issues, whether their roots are in problems of entitlement or delimitation, form a large part of the Kashmir dispute. They played an especially prominent role in its earliest stages, and their importance has been little diminished since then. Some of the reasons for their continued importance are to be found in the external environment of the dispute—in its long-standing and nearly inevitable entanglement in the contemporaneous struggles among the great powers for influence and control over the Asian landmass. All along, in fact, we have observed that the "boundary" issues being examined had significant military and security content and that they raised serious questions about Kashmir's external environment, not just about the immediate circumstances of its internal boundaries. We shift our attention now specifically to this *strategic* side of the boundary problem.

KASHMIR AND GREAT POWER RIVALRIES

As much as for its natural beauty, the state of Jammu and Kashmir has long been regarded as a place of great strategic importance. It owes this reputation, acquired over a lengthy and turbulent history of conquest and reconquest by warring Asian powers, in large part to its position alongside or astride traditional invasion routes leading into the subcontinent from the west and north. In the nineteenth century, the growing rivalry between the advancing Russian and British empires for control of the marchlands of Central Asia led to intense competition for these routes. The huge territorial stakes in this rivalry, whose relentless intrigues and high adventure won it renown as "the Great Game," focused British strategic planning for the defense of India's lengthy land frontier to an increasing extent on Kashmir. Indeed, by the latter part of the nineteenth century denial of access to Kashmir by hostile powers had become a matter "of consummate interest to India's British rulers," who considered Kashmir "Britain's territorial buffer behind the mountains."[1] A series of Anglo-Russian agreements near the turn of the century laid the foundation for the development of more stable spheres of interest in the region; but Russia's conversion to Communist rule in the second decade of the twentieth century and the threatened resumption of the Great Game inevitably rekindled acute British interest in India's northern frontier. Thus, Kashmir continued to occupy a central place in British strategic policy right up to the transfer of power—central enough, in any event, to prompt one historian to claim that "everything that happened in the State of Jammu and Kashmir between 1846 and 1947 was in some way a product of this strategic policy."[2]

Kashmir's reputation for strategic importance easily survived the transfer of power. Its geographic position alone, since it egregiously exposed the state to the threat both of Soviet and, after 1949, of Chinese Communist expansionism, guaranteed this reputation;[3] and Indian and Pakistani leaders were themselves quick to reaffirm it. Prime Minister Nehru of India had reminded Lord Mountbatten even before independence of "the great strategic importance of that frontier state";[4] and on 25 October, in a cable to Prime Minister Clement Attlee of Great Britain explaining India's decision to render military assistance to the beleaguered maharaja, Nehru stressed the fact that "Kashmir's northern frontiers . . . run in common with those of three countries, Afghanistan, the U.S.S.R. and China. Security of Kashmir . . . is vital to security of India, especially since part of southern boundary of Kashmir and India are common."[5] Liaquat Ali Khan, the Pakistani prime minister, for his part invoked much the same theme. In a radio broadcast made within days of Kashmir's accession to India, he described the accession as a "threat to the security of Pakistan";[6] and in a cable to Nehru on 16 December 1947, he observed that "the security of Pakistan is bound up with that of Kashmir."[7]

Postindependence appraisals of Kashmir's strategic importance differed in at least two major respects, however, from those that had preceded independence. One of these differences was visible in comments made by Liaquat Ali in the course of an interview with David Lilienthal in 1951. Said the prime minister: "The very position—the strategic position of Kashmir—is such that without it Pakistan cannot defend itself against an unscrupulous government that might come in India."[8] The difference was plain enough: Now that India and Pakistan had one another to contend with, Kashmir's strategic importance had to be evaluated in terms of a whole range of threats to Pakistan originating *within* the subcontinent, not only in terms of threats coming from beyond the northern frontier. Mahnaz Ispahani, a perceptive student of South Asian geopolitics, explained it thus:

> With the partition of the subcontinent, Kashmir itself became of even greater strategic value than in imperial times. Its military relevance for both India and Pakistan lay in its location and in its usefulness for each state's defense posture. For India, control of the Kashmir Valley, in particular, became essential for the protection of remote Ladakh, next to the Chinese borderlands. In a war with Pakistan, too, India could be vulnerable to a fast penetration of Kashmir by Pakistani armor and tactical airpower aiming to sever the territory off from India proper. Kashmir, however, had numerous links to Pakistani territory: its partition had meant economic disruption, since its waters were essential to the irrigation and power supplies of (Pakistani) west Punjab; its timber resources were rafted down west Punjab's rivers; its willow and resin were used in Pakistani industry; and the natural access routes from Kashmir led mainly to west Punjab.[9]

The second major difference between pre- and postindependence assessments of Kashmir's strategic importance was linked to the onset following World War II of the global Cold War. Begun at about the same time that India and Pakistan achieved independence from Britain, the Cold War intruded upon the Kashmir dispute fairly rapidly and, in the process, by superimposing the global upon the regional conflict, fundamentally transformed its geopolitical context. The effects of this transformation on India and Pakistan, while equally great on both, took rather different forms.

Insofar as Pakistan's political leadership was concerned, the Cold War came more as a blessing than a curse. The reason for this was to be found in Pakistan's relatively disadvantaged birth. Pakistan had begun its existence economically and militarily much weaker than its Indian rival. At partition, Pakistan commanded only about 18 percent of the population, less than 10 percent of the industrial base, and barely more than 7 percent of the employment facilities of undivided British India. Its total industrial assets had an estimated worth at the time of about $112 million. It "was the quintessential agrarian economy"—grossly deficient in sources of revenue for the promotion of industrialization and yet self-sufficient in little else but food grains.[10]

Things weren't much more promising on the military side. Pakistan had inherited a disproportionate share of British Indian military personnel—30 percent of the army, 40 percent of the navy, and 20 percent of the air force. It was burdened, however, with "a resource endowment which was insufficient to meet even the most basic internal security needs," let alone satisfy its rapidly escalating external defense requirements.[11] Brave words to the contrary, Pakistan was not able to prevent Indian military takeover of either Junagadh or Kashmir—episodes that had very early exposed the "hopeless inadequacies" of Pakistan's defense forces.[12]

In view of these harsh realities, Pakistani policymakers were from the outset of the Kashmir dispute under few illusions that Pakistan could, entirely from its own resources, compel a satisfactory settlement of Kashmir through direct dealings with India. They knew that the regional balance of power leaned visibly in India's favor and that Kashmir was as much as lost unless something could be found to offset Indian preponderance. Frustration with these circumstances "provoked Pakistan into a constant search for arms and alliances."[13] Sensing opportunity in the onset of the Cold War and the emergence of rival political-military blocs eagerly on the lookout for would-be clients, Pakistan's rulers hastened to present their country to the Americans as an "Islamic barrier against the Soviets."[14] The appeal eventually succeeded; and in less than a decade of Pakistan's creation, it had achieved a rather spectacular standing as Washington's "most allied ally" and as a lynchpin of the West's anti-Communist alliance system on the rimland of Asia.

Alliance with the West promised at least two Kashmir-related benefits for Pakistan: on the one hand to bring military assistance from the United States desperately needed to contest for control over Kashmir, and on the other to acquire U.S. diplomatic backing "necessary to force the Indians to hold a plebiscite in Kashmir."[15] As for the first of these, Pakistan was no more than modestly successful; U.S. arms deliveries in the 1950s, though they clearly gave Pakistani forces a lethal bite, never came close to the level needed to wrest Kashmir from Indian control. As for the second, Pakistan was almost wholly unsuccessful; U.S. diplomatic support no doubt assured Kashmir's inclusion on the agenda of the UN Security Council, but this support was never exercised to force a plebiscite on an unwilling India. Pakistanis had to confront rather quickly, in fact, the unpleasant discovery that while the Cold War offered an opportunity to build a formidable defense capability, it contained no firm assurances whatsoever for the acquisition of Kashmir.

The Cold War clearly presented India, too, with opportunities. Having inherited far greater self-sufficiency than their counterparts in Pakistan, India's leaders were able to piece together an independent or nonaligned foreign policy that avoided at least formal commitment to either the Communist or the non-Communist bloc while at the same time facilitating far-ranging contacts with both. It did not, however, preclude development at a fairly early point in the Cold War of an exceptionally close and, in many respects, rewarding strategic partnership with the Soviet Union. There were solid grounds for partnership: Both countries shared long and disputed borders with China and were thus bound to be somewhat apprehensive in regard to China's future intentions; and both could hardly look upon Pakistan's step-by-step inclusion in the period from 1953 to 1955 in a widening arc of U.S.-sponsored military alliances with anything other than disfavor. With astonishing rapidity, early distrust between them yielded to extraordinary cooperation. In February 1955, large-scale economic assistance to India was inaugurated with the Soviet agreement to construct the huge Bhilai steel plant in Madhya Pradesh. Then, in June, Nehru was received in Moscow with a welcome that was unprecedented not only in its warmth but in the amount of respect shown to a Third World leader.[16] It was during the return state visit to India by Soviet leaders Nikita Khrushchev and Nicolai Bulganin in November–December the same year, however, that an event occurred—Khrushchev's public and unreserved endorsement of Kashmir's accession to India—"that was to transform the Indo-Soviet relationship."[17] The endorsement topped what Nehru described as "this feast of friendliness between the Soviet leaders and the people of India."[18] Since Soviet policy up until then had seemed to favor political independence for Kashmir, Khrushchev's declaration came as a stunning surprise.[19] It was an early and important milestone in a relationship that was to bring India numerous political and military benefits over the next several decades.

The Cold War brought a number of unwelcome consequences for India, of course, as it had for Pakistan. Among the most notable of them was America's Soviet-motivated arms aid to India's arch-rival Pakistan. Carried out in blunt disregard of Indian complaints, this aid exposed to view the fact that India's ability to trade in the currency of the Cold War was far from unlimited. Equally revealing in this regard, however, was the equivocal and somewhat double-edged American response to India's short but brutally disastrous border war with China in November–December 1962. In the initial phase of that response, Washington's emergency airlift to India on an around-the-clock basis of some 60 planeloads of automatic weapons and ammunition seemed to signal what many in India expected, or at least hoped, would develop into a long-term military relationship between the two countries. The airlift had begun on 3 November; and on 14 November, only days before China launched its major offensive in India's northeast, India formalized a defense assistance agreement with the United States. Thrown into panic by China's palpable threat to India's territorial integrity, New Delhi seemed prepared to upend its long and very vocal commitment to nonalignment. The stage seemed set, in fact, for the full-scale and West-subsidized modernization of Indian armed forces. However, with China's announcement on 20 November of a unilateral cease-fire and its intention to begin withdrawing its troops on 1 December, expectations fast receded. Less than a month following India's crushing defeat, Washington's explicit concerns had shifted away from the Chinese threat to India's territorial integrity and toward "a new emphasis on the urgency of a Kashmir settlement."[20] Both the United States and the United Kingdom launched major diplomatic efforts at this time, in fact, to persuade India to reopen the Kashmir question and to explore with Pakistan the idea of joint subcontinental defense. These efforts, as we will have occasion to take note of again in Chapter 7, were not received with enthusiasm in India and didn't prosper. Western interest in India's security problems quickly faded. In the end, as against an expressed Indian request for a Western financial aid commitment of $500 million to a five-year defense modernization program, the sum total of U.S. military aid supplied to India between October 1962 and September 1965 came to $80 million—an amount, according to the Indian scholar Shivaji Ganguly, that was no more than 36 percent of American aid promised at the time, only 4 to 5 percent of India's declared defense needs, and "about one-twentieth of [U.S.] military assistance to Pakistan during the preceding ten years."[21]

Assessing the consequences of the Cold War for either India or Pakistan is thus clearly problematic. On the one hand, there can be no question that a sturdy linkage existed between the global (great power) and regional (India-Pakistan) rivalries and that this linkage was among the factors that determined, in particular, the course of the Kashmir dispute. On the other hand, "local" forces, stemming entirely or mainly from the hostility of India and Pakistan, were no less conspicuous in the jumble of events that shaped the Kashmir dispute in the years of Cold War than were "extralocal" forces arising from the hostility of the great powers. Most authors conceded that both of these forces played some role.[22] As to which of them—the local or the extralocal—greatest responsibility was to be assigned for the persistence and seeming intractability of the Kashmir dispute, opinion was sharply divided. Some contended that Pakistan's joining of U.S.-orchestrated defense pacts in the early 1950s was primarily at fault, in that it brought the threat of military aggression to India's doorstep, drew "India involuntarily into the Cold War,"[23] and, in particular, forced Nehru to renege on his commitment to a plebiscite in Kashmir.[24] Others argued, however, that Pakistan's growing alliance with the United States in the 1950s, since it supplied an informal but vital external guarantee of the integrity of Pakistan's borders, was precisely the factor that kept India and Pakistan from one another's throats.[25] Of "great power intrusion" in the subcontinent's affairs, in other words, there could be no doubt; but about the short- and long-term impact of the intruders on the Kashmir dispute there was plenty of room for disagreement.

None of the great powers has been more intrusive in the Kashmir dispute than China. This has been a function, in part, simply of its geographic proximity, which would assure it a role in this dispute under virtually any circumstances. But the prominence of that role obviously owes a lot to the existence of controversial Chinese claims to mountainous terrain straddling Kashmir's outer or international borders with China's two westernmost provinces—Xinjiang (traditionally Chinese Turkestan, formally the Xinjiang Uighur Autonomous Region) and Tibet. These claims, which became the focus of major international concern only after the Tibetan uprising of 1959, embraced territories on both sides of the CFL/LOC. Conflict over them led, on the Indian side, to the Sino-Indian border war of 1962 and, on the Pakistan side, to the peaceful negotiation of the Sino-Pakistan Border Agreement of 1963. The Border Agreement, which for the first time expressly signaled China's support for the Pakistani contention that Kashmir was *disputed* territory, implicated China directly in the Indo-Pakistan boundary dispute over Kashmir. The border war, fought largely for possession of a remote and scarcely visited place called the Aksai Chin, seemed, in contrast, to involve China only tangentially in the Indo-Pakistan dispute. A desolate and uninhabited high plain framed by massive mountain ranges at the junction of Tibet, Xinjiang, and eastern Ladakh, the Aksai Chin in and of itself held no obvious attraction at all for Pakistan; and even for India its value seemed more symbolic than anything else. Events were to show, however, that the struggle for control of the Aksai Chin would continue to cast a long shadow over the whole of the Kashmir dispute years after the fighting had ended.

The Communist regime that established control over mainland China in 1949 did not at once take sides in the border dispute over Kashmir between India and Pakistan. For over a decade, in fact, the People's Republic of China (PRC) maintained a position of official neutrality in regard to that dispute. China moved away from that position at the end of the 1950s, when mounting tensions with both the Soviet Union and India led to major policy changes in respect to the security of western China's frontiers. Signs had existed all along, however, of potential future difficulties in Sino-Indian relations. In late 1950, when the Chinese People's Liberation Army (PLA) carried out its "peaceful liberation" of Tibet, India was abruptly deprived of a vital northern buffer. Tibet was allowed to retain no genuine autonomy; and India's extraterritorial rights there, inherited from the British period, were rudely swept away. The loss of Tibet, which obviously added to the strategic pressures on Kashmir, carried an implicit threat as well to Kashmir's borders. Little noticed at the time, one of the key invasion routes used by the PLA to overpower Tibetan defenses was in the far northwest of

Tibet—the rarely traveled route from Xinjiang through the Aksai Chin in Ladakh.[26]

Both India and Pakistan had moved very quickly following the Communist takeover to establish friendly relations with China's new rulers. India had been the second state and Pakistan the first Muslim state to extend diplomatic recognition to Communist China. India seemed to have the greatest initial success. In April 1954, a high point of sorts was reached when the Sino-Indian Agreement on Tibet was signed declaring the Panch Shila, or "Five Principles," of peaceful coexistence to be the basis of future Sino-Indian relations. This agreement, however, and the profuse public expressions of goodwill and friendship put out in those days in the name of Sino-Indian brotherhood only papered over the deep suspicions the Chinese and Indians were acquiring of one another's intentions. The Chinese government maintained that there were no territorial disputes between India and China; but the obvious discrepancy between the government's assurances and its maps naturally upset the Indians.[27] For its part, the Indian government quietly began issuing Survey of India maps in 1954 that showed the eastern corner of Ladakh (including the entire Aksai Chin region) wholly within India's boundaries.[28] Sino-Indian camaraderie at the 1955 Bandung Conference temporarily smoothed things over. Soon thereafter, however, Sino-Indian relations began to show public signs of wear. These signs increased dramatically in September 1957 upon the Indian government's discovery that the Chinese had constructed a road traversing the Aksai Chin plain in territory claimed by India. India's formal complaint in 1958 about this seemingly blatant violation of Indian sovereignty was rebuffed by the Chinese, who claimed the territory as their own. In March 1959, when Chinese forces moved to crush a popular uprising in Tibet, ending the fiction of Tibet's autonomy and forcing the Dalai Lama and thousands of his countrymen to seek refuge in India, any remaining traces of Sino-Indian friendship evaporated.

Pakistan's strategic position in relation to China in the early 1950s was hardly less awkward than India's. Conscious of the need to prevent India from preempting Beijing's sympathies, Pakistan took China's side on a number of key issues, including, initially, the PRC's claim to the China seat in the UN Security Council. Equally conscious, however, that its search for vital Western economic and military aid depended very heavily on the goodwill it was able to generate in the United States, it prudently straddled other sensitive issues.[29] Sino-Pakistani relations, consequently, achieved a modest cordiality in the early 1950s, though the deference with which each side treated the other was inevitably mixed with suspicion.[30] Alliance with the United

States toward the middle of the decade compelled Pakistan to move perceptibly to more patently pro-Western positions. The Chinese reciprocated by resisting appeals that they take a stand on Kashmir more sympathetic to Pakistan. As a result, Pakistan's relations with China were occasionally strained in the latter half of the 1950s. Both countries recognized, however, that there existed no inherently irreconcilable problems between them. Pragmatism prevailed, and no serious break occurred.

In a space of four years, between the onset of the Tibetan rebellion in March 1959 and the signing of the Border Agreement between China and Pakistan in March 1963, a fundamental turnabout occurred in the pattern of relations among the three neighboring states—China, India, and Pakistan. By the latter date, China had dealt a humiliating defeat to India in the border war of October–November 1962, while at the same time having entered into a multifaceted informal alliance with Pakistan. This turnabout undid the fairly straightforward bilateral contest over Kashmir between India and Pakistan that had existed at the start of the 1950s, replacing it in the early 1960s with a three-cornered, trans-Himalayan "security complex"[31] that was infinitely more complicated than the preceding arrangement. For better or for worse, China had become (and remains today) a direct and partisan participant in the Kashmir dispute.

Befitting its huge size and political importance, China's role in the Kashmir dispute has generated particularly heated controversy among scholars. Much of the debate has centered on pinpointing responsibility for the development of enmity between India and China. Admirably detailed accounts of the historical origins of this enmity have been produced, and there is no need for us to repeat the exercise here.[32] Instead, our focus at this point in the discussion is on the controversy itself—on the arguments and counterarguments that have been made for over three decades over "India's China war." An examination of this controversy will help to enrich our perspective not only on the basic question of linkage between the "local" Kashmir dispute and the "extra-local" Cold War, but on the related and even more intriguing question, now that the world is exiting from the Cold War era, of the probability of change in China's Kashmir role. That question is the focus of discussion in the following section.

China in Kashmir: The Aksai Chin Issue

Academic literature on the Sino-Indian border problem, as the American political scientist Steven Hoffmann recently pointed out, has conventionally been divided between "pro-Indian" and "pro-Chinese" schools of thought—the former describing the Indian side "as the victim of Chinese betrayal and expansionism," the latter casting China "as a victim of India's self-righteous intransigence . . . provoked into practicing a justifiable form of realpolitik."[33] The judgment of the pro-Indian school that the Indian side was in large part the victim of Chinese aggression was put forth by many observers in the years immediately after the 1962 border war and is still current, especially with Indian writers. Among the many and varied themes advanced by this school, three were most fundamental. One was that the PRC had come bursting upon the scene equipped with a worldview that was uniquely incompatible with the established norms of international society. This worldview combined a militantly nationalistic strategic outlook with an intolerant revolutionary ideology that envisioned the world divided into two implacably hostile camps. To these abrasive attitudes it added an "inbred historical arrogance" and unquestioned sense of cultural superiority that made reasoning with the Chinese immensely difficult if not impossible.[34]

A second theme was that China's border policy toward India, anchored in deceit, provocation, and bullying, reflected deeply sinister designs against not only Indian territory but against India's independent standing in the world. China's military assault on India in autumn 1962, according to this view, was indeed meant to tighten China's grip on the strategic Ladakhi corridor linking Xinjiang and Tibet. It was also meant, however, to discredit India among Asian and African nations, to put the "imperialist stooge" Nehru in his place—in brief "to demolish Indian prestige."[35] The magnitude of the menace faced by India left it with no alternative, in other words, but to counter Chinese designs with a firm and resolute policy of its own.

The third theme of the pro-India school—one to which the adherents of this school seem to have applied the greatest intellectual energy and which may well have set it apart most fundamentally from its rivals—was that India's case for its territorial claim in Ladakh "was not only far stronger than the Chinese, but also possessed a solid basis quite apart from any questions of 'British imperialism.'"[36] The history of India's northern frontier, seen from this point of view, was not to be ignored in establishing the legality of claims. Neither was its history to be understood as having begun with the coming of the British. The location of the frontier between India and China was certainly not a matter that could be settled by comparing old maps produced by the British and Chinese governments. Such maps revealed only the immediate strategic imperatives of their imperial drafters, not the accumulated record of preimperial frontier history. As put by Sarvepalli Gopal, a historian whose semiofficial biography of Nehru contains one of the most recent pro-Indian expositions on the Sino-Indian border problem, there had been an India long before British rule, and it was to the evidence of *that* India's outermost boundaries that one had to turn to establish the legitimacy of present-day claims. "To set aside the considerable and varied evidence of tradition, custom and administration stretching over centuries and look solely at some odd maps of the last hundred years," he said,

> is to miss the wood for some of the nearest shrubs. To assume that nothing mattered in India before the arrival of the British, to revel in the details of policy-making during the [British] raj and to recommend compromise alignments whose sole claim to consideration is that they were suggested by Englishmen is to exhibit intellectual shallowness. The inclination of some British officials at the end of the nineteenth century to relinquish Indian sovereignty over parts of the Aksai Chin plateau does not provide China with traditional rights to this area.[37]

The Chinese, he pointed out, "are imprecise about their alignments, can produce no evidence even faintly substantiating their demands and base their case solely on occupation of territory which they knew India regarded as hers."[38] The Chinese claim had only lately been concocted to justify Chinese aggression. As a matter of fact, he said, there was no genuine "territorial dispute" to negotiate.

The second—revisionist and more or less pro-Chinese—school of thought focused the search for the precipitants of the border conflict very largely on India's border policy, on the strategic assumptions that underlay it, on the processes of decision making that led to it, and, to no small extent, on the shortcomings of the decision makers who shaped it. According to the adherents of this school, India's territorial claim to the Aksai Chin was on the face of it lacking in substance; and the Indian government's efforts, between the discovery of the Chinese-built road and the outbreak of war with China, to force the Chinese to yield to this claim were based not only on a dangerously flawed understanding of the Chinese strategic outlook but on wholly unrealistic assessments of the comparative capabilities of the Chinese and Indian armies. The problem faced by India, from this perspective, was not one of Chinese expansionism but of a poorly defined frontier. Unwilling to accept that fact and to negotiate with the Chinese on the basis of it, New Delhi adopted a reckless confrontational policy that the circumstances neither justified nor required.

Alastair Lamb's 1964 study of the historical origins of the Sino-Indian border conflict was the first authoritative account to give some credence to China's territorial claims against India. According to Lamb, by far the greater portion of these claims—some 38,000 square miles out of a total claim of over 45,000 square miles—rested on dubious grounds. He reckoned the 700-mile-long, British-negotiated and Indian-claimed McMahon Line (constituting the so-called Eastern Sector of the disputed boundary) to be "on the whole, quite a fair and reasonable boundary between China and India along the Assam Himalaya."[39] As far as that stretch of the boundary was concerned, he said, "the Chinese claim can only be described as absurd," presumably "no more than a bargaining device."[40] In regard to the over 1,000-mile-long Western Sector of the boundary, however, Lamb took a considerably more favorable view of Chinese claims. This sector, in Lamb's judgment the real focus of the boundary dispute between India and China, held over 15,000 square miles of territory claimed by India and controlled by China. Most of this territory lay in the Aksai Chin. To the northern half of the Aksai Chin (about 7,000 square miles) the Chinese, according to Lamb, had a respectable claim. British alignments of India's northern boundary had varied considerably over the years, he pointed out, expanding and contracting with changes in Britain's strategic outlook. The "forward" alignment in Aksai Chin favored by independent India was the product of an expansionist period. It survived beyond the British withdrawal from India, Lamb argued, more by default than anything else. It appeared to be based in part on misunderstanding and misquotation.[41] It was perfectly substitutable, he suggested, by the so-called Macartney-MacDonald alignment of 1898–99, an earlier attempt at a compromise adjustment that would cut the Aksai Chin about in half, leaving the northern portion (containing the Xinjiang–Tibet motor road) entirely in Chinese hands.

The best-known and by far most devastating of the revisionist critiques of New Delhi's northern border policy was Neville Maxwell's *India's China War,* which appeared in 1970. Aimed against "the general view of China as a bellicose, chauvinist and expansionist power,"[42] this study drew heavily on the author's firsthand observations of the border war as correspondent for a British newspaper as well as upon classified Indian documents supplied to him by anonymous Indian sources. The portrait Maxwell drew of Indian policy and actions leading up to the outbreak of war with China in 1962 was far from flattering. Utterly persuaded of the righteousness of its own position on the alignment of India's northern boundaries, Nehru's government, according to Maxwell, adopted an absolutist, irrational, and uncompromising stance. Badly misinterpreting Beijing's intentions, it passed up numerous opportunities for negotiating a mutually agreeable settlement and then, when its diplomatic importunings failed to elicit a positive response from Beijing, initiated provocative military actions along the border with China that recklessly exposed its army's unpreparedness. "At no time," said Maxwell, "were the implications thought through in New Delhi. The policy was legalistic, assuming that as possession is nine-tenths of the law India had only to go and stand on as many parts of Aksai Chin as possible to turn the tables on China, or at least attain a position of equality with her."[43]

In sharp contrast with the Indian position in regard to the Sino-Indian boundary, China's seemed to Maxwell to be essentially reasonable. "The Chinese position," he said, "was that the boundary had never been delimited, that there were disputes, and that these could only be settled by mutual consultation and joint survey." In the meantime, progressive development of Sino-Indian relations should not be affected.[44] The Chinese, he said, had seized numerous opportunities in the late 1950s to castigate Nehru in Marxist-Leninist terms for what seemed to them to be India's steady rightward drift both in domestic and international affairs. But their policy and actions in regard to the border with India, Maxwell insisted,

> remained, from beginning to end, reactive—determined by India's actions towards China, not by the dialectical interpretation of the class character of the Nehru Government. Communist China's record in foreign relations is clear in this regard. Policy towards other governments springs from how they act towards China, not from their political character.[45]

The Chinese, according to Maxwell, did not direct the full fury of their ideological denunciation against Nehru until a very late stage in the evolution of the Sino-Indian dispute; and until that stage arrived, he said, they consistently strove to minimize the boundary question. In no sense was the border war ideologically preordained. "There is no reason to believe," maintained Maxwell, "that if at any time before mid-October 1962 India had changed her policy towards China, either by agreeing to negotiate a general boundary agreement or even by simply suspending the forward policy, China would not have responded and encouraged Sino-Indian relations to simmer down."[46]

Maxwell's transparent onesidedness and seeming inclination to take the Chinese—but not the Indians—at their word must be reckoned as potentially serious shortcomings in his analysis. After all, were more known of Chinese motivations and decision making at the time, it is wholly conceivable that they would fare no better than the Indians have in the assessment of responsibility for war.[47] There is no denying, however, that subsequent studies have done remarkably little injury to Maxwell's caustic characterization of Indian foreign policy decision making and, in a number of cases, appear to have strengthened it. Israeli scholar Yaacov Vertzberger's 1984 inquiry into the Sino-Indian conflict, for instance, asserted that both sides had behaved somewhat recklessly and that on both sides there had been misperception and faulty evaluation of the situation. Nevertheless, his study, no less than Maxwell's, had as its central theme that Indian geostrategic and geopolitical assumptions, evaluations, calculations, and expectations at all levels and in all aspects of its relationship with China were absolutely littered with misperceptions.[48]

Even the very recent attempt by Hoffmann to reconcile conflicting academic perspectives on the Sino-Indian dispute, though unusually evenhanded in its treatment of the two countries, falls well short of exonerating Indian decision makers. Questioning Maxwell's contention that the Indian government committed a grave error in refusing to negotiate the border dispute with China, Hoffmann argued that by 1962 the two governments held fundamentally different conceptions of what was to be negotiated. "From the Indian side," he suggested,

> the most immediate and pressing subjects were the method and timing of Chinese withdrawal from occupied territory, so that border claims could then be considered again, in the light of historical evidence. From the Chinese perspective the most pressing need was to negotiate a halt to India's forward policy. The Chinese then would try again to create a new Sino-Indian border by means of a barter arrangement that took account of the military realities the Chinese had created on the ground.[49]

More than that, he pointed out, the two nations clung to basically different national psychologies. Nehru, for his part, erred in believing that the Chinese were motivated principally by anti-Indian hostility and expansionist designs. But the Chinese, said Hoffmann, were no better prepared to understand Indian border psychology. "Few self-respecting governments," he observed, "would consider a 2,000-mile border open to barter, even if they were assured of a favorable negotiating outcome and no expansionist designs on the other side."[50]

Hoffmann's study was consciously aimed at the avoidance of imbalance. Like both the Vertzberger and Maxwell volumes, however, it was focused on the *Indian* response to the border crisis. Inevitably, therefore, it revealed, as did the earlier studies, much more about the shortcomings of foreign policy decision making in New Delhi than in Beijing. Indian decision making, Hoffmann made clear, was riddled with imperfections, including Nehru's arrogance, a strong tendency toward groupthink, and "an absolute conviction of the righteousness of India's cause."[51] Thus, Hoffmann's commendable effort to reconcile rival interpretations in the academic debate over the Sino-Indian war, while a highly useful corrective, did not fully succeed in rescuing Indian foreign policy from its critics.

Surprisingly, some of the strongest reinforcement of the revisionist school has come from Indian writers, including some with seemingly impeccable credentials. One of these was John Lall, a senior Defence Ministry bureaucrat in New Delhi during the period of the Sino-Indian war, whose detailed and authoritative study of the historical origins of the Aksai Chin dispute appeared in 1989.[52] Lall placed blame for the border crisis primarily on the British and Chinese imperial governments, whose irresolute and irresponsible statesmanship at the end of the nineteenth century, according to him, unnecessarily left the problem of Aksai Chin to fester on into the twentieth.[53] In 1899, he pointed out, the British government had proposed to the Chinese a boundary alignment (the so-called Macartney-McDonald line) which, had it been effectively pursued diplomatically, would have split the Aksai Chin roughly in two between the British and Chinese. Taking a position remarkably at odds with the official stance of the government of India, Lall concluded that the Aksai Chin was fundamentally a no-man's land, that it "was neither Chinese nor Indian," that the provocative claim to all of Aksai Chin advanced by the Nehru government lacked even a shred of justification, and that the fairest way to resolve the problem—urged all along, we might note, by Alastair Lamb—was to resurrect the Macartney-McDonald line, a compromise solution that would leave the Xinjiang–Tibet motor road securely within China.[54]

A yet more recent and perhaps more important addition to the revisionist literature by an Indian writer was that of D. K. Palit, a retired major general and respected military historian, whose book on the Sino-Indian war first appeared in 1991.[55] Palit, who was serving as director of military operations at Indian army headquarters in New Delhi when the war broke out, had uniquely privileged access to military policymaking both before and during the war.[56] Hence, his profoundly critical account of organizational disarray and irrational decision making in Nehru's government cannot lightly be dismissed. Pointing to a fundamental "organic deficiency" in civil-military relations in India, Palit described the handling of the 1962 crisis by both civilian and military branches of the government as "incomprehensible," "inexplicable," as "so inept that it verged on the bizarre." He wondered how that government "could have made such gross misjudgments and breaches of established procedure." Restraint and calculated consideration of policy alternatives, he said, were abandoned

> in preference for emotional posturings and untenable assumptions. Nor did the army high command live up to expectation. Its strategic perceptions were unsound; it failed to withstand or moderate ministerial directives that patently foreboded disaster; and it abjectly accepted political over-reach in operational supervision.[57]

Palit was just as blunt when it came to India's territorial claim to the Aksai Chin. Decisively breaking ranks with India's official position, he traced the origins of the Indian claim in terms scarcely distinguishable from those of Alastair Lamb and John Lall. The British, he said, had left India hurriedly, leaving behind an imprecise definition of the territories they were passing on. The successor states were faced with the task of delimiting the outer boundaries on their own. "If the British," wrote Palit,

> had made even a suggestion that Kashmir's boundary should follow the only formal proposal ever to have been made to the Chinese government (in 1899 . . .) at that juncture it would have certainly been accepted by the Nehru government. This would have placed the strategic road subsequently built by the Chinese in the 1950s well outside India's borders. It was this road that was China's real interest in the Aksai Chin and became the main cause of the Sino-Indian confrontation.

Instead, Palit observed, the Indian government defined the border in Kashmir unilaterally, ignoring the Chinese. "Almost everywhere," he said, "it accepted the forward-most claims of the British. . . . No heed was taken of the British proposal to the Chinese government of 1899."[58]

These commentaries on the origins of the border dispute between India and China over the Aksai Chin, while they obviously do not rule out the Cold War from among the causal factors of the dispute, compel us to consider the strong likelihood that its impact may have been considerably less central than was once argued. The outbreak of the Sino-Indian border war in 1962 very likely had more to do, in other words, with local circumstances—the youthfulness and political immaturity of the Indian and Chinese regimes, for instance; or the military balance (or imbalance) between them; or the natural fears that both these countries would have, whatever the surrounding geopolitical circumstances, for the security and integrity of the lengthy and ill-defined border between them (not to mention the inevitable misperceptions and misunderstandings that these fears would generate)—than with extralocal considerations relating to the emerging Cold War alliance systems.

Now that these Cold War systems no longer even exist, what changes should we expect in Sino-Indian and Sino-Pakistani relations? Are today's "local circumstances" sufficient by themselves to sustain, on the one hand, the enmity between India and China and, on the other hand, the friendship between Pakistan and China? In the new and turbulent geopolitical environment in which Kashmir now finds itself, do established beliefs about its strategic importance continue to apply? With the end of the Cold War, will at least Kashmir's *external* boundary finally be settled?

After the Cold War: The Encirclement Issue

Whatever may have motivated Beijing's policy toward India in the years leading up to the 1962 border crisis, there can be little doubt that its South Asian policy over the next 30 years or so—up until the end of the Cold War, that is—bore the unmistakable imprint of China's triangular and global relationship with the Soviet Union and the United States, and indeed that this relationship, as Yaacov Vertzberger put it, "became the preeminent component in China's strategic calculus with regard to the [South Asian] region."[59] This calculus, according to Vertzberger, was rooted in the Chinese conviction that Soviet strategy in regard to the southern rimland of Asia was aimed at construction of a belt of influence stretching in a broad arc from the Middle East all the way to Northeast Asia. South Asia was the land bridge and the Indian Ocean the sea bridge connecting these regions. The scheme had to be blocked, as the Chinese saw it, because its fulfillment would permit the Soviets "to complete the pincer movements, from west and east, and lock both arms of their pincer around China."[60]

Just how the Chinese went about blocking this scheme has been the focus of some controversy. One "Pakistan-centric" school of thought has maintained the singular importance of Pakistan in China's strategy. Vertzberger, for instance, argued that blocking took three main forms: One of them was aid to the Afghanistan resistance following the Soviet takeover in Kabul in late 1979; and a second, which had begun in the 1970s, was increased attention to Chinese naval power and influence in the Indian Ocean. The third and most important element by far in China's "counterencirclement" strategy, he asserted, was development of the "enduring entente" with Pakistan.[61]

Pakistan's pivotal importance in Chinese counterencirclement strategy, as described by Vertzberger and other adherents of this Pakistan-centered school, first became visible in the conclusion by China and Pakistan in 1963 of both border and civil aviation agreements. Thereafter, it was reinforced by a steadily augmented panoply of cooperative endeavors, including prolonged collaboration, beginning around 1965, on the construction of strategic highways linking the two countries; the launching by China in 1966 of a major and sustained military assistance program designed to help modernize Pakistan's naval, air, and ground forces; Chinese assistance in the development of Pakistan's small indigenous defense production capability; Chinese diplomatic support of Pakistan at the time of both the 1965 and 1971 wars between Pakistan and India; and, it seems, even covert assistance by China to Pakistan's nuclear weapons development program.[62] Of these, two—the 1963 Border Agreement and joint construction of the strategic Karakoram Highway—had the most explicit and material relevance to Kashmir.

The Border Agreement, as we have already noted, for the first time signaled China's acceptance of Pakistan's claim that Kashmir was disputed territory. It covered a stretch of China's common border with Pakistan's Northern Areas that extended over 200 miles from the trijunction of Afghanistan, Pakistan, and China's Xinjiang province eastward to the Karakoram Pass. Under its terms, Pakistan relinquished claims to over 1,500 square miles of territory, no part of which was under its actual control, while the Chinese ceded to Pakistan about 750 square miles of territory (including access to the prestigious peak K-2) actually administered by China.[63] The accord, which was explicitly acknowledged to be provisional pending Pakistan's final settlement of the Kashmir dispute with India, concretely settled very little. It came, however, at a time of fading U.S. interest in its subcontinental ally as well as of badly worsened relations not only between China and India but between China and the Soviet Union. It was thus, at least in terms of building strategic momentum between them, of considerable significance for both Pakistan and China.

Best symbolizing the growing strategic nexus between China and Pakistan, however, was the network of strategic highways, in particular the 500-mile Karakoram Highway, that they began constructing together in the late 1960s. Built in and through the disputed territory of Kashmir and vastly improving the Pakistan military's access to remote portions of the LOC, these roads unquestionably reinforced Pakistan's hold on its share of Kashmir. Indian officials naturally rejected Pakistani and Chinese contentions that the roads served none but commercial purposes; understandably, they described them as a potential military threat to India's own rather tenuous hold on Ladakh. Together, said the author of an illuminating study of Sino-Pakistani cooperation in the construction of roads, the earlier Border Agreement and the strategic highways

> complicated China's stand on the Kashmir problem. In effect, China recognized Pakistan's practical control over the Northern Areas. And in its highways China made a discrete physical investment in the region. . . . China's concrete investments in the region have retained their original importance. Despite its protestations, in a brilliant illustration of the enduring meaning of access China had insinuated itself into the Kashmir quarrel.[64]

Considerable scholarly effort has been expended in recent years to show that China's strategy toward South Asia during the Cold War era, while unquestionably founded upon counterencirclement, was far less partial to Pakistan, and in particular far less supportive of Pakistan's stand on Kashmir, than had been implied by supporters of the Pakistan-centered approach. The sinologist

John Garver argued, for instance, that Chinese foreign policy toward South Asia in the years between 1977 and 1988 did indeed fit very well into the broad pattern of Beijing's antihegemony diplomacy directed against the Soviet Union. But this policy, he suggested, far from banking solely or even chiefly on the cultivation of a special relationship with Pakistan, had been driven throughout this period to a considerable extent by Beijing's desire to improve its relations with India. He accounted for this motivation in a number of ways: First, Beijing recognized that India, following its dismemberment of Pakistan in 1971 and successful nuclear test in 1974, was clearly the preeminent power in South Asia and that a policy aimed at balancing Indian power by supporting a combination of its small South Asian rivals "was simply not sound."[65] Second, Beijing gradually began perceiving Indian foreign policy after the 1971 war as more independent of the Soviet Union than may have been the case earlier. Third, Beijing, worried by Moscow's seemingly more aggressive foreign policy in the wake of America's defeat in Vietnam as well as by America's apparent drift toward isolationism, sought to compensate in part by making friendly overtures to India. And fourth, Beijing's avid pursuit of multifaceted development goals (the Four Modernizations) in the 1980s stimulated a general foreign policy campaign "to reduce tension and expand relations with most of China's neighbors, including India."[66]

One of China's "friendly gestures" cited by Garver was the launching in 1981, following the visit to New Delhi of Chinese foreign minister Huang Hua, of a series of exploratory talks on the border issue. Another, of equal pertinence to the present discussion, was a shift in China's position on the Kashmir issue. Beginning in 1964, Beijing, according to Garver, had consistently endorsed Pakistan's demand for a plebiscite as called for in the Security Council resolutions of 1949. But by 1980, according to him, the Chinese had dropped their support for Kashmiri self-determination and were instead describing Kashmir as a bilateral issue that should be settled peacefully in accord both with the Simla agreement *and* the relevant UN resolutions—a fence-straddling position that managed to appease India without necessarily alienating Pakistan.[67]

The fundamental *inconstancy* of China's policy in regard to Kashmir is argued even more insistently by the Pakistan-born scholar Samina Yasmeen. She agrees with the proposition that China's South Asia policy has for long been part of its broad anti-Soviet counterencirclement strategy. From her survey of China's public statements in regard to Kashmir, she draws the conclusion, however, that China's policy on Kashmir during the roughly four decades since the Chinese Communists came to power in Beijing showed very little consistency. "As Beijing's perceptions of, and responses to, the threat along its borders has altered," she observed, "so has its South Asia policy and its stand on the Kashmir dispute. China's policy towards the Indo-Pakistani deadlock over Kashmir has not been consistently and rigidly pro-Pakistan, not even after the 1962 Sino-Indian War, or after the Indo-Pakistan Wars of 1965 and 1971."[68] Yasmeen argued that Beijing's Kashmir policy had, in fact, been drifting steadily closer to evenhandedness ever since the mid-1970s. By the early 1990s, she said, it had come full circle: It was less and less willing now to side with Pakistan on the issue, and its position in regard to Kashmir was scarcely distinguishable from the neutralism it espoused in the earliest years of the Communist regime. The presumed "permanence" of Sino-Pakistani friendship, she concluded, had little basis in fact.

These revisionist critiques of the standard Cold War versions of Chinese involvement in South Asia are not without merit. It seems to me, however, that if one accepts their fundamental proposition—namely that Chinese determination to reduce the threat of Soviet encirclement produced a flexible, reactive, and not altogether coherent set of policies in regard to India, Pakistan, and Kashmir (that these policies changed, in other words, when circumstances as well as Beijing's understanding of them changed)—establishing the probable path of *post*-Cold War Chinese policy toward this region is certainly rendered no easier.

The enduring character—the *continuity*—of China's Cold War relationships expressly argued in the standard versions inevitably implied that when and if the compulsions of the Cold War died, so too would the rationale for these relationships. Remove the external props, in other words, and these relationships would naturally be rearranged. Political scientist Raju Thomas suggested precisely this well before the Cold War's demise. "From the Indian standpoint," he said,

> a lowering of great-power tensions and a relatively cooperative tripolar world may suggest less external interest in the [South Asian] region and the elimination of great-power military commitments from the subcontinent. . . . [T]he present phase may imply coming to terms with the regional dominance of India and the acceptance of disputed claims on India's terms.[69]

The Cold War had perpetuated an "unnatural" pattern of alignments in South Asia, in other words, and had sustained Pakistan's claim to Kashmir. The sharp break—the *discontinuity*—inherent in the end of the Cold War, from this point of view, would very likely render both the pattern and the claim untenable.

If the pattern of alignments during the Cold War was *not* so rigidly set, however, as the revisionists tend to argue, then the global break with the past represented in the end of the Cold War might not be mirrored very clearly—or at least might not be as quickly or as unambiguously defined—in China's now-evolving strategic moves toward the South Asian region.

These moves, in fact, fit neatly into no obvious grand design and pointed unequivocally in no particular direction. On the one hand, there appeared to be no marked curtailment of the military collaboration that had characterized Sino-Pakistani relations since the mid-1960s. There were repeated allegations in early 1993 by American intelligence officials, for instance, of continued major Sino-Pakistani collaboration in the sensitive nuclear field. The Chinese and Pakistanis, it was claimed, were exchanging nuclear weapons scientists; the Chinese were also said to be providing Pakistan with equipment needed to manufacture nuclear weapons and to make fissile materials; and, in particular, the Chinese were charged with being in violation of the Missile Technology Control Regime (MTCR) by having supplied Pakistan, near the end of 1992, with components for making M-11 intermediate-range ballistic missiles.[70] While China's greed for foreign capital was widely accepted as a likely (nonstrategic) motive for the deal, its wish to balance Indian nuclear capability by arming Pakistan could hardly be ruled out. In any event, Washington's suspicions in regard to the M-11, a missile capable of carrying a payload of 1,100 pounds over a distance of nearly 200 miles, were serious enough to lead on 25 August 1993 to the imposition of sanctions against both China and Pakistan.[71]

On the other hand, there were equally compelling signs in this same time period of progress in Sino-Indian relations. In late June 1993, the sixth round of meetings of the Sino-Indian Joint Working Group, formed in 1988 to give fixed institutional focus to the border question, met in New Delhi; and soon thereafter, in September, Beijing extended an unusually warm welcome to visiting Indian prime minister Narasimha Rao. No major breakthroughs were announced; but on 7 September a number of potentially significant agreements, including an accord pledging both sides to troop reductions, respect for cease-fire lines, and other confidence-building measures relating to the "line of actual control" separating their forces along their 2,100-mile border, were signed.[72]

These somewhat puzzling and potentially contradictory moves by Beijing should surprise no one: The end of the Cold War and the disintegration of the Soviet Union are extremely recent events, and there has hardly been time for the Chinese or anyone else to assess their full potential impact, much less to develop and implement a full slate of new policies. It is doubtful, however, that the mere passage of time itself will wholly dispel the confusion or give a radically new and cooperative orientation to China's South Asian policies. For a number of reasons, in fact, the expectation that the seemingly vanished requirement for a Chinese counterencirclement strategy would lead in due time to a major overhaul in China's South Asia policy, to a less friendly relationship with Pakistan, perhaps to the rapid resolution of its border dispute with India, and, thus, to the elimination of a major *strategic* obstacle to settlement of India's dispute with Pakistan over Kashmir, seems largely unwarranted.

In the first place, prospects for China's wholehearted and durable conversion into a benign, cooperative, and "low-politics" oriented player in Asian politics are fairly modest. Only one-half of China's Cold War, that with the Soviet Union, is over. The other half, with the United States, is not. Between China and the United States, relations "remain complex and contentious,"[73] with about as much potential for deterioration as for improvement. Some of China's military leaders appear convinced, in fact, that the United States will one day be China's principal military adversary.[74] Furthermore, China's traditional regional rivalries could well be resurrected if, as some deem likely, China selects a more assertive and confrontational path. Its *capacity* to select this path, in terms both of military and economic muscle, is unquestionably expanding. In recent years it has sustained a stunning rate of economic growth, leading the world in 1992 (at 13 percent) and expected to expand even further (to 13.4 percent) in 1993.[75] The expansion was enough, in any case, to stimulate predictions that "by the year 2000, parts of coastal China may reach a level of modernity commensurate with the newly industrialized nations of East Asia."[76] The modernization of China's military forces, moreover, while obviously facing a long and uphill struggle, shows no slackening of will: In the three years (1990–1992) following the Tiananmen incident in Beijing, the net real increase in China's military budget came to more than 50 percent.[77] Faced with rapid growth in China's economy, defense spending, and power projection capabilities, Indian leaders, along with the leaders of China's other neighbors, naturally react with alarm. China, observed the chief of the Indian air force in a public address in New Delhi near the end of 1993, had emerged as India's primary long-term security challenge. In spite of the recent trend toward reconciliation, he said, China's military modernization program was disturbing the Asian strategic balance. "India," he pointed out, "is thus placed with twin contrasting security dilemmas. On the one hand, the probability of an armed conflict with China has been reduced in the short term, but in the long term, by 2005, the threat from China will be of a different magnitude altogether."[78] In very similar terms, David Shambaugh, editor of *The China Quarterly,* concludes that

> by the turn of the century, it is quite likely that regional rivalries will emerge between China on the one hand, and Japan, Vietnam, India—and perhaps Russia—on the other. China's growing economic and

> military strength, central geographic location in Asia, enormous population, assertive nationalism and desire to become the pre-eminent power in Asia all suggest that in the medium and long terms, international politics in Asia will again become conflict-ridden. China may be at the centre of these conflicts.[79]

In the second place, Pakistan is likely to remain an unusually useful and, indeed, essential ally. The Chinese have long valued Pakistan as a counterweight to Indian power in South Asia; and this role hardly seems to be declining in importance. Readily visible, of course, is the fact that, much to China's advantage, by far the greater proportion of the Indian army is tied down in the defense of India's western border with Pakistan. Beyond this, India's military strength, like China's, is steadily growing. Its ability to manufacture nuclear weapons is undoubted; some estimates suggest that it now owns enough weapons-grade plutonium for almost 60 weapons.[80] In recent years, it has developed and successfully tested five ballistic missile systems, including the intermediate-range *Agni;* and the suspicion is strong among Western nuclear experts that its plans include development of long-range delivery capability for nuclear weapons—a development Beijing clearly recognizes as a distinct threat to China.[81] Like China, India hopes to streamline its military, to produce a smaller, higher-tech force. But the expectation, apparent in some quarters,[82] that the current dip in Indian defense spending signals a long-term pacific trend is not supported by careful studies of Indian defense expenditure patterns. According to the Australian defense analyst Sandy Gordon, for instance, a substantial portion of the alleged decline disappears when one takes into account the roughly 20 percent of defense spending that isn't listed in the budget under the defense heading; and a large part of the cuts that have been made have fallen most heavily on the navy (of least immediate relevance to Sino-Indian relations). Gordon observes that the recent "fall in expenditure does not mean that the process of military modernization in India has ceased, or that New Delhi has assessed that it should dispense entirely with the acquisition of additional military power and instead direct resources to economic development." On the contrary, he says, "the structure of the cuts suggests that New Delhi is still intent upon preserving the basic fabric of the force structure against a time when the financial position has improved and the defense budget can again grow in real terms."[83]

One should also bear in mind in this connection that Pakistan is the most populous of five Muslim states bordering on western China and it is also an important member of the economic bloc (the Economic Cooperation Organization) formed in early 1992 from the Muslim states of Central and Southwestern

Asia. While China may have fewer reasons to panic over the so-called Islamic resurgence in this area than some observers have suggested, prudence clearly dictates that Beijing, even if there is some downgrading in the relationship, not casually discard Pakistan. Faced with potential disaffection among its own Muslim minorities as well as with rising competition (from Russia, Turkey, Iran, the United States, and India, among others) for the friendship of the countries in Asia's Islamic belt, China would seem more likely to focus on retaining and, indeed, building upon whatever influence it already has there.[84] Highly dependent on China for military and other assistance, Pakistan, moreover, is more likely than most states in the area to be a dependable ally. China unquestionably values its improved relationship with India and is unlikely to provoke New Delhi unnecessarily by pushing too hard its friendship with Pakistan and the other small states of South Asia. "It would probably be wrong to conclude, however," observes Garver, "that China has made, or is likely to make, a conscious decision to concede South Asia as an Indian sphere of influence. Such a move would spell the virtual end to Chinese aspirations of being the leading Asian power and would greatly weaken China's position against Indian power."[85]

Third, China simply does not have an especially strong incentive to settle its border dispute with India. The Chinese acquired the territory they wanted in the 1962 border war; and, while they would no doubt prefer to have their sovereignty over this territory formally recognized by India, they are clearly in no danger of losing it. As the recent summit meeting in Beijing between the leaders of India and China makes clear, moreover, settlement of the border dispute between these countries is not an absolute precondition to improved relations: Demonstrably, they can make incremental progress in less sensitive areas without settling it.

Neither, we should note, does China have any very good reason to go out of its way to help settle the border dispute over Kashmir between Pakistan and India. There are no Kashmiri coethnics in China; and the danger of cross-border contagion, given geographic circumstances alone, seems very meager. Furthermore, slightly over half of India's regular army, according to the army's new chief of staff, is currently employed on internal security duties, many of them, as we will note in Part II of this study, in Kashmir. This commitment, he concedes, is hurting troop training and war preparedness.[86] Sustained Indian vulnerability to separatism in Jammu and Kashmir state, the Chinese could not help but conclude, is for China nearly cost- and risk-free insurance against Indian adventurism in Chinese Tibet or Xinjiang.[87]

The all-too-direct relationship claimed in earlier years between the Cold War and Sino-Indian hostility has its parallel today in the frequent assertion of an equally powerful relationship between the Cold War's end and the potential for Sino-Indian friendship. That potential obviously exists; but so does the potential for sustained, or even increased, enmity. Available evidence is insufficient to establish conclusively which potential is the more probable. Of two things, however, we can be sure. One is that China's policies in South Asia will stem from far broader considerations than those arising solely from the rubble of its collapsed counterencirclement strategy. The other is that the end of the Cold War, by itself, does not spell the end of the Kashmir dispute.

Part II

The Separatist Problem

In Part II, our attention is drawn largely to the Indian side of the Line of Control and to current events—specifically to the separatist unrest that began in earnest around 1988 in the Indian state of Jammu and Kashmir. This focus will require that we continue to pay some attention to Pakistan, the scale and nature of whose role in this unrest is the focus of enormous controversy. The bulk of discussion, however, will concern India, for whom "the Kashmir problem" has recently become as much an internal as an external issue.

The discussion is grouped into three chapters. Chapter 4 focuses on the Kashmiri uprising itself, on its origins, character, and impact. Chapter 5 examines the role of Indian security forces in Jammu and Kashmir, paying particular attention to the human rights issue that has emerged from the employment of these forces in counterinsurgency operations. In Chapter 6, the discussion shifts to the policy level of the separatist problem and to the political dilemmas facing Indian policymakers as they attempt to cope with the separatist challenge. Our purpose is again mainly diagnostic, aimed at narrating neither the history of Kashmiri separatism nor of India's repression of it but at unraveling its various segments to gain insight into the relationship of separatism both to the India-Pakistan boundary dispute over Kashmir and, of course, to the problem of its settlement.

CHAPTER

·4·

THE KASHMIRI MUSLIM UPRISING

This chapter examines the Kashmiri Muslim separatist movement in the Indian state of Jammu and Kashmir. Its focus is the sustained violent uprising or insurgency into which this movement developed in the late 1980s.* It considers (1) the origins and precipitants of the uprising; (2) Pakistan's role in the uprising; (3) the scale, organization, and capabilities of the separatist forces; and (4) the impact (casualties; physical damage; administrative, social, and economic costs) on Kashmir of prolonged violent struggle.

ORIGINS AND PRECIPITATING FACTORS

Accounts of the Kashmiri Muslim separatist uprising in the popular media generally date its formal onset to a series of antigovernment demonstrations, strikes, and sporadic violent attacks on isolated government targets that began at scattered locations in the Valley of Kashmir in July 1988. These incidents developed into a major political confrontation between the central government and the separatist militants with the kidnapping in December 1989 of Dr. Rubaiya Sayeed, the daughter of Home Affairs Minister Mufti Mohammad Sayeed, himself a Kashmiri Muslim and a leading contender for political leadership in the state of Jammu and Kashmir. This confrontation ended when the central government freed five detained militants in exchange for the minister's daughter. In January 1990, with bloody clashes between Indian paramilitary troops and the militants becoming daily affairs, and with the state's placement under Governor's Rule following dissolution of the elected state assembly, the unrest spread to the entire state. A serious police strike late in

* Kashmiri Muslim separatists are with equal validity described as militants, secessionists, or insurgents; and these terms will be used more or less interchangeably in this study. However, describing the Kashmiri Muslim movement as a terrorist, freedom, or liberation struggle, while common practice in South Asia, displays obvious partiality and is avoided here.

January dramatized the near collapse of the government's authority; and the exodus into Pakistan at this time of thousands of severely disaffected Kashmiri youths signaled a depth of open resentment against India unknown in the state until then.

Debated ever since those events took place has been the relative importance in the onset of the uprising of *foreign* as opposed to *indigenous* factors. Did Pakistani cunning underlie the attacks on Indian rule in the state? Or had the Indian government, with its drift and indecision, heavy-handed interference in Kashmiri politics, and seeming disregard for the aspirations of Kashmiri Muslims, accomplished the erosion of its authority in the state largely on its own? These are obviously questions that cannot be answered very confidently with available evidence; indeed, a fully satisfactory answer to them may never be given. At least the rough outlines of an answer must be hazarded, however, since these questions bear heavily on the dispute currently under way in India over what the government ought *now* to be doing about Kashmir.

As a first step, we can dismiss outright the argument that Kashmiri Muslim separatism in its latest and most violent phase was exclusively or even primarily the product of a craftily designed and skillfully executed conspiracy hatched by Pakistan's military intelligence (primarily the Inter-Services Intelligence Directorate, commonly designated the ISI) and developed in collusion with expatriate Kashmiri Muslim subversive forces and their allies both abroad and in Pakistan. This notion, always popular in some quarters in India, gained fairly wide respectability there in a rather bizarre manner following publication in July 1989 in the New Delhi–based journal *Indian Defence Review* of an article addressing Pakistan's role in Kashmir. The article, whose authors were identified only as "IDR staff members," described a clandestine operation—codenamed "Op Topac"—that had allegedly been outlined to key Pakistani generals and intelligence officials at a secret convocation in Rawalpindi and then set in motion by the Pakistani leader General Mohammad Zia ul-Haq in the months immediately prior to his death in an air crash on 17 August 1988. A preambular paragraph described the article unequivocally as "part fact, part fiction," as an intellectual exercise developed by the journal's staffers in which "the scenarios visualized have been based on the trends which have become manifest in the subcontinent in the last few years." The way in which the article was written gave no hint of fiction, and many readers, including a number of leading journalists and think-tank analysts who seemed to have missed or simply ignored the disclaimer, declared the article's contents to be wholly factual.[1]

Dismissal of Op Topac–like versions of events leaves intact, of course, the argument that Pakistan, whether it engineered the uprising or not, took maximum advantage of it once it was in progress. To this issue, here designated the infiltration issue, we return in a moment. Also left intact is the extremely strong probability—indeed, near certainty—that Pakistani intelligence organs took advantage of discontents developing among Kashmiri Muslims in Indian Kashmir *prior* to the onset of the uprising and, in so doing, exerted some influence on its scale, timing, tactics, and objectives. By the middle of the 1980s, the ISI had accumulated abundant experience with covert operations in Afghanistan;[2] and it would have taken little imagination and no great investment of resources for its managers to undertake parallel operations in Kashmir—to try to be the "master switch," as a Kashmiri Muslim journalist in Pakistan described it, lighting up the valley with armed insurgency.[3] The incentives to do so had been present since 1947 and clearly had not diminished with the passage of time.[4]

To acknowledge Pakistan's involvement in this way is not meant, however, to commend the argument, commonly made in India, that the current problem in Kashmir is largely one of "sponsored terrorism," that this terrorism is evolving in programmed stages in line with a blueprint drawn up in Pakistan, and that once its Pakistani masterminds are induced to call off their terrorist underlings violence will end and a peaceful settlement be achieved.[5] This argument very conveniently deposits at Pakistan's doorstep major responsibility for the misfortunes currently befalling the Kashmiri people. It essentially exonerates Indian leaders of political mismanagement and of responsibility for violence and brutality in the state. And it flies in the face of the admissions of Indian government officials in Srinagar—including the present governor (a Hindu, the erstwhile chief of army staff, and an occupant of his present position at the time major insurgency surfaced in January 1990)—that on the eve of the insurgency (in 1989), years of effort by Pakistan had produced a maximum strength of 300 Kashmiri militants and that it was New Delhi's mistaken response, its understanding of Kashmir as a law-and-order problem to be dealt with by "brute force," that enabled separatism to gain real headway in 1990. Pakistan's success, he observed, came *subsequent* to India's failure.[6]

As a second step, we can also dismiss efforts to lay the blame for India's *political* failure in Kashmir on any single political incident or electoral event. In a state and in a country where *un*rigged elections have been the exception and where public cynicism arising from political chicanery and electoral malpractice runs very deep, it is difficult to believe that the recent resurgence of Kashmiri Muslim separatism—leaving aside the violent insurgency—sprang wholly or even largely from the rigging of the 1987 state elections, for instance, or from New Delhi's blatant interference with the state's administration in 1984. This was the explanation, for instance, of one senior (non-Muslim)

Indian bureaucrat, with long years of service in Indian Kashmir, who told the author that the "critical event" in triggering the militancy occurred in July 1984 when the state's popular chief minister Farooq Abdullah was toppled from power with the behind-the-scenes assistance of New Delhi. At that point, he said, the Kashmiri people's psychological alienation began. "Many Kashmiris," he said, "up until then felt that the Kashmir problem was over." From 1975 to 1984, he maintained, there had been a decade of reasonably genuine democracy. Congress's defeat in the 1983 state election had been "thrilling" for Kashmiris; it confirmed that democracy worked. In the meantime, economic development was in progress and life was improving. Then came 1984, a traumatic year, he said, in the state's recent political history. That year's events plus the rigged elections of 1986 and 1987 pushed Kashmiris over the political brink.[7]

No doubt, these things helped to vitiate public trust in the state's political leadership and institutions; but an uprising on the scale and of the duration of the one in Kashmir requires much more than a rigged election or a sacked chief minister to explain it. Kashmiri politicians themselves, after all, do not have a reputation for ethical behavior any better than their counterparts in New Delhi. As a Ministry of Home Affairs bureaucrat expressed it in July 1993, the beneficiaries of New Delhi's manipulations were usually Kashmiri Muslims, willing accomplices to the last man of the wielders of power in New Delhi. Complaints of rigged elections, he said, echoing the judgment of a seasoned Kashmiri Muslim publicist in Pakistan, vastly exaggerated their role (and underrated Pakistan's, by the way) in precipitating the insurgency.[8]

By the same token, main responsibility for India's political failure in Kashmir should not be assigned to any particular political leader or political party. The temptation for Indian politicians to do precisely this is, of course, nearly irresistible; and the practice, admittedly, is just about universal. Nothing has enlivened the debate over Kashmir more, or contributed less to reasoned discussion of it, than this.

No one, it seems, has engaged in this blame-laying pursuit more avidly—or been paid back in the same coin so fervently—than Malhotra Jagmohan, an erstwhile civil servant who was twice named governor of Indian Kashmir. Appointed initially by the Congress government of Prime Minister Indira Gandhi, his first tour, lasting five years (April 1984–June 1989), coincided with a number of developments (the sacking of Chief Minister Farooq Abdullah in 1984, for instance, and the imposition of Governor's Rule for a number of months in 1986) that marked him in the eyes of many as an obedient stooge for New Delhi. He emerged from that tour relatively unscathed, however, with his reputation for evenhanded and efficient administration still mainly intact. His second appointment, by the Janata government of Prime

Minister V. P. Singh, came in January 1990 at that insalubrious moment in the state's history when it was sliding rapidly into massive unrest and violence. This appointment lasted only five months. It began with his politically risky decision to dissolve the elected state assembly and to vest supreme authority in his own hands under the state constitution's provision for Governor's Rule; and it ended with his forced resignation and with his reputation mired in mud. A victim as much of New Delhi's byzantine and backbiting politics as of his own extraordinarily single-minded (by some accounts, narrow-minded) determination to set things right in the valley, Jagmohan relinquished the governorship in May, replaced by ex-intelligence chief Girish Saxena.

Provided with heavy, round-the-clock police protection, Jagmohan devoted much of the next year, ensconced in the library of the India International Centre in New Delhi, to authoring a book filled with uncommonly revealing, often bitter, self-exculpatory, and rarely dull narration of his trials and tribulations as governor.[9] In it, he comes down heavily on Pakistan's "Connivance, Collusion, Conspiracies" in Kashmir; but his choicest criticisms are directed at India's own ruling class —in particular, those in it who were center-left in political outlook—and at what seem to Jagmohan to be the dangerous rot and decay of India's political system that have set in under its tutelage. While he wrote the book, he engaged in a running battle in the press with his political adversaries, who accused him of megalomania, of virulent hatred of Islam, of deliberate incitement of Hindu-Muslim communalism, and, in general, of ruthless management of New Delhi's campaign to crush militancy in the valley by whatever means.

Jagmohan unquestionably has an exceptional appetite for controversy, and there is little doubt that he brought some of the vituperation of his critics down upon his own head. There is equally little question, however, that his were not the only—and they were certainly not the most important—decisions taken by India in regard to Kashmir in the years he presided as governor. The key decisions—including, of course, his own appointments—were with very few exceptions taken in New Delhi, in fact, not in Srinagar. And they were customarily taken as part of a cumulative policy fashioned over many years, not normally in one gulp and on the spur of the moment by this or that leader. As parliamentarian and prominent spokesman of the opposition Bharatiya Janata Party (BJP, or Indian People's Party), Jaswant Singh observed to the author in this regard, one needed to distinguish between style and substance.[10] One could quibble with Jagmohan's *style,* he said, but the *substance* of his policy shouldn't have been his to define in any event. That responsibility fell to the union government in New Delhi. If it failed to supply adequate policy guidance to the governor, that was the government's fault, not his. Jaswant Singh added, getting in a lick of his own at the alleged indecision of his Congress adversaries, that none of Kashmir's governors could possibly have implemented what didn't even exist.

As a third step, it has to be recognized that the Kashmiri Muslim uprising is not just a contingent phenomenon—a product, on the one hand, of New Delhi's political mismanagement or, on the other, of Islamabad's sinister designs. It has roots and a life of its own arising, on the one hand, from a lengthy history of separatist politics as well as, on the other, from the Kashmiris' very distinctive culture and strong sense of identity. This identity is being significantly inspired and reinforced in our day by the experiences of other separatist movements, many of them in India itself—and one of those, Sikh separatism, in immediately adjacent Punjab; and it is being refashioned, perhaps fundamentally, by the cultural assertiveness and antisecularism of the powerful Islamist elements that are also present in the neighborhood and, indeed, in Kashmir itself.

The Kashmiri uprising's semiautogenous (or noncontingent) origins deserve more attention than they ordinarily get: They are the aspect of the movement emphasized most often by Kashmiri separatists themselves; they are characteristically ignored or underplayed in the prescriptions for relief written out either by the Indians or Pakistanis; and yet they alone can account very well for the profound alienation of the Kashmiri people from India or for their surprising tenacity and sheer physical endurance in the present difficult circumstances.

The roots of the Kashmiri uprising are thus clearly multiple, some of them readily traceable to policy failures in New Delhi, others to political and social currents in Kashmir, and still others, inevitably, to the designs of leaders in Pakistan. Overemphasis upon or selective neglect of any one of these will only cloud analysis. The Kashmir dispute's separatist dimension, like its boundary dimension, is unavoidably complex.

We suggested earlier that Pakistan's role in the separatist uprising *since* its onset deserves to be considered apart from whatever role it may have played in the years *before* its onset. The discussion turns now to this issue of infiltration since the uprising began.

PAKISTAN'S ROLE: THE INFILTRATION ISSUE

The issue of cross-border infiltration—the armed violation of the LOC through covert dispatch of regular or irregular forces (Indian or Pakistani) across it—has persisted with greater or lesser severity ever since the CFL was first drawn in 1949. Pakistan's open diplomatic and political support of the recent Kashmiri uprising, together with widespread accusations that its intervention included covert military support of infiltration and insurgency in the Valley of Kashmir, has brought this issue once again to the forefront in India-Pakistan relations. Included in this issue is the question of the extent of Pakistan's official intervention, of Pakistan's motivations, of the extent to which India's continuing problems in restoring peace in Kashmir may reasonably be attributed to Pakistan's activities, and of India's capacity for effective counterinfiltration and retaliation. The first two of these questions we deal with now, the second two in Chapter 5.

The CFL/LOC has been violated from both sides and in countless ways on a continuing basis ever since its establishment in 1949. In only two cases, however, has violation of the boundary taken the form of large-scale covert infiltration by guerrilla forces.[11] The first such case was in July–August 1965, when Pakistan attempted to infiltrate several thousand armed men (most of them drawn, in fact, from the regular Azad Kashmir armed forces) across the CFL into Indian Kashmir. Most of the would-be infiltrators were stopped at the border by Indian forces; and the effort (codenamed Operation Gibraltar) has generally been judged a failure.[12] It led directly to full-scale war between India and Pakistan.

The second case of major cross-border infiltration developed only in the last several years. It has involved large numbers of disaffected Kashmiri Muslim youths; and both in its duration and magnitude it has clearly exceeded Pakistan's ill-fated Operation Gibraltar.

It was this author's view, set forth in a report prepared for the U.S. Department of State in late 1991, that Pakistan's official involvement in this second round of infiltration was far from insignificant; that Pakistan supplied substantial political, diplomatic, *and material* support to the Kashmiri uprising; that the material support took various forms, including the training, indoctrination, arming, and cross-border movement of the infiltrating forces; that the exfiltration of Kashmiri Muslims across the LOC into Pakistan or Pakistan-controlled Kashmir and their covert reinfiltration, following training in light arms and guerrilla tactics, played a very important role in maintaining the tempo of the insurgency; that the support was planned and coordinated in large part by Pakistan's ISI; and that all this was carried out with the full knowledge and under the auspices of the Pakistan army.[13] These judgments have to be modified now to take account both of changes in the pattern of Pakistan's support and of an apparent sharp decline in the past year or so in the rate of infiltration. (See Chapter 5.) Nevertheless, nothing the author has discovered about the Kashmir conflict since this view was initially expressed would warrant overturning the basic contention.

Those in command of the Indian army in Kashmir, as gleaned by the author from interviews and briefings during escorted visits to the Indian side of the

LOC in 1991 and 1993, seemed to have not a shred of doubt that the Pakistan army, in particular the ISI, was masterminding the infiltration. Intelligence briefers in 1991 claimed, for instance, that the ISI was maintaining at that time approximately 48 training camps in Azad Kashmir (called Pakistan Occupied Kashmir, or POK, by the Indians), in which fundamental instruction in light arms and guerrilla warfare tactics was imparted, generally by retired army non-commissioned officers, to Kashmiri Muslim recruits.[14] Exfiltration and infiltration of the recruits across the LOC, according to the Indians, was arranged at five ISI base camps located in Azad Kashmir. From forward ISI staging posts near the LOC, they said, the militants, sometimes under covering fire meant to distract Indian troops from the chosen crossing point, were dispatched across the border. The ISI appeared, according to them, to be the principal vehicle for the supply of weapons, cash, and guidance to the Kashmiri militants; and, in general, it was an indispensable vehicle in the entire infiltration operation.

Pakistani officials deny, of course, that Pakistan's support included *military* assistance of any kind; and, over time, a variety of artful defenses—including the contention that the infiltrators are "privately" sponsored, that no *serving* military personnel are delivering any training, and that the Kashmiris' access to weapons is impossible to control amid the wild-and-woolly arms traffic that now characterizes Pakistan—have been adopted to give this claim at least a veneer of credibility. These defenses are certainly plausible. No doubt, groups other than the Pakistan army (the powerful, right-wing Jama'at-i-Islami party, for example) have operated their own training camps for Kashmiri militants (including at least a few inside Afghanistan); and, unquestionably, funds have flowed to the militant organizations from a variety of foreign sources, including Gulf Arab states. When all is said and done, however, there is very little likelihood that many infiltrators have made their way across the LOC into Indian Kashmir without the knowledge and active cooperation of the Pakistan army, of the Afghanistan-seasoned ISI, and, indeed, of key elements in the civil bureaucracies of Pakistan and Azad Kashmir.

The LOC, after all, is heavily fortified, and patrolling is extensive on both sides. Topographic perils, including, for example, the swift-flowing, freezing, and extremely turbulent Kishanganga River (called Neelam on the Pakistan side) that abuts one lengthy stretch of the LOC, are many; safe crossing points are limited; and extraordinary precautions are essential to secure passage through the thicket of Indian checkpoints. Kashmiri Muslim militants themselves have given countless testimonials of the Pakistan army's assistance; and the circumstantial evidence—even when one discounts the inevitable distortion and exaggeration coming from the Indian side—seems pointed overwhelmingly in this direction.

For the most part, at least in this author's opinion, the infiltration has been *necessarily* a Pakistan-directed operation. It has *not* been an ISI rogue operation. And it most certainly has *not* been, as Pakistani civil and military officials naturally continue to claim, a largely spontaneous affair.

Pakistan has had several objectives in supporting the Kashmiri uprising. Promoting Kashmiri liberation has clearly been among them. Even a few years ago, this objective did not have much of a following in policymaking circles in Pakistan, least of all among those most familiar with the discrepancy between Indian and Pakistani military capabilities. To them, India's power to protect its claim to Kashmir seemed insuperable, and Pakistan's eventual capitulation to the LOC's conversion to a permanent border, even if not publicly admissible, seemed inevitable. The emergence recently for the first time in modern history of a powerful and widespread Kashmiri Muslim separatist impulse has unquestionably altered perceptions. And these perceptions have obviously been reinforced by the collapse of the Soviet state and the almost overnight acquisition of independence by the Muslim republics of Central Asia. Articulated nowadays at all levels of the civil and military leadership, in fact, is the view that history is marching against the world's remaining multinational conglomerate or "imperial" states, such as India, and that patience in regard to its Kashmir territorial claim will ultimately reward Pakistan. India, it is often claimed, is in the early throes of a process of disintegration that may require decades to materialize but that is virtually certain to result in its breakup into several separate states. Kashmir, the argument goes, is very likely to be one of these breakaway segments.

As frequently vocalized as this argument has been in some quarters of Pakistani society and government, unqualified commitment to it in Pakistan's policymaking community remains quite rare. Promoting Kashmiri liberation has a ring of wishful thinking about it; few Pakistani policymakers believe that Pakistan can bring it off soon or single-handedly; and for most of them, in any event, it simply is not the most important, certainly not the most practical or immediate of Pakistan's objectives. These, including the "bleeding" of Indian resources, the demoralization of its army, the undermining of India's reputation abroad, the acquisition of diplomatic leverage against India, retaliation for Indian meddling in Pakistan's own ethnic unrest, and, not least, the disarming of the Pakistan government's domestic political opponents, surely have dominated Pakistan's day-to-day strategy.

The truth is that Pakistan has done very little to lay the groundwork for an effective, long-term, and sustained insurgency in Indian Kashmir. Such evidence as we possess, for example, in regard to the management in Pakistan of Kashmiri recruits to the separatist movement hardly supports the thesis that

Islamabad has made an unequivocal commitment to Kashmiri liberation. Most Kashmiri recruits appear to have been given extremely limited training in Pakistan, often only a few weeks in duration, and have often been infiltrated across the LOC improperly equipped and under conditions that virtually guaranteed their failure, capture, or slaughter by Indian forces. While obviously needing to be interpreted very cautiously, the author's interviews in June 1991 with two groups of Kashmiri infiltrators recently apprehended by Indian forces indicated that many of them were very poorly motivated, barely conversant with the weapons supplied to them, and disillusioned with Pakistan.[15] Some described their training in Pakistan as a joke. Some confessed, with seeming sincerity, that they had been lured to Pakistan largely by promises of generous pay, others that they had been used by Pakistan simply to generate bad publicity for India. They told of colleagues who had been sexually or otherwise abused in the training camps, and of so-called guides who, once having led the recruits across the LOC, had stripped them of their weapons and fled, leaving the hapless infiltrators to fend for themselves.

Concealed in the torrent of pro-Kashmiri slogans pouring from the Pakistani propaganda machine is the ironic fact that the motives of the Kashmiri insurgents are viewed with nearly as much suspicion in Pakistan as they are in India. As a consequence, Pakistan's support of the uprising, in terms of militant organizations financed, trained, and equipped, has grown increasingly selective since the separatist movement broke out in full fury in January 1990. A conscious policy decision appears to have been taken very quickly in Islamabad, in fact, to curb the *independence* sentiment that clearly lay at the foundation of the movement. A generally very well informed Kashmiri observer, resident in Pakistan, put it this way to the author:

> While the People's Party was yet in power, Pakistani leaders became aware of the need to assert more Pakistani control of the uprising. The movement was getting huge in size and the cry for *azadi*—independence of *both* India and Pakistan—was growing loud. In early February 1990, a meeting was held in Islamabad, with Prime Minister Benazir Bhutto in the chair, and with the Chief of Army Staff general Aslam Beg, and the president and prime minister of Azad Kashmir in attendance. They considered the possibility that the uprising could boomerang on Pakistan, and that Pakistan could lose not only Jammu and Kashmir but the Northern Areas as well. They decided they had to curb the *azadi* forces, meaning they would not equip them and not send them into the valley. It was decided that the Pakistan army should take over the training camps and that the private camps that had sprung up be shut down. Bhutto addressed a press conference later that month, on returning from a visit to Muzaffarabad. She said at this

> conference that accession to Pakistan was the only option open to Kashmiris. That understanding of the issue then became the policy of Pakistan, which was then focused on restricting both access to the valley and supply of arms to pro-accession forces.[16]

Having decided to curtail the mounting popularity of pro-independence groups in the valley, the Jammu and Kashmir Liberation Front (JKLF) and Operation Balakot, for instance, the Pakistan government has swung its support largely to the apparently less popular but pro-accession (meaning pro-Pakistan) groups such as the Hizb-ul Mujahideen and Muslim Janbaaz Force.[17] Funds and weapons have dried up substantially for the pro-independence groups, and the access of their Pakistan-based leaders (and followers) to the valley has been made more difficult. Pakistan's support of the militants has gradually been more carefully focused, in other words, to reflect its own political interests.

Naturally, Pakistanis interpret these developments in a rather different way. They claim that national liberation takes both time and sacrifice; Kashmiri victims of the Indian military meat grinder are the necessary price, they say, of eventual Kashmiri freedom. Unacknowledged, of course, is the strong possibility that Pakistan's interest in the Kashmiri uprising falls short of liberation, possibly even of Kashmir's union with Pakistan. Pakistani motives are certainly mixed. There is, however, an undeniable element of calculated, in some respects ruthless, self-interest underlying Pakistani support of the Kashmir uprising.

Pakistan's self-interest and fundamental pragmatism when it comes to Kashmir were made painfully apparent in February 1992, when Pakistani troops and riot police, according to press reports, opened fire on unarmed Kashmiri separatist protest marchers threatening to force their way across the LOC into the Indian-controlled portion of Kashmir. Amanullah Khan, the Pakistan-based chairman of the JKLF, had jolted Islamabad weeks earlier with the announcement of his plan to lead thousands of his followers from Azad Kashmir to the Indian border, which he said he intended to storm in a demonstration of solidarity with the Kashmiri militants fighting to end Indian control of the state of Kashmir. In an increasingly tense atmosphere, which included threats by the Indian army to shoot any marchers attempting to cross the LOC, negotiations between the Pakistan government and the protesters came to naught. The government resorted to extraordinary measures to stop the march, including the setting off of landslides and the dismantling of bridges; and when these efforts failed, they allegedly fired into the oncoming marchers, killing at least 12 and wounding many more.[18]

The February march was a repeat, on a much larger scale, of a less-publicized procession taken out near Muzzaffarabad a year earlier, on March 15, 1991, by the JKLF, Operation Balakot, and their allies. The motivation of these groups then was much the same as it was for the 1992 demonstration—to pressure Pakistan into lifting curbs on the infiltration across the border into Indian Kashmir of independence-minded Kashmiri separatists. On that occasion, the Pakistan government succeeded in persuading the marchers to disband before reaching the border, and violence was avoided.[19]

Justifying its decision to halt the February march with whatever force necessary, the Pakistan government declared in the days preceding the event that it had no choice in the matter: It did not want another war with India, and it could not permit the marchers recklessly to provoke an incident at the border that might have explosive consequences. Though one could hardly argue with this reasoning, there was a strong possibility that the incident developed in the first place at least in part because of the considerable gap that had grown between Pakistan's public profession of unqualified support for the Kashmiri separatist movement as a whole and its private preference of more narrowly focused support for a select group of pro-Pakistani parties within that movement. Widely believed to have the bulk of Kashmiri opinion in the Valley of Kashmir on their side, JKLF followers naturally resented being shunted to the sidelines. For them, the traumatic events of February exposed a hollowness in the Pakistan government's claim that it backs the self-determination of Kashmiris. They were, in fact, a brutal reminder that Kashmir's political future could not be charted without due regard not only for the national interests of India but for those as well of Pakistan. When these interests hung in the balance, Pakistanis, like Indians, might not hold back from shooting independence-minded Kashmiri Muslims.

PROFILE OF SEPARATIST FORCES

Scale

As separatist movements go, the Kashmiri Muslim edition is in a number of respects fairly small in scale. Territorially speaking, it has been confined for the most part to Kashmir Valley (or Vale), the smallest of three administrative subdivisions (Ladakh and Jammu being the other two) in India's Jammu and Kashmir state. (See Map 2.) Formed of an intermontane plain cut by the Jhelum River and enclosed on its south and west by the Pir Panjal Range and on its north and east by the Great Himalaya Range, the valley embraces about 8,000 square miles, if measured ridge to ridge, but hardly 3,000 square miles if only the valley floor is included. Measured against the whole of the old princely state as it stood in 1947—an area of about 85,809 square miles—the valley's share, however reckoned, is less than 10 percent.

Demographically, the picture is only marginally more favorable to the valley. With over 3 million people (52.36 percent of the state's 1981 population of

Map 2

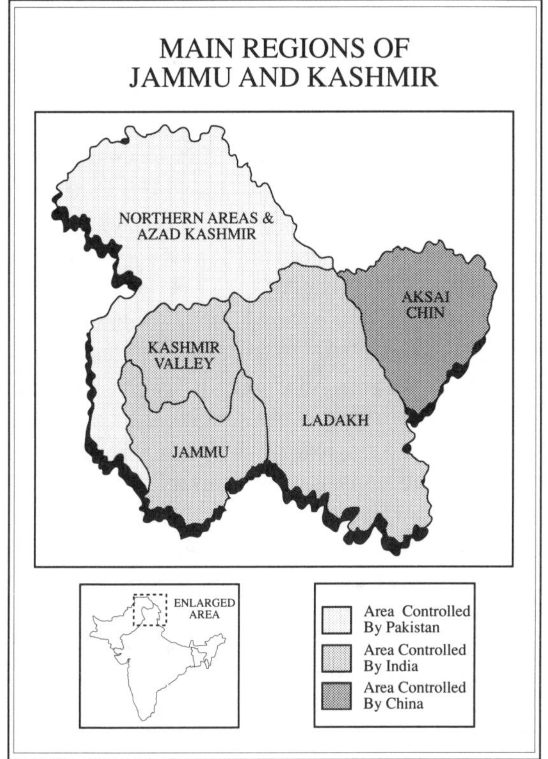

Table 4.1 Area, Population and Religion, J and K State (1981)

Region*	Area (sq/m)	Population	%Muslim	%Hindu	%Other
Kashmir Valley	8,639	3,134,904 (52.36%)	94.96	4.59	0.05
Jammu	12,378	2,718,113 (45.39%)	29.60	66.25	4.15
Ladakh	33,554†	134,372 (2.24%)	46.04	2.66	51.30‡
TOTALS:	**54,571**	**5,987,389**	**64.19**	**32.24**	**3.57**

Sources: Ministry of Home Affairs, Government of India; and *Census 1981*, Government of India.

*India's Jammu and Kashmir state contains 14 districts: Kashmir Valley has six (Anantnag, Badgam, Baramulla, Kupwara, Pulwama, Srinagar), Jammu also six (Doda, Jammu, Kathua, Poonch, Rajouri, Udhampur), and Ladakh two (Kargil, Leh).

†This figure includes areas of Ladakh (Aksai Chin) held by the Chinese.

‡Mainly Buddhist.

5,987,389), it is by far the most densely populated of the three subdivisions on the Indian side of the LOC. (See Table 4.1.) If it is measured against the population of the entire undivided state, however, which came to nearly 8.5 million in 1981, its share is not nearly so impressive.[20]

The Kashmiri Muslim separatist movement faces a number of limitations also in ethno-religious terms. Some of these limitations arise from ethnographic changes in the state's population since 1947. The most marked of these—the product of heavy migrations in and out of the territory during the partition crisis at independence and in the years of Indian control since then—is the sharp decline in the Muslim share of the population of Jammu division, from 61 percent in 1941 to 29.6 percent in 1981. The decline left only three of Jammu's six districts (Doda, Poonch, Rajouri) Muslim-majority areas. Far more of these limitations, however, arise from the fact that Jammu and Kashmir, as it now stands, came into existence under a single administration only during the course of the nineteenth century; that its population remains today conspicuously polyethnic and polysectarian; and that, even excluding all but the Indian-controlled portion of it, the *Kashmiri Muslim* share—those who are Muslim, Kashmiri-speaking, and who live in accord with Kashmiri culture—barely surpasses half of the total.

In the 1981 census, Kashmiri Muslims accounted for an overwhelming majority—nearly 95 percent—of the valley's population. The exodus from the valley since then of between 150,000 and 200,000 Kashmiri (Hindu) Pandits has driven that percentage even higher. The non-Muslim majorities of Jammu (70.4 percent) and Ladakh (53.96 percent) substantially dilute the Muslim percentage of the total state population, however, bringing it down (1981) to about 64 percent. (See Table 4.1.)

Even that figure requires some disaggregation, since Jammu and Kashmir state's Muslim population is, in ethno-linguistic and even sectarian terms, less than homogeneous. The state's Muslims are very largely Sunni, but the Shi'a minority, which is overwhelmingly dominant—as much as 95 percent—in Kargil district (Ladakh) and which has considerable numerical strength in Badgam district (Kashmir), is influential in some localities. The state's Kashmiri-speaking element clearly outstrips all other ethnic groups in size; but there are healthy numbers of Gujri-, Dogri-, Balti-, Pahari-, Potohari- and Hindko-speaking peoples contending for cultural space. The actual extent of cultural difference between any of these and the valley's Kashmiri Muslims clearly varies: Some of Jammu's Muslims, for instance, especially those in Doda district, have considerable cultural affinity with the Muslims of the valley; but most of them, like the numerous Rajputs of Rajouri and Poonch districts, have much more in common with the peoples of Pakistan-controlled Azad Kashmir and the Punjab than with the Kashmiri Muslims of the valley.

Jammu and Kashmir state's non-Muslim officials are likely to exaggerate these differences among Muslims; separatist-minded Kashmiris, for their part, are bound to play them down. Non-Kashmiri Muslims themselves are minorities in whichever of the three regions of the state they dwell, and that fact alone may induce skepticism among them about the benefits to be gained from successful Kashmiri separatism.

The Kashmiri separatist movement no doubt enlists individuals from other of the state's Muslim communities. The movement's organizational counterparts abroad, as in the case of the Pakistan-based wing of the JKLF, consist overwhelmingly of non-Kashmiris.[21] Moreover, the valley's separatists maintain an extremely close alliance with—and draw important support from—the political leadership of Azad Kashmir, very little of which has ever been ethnically Kashmiri. Clearly, ethnicity is not an absolute barrier to cooperation against Indian rule among Muslims of differing ethnic backgrounds: The huge Muslim-Hindu divide remains intact whatever may be the differences among Muslims.

Still, the *ethnic* component in Kashmiri separatism is deeply problematic for the movement. As outlined by a Hindu official with lengthy service in Indian Kashmir (and with no obvious animosity for Kashmiris), ethnicity is a major problem because Kashmiris are, he said, unusually insular; they have a feeling of uniqueness, indeed of cultural superiority.[22] *Kashmiriyat* (Kashmiri culture or "Kashmiri-ness"), he suggested, boils down to the Kashmiris' sense of themselves as a Chosen People and of their land as the Promised Land. He conceded that the Kashmiri claim to ethnic affinity with many of the Muslims of Doda district in the Jammu region had some truth. On the whole, however, he felt that the Kashmiri territorial claim to Greater Kashmir, including all of the prepartition state, apart from being based on a profound misreading of Kashmir's (disunified) history, inevitably aroused in the state's other peoples, both Muslim and non-Muslim, the threat of Kashmiri imperialism. It complicated the Kashmiris' situation, he argued, by bringing too many potential rivals *other than the already formidable Indians* to the negotiating table. The Balti-speaking (and Shi'a) Muslims of Kargil might, he said by way of example, side with the Kashmiri separatist program, provided it was not cast in overtly ethnic Kashmiri terms; but even then not without some reservations or calculated bargaining.

Aside from its territorial, demographic, and ethnographic scale, the Kashmiri separatist uprising needs also to be viewed in terms of the level or scale of violence it has generated. A difficulty in this connection is that the only set of seemingly comprehensive statistics available to the author is that supplied by the Ministry of Home Affairs in New Delhi. While the author has no good reason to doubt the general accuracy of these statistics, they obviously exclude a fair amount of *security force*–generated violence and may give a particular slant to *separatist*-generated violence. It is essential, of course, to read them with care and to withhold final judgment in regard to them pending comparison with data drawn from alternative and more neutral sources.

We may infer from the data presented in Tables 4.2 and 4.3 (1) that the *frequency* of violent incidents arising from the separatist insurgency in Kashmir has been high, has shown a general increase since the insurgency's onset, and shows no signs of abating; and (2) that there is some change in the *pattern* of violent incidents, namely a shift from bombings in public places to direct attacks on the security forces. The first finding was confirmed in numerous interviews with senior government officials in New Delhi and Srinagar, all of whom agreed that violent incidents had become commonplace and that there were no signs of a significant decline in them. In addition to other possibilities, the second may indicate recognition by the separatist militants that detonation of explosives in public places (roads, markets, buildings, transport vehicles) is more likely to victimize Kashmiris—and to alienate them—than to win them to the separatist cause.

Table 4.2 Separatist Incidents, J and K State
(1 January 1988–31 May 1993)

Year	Total Incidents	Attacks on Security Forces	Attacks on Others	Explosions & Arson	Other Incidents
1988	390	6	1	142	241
1989	2,154	49	73	840	1,192
1990	3,905	1,098	485	1,810	512
1991	3,122	1,999	321	611	191
1992	4,971	3,413	507	744	307
1993 (5/31)	2,113	1,203	245	445	220
TOTALS:	**16,655**	**7,768**	**1,632**	**4,592**	**2,663**

Source: Ministry of Home Affairs, Government of India.

Table 4.3 Explosions in Public Places, J and K State
(1 January 1988 – 31 May 1993)

Year	Total Incidents	Killed	Injured
1988	24	15	69
1989	506	7	125
1990	1,164	16	500
1991	220	24	85
1992	180	89	400
1993 (5/31)	83	27	182
TOTALS:	2,177	178	1,361

Source: Ministry of Home Affairs, Government of India.

A glance at maps 3 and 4 indicates that every district in the state has experienced violent incidents to some extent, but that, apart from Doda and Jammu districts in the Jammu region, the violence is concentrated overwhelmingly in the valley. No place in the valley has been free of widespread violence. Noticeable, however, is the greater frequency of violent incidents in the more urbanized districts (Srinagar, Baramulla, Anantnag). This is not surprising, given the greater number of targets, the concentration of political power, the greater psychological impact, and the greater publicity achievable in the ten or so towns and cities in the valley. Obviously, not all of the incidents depicted, either in Ladakh or in Jammu, are traceable solely to *Kashmiri* separatists.[23]

Mounting separatist violence in the Hindu-majority Jammu region, though still of far lesser scale than in the valley, clearly had Indian officials worried. Concern appeared greatest in regard to Doda (as we observed earlier, one of the region's three Muslim-majority districts). A senior bureaucrat in the Ministry of Home Affairs acknowledged to the author in July 1993 that the insurgency was spreading there, that the frequency of bombings was increasing, and that the number of killings was going up. In his opinion, the militants' aim there was, on the one hand, to create a communal (anti-Muslim) backlash—useful for its publicity value—and, on the other hand, to inspire a Hindu exodus. The militants, he said, had been only modestly successful in achieving the first, and there was no sign, so far, of any success in regard to the second.

Finally, under the heading of scale we need also to take a look at the size of the uprising itself—at the number of Kashmiris who have been drawn into active separatist militancy. A senior police official in Srinagar gave the figure 10,000 to the author in July 1993 to describe the total number of Kashmiri

Muslim militants then under arms in the valley. Of these, he said, only about one-third were active at any given time. These figures come close to those given the author by Indian military intelligence officials two years earlier,[24] and they square with most estimates given the author by other informed observers. The figures indicate a movement that has perhaps achieved a certain stability of membership and whose proportions, relative to the Valley's geographic size (if not to the number of government troops it faces), are quite substantial.

Map 3

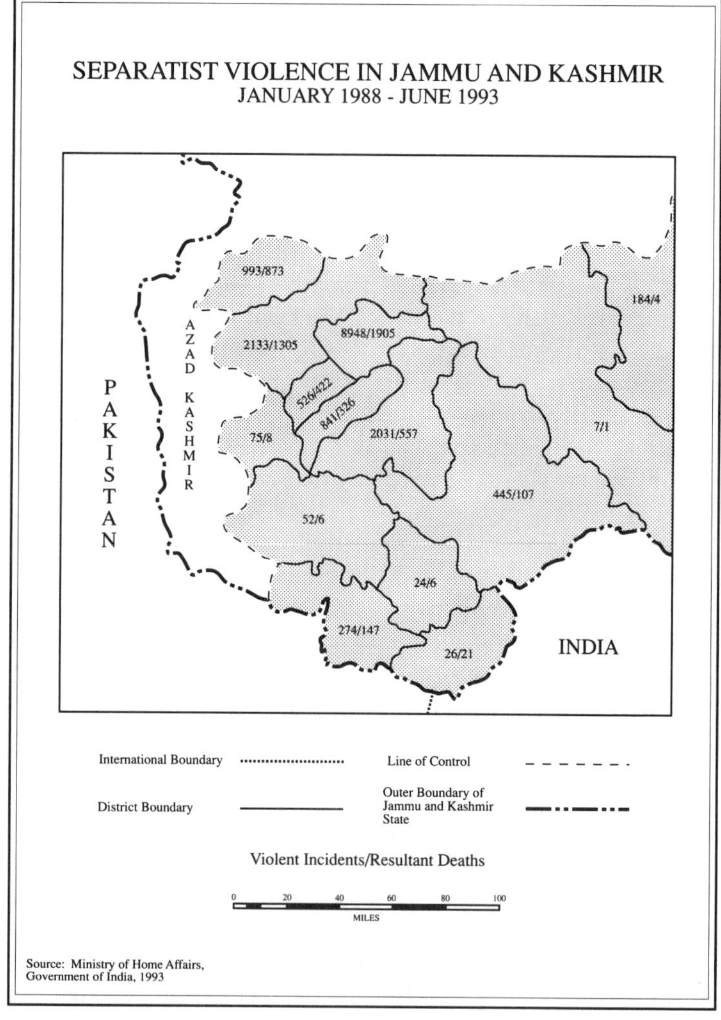

Map 4

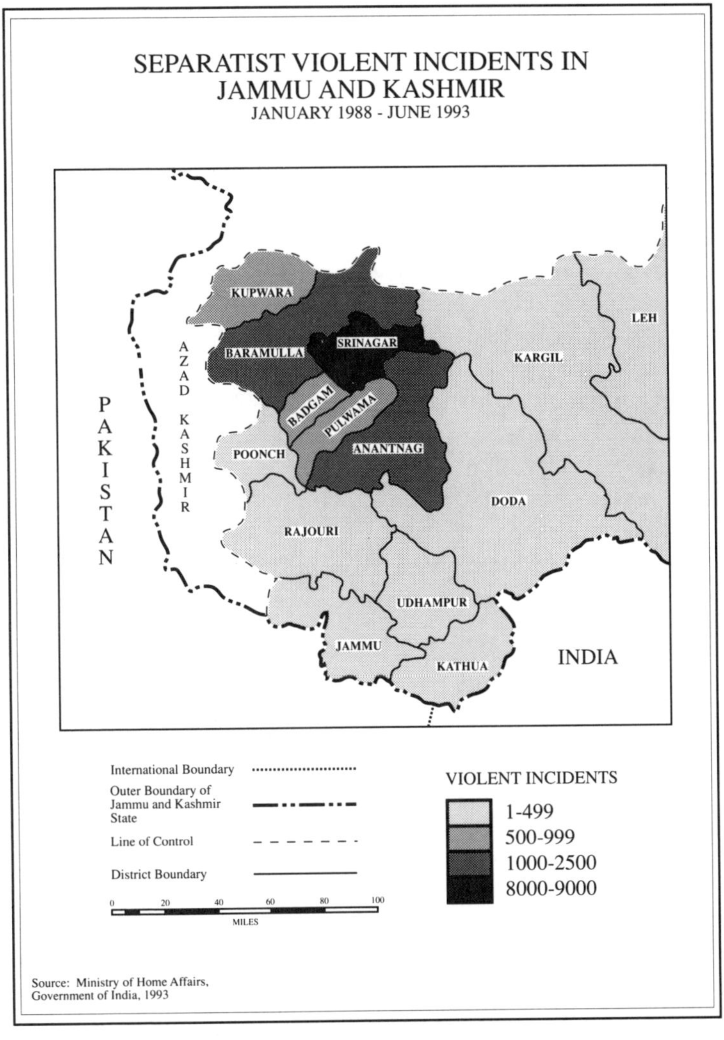

SEPARATIST VIOLENT INCIDENTS IN JAMMU AND KASHMIR
JANUARY 1988 - JUNE 1993

Source: Ministry of Home Affairs, Government of India, 1993

Organization

Commonly expressed views on the Kashmiri Muslim separatist movement, organizationally speaking, are that it is highly fragmented; that it has no central or apex command; that the most fundamental division within it is between the pro-Pakistan elements (those favoring accession of the state to Pakistan) and the pro-*azadi* elements (those favoring Kashmir's complete independence from both India and Pakistan); and that attempts to forge alliances or in some other way to build unity among the major groups have mainly foundered. While these views seem in general to be accurate, they require some qualification.

If on nothing else, Indian officials and separatist leaders agree that the movement is badly fragmented. Ex-Governor Jagmohan has listed in his book 44 different "terrorist" organizations that he says were active in the state at the time he assumed the duties of governor in January 1990;[25] and JKLF chairman Amanullah Khan says there were 60 to 70 groups active in the valley in 1991.[26] Media reports nowadays commonly speak of "about two dozen" underground organizations operating in the state; and that estimate comes very close to the author's own recent tabulation. Most of these organizations are splinter groups, however, based in particular localities, enrolling few followers, and habitually moving in and out of loose alliances and mergers with other groups. In some cases, their independence from one another appears more nominal than real. Loose coordination of militant group activities is reported; but no central command for the formal integration of military operations appears to exist.

Well-armed and powerful groups, having more than scanty followings, are, in fact, quite few. Most observers identify four to six underground militant organizations that currently really count. Most often identified are:

Pro-independence:	**Pro-accession:**
1. JKLF	1. Hizb-ul Mujahideen
	2. Al Jehad
	3. Al Barq
	4. Ikhwan ul-Musalmeen
	5. Al Umar Mujahideen

The first groups listed in the two columns—the JKLF and the Hizb-ul Mujahideen Jammu Kashmir (HMJK)—are widely judged the two most important militant organizations in the valley. The JKLF, by virtue of its espousal of Kashmir's independence and a more moderate brand of Islam, is generally held to be the more popular of the two; but the HMJK, considered by most the better patronized by Pakistan, hence better trained and funded, and with greater firepower, is probably the more effective and feared. The split between them has had a major impact on the separatist movement's development. The pro-accession side has emphasized the movement's newer and increasingly potent Islamist orientation, the pro-independence side its long-standing identity with secular Kashmiri nationalism. On both sides, there is an element of political opportunism in these orientations: Their strategic appeals to faith or ethnic nationalism conveniently conceal their mutual (but unpopular) dependence on Pakistan. On neither side is the formal ideological orientation wholly exclusive: Many members of both organizations could readily cross to the other without any serious deflation of personal ideological commitment. Nevertheless, political and ideological differences between these organizations are by no means inconsequential.

On a number of occasions, the rivalry between these groups has led to open violence and, even more troublesome, has supplied India with numerous opportunities for leveraging one side against the other. The assassination in Srinagar on 31 March 1993 of the popular Kashmiri physician Dr. Abdul Ahad Guru was one such opportunity. Dr. Guru was abducted and shot dead on his way to a meeting of the central council of the JKLF, with which he had long been closely associated. No one claimed responsibility for the killing. However, Dr. Guru, acting as a channel of communication between the militants and the government, had been instrumental in 1989 in securing the release of Dr. Rubaiya Sayeed; and there were rumors that he was among those the government was contacting in the early months of 1993 in its renewed efforts to find a solution to the unrest. (See Chapter 6.) The Pakistan-backed HMJK, presumably keen to undermine any reconciliatory moves between the militants and the government, had an obvious motive to eliminate him; but so, too, did the Indian government, not to mention rival factions of the JKLF. In the absence of proof, one way or the other, the government's contention that it was an HMJK-engineered assassination was bound to raise at least some suspicion within the JKLF.[27] Fear of precisely such a development probably underlay the signing on 2 April, within days of Guru's killing, of a "peace" agreement between the leaders of these militant groups, committing them to full moral, political, and military cooperation against India and to full respect for one another's ideological orientation. There were strong grounds for doubt, however, that the agreement, signed in Islamabad by the leaders of the Pakistan-based branches of these organizations, would have very great or lasting impact on their Kashmir-based and far-from-subservient colleagues.

The fragmentation that characterizes the state's militant organizations shows up also in the *political* organizations active in the state. In fact, most of the major political parties covertly sponsor or at least maintain close links with one or the other of the armed militant groups: The Jama'at-i-Islami, for instance, is closely tied to the HMJK, the People's League to Al Jehad, the People's Conference to Al Barq, and so on. The JKLF organization in the valley is viewed in some quarters as the militant wing of the erstwhile ruling party in the state, the National Conference; but since that party has a collaborationist reputation and is, at least temporarily, defunct in the valley, the linkage, if it exists at all, is strictly tacit.

There have been a number of efforts since the uprising began to forge a common aboveground pro-separatist movement from the valley's political, religious, student, intellectual, professional, and social organizations. The first of these was the Tehreek Hurriyet-e-Kashmir (THK/Kashmir Liberation Movement), an Islamist-leaning umbrella organization that was the successor in some respects to the Muslim United Front coalition that had developed in the valley in the mid-1980s.[28] This organization excluded groups allied to the JKLF, however, as well as the badly discredited National Conference; and by early 1993 it was barely functioning. In April 1993, it was replaced by a larger alliance that combined two dozen or more groups. This organization, the All Party Hurriyet (Freedom) Conference, included the JKLF and, on the surface at least, appeared to bridge the ideological divide. Led nominally by Maulawi Omar Farooq, a 17-year-old *pir* (hereditary saint in the Sufi tradition), and joining together most of the valley's best-known separatist politicians, the Hurriyet shot into prominence during the month-long crisis in October–November 1993 over the militants' seizure of the Hazratbal shrine in Srinagar. It organized strikes, boycotts, and mass public demonstrations to protest against the government's siege tactics. Its influence in the valley seemed to rival that of the militant organizations. Called upon by government officials to mediate between them and the militants holed up in the mosque, the Hurriyet appeared to some observers to contain precisely the kind of moderate—and potentially independent—leadership with which the government could one day negotiate an end to the strife.[29]

Pakistan's support (or withholding of it) has unquestionably been a key organizational variable in Kashmir; and its patronage has no doubt exerted a powerful influence on the rise and fall in fortunes of practically every militant group active there. Some of the militant organizations may be largely or even entirely the creatures of the ISI, and all of the principal groups, according to most informants, are dependent to some extent for their financing and supplies on the resources of that intelligence unit. Nevertheless, the separatist movement as a whole, as we have already observed, has strong indigenous motivation. The Hurriyet's actions during the Hazratbal crisis, in particular its willingness to help mediate an end to the crisis, were, perhaps, a display of this. In any event, Pakistan's ability to compel both its militant and political arms to remain in step with music broadcast from Islamabad, while exceedingly difficult to measure, should not be overstated.

Capabilities

Indian officials use the word "massive" to describe the quantity of weapons in the hands of the Kashmiri militants; and if the figures released by the government in regard to *weapons recovery* are authentic (see Table 4.4), there is clearly no shortage of light arms, in particular of automatic weapons and grenades, available to them. Asked to cite recently detected *qualitative* improvements in militant weaponry and equipment, if any, knowledgeable civil and military officials in the valley listed sniper rifles, 60mm (light) mortars, advanced walkie-talkies, and heavy-caliber (12.7mm) machine guns. However, there had been no confirmed use (up to July 1993) of the mortars; and the machine guns had been reported but were not then confirmed. The mortars have a range of about 2,000 meters and are most useful for antipersonnel (or antilight-vehicle) missions. The machine guns, which are barely man-portable, can destroy light armored vehicles and are excellent weapons against some kinds of aircraft. The possible introduction into Kashmir of these particular weapons is, therefore, naturally a matter of great concern to the Indian army.

Table 4.4 Recovered Kashmiri Separatist Weapons, J and K State
(1 January 1988–31 May 1993)

Weapon/Explosive	1988–90	1991	1992	1993 (5/31)	TOTAL
Rocket launchers	141	140	174	31	486
Machine guns	124	176	174	59	533
AK series rifles	1,474	2,602	3,775	953	8,804
Sniper rifles	1	3	13	11	28
Pistols/revolvers	858	946	808	244	2,856
Ammunition (in 1000s)	242	318	343	169	1,072
Grenades	2,994	2,236	2,818	2,991	11,039
Rockets	370	329	267	59	1,025
Rocket boosters	156	203	144	35	538
Mines	1,101	217	307	170	1,795
Guns	30	79	81	45	235
Explosives (in kgs)	1,966	588	436	191	3,181
Bombs	708	72	228	150	1,158
Walkie-talkie sets	22	36	68	62	188

Source: Ministry of Home Affairs, Government of India.

Both in 1991 and in 1993, the author encountered rumors in Kashmir that the militants were in possession of surface-to-air missiles (SAMs). One of the best-informed and seniormost officials in Srinagar stated flatly to the author in July 1993, however, that the militants did not possess SAMs and that if they did, they would have used them by then. Indian army helicopter pilots in the valley do now conduct evasive takeoff and landing procedures; but these are obviously of the sort to counter the possibility of small arms ground fire, not long-range missiles. Much like the Afghan mujahideen in the first years of their struggle against Soviet and Soviet-backed Afghan army troops, the Kashmiri militants are armed and equipped in large part for hit-and-run missions against lightly protected targets; for raids on isolated army or police outposts; for ambushes; for mining of roads and sabotage of power, communications, and transport facilities; for sniper, bombing, and rocket attacks designed for their propaganda value; but—so far at least—not for head-on clashes with India's regular or paramilitary forces.

Indian police officials in the valley distinguish acronymically among PTMs (Pakistan-trained militants), KTMs (Kashmir-trained militants), and LTMs (locally trained militants). They claim that anywhere from 10,000 to 15,000 Kashmiri men have crossed the LOC to Pakistan for arms training between 1986 and the present, and that as many as 75 percent of the core fighters in the valley now are PTMs. As noted earlier, the issue of training camps—of whether Pakistan officially sponsors them, of where or even whether they exist—has been the focus of much controversy. Pakistanis have insisted, of course, that they maintain no training camps for the militants (or that if any once existed, they have been shut down). Indians contend, however, that the Pakistanis continue to operate training camps, in Azad Kashmir and in Pakistan itself, and that, in fact, they have streamlined and upgraded their training programs, laying greater emphasis than in the past on physical conditioning and specialized training, including more sophisticated communications.[30] In sharp contrast with militants captured attempting to cross the LOC in the first two years of the insurgency, many of whom were scarcely prepared to face either the Indian army or the rugged terrain, the newer breed, according to many senior Indian army officers interviewed by the author, is generally better trained, better equipped, and better motivated—better able, in short, to survive. The Pakistanis, say the Indians, have obviously gained experience in training and motivating men; and so the militants—at least the hardcore fighters—naturally now show more military proficiency.

Aside from some likely improvement in military proficiency, the militants in virtually every other respect retain today the low esteem of observers they acquired very early in the uprising. Obviously, some of the criticism is standard propaganda fare put out by Indian information services; and no small part of it is politically motivated. A spokesman for the National Conference party, for example, a Kashmiri Muslim but an exile from the state like most of his colleagues in that now-fallen party, characterized the uprising in these words:

"There was a point," he said, "when it was a people's movement, in January, February . . . up to May 1990, but not thereafter." The movement today, he said, consisted mainly of "riffraf, hooligans, pickpockets . . . [people] guiltier—or as guilty—of killing the people than the security forces. . . . Now it is not a people's movement. . . . Human rights violations by the militants are as bad as those committed by the security forces." There are no leaders, he said, worthy of the name. So-called leaders are bad types: Some are totally illiterate and hardened criminals. They practice extortion, rape, and murder; and the people live in fear of them. Their defenders will say: Our boys are not violating human rights. The fact is even these people get "vicarious pleasure" from the killings. The JKLF, he observed, is some better than the other groups in this respect; the Al Umar Mujahideen and Hizbul Mujahideen, he said, are the worst in Srinagar.[31]

Even when one discounts for propaganda or political bias, however, the militants do not emerge unscathed. Practically all informed observers, including those with strong pro-Kashmiri sympathies, maintain that many, perhaps most, of the militants are very poorly motivated and poorly disciplined, that they routinely inflict upon the Kashmiri people the same sorts of brutality as the Indian troops, and that a worrisome criminalization of the movement has set in. A senior Indian (Hindu) bureaucrat, for instance, with lengthy experience in Srinagar and with evident sympathies for the Kashmiris, insisted to the author in July 1993 that the insurgency had become something of a commercial enterprise, indeed that "making a business of it" had increased strikingly in the past two years. This commercialization, he said, had corrupted the freedom movement, weakened it, diverted it from its goals, and spoiled its popular image. The militants, he emphasized, were engaged in *widespread* extortion rackets, having turned abductions of government employees, for example, into a profitable business.[32]

The subject remains highly controversial, but the exodus from the valley in the first year of the uprising of large numbers of the minority Hindu community (mainly Kashmiri Pandits) was almost certainly a result in part of the militants' deliberate policy of threat, intimidation, and "ethnic cleansing."[33] The reported slaughter by Muslim guerrillas on 14 August 1993 of 15 Hindu civilians, all of them passengers yanked from a bus bound from Kishtwar (Doda district) to Jammu city, may conceivably have been inspired by the same policy.[34]

IMPACT OF THE UPRISING

Estimates of the death toll in Kashmir stemming from the uprising have varied enormously, ranging (by midyear 1993) from the government figure of nearly 6,000 (see Table 4.5) to figures as high as 35,000 given by militants and their sympathizers. Depending on the sources consulted, international wire-service estimates at that time also varied, though less extremely, from about 7,500 to 12,000. Fairly systematic reckonings by neutral diplomatic sources, and the author's own tabulation entirely from media sources, tend to confirm the greater accuracy—albeit likely understatement—of the government estimate. What is clearly contestable, given the evident broad latitude that exists in making these distinctions, is the government's claim that of the total non-security force personnel killed between the eruption of major fighting in January 1990 and the end of May 1993 (5,093) roughly 2,800 were civilians and 2,200 were militants.[35] Even more contestable, of course, is the government's claim that practically all of the civilians killed lost their lives (accidentally) in crossfire. The distribution of deaths is shown by district in Map 5.

Table 4.5 Death Toll in Separatist Uprising, J and K State
(1 January 1988–31 May 1993)

	1988	1989	1990	1991	1992	1993 (5/31)	**TOTAL**
Total killed	31	92	1,177	1,393	1,909	1,086	**5,688**
Security forces	1	13	132	185	177	87	**595**
Govt. officials	1	3	62	57	36	13	**172**
Politicians	-	3	24	10	4	10	**51**
Judges	-	3	1	1	-	-	**5**
Press/media	-	-	2	1	1	-	**4**

Source: Ministry of Home Affairs, Government of India.

By the standards of other separatist-inspired upheavals in our time, including the East Bengali breakaway from Pakistan in 1971, the Kashmiri uprising so far has taken *relatively* few lives. These figures are substantially magnified in the public's mind, however, not only because they are given fairly wide publicity in the local, Indian, and foreign press (more, certainly, than many other equivalent uprisings have received), but because of the valley's small size, in both territory and population, and unusually strong ethnic solidarity. Especially noticeable in the figures, however, is the steady annual *increase* in the death toll, a fact which will weigh heavily, of course, upon the prospects for resolution.

The complete absence so far in the uprising of pitched battles between the security forces and the militants, fought door-to-door in towns and cities over prolonged periods, has meant that physical damage to property, too, has been relatively modest. By far the greatest destruction has come from widespread fires in some urban areas, conveniently said by the government to result entirely from deliberate torching by separatist militants, but with private homeowners obviously the principal victims. (See Table 4.6.)

Map 5

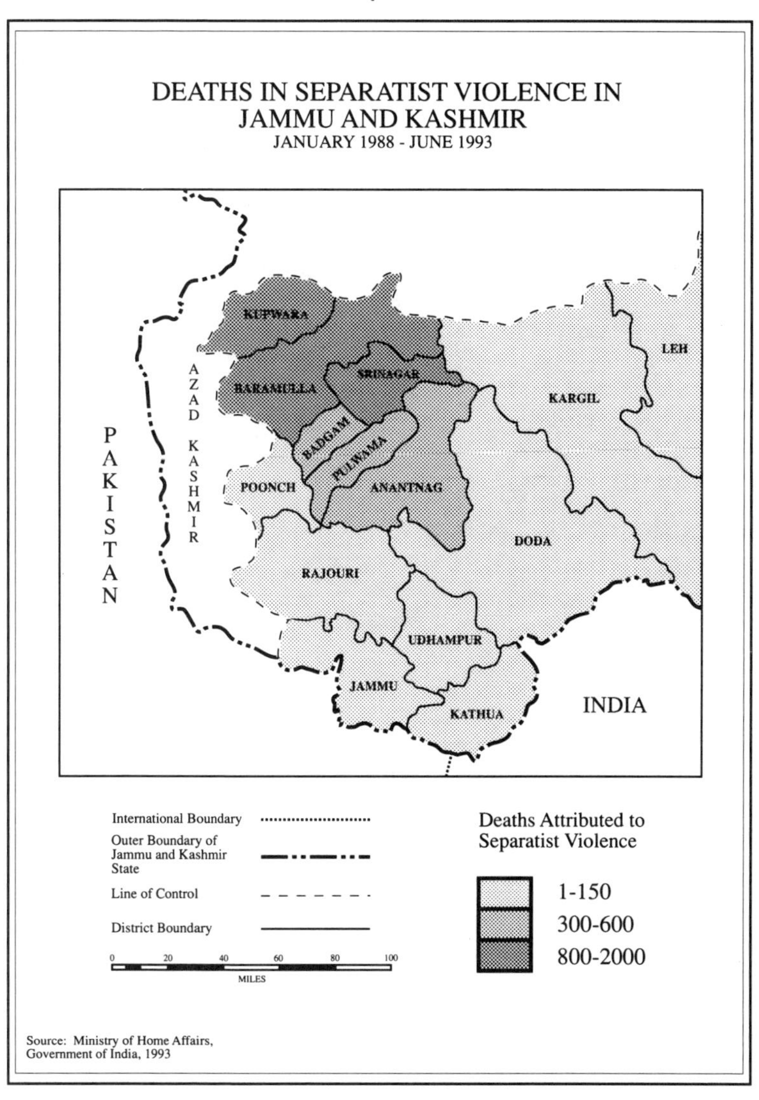

Table 4.6 Major Attacks of Arson, J and K State
(1 January 1988–31 May 1993)

Year	**Total Incidents**	Government Buildings	Educational Institutions	Private Houses	Bridges
1988	**128**	4	4	19	1
1989	**294**	191	172	427	16
1990	**646**	501	129	1,242	172
1991	**391**	45	24	819	24
1992	**564**	67	57	2,510	28
1993 (5/31)	**362**	50	24	657	20

Source: Ministry of Home Affairs, Government of India.

Table 4.7 Exodus of Non-Muslim Minorities from Kashmir Valley
(1 January 1990–31 May 1993)

Destination	Hindu Families	Sikh Families	Other	Total
Jammu Region	23,653	2,836	3,120	**29,609**
Delhi	11,391	50	-	**11,441**
Other	2,014	740	17	**2,771**
TOTAL:	**37,058**	**3,626**	**3,137**	**43,821**

Source: Ministry of Home Affairs, Government of India.

Table 4.8 Death Toll of Non-Muslim Minorities, J and K State
(1 January 1990–31 May 1993)

	1990	1991	1992	1993 (5/31)
Hindus Killed	177	45	67	37
Sikhs Killed	7	9	10	-

Source: Ministry of Home Affairs, Government of India.

As noted earlier, one of the major impacts upon the state of the uprising has been the mass exodus from the valley of large numbers of the area's non-Muslim minorities—Hindus and Sikhs in particular. Responsibility is debated, the government charging the Kashmiri militants with terrorizing the minorities and with deliberate ethnic cleansing, the militants responding that the government provoked the exodus in order to give the separatist movement a distinct communal complexion. Anywhere from 150,000 to 200,000 Kashmiri (Hindu) Pandits, as pointed out, have fled the valley (see Table 4.7); and a fairly substantial number have perished (Table 4.8). The political exploitability of these losses is far greater than these numbers might suggest. Kashmir, long celebrated as a mecca for tourists, has unquestionably suffered a severe economic setback as a result of the uprising. Before the unrest began, the annual influx of *Indian* tourists to the state generally ran between 500,000 and 600,000. Of these, there are practically none today. *Foreign* tourists, more often the big spenders and thus a special target of government promotional efforts, generally ran around 60,000 per annum. Currently, according to a government tourism official, their number was down by over 80 percent.[36] About 10,000 were expected to visit Srinagar during the current (1993) tourist season. The tourist industry, in other words, was clearly hurting. All but one hotel had been shut down (most now were sheltering paramilitary forces or civil servants); and of the nearly 2,000 houseboats registered in Srinagar, only about 20 or 30 were currently being rented out each day. Restaurant, sightseeing, souvenir, taxi, and other tourist-oriented enterprises have been badly affected.

Apart from the tourist business, however, the Kashmiris have clearly not been crushed economically by the separatist uprising. According to a former senior adviser to the Jammu and Kashmir state government, less than 10 percent of the valley's economy was ordinarily tourism-dependent; and those most affected by the decline in tourists have been absorbed economically, one way or another, by their extended families. About 80 percent of the area's economy, he said, was agriculture-based, and that sector so far had not been much affected. The other 10 percent of the valley's economy, he observed, consisted largely of the handicraft industry, and some sectors of that industry, he said, had actually registered gains in recent years. Carpet sales, for instance, were up 40 percent (in 1992) over 1990; and carpets were being sold as rapidly as they were made. A further positive economic factor, he pointed out, was the number of Kashmiri Muslims who were on the public payroll: Of the 3.5 million Kashmiris in the valley, about 150,000 were state employees—an exceptionally high proportion by all-India standards, he pointed out, and a group insulated from at least some of the consequences of the uprising. Unlike other parts of India, he noted, there were no starving people in Kashmir, and there were no beggars.[37]

Among the most badly affected sectors in Kashmir is government administration. Some agencies had collapsed almost entirely: The Forestry Division, for instance, an especially important branch of administration in the state but one that was by the nature of its work acutely vulnerable to the militants, had virtually suspended operations. According to a senior administrator in that division, forestry officers were completely restricted in their movements. The forests, as a result, were suffering serious degradation from indiscriminate cutting. Progressive conservation policies had simply been put on hold for the duration. In the meantime, almost nothing could be done to protect the forests.[38] Other agencies—the public schools, for instance—seemed to be operating at half-speed. As an Indian journalist put it, the administration is best said to be in a state of *semi*collapse or *partial* paralysis: Most taxes haven't been paid for three years; the supply of electricity is erratic at best; and yet schools are open and the hospitals, one way or the other, continue to function. The police and army were filling the administrative vacuum where the civil administration had ceased to function.[39]

CHAPTER

·5·

INDIAN SECURITY FORCES IN JAMMU AND KASHMIR

This chapter examines the deployment and employment of Indian security forces in relation to the Kashmiri Muslim separatist uprising in the Indian state of Jammu and Kashmir. It considers (1) the type, number, and operational roles of these forces; and (2) the character, extent, and effectiveness (a) of border-sealing and counterinfiltration operations at the LOC, and (b) of counterinsurgency operations within the state. The human rights issue is examined in relation to these counterinsurgency operations.

TYPE, NUMBER, AND OPERATIONAL ROLES

There are three main categories of Indian security forces in Kashmir: the local (state) police, the paramilitary forces, and the regular army. There is some overlap in the operational roles of these forces in regard to the insurgency. There are major differences among them, however, in training, organization, function, ethnic composition, and day-to-day employment that relate in significant ways to the manner in which counterinsurgency operations are conducted. In regard to some of these differences, there is considerable controversy. Reliable information is fairly scanty.

The state police (JKP) number about 34,000. They are organized into three main divisions—the armed police (JKAP), the civil police (including traffic police), and criminal investigation (CID) and security. Each division enrolls roughly the same proportion (one-third) of the total force. On paper, the police bear primary responsibility for maintenance of law and order in the state; and in certain key respects this responsibility has been substantially enlarged since the insurgency's onset in the late 1980s. Investigation and prosecution of thousands of cases registered in the state under the Terrorist and Disruptive Activities (Prevention) Act (TADA), for instance, have been the responsibility almost entirely of the JKP.

In large measure, however, the JKP have been mainly sidelined since the insurgency began, not only because they have neither the training nor the equipment for counterinsurgency operations but because some of their midlevel officers and many of the rank and file were widely suspected of harboring ambivalent feelings about, if not actively sympathizing with, the Kashmiri militants. This suspicion—and the intense resentment it has generated among the Kashmiri Muslims in the JKP against the other (overwhelmingly non-Kashmiri) security forces deployed in the valley—was brought to the surface in a spectacular fashion in late April 1993 when a week-long police strike, involving at least 1,400 police officers, broke out among the JKAP in Srinagar. Inspired by the alleged torture and killing in the custody of paramilitary troops of a local police constable, who had apparently been detained on suspicion of aiding underground Kashmiri Muslim militants, the mutiny was finally crushed on 28 April when army and paramilitary troops seized control from the rebels of police headquarters in Srinagar. Nearly 200 policemen who had participated in the strike were dismissed from service, at least 50 were arrested, and others were posted out of Kashmir or transferred to less sensitive positions.[1]

About half of the JKP, according to a senior (non-Kashmiri) police official interviewed by the author in early July 1993, is ethnically Kashmiri Muslim. Top police officials, however, both in the state police administration and in the state's 14 districts, are almost invariably Hindu or Sikh.[2] As insiders in Kashmir with intimate knowledge of the valley's inhabitants, the Kashmiri Muslim officers are in theory a potential asset to the counterinsurgency forces, the great bulk of whom are ethnic outsiders ill-equipped to develop channels to the local population that are ordinarily vital for successful police work and for intelligence collection. In practice, however, and regardless of their feelings about the insurgency, the police are extremely vulnerable to local pressures and to reprisals by the insurgents. Not more than 20 percent of JKP families are housed in more-or-less secure police colonies. For the rest, security is obviously contingent upon the insurgents' judgment of the police officials' "political correctness." By and large, the JKP has not been the target so far of sustained and systematic killings, as was the pattern up until recently in the Sikh insurgency in the Punjab. A total of about 60 police have been killed in the state, however, since January 1990, enough certainly to remind their colleagues to avoid taking unnecessary risks.

At least four separate branches of India's multitude of paramilitary forces were deployed in 1993 on counterinsurgency duties in Kashmir—the Border Security Force (BSF), the Central Reserve Police Force (CRPF), the Indo-Tibetan Border Police (ITBP), and the Rashtriya (National) Rifles (RR).[3]

Jointly referred to as Central Police Organizations (CPOs), these forces report to the Home (Interior) Ministry in New Delhi. Estimates of their number vary, but most sources place the total of CPO forces in Jammu and Kashmir at between 100,000 and 150,000.[4] The largest and most important of these organizations—the BSF and CRPF—have experienced roughly tenfold growth in the state since 1989.[5]

CPO troops are drawn very largely from outside the state of Jammu and Kashmir and are overwhelmingly Hindu. According to a senior official in the Ministry of Home Affairs in New Delhi, over 5,000 Kashmiri Muslims had been recruited to the paramilitary forces since 1990; their posting to the valley seemed, however, extremely improbable.[6]

The CPOs have primary responsibility in Kashmir for *internal* security. Along some stretches of the LOC, the BSF has limited responsibility, together with the regular army, also for *external* security, that is, for guarding the border with Pakistan-controlled Kashmir. It is the only CPO in the state today, however, directly involved in counterinsurgent operations, having *sole* responsibility for the conduct of combing (cordon and search) operations in Srinagar and *primary* responsibility for them in most other parts of the state. Unlike the BSF, which is both trained and equipped for counterinsurgency duty, the other CPOs (the CRPF, ITBP, and RR) are today assigned largely to guard (that is, static defense of roads, bridges, communications and power facilities, government and military installations) and escort duties. Until early 1993, the CRPF was employed to some extent in active counterinsurgency operations in the valley, including supervision of some of the notorious interrogation centers. But traditionally tasked, trained, and equipped for riot and mob control, the CRPF of late—and in part for reasons relating to the controversy over human rights violations, dealt with later—has been assigned more limited responsibilities.[7]

The Indian army has been deployed in Jammu and Kashmir since the state's accession to India in late October 1947. From then until the present, its primary assignment there has been to prevent violation of the state's external boundaries, principally the CFL/LOC that runs through the center of the prepartition state and that divides Indian from Pakistani forces. The army has also been heavily involved in internal security (that is, counterinsurgency) duties, however, right from the beginning of the insurgency. This part of its duties has steadily expanded over the past three years or so. (See Chapter 6.) The army does not have exclusive responsibility for internal security, however, anywhere in the state; and, for the most part, its role in counterinsurgency operations is generally performed in company with the BSF. Like the BSF, the regular army is overwhelmingly Hindu. Muslim troops are fully integrated among the rank and file; but Muslims in senior command positions, with the notable exception of Lieutenant General Mohammad A. Zaki, the recently retired 15th Corps commander, have been few and far between.

Estimates of the total strength of *regular* Indian army troops in Jammu and Kashmir state vary substantially. Pakistani military sources put the total in mid-1993 at about 250,000. Third-country observers put the figure closer to 150,000. Either way, the total for army plus paramilitary forces in the state bulked large—between 300,000 and 400,000.

In 1993, the army was headquartering one of its five regional commands (Northern Command), two of its ten corps (15th and 16th), and seven of its 30 infantry (or mountain-light infantry) divisions in Jammu and Kashmir state. While these divisions were conventionally said to have between 10,000 and 12,000 troops, in fact they appeared to vary considerably in size—most containing more than the standard complement of brigades and additional special units.[8] Complicating the picture was the fact that one division (29th) of the 16th Corps, albeit headquartered just across the state border in the Punjab, fielded substantial forces in Kashmir; and another division (3rd), based near Leh in Ladakh, faced Chinese forces in the Aksai Chin while fielding a force of thousands in the Saltoro Range (Siachen Glacier) at the extreme northern end of the LOC. Also attached to the two corps headquarters in mid-1993 were some 12 independent brigades, whose numbers vastly enlarged the total.

Major unit deployment (in June 1993) was as follows. (See Appendix II for Map—"Indian Security Forces in Indian Held Kashmir.")

15th Corps (Srinagar; Kashmir and Ladakh subdivisions):

3rd Infantry Division	Leh (Ladakh)
8th Mountain Division	Sharifabad (Kashmir)
19th Infantry Division	Baramulla (Kashmir)
28th Infantry Division	Kupwara (Kashmir)

16th Corps (Nagrota; Jammu subdivision and Punjab):

10th Infantry Division	Akhnur (Jammu)
25th Infantry Division	Rajouri (Jammu)
26th Infantry Division	Jammu (Jammu)
29th Infantry Division	Mamun (Punjab and Jammu)

There were numerous credible reports, emanating both from Pakistan and from India, that the Indian army was reinforcing these units in summer 1993 with "elements" of two additional mountain divisions—the 6th and 39th.[9] Reports varied on the exact scale of the induction, on whether it was part of seasonal rotation or permanent, and on whether the new units would be tasked for border-sealing or internal security duties. One way or the other, the induction seemed to represent a fairly substantial increase (one informed guess was 25,000 new troops) in the army's deployment figures for the state. There were also unconfirmed reports in September 1993, following the signing in Beijing of agreements in regard to troop reductions on the Sino-Indian border (see Chapter 3), that India planned to shift some of its troops from that border to Kashmir.[10] These reports obviously held serious implications—ominous from the perspective of the Kashmiri militants—both for India's counterinsurgency capabilities and its intentions in Kashmir.

Pakistani military intelligence sources claimed to the author in June 1993 that one full division (8th Mountain), plus nine additional brigades (52nd, 53rd, and 160th Infantry; 33rd, 68th, 79th, and 323rd Mountain; 19th and 39th Artillery) and one airborne battalion (9th Paratroop) were designated for internal security duties, mainly in the Valley of Kashmir. (See Appendix II.) Only the 8th Mountain Division's employment in this capacity was confirmed to the author by other observers.

BORDER-SEALING AND COUNTERINFILTRATION OPERATIONS

Indian counterinsurgency strategy is fundamentally two-pronged, aimed, on the one hand, at direct liquidation of the insurgents and their support base *within* Kashmir and, on the other, at the elimination of support of all kinds, but especially of the influx of armed insurgents, from sources *outside* the state. Border-sealing operations, while at all times an intrinsic element of the Indian army's territorial defense mission on all of India's frontiers, are thus of particular importance in the present context, given Pakistan's conspicuous presence on the LOC and the certainty of hostile infiltration across it. We shall have occasion to observe later on (Chapter 6) that Indians, not excluding some with key roles in counterinsurgency planning, not infrequently dissent from their government's official accent on the overarching importance of the "foreign hand" in the Kashmir insurgency; practically everyone of some consequence in the Indian civil and military hierarchy, however, attaches at least some weight to the importance of countering cross-border infiltration in counterinsurgency strategy.

India's counterinfiltration efforts have been seriously handicapped by a number of factors. Terrain, climate, and costs have thus far prohibited either full fencing or extensive mining of the lengthy LOC. Patrolling of the LOC is extremely difficult at higher elevations, where deep snows hinder movement most of the year, and cannot by itself seal the border against scattered bands of determined infiltrators. Hazardous as is their mission, the infiltrators are at severe risk of detection only for a relatively short period of time after they cross the border. As the commanding officer of the 19th Infantry Division, guarding a stretch of the LOC west of Baramulla, explained it, the distance between the LOC and the Indian-defended mountain ridges to the east varied anywhere from about 1.8 to 18 miles.[11] The infiltrators tended to make their crossing where the distance was least. Key objectives for them were the fairly numerous small passes, actually gullies or ravines, numbering about 15 in the nearly 168-mile-long sector of the LOC defended by this division, that cut through the ridgeline at elevations running between 11,000 and 12,000 feet. Ordinarily, the infiltrators required about six to eight hours—one night, in other words—to make it from the LOC, across the Indian-defended ridgeline to the safety of the thickly pine-forested slopes on the other side. Even fairly large groups of infiltrators have apparently been able to make it across from time to time. Discovery by an Indian army patrol of an especially large group of infiltrators attempting to cross the Shamshabari ridge near Baramulla on 5 May 1991, for instance, seems to have resulted in large part from the failure of the infiltrators to get past the ridgeline before daybreak.[12]

The LOC is by no means impenetrable. Indeed, natural geographic barriers form only parts of it. There are no mountains, for example, to obstruct passage for about 15 to 20 percent of the sector guarded by the 19th Infantry Division. Even where natural barriers exist, moreover, they are not uniformly formidable. A short stretch of the LOC is formed, for example, by the Poonch River, which is relatively shallow and fairly easily crossed, winter or summer.

Geography aside, Indian troops themselves are a less than perfect screen against surreptitious border-crossers. When asked whether the troops guarding the LOC were open to bribery, an Indian general in command of troops on the LOC replied: "It is absolutely impossible to bribe an Indian army man." But a senior Indian government official with decades of experience in Kashmir insisted vehemently that the movement of armed infiltrators across the LOC was the product in large measure of what he called the "massive corruption of Indian troops."[13] Even the general confessed, with a grin, that his statement did not necessarily blanket the paramilitary forces.[14]

India's counterinfiltration efforts have taken many forms during the insurgency, including the laying of additional minefields; the passage of new emergency legislation governing disturbed areas to facilitate preventive arrest and detention by the armed forces; the establishment of an elaborate informant apparatus throughout the valley; clearance of civilians, when they still remained, from a "dead zone" immediately adjacent to the LOC; the erection of a three- or four-tiered security belt (Forward Defended Area) stretching back about three miles from the LOC; more aggressive air and ground patrolling; imposition of dusk-to-dawn curfew in the border security zone, as well as a system of mandatory identity cards and security passes plus constant security checks on locals living in or near this zone. While these devices most certainly have raised the risks of infiltration very substantially, they have clearly not ended it.

The idea of *complete* interdiction of infiltration—in particular by fencing the entire LOC in the same way as has been done on the international border in the Punjab—continues to have some advocates in India. Knowledgeable observers are almost uniformly of the view, however, that full sealing of the border, in general, and fencing of it, in particular, are not practical options.[15] Not only the extremely rugged character of the landscape and the "illogical" path followed by the LOC account for their view. As a Pakistani brigade commander in the Poonch sector of the LOC put it to the author in June 1993, fencing isn't really an option at all for the Indians because, quite unlike the situation in the Punjab, where the fencing was done on an agreed *international* border, there has never been a demarcation (marking on the ground) of the LOC *and the Pakistani army, governed by the existing protocol that limits fortifying the LOC, would unquestionably fire upon anyone who attempted to build one!* Nothing as conspicuous as a fence, in other words, can be built at or near the LOC; and the Indians, the Pakistani brigade commander pointed out, are not likely to construct it much to the *rear* of the LOC not only because that would obviously interfere greatly with the present Indian defense system on the LOC but also because, in doing so, they would risk its becoming at some future point the de facto LOC.

Mining, under the circumstances that obtain along most of the LOC, is, according to most sources, also a very limited option: The LOC for much of its length follows no logic in terms of terrain and presents relatively few opportunities for discriminate, permanent, and effective mining. Where mining has been done, its victims have probably more often been innocent villagers—stepping on mines washed down from the hillsides in the massive flooding that often follows the monsoon rains—than sinister infiltrators.

Since the LOC is a "live" and militarily contested border, the Indian defense line naturally adheres to a military logic, not to the LOC itself. This means that Indian pickets lie mainly along the crests. In some areas, this leaves Indian villages (according to one source, about 40 of them) *ahead* of the pickets, an obviously complicating feature whether one is contemplating mining or fencing of the border.

These cold facts appear to have inspired at least three different forms of response on the Indian side of the LOC, one of them diplomatic (appeals to the international community to condemn Pakistan's support of infiltration as an act of state terrorism), the other two relating directly to the Indian security forces.

One of these, clearly the most important, has been to "thicken" Indian defenses on the LOC, to intensify patrols, and, in general, to sharpen techniques of detection. Pakistani military intelligence officers claimed in a briefing for the author in June 1993 that the Indian army deployed on average about 300 troops per kilometer along the LOC. While this figure, interpreted literally, would obviously not stand scrutiny (Indian troops are not, by any stretch of the imagination, standing shoulder to shoulder on the LOC), there is little doubt that the Indians have substantially beefed up their forces positioned directly on the LOC, that in most sectors they retain a distinctly advantageous force ratio (some claim in the vicinity of 3:2) over Pakistani troops, but that, importantly, this lopsidedness is efficient militarily only in so far as it contributes to the success of counterinfiltration operations. It is not, as Pakistani military observers see it, a militarily sensible (or unusually threatening) deployment of Indian forces *relative to themselves.* The Indians, in other words, have drawn down their reserves in order to better police the infiltration routes.

Indian security forces have also responded to cross-border infiltration from Pakistan with both heavy and small arms fire at targets across the LOC in Azad Kashmir. Such fire, in both directions, is hardly without precedent. In some sectors, in fact, the exchange of fire across the LOC has been a fairly commonplace feature of the Kashmir dispute from its inception, occurring, on average, every few weeks or so. According to Pakistani sources, they usually began with small arms fire, but they almost invariably would escalate to heavy mortar and artillery exchanges lasting, normally, one or two days. The frequency of these exchanges increased with the onset of the insurgency; and by late spring 1991, when they began to include prolonged heavy mortar and artillery bombardments, so had their ferocity. Unmistakable in the pattern of heavy arms fire coming at that time from the Indian side of the LOC was its retaliatory motivation *and* its apparently deliberate targeting of civilian settlements.

The great bulk of these bombardments occurred along the stretch of the LOC that runs roughly parallel to and in some portions very close to the Neelam Valley road—a major artery that follows the Neelam (Kishanganga) River in a northeastward direction for about 100 miles from Muzaffarabad (the capital of Azad Kashmir) to Kail. At three points on this route, Indian forces occupy distinctly advantageous positions in the heights overlooking the road from which they can bombard the highway and civilian settlements, as well as delicately suspended footbridges across the raging Kishanganga. Since virtually all supplies to Pakistani forces and civilians in the adjacent areas must travel via this road, India is obviously in a position to inflict serious damage on Pakistan virtually at will. "To be difficult," said the Indian army general whose forces manned the artillery batteries in the mountains overlooking the

Neelam Valley road, the Indian army can easily choke this key artery. Beyond Kail, he said, there are no all-weather, all-year roads.[16] In one episode of shelling, from 2 to 8 May 1991, Pakistanis claim that Indian guns (120mm mortar, 130mm and 155mm artillery pieces) fired thousands of rounds at one cluster of villages in Athmuqam subdistrict, flattening many homes and shops.[17] Pakistani forces focused their own heavy fire on the Indian gun batteries. Which side actually precipitated the firing is unclear. It was at exactly this same time, however, that massive infiltration efforts appear to have been launched from the Pakistan side, suggesting a possible correlation between the two. Indians typically argue that the Pakistanis initiate such exchanges as "cover" for infiltration operations. Pakistanis retort that Pakistan's vulnerability to Indian artillery placed along the Neelam River road presents the Indians with an especially tempting point at which to apply pressure on Pakistan for any number of diplomatic or military purposes. According to a Pakistani officer in command of a Mujahid Force (paramilitary) battalion at Athmuqam, for instance, the Indians simply wanted to make the point: "We can close this road whenever we want."[18] On this point, at least, the two sides seemed in perfect agreement.[19]

These heavy artillery and mortar barrages across the LOC unquestionably added an ominous wrinkle to the Kashmir dispute. Their ferocity suggested that whatever constraints on violation of the Kashmir boundary may once have existed were in grave danger of breaking down. On both sides of the LOC, civilian and military leaders seemed prepared to vent their wrath against the other side through increasingly direct and sustained military assault.

All sources, Indian and Pakistani, confirm that heavy weapons (mortar and artillery) firing across the LOC was suspended entirely in summer 1992, following an understanding reached at that time between the army headquarters of the two countries.[20] A *limited* cease-fire has thus been restored on the LOC. Indian military sources claim that they want a full cease-fire but that the Pakistanis won't go along.

Not suspended at that time was small arms fire (rifle, light and medium machine gun), which apparently has averaged several thousand rounds a day in both directions ever since. Pakistani military officers charge that much of the Indian fire is directed deliberately at civilian settlements, at civilian homes and livestock, *and at civilians themselves—whether men, women, or children.* This author's fairly extensive personal observation, inspection, and interviews with scores of civilians in villages of Azad Kashmir at widely separated points on the LOC over three days in June 1993, taken together with the corroborative private testimony of other expert and neutral witnesses interviewed by the author, give strong support to these charges.

According to a Pakistani brigade commander on the LOC, routine small arms firing across that line, particularly in the mountainous Poonch sector (in Jammu division), had grown far more intense by summer 1993 than it had ever been in the past. This sector was one of the "most active" in terms of cease-fire violations, he said, of the entire border. Indian firing, he said, occurred virtually every day on the 50-kilometer stretch of the LOC for which his brigade held responsibility. It usually took the form of machine-gun fire, as many as 1,000 bursts per night. Civilian casualties, he said, were heavy and gaining in frequency: In 1992, in this sector, there was one civilian killed, he indicated, and 21 wounded; in the first six months of 1993, in contrast, eight civilians had been killed and 36 wounded.[21]

The impact on the civilians living adjacent to the LOC in Azad Kashmir was obviously severe: Apart from the killed and wounded (including a number of small children who have been badly crippled and disfigured), the villagers, to protect themselves, have been forced to shift their residences, locate new sources of water supply, dig trenches, lay new access roads, tend their fields at night, and pasture their livestock in concealed areas. In village after village, the story was the same: Prior to 1990, Indian small-arms fire was almost invariably directed at Pakistani army outposts near the LOC; since then, it has often—and deliberately, it seems—been directed at the villages and at the villagers themselves.[22] Pakistani military officials attributed three motives to the Indian side for this firing pattern: (1) to reduce civilian assistance to the infiltrators by clearing civilians from the corridor adjacent to the LOC on the Pakistani side; (2) to drive a wedge between the militants and the harassed civilians; and (3) to multiply problems of administration for the governments of Pakistan and Azad Kashmir.

Rates of cross-border exfiltration and infiltration reported by India in 1993 showed a steep decline for the period since 1991. According to a set of figures compiled by India's Ministry of Home Affairs, encounters with infiltrating militants at or in the vicinity of the LOC numbered 382 in 1990, 164 in 1991, and only 39 in 1992.[23] Official figures in regard to encounters in 1993 were not made available; but estimates given to the author in July 1993 by Indian military and police officials in Srinagar of the rate of infiltration up to that point indicated the strong likelihood that the decline in encounters would not be reversed.[24] Totals for exfiltration and infiltration, as well as for interceptions, arrests, and killings by Indian forces at the LOC, for the entire period of the insurgency, as supplied to the author by the Ministry of Home Affairs, are given in Table 5.1.

Table 5.1 Exfiltration and Infiltration on the LOC
[1 January 1990–30 June 1993]

	Exfiltration	Infiltration
Total number (est.):	18,750	16,900
Groups intercepted on border*:	121	301
Arrests on border:	725	863
Killings on border:	153	836

Source: Ministry of Home Affairs, Government of India.

*These numbers do not correspond exactly with the figures on encounters mentioned in the text.

The reported decline in the rate of infiltration could be due to a number of factors. One is an increase in Western pressures on Pakistan to curb its support for cross-border infiltration attempts. While recent reports that "U.S. pressure has forced Pakistan to stop arming and training Kashmiri militants fighting Indian rule"[25] should be treated with some caution, these pressures have very likely had an impact. Another possibility is the greater success of infiltrators in eluding detection. The decline is more likely due, however, to a considerable extent to India's increasingly aggressive and energetic efforts to police the border and to raise the costs of interference by its adversary by bringing direct military pressure to bear on the Pakistani side of the LOC.

Also apparent in the figures given in the table is the suggestion that apprehension of infiltrators (arrests and killings) runs at about 10 percent of the total—a rate that is probably fairly close to the truth. These figures contrast markedly with routine (and vehement) insistence by practically all Pakistani officials, civil and military, that the uprising in Kashmir is entirely (or largely) indigenous, that the Pakistani army provides no material support to the militants, that any militants who make their way across the LOC do so with the support of private organizations only, and that, in any event, penetrating the thicket of defenses erected by the Indians is next to impossible. They compare reasonably well, on the other hand, with the insistence of a very senior government official in Srinagar that the security forces didn't *want* to seal the LOC effectively since they were engaged in very lucrative smuggling operations across it, not infrequently in cooperation with the militants![26]

A one-day air and surface tour in June 1993 of Indian border installations in the Kupwara sector of the LOC (about 55 miles west of Srinagar), including observation of an allegedly in-progress encounter between infiltrating militants and troops of the 28th Infantry Division, reinforced the author's already strong conviction that the price of detection could be very high but that—adequately trained, equipped, and guided—determined infiltrators certainly could, and apparently often did, penetrate Indian defenses.[27]

COUNTERINSURGENCY OPERATIONS: THE HUMAN RIGHTS ISSUE

Almost all foreign and not a few Indian visitors to Kashmir describe Indian military and paramilitary forces there, not only in the way they are garrisoned, convoyed, and deployed but in terms of their attitudes toward the local Kashmiris, as an army of occupation. And from the moment one sets down at the airport in Srinagar, to be confronted immediately with layer upon layer of security detachments, screening precautions, and fortified guard posts, the feeling is inescapable that this is not an entirely inappropriate comparison. The situation in Kashmir is very unlike the Punjab, where the inevitable aggravations of counterinsurgency operations were bound to be mitigated in Sikh eyes, at least to an extent, by the obviously disproportionate representation of Sikh men at all ranks in the police, army, and paramilitary forces. In Kashmir, the distrust of the people for the security forces seems nearly complete; and the security forces unquestionably reciprocate it.

Not surprisingly, the security forces' counterinsurgency operations on a daily basis deepen and widen this distrust. These operations take many forms. For convenience's sake, however, we can categorize them under three broad headings: (1) the creation and maintenance of *secure zones,* (2) the mounting of *combing* (cordon and search) *operations,* and (3) the administration of both *judicial and extrajudicial punishments.* All three, but especially the second and third, contribute to the climate of fear and hostility that pervades the relationship between the local citizens and the security forces.

Secure zones. As Indian security forces view it, the Valley of Kashmir has been sharply divided by the uprising into two spatially fragmented but otherwise perfectly visible sectors—an insecure zone, the one in which most of the people dwell and the one, of course, in which the militants move with relative freedom; and a secure zone, holding government offices, military installations, and the roads that connect them, but not much else, and the one, of course, from which the militants are largely excluded. The insecure zone is by far the larger of the two; entry into or passage through it by the security forces is always undertaken with some degree of risk and never without arms at the ready. Government officials and the government's civilian allies (including, as we will see in Chapter 6, the erstwhile political leaders of Kashmir), with some few exceptions, and with notably deleterious effects on state administration, stay entirely out of it. The secure zone itself is secure only in a relative sense: Fortified sandbag bunkers and intense patrolling keep most main arteries in it open by day; but even police officials hasten to reach their homes in it before nightfall. Spectacular measures are required to guard VIPs and senior officials in the government and police who visit or work in it, and there is a constant (and entirely valid) fear that this zone's perimeter defenses work very imperfectly.[28] It is the government's expectation, naturally, that this bifold arrangement of the valley will end in due time and that the two zones will merge into one—secure—area. In the meantime, and regardless of whether that expectation is realistic, the arrangement has highly abrasive effects on both sides and is a standing physical reminder of the alienation that is present between the Indian government and its Kashmiri Muslim citizens.

Combing operations. Antipathy between the security forces and the valley's inhabitants has been exacerbated on a much grander scale by the cordon and search operations that have been conducted by the security forces on a routine basis throughout much of the valley for most of the period since the uprising began in earnest in January 1990. These operations, which to date have fallen largely under the responsibility of the BSF, are basically unannounced raids on either urban or rural settlements designed to uncover hideouts and to net weapons and militants, both the hardcore cadre as well as their softcore collaborators. As described to the author by an Indian army division commander in July 1993, the targeted area is generally surrounded by troops in the predawn; all persons within the area—whatever their age or gender—are commanded to vacate their dwellings or business establishments and to assemble in a designated area, where they are held under guard; a meticulous house-to-house search, often requiring four to six hours to carry out, is then conducted; and in the meanwhile a so-called parade of the inhabitants, following segregation of women, small children, and aged males from teenage and adult males, is held, in which hooded informers are invited to identify suspects. Suspects, if any, are then led away for interrogation and possible detention.

This process, endlessly repeated, is obviously tremendously disruptive of households, patently humiliating, bound to produce massive injustice, and—to say the least—frightening to those who must endure it. It presents opportunity for abuses of every kind, physical and otherwise, by the security forces; and these have by now been so well filmed and documented that most Indian officials do not even attempt to deny them.[29] They argue that so long as the public insists upon concealing the militants in their midst, the security forces have little choice but to round up the innocent along with the guilty.

Judicial and extrajudicial punishments. It can be said without qualification that nothing generates quite as much antipathy between the security forces and the Kashmiri public as the judicial and extrajudicial punishments meted out by the former upon the latter. It can further be said that while it is the extrajudicial—by most standards, illegal—punishments that have earned the greatest notoriety, it is the quite legal, judicial punishments that may have had the greatest negative impact on Kashmiri Muslim attitudes both toward the security forces and toward India.

Judicial punishments, periods of detention or imprisonment mainly, would under ordinary circumstances fall largely within the jurisdiction of the state courts, not that of the security forces. However, placement of the state under emergency rule on 5 July 1990 brought into play a number of statutes, in particular TADA, mentioned earlier, the Armed Forces Special Powers Act, granting the security forces substantial immunity from prosecution, and the Public Safety (Preventive Detention) Act (PSA), that have created a military-dominated regime that resembles martial law and which vests extraordinary powers in the security forces. These powers are, of course, not difficult to justify under the circumstances prevailing in Kashmir,[30] and there is nothing very unusual about them: These same statutes, or ones like them, have been on the books practically everywhere in India, indeed everywhere in South Asia, for most of the twentieth century. Their prototypes were introduced by the British during the colonial period, and their offspring have remained highly popular with the often-beleaguered governments of this region ever since. It is equally obvious, of course, that these laws by their nature threaten at all times to eviscerate the protections against arbitrary exercise of police authority embodied in the Indian constitution; and in Kashmir, with representative political institutions dissolved and the domain of the courts brutally truncated, they threaten to destroy these protections entirely.

TADA, a federal enactment, makes it a crime to commit certain actions that have been defined as terrorist. Under this law, detention on suspicion of guilt is sufficient for the accused to be remanded to the state's custody for up to one year, without charges, without trial, and with bail rarely granted. Confessions, even if recorded by a police officer while the accused is in police custody, are accepted as evidence of guilt without any safeguards against false or coerced confession. Should the accused file for bail, he must prove his innocence, and the judge, if bail is approved, must certify that the accused will not repeat the offense—a guarantee that few judges are likely to make. At the end of the year of incarceration, the accused may get a release on paper, but in practice is often rearrested under a different law and the whole process repeated.[31]

The PSA, on the other hand, is a piece of preventive detention legislation enacted by the Jammu and Kashmir state assembly. Under it, the state can detain a person without trial for up to 24 months. Its preventive feature means that an individual may be detained simply on *apprehension* that a crime might be committed. No legal remedy is provided to the detainee. The maximum sentence is two years, and that, according to a number of Kashmiri Muslim attorneys interviewed by the author, is what the average detainee gets. Unlike those arrested under TADA, who must by law be held in Jammu and Kashmir state itself, PSA detainees, by virtue of an action taken by the New Delhi–appointed governor in 1990, can legally be held in any state of India.[32] The Bar Association of Jammu and Kashmir state, according to the attorneys, has filed over 5,000 habeas corpus petitions with the state courts since January 1990; few of them, they say, were ever even considered by the courts.

How many Kashmiri Muslims are presently under preventive detention or serving sentences, either in Jammu and Kashmir or in India proper, under these laws? When Rajesh Pilot, Minister of State for Home Affairs (Internal Security) and the man designated by Prime Minister P. V. Narasimha Rao in January 1993 to chair the central government's Kashmir Cell and to act as the government's overall policy coordinator in regard to Kashmir, was asked at a press conference in late June 1993 how many Kashmiris were then in custody, he responded after a pause that the number was "under 5,000."[33] Senior (non-Kashmiri) police officials in Srinagar placed this figure (early July 1993) at under *3,000* (2,870 to be exact), the same number given the author in a briefing at the Ministry of Home Affairs in New Delhi at about the same time.[34] These figures obviously cannot be independently verified. They fall far below the figures given this author by most nonofficial observers, whose estimates rarely fell beneath 15,000 and reached as high as 36,000; and they were substantially below the figure of 8,000 to 10,000 given to the author by one of Kashmir's most senior bureaucrats.[35] On the other hand, several estimates by generally well-informed observers, including a number of Indian journalists quite sympathetic with the militants, were not greatly larger than the government's figures. The highest figures are almost certainly vastly inflated; but even if the government's low figures are technically accurate, they probably conceal a fairly large number of Kashmiri Muslims who languish in detention centers, uncharged and unacknowledged, awaiting disposal of their cases. Until Indian arrest, detention, and penal procedures achieve vastly greater transparency than they now have, however, the Kashmiri Muslim prison population must remain a matter largely of conjecture.

Extrajudicial punishments meted out by the security forces are, of course, the focus of the greatest amount of controversy not to mention publicity.

They allegedly include revenge killings (of both militants and innocents); summary executions and assassinations; staged encounters; sexual molestation and rape; deliberate torching of homes, markets, and mosques; systematic torture and custodial deaths. The occurrence of most of these is acknowledged by the government; debated are their frequency, allocation of principal responsibility for them among the security forces, earnestness of government efforts to stop them and to punish the guilty, and how to account for them.

Kashmiri Muslims and their allies in Pakistan and in both Indian and foreign human rights groups declare with near unanimity that these activities have been a matter of routine and that the government's efforts to curb them have been wholly inadequate.[36] Skepticism in regard to some of the more extravagant claims in this regard is essential. The Kashmiri militants and their supporters know well the political appeal to Westerners of human rights issues and naturally they make the most of this. There can be no doubt, in other words, that reports of human rights abuses are often exaggerated. Neither, however, can there be any doubt—the evidence is simply overwhelming—that brutality, at times in its most egregiously repugnant forms, has been institutionalized by the security forces in Kashmir; that violating human rights has been the norm all along in security force operations against the militants; and, furthermore, that curbing these violations would take a far more massive and sustained effort than the government, at any level, has thus far seemed willing or able to make.

The statement to the author in July 1993 by a senior adviser to the governor of Jammu and Kashmir state that most reports of human rights abuses were "a figment of the imagination" and that the government, in fact, was "very particular about the human rights aspect" bears little relationship to reality. His claim got extremely meager support even from others on the governor's advisory staff—and not much support, in fact, from the governor himself. To be sure, the governor gave the author the clear impression of deep and sincere concern about the reports of violations. He freely conceded that the security forces had badly alienated the Kashmiri public, and he outlined steps he was taking to overcome that. The bulk of his comments, however, focused on the sorry condition of the state administration—of its extremely deep corruption, dishonesty, and tradition of unresponsiveness to the public—and of the great difficulty he faced as governor in trying to get the local police and CPOs to cooperate with him in disciplining those against whom complaints of violations were brought. The Indian army, he said, had a strong tradition of discipline. "The only problem," he said, "is the police forces—the CRPF, BSF, and JKP." These organizations, he observed, do not share the same ethos as the regular army. While the army, at least its senior officers, willingly cooperated with his efforts to bring human rights violators to book, the police and paramilitary forces were proving tougher to discipline.[37]

In interviews with the author, a number of well-placed observers with inside knowledge of the security system in the state of Jammu and Kashmir disputed the governor's contention that there was a human rights hierarchy among the security forces—the regular army, the "cleanest" of them, at the top, then the BSF, followed by the CRPF, with the JKP huddled at the bottom. They argued very persuasively that the CPOs got their reputation for nasty behavior (for being particularly brutal, corrupt, and ruthless) primarily because of the role they were assigned to play—one that placed them, in contrast with most of the regular army troops in the state, in direct, constant, and stressful confrontation with the Kashmiri militants *and* with the Kashmiri public. Whenever and wherever the army took on internal security duties, they said, its behavior—including the routine use of torture to extract intelligence—was little different from that of the CPOs.

Taking a position midway between the governor and his critics, a self-styled consultant to the Indian army on counterinsurgency maintained to the author that there was a clear difference in behavior between the army and the paramilitary forces. The army, he said, was generally well officered and still showed considerable professionalism. The paramilitary forces in Kashmir, on the other hand, were suffering from a severe shortage of both commissioned and noncommissioned officers and were thus structurally handicapped when it came to maintaining discipline. Army and BSF troops were drawn essentially from the same stock, he pointed out; and both types of troops received much the same military training. Differences in their behavior were thus due more to shortcomings in command than in moral character. In a typed and untitled paper supplied to the author, he wrote that the BSF troops were, in fact,

> better equipped and provisioned [than regular army troops] for the task on hand. The difference comes in the manner they are organized and led. A BSF battalion is supposed to have eleven officers. This is rarely the case. Most battalions make do with four or five officers. For instance, the BSF's 22nd battalion, entrusted with the critical task of policing Srinagar, is short of five officers. Its commandant, an ex-serviceman with a distinguished record in the BSF and IB [Intelligence Bureau] and who is credited with some very notable successes in the current post, does not have a second-in-command. The battalion is also short of two each of deputy commandants and assistant commandants. To compound matters a BSF battalion generally has six companies as opposed to its Army counterpart which normally has four companies. In addition to this the Army's battalions have seventeen

> officers. Thus, whereas no army unit goes into action in the valley without an officer in command, the BSF has often to make do with noncoms in command. The BSF unit which torched and shot up Sopore [in early January 1993] was led by an Assistant Sub-inspector.[38]

In regard to torture itself, it is hard to dispute the statement of a renowned civil libertarian in New Delhi who stated to the author in early July 1993 that torture was "absolutely universal" in Kashmir. Everywhere in India, he said, echoing practically all Indian and international human rights organizations that have investigated the matter, torture was the *normal* practice of the country's security personnel; in Kashmir it was simply more systematic and extreme. The circumstances in Kashmir, he suggested, hardly allowed for anything else. How could the interrogation of detainees live up to the textbook standards of police interrogation taught at police academies in the West, he queried, when the interrogators were under few restrictions, were being pressed hard for quick results, and could barely, if at all, speak the local language?

Each of the security forces maintains its own interrogation centers. Some of these are permanent facilities, others are temporary, set up on the spot in any available structure in the course of combing operations. Detainees who are not cleared in preliminary screening at these centers may be sent on to interservice units, the so-called Joint Interrogation Centres, where detention may extend over months.[39] The Kashmiri Muslim attorneys interviewed by the author in Srinagar claimed that there were more than 30 permanent interrogation centers in that city alone, and that in the entire state they numbered between 200 and 300. These particular estimates may well be inflated; no outsider is in a position, in any event, to count, much less to visit, these installations. Their existence is not generally concealed from public knowledge, however, and some of the most notorious of them in Srinagar—Hari Niwas Interrogation Centre, a small palace that once belonged to the maharaja of Kashmir, and the somewhat perversely named Papa I and Papa II—are conspicuously located within minutes of the governor's mansion.

The interrogation centers are not a new institution in Kashmir; they were a staple of the military intelligence collection apparatus there, according to a retired army officer with intimate knowledge of these centers at the time, at least as early as 1987. The number of interrogation centers in the Valley of Kashmir and the scale of torture that went on in them even then, he said, was vast, "beyond the imagination of the Indian public."[40]

As for the problem of custodial deaths in Kashmir, while Indian officials will dispute its scale, all concede its existence. One senior civil servant in the state government, though insisting vehemently that the militants violated human rights on a far greater scale than the security forces,[41] speculated in an interview with the author in Srinagar in July 1993 that the custodial deaths occurring in Kashmir were part of a deliberate strategy learned from the experience of the security forces in the Punjab. There, he said, faked encounters had been widely used by the security forces to conduct summary executions of hardcore Sikh militants. It was a brutal device, he admitted, but it had the desired effect: Abduction and assassination of security personnel, which had been up until then very common, were dramatically curbed. The model, he guessed, had been imported into Kashmir as a strategy for curbing attacks upon and abductions of BSF personnel and their families by Kashmiri militants. An Indian civil libertarian, commenting to the author on the same phenomenon, suggested that many Indian officials, whatever they might say in public, believed that extrajudicial killing of suspects was the most *efficient*—in fact, the *only* efficient—means of contending with the insurgency. Public trials in India, after all, were notoriously slow, costly, and of very uncertain outcome.

From all this we may come to three conclusions. First, rapidly mounting worldwide allegations that Indian security forces are guilty of grave violations of human rights are recognized by all parties to the Kashmir dispute as a major issue in it, as a potentially serious political liability in India's position in Kashmir, and thus as a focal point of a propaganda battle as intense and hard-fought in its own way as the physical struggle between these forces and the insurgents in the valley. The strenuous efforts either to assail or to defend the reputation of the security forces in this regard are symptomatic of this battle.

Second, it is extremely difficult, on the basis of evidence now publicly available, to confirm or disconfirm the government's contention that human rights violations have been brought under control and that violators in the security forces are being systematically and conscientiously weeded out and punished. Such figures as were supplied to the author by Home Ministry officials in New Delhi, specifically that up to 31 May 1993, 146 security force personnel had been punished—nearly 50 of them imprisoned and about 25 kicked out of the services—for violations of human rights in Kashmir, reveal scarcely anything about the actual scale of the problem or of its remedy and clearly give no hint of current trends.[42] Rajesh Pilot, in the press conference cited earlier, maintained that there was a "communications gap" between the security forces and their critics, that the government *was* taking forceful action to curb violations, and that custodial deaths, in particular, were no longer tolerated. But his claims were heatedly denied by Kashmiri Muslims and their supporters; and more than one senior official in the state government privately expressed strong skepticism about them as well.

Third, human rights violations committed by the security forces in Kashmir take many forms and arise from a variety of circumstances. These circumstances include (1) the *international* character of the Kashmir dispute, the fact that India's principal adversary is actively intervening in the insurgency, and that there are major and unavoidable strategic and military pressures on the security forces resulting from this intervention; (2) the character of the *security forces* themselves, the fact that brutality and torture have a very lengthy and deeply ingrained tradition within them; (3) the *ethno-religious differences* that divide the security forces from most of the residents of the valley and that intensify the distrust between them; and (4) the inevitably harsh nature of the *counterinsurgency operations* themselves. These operations unquestionably multiply opportunities for human rights violations; and so long as they continue, no doubt so will the violations. The abuses are not just the result of these operations, however, and they would not all disappear even if the insurgency were to end. The abuses are clearly not all equally amenable to rapid or uncomplicated remedy.

CHAPTER

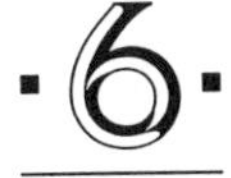

INDIAN POLICY IN JAMMU AND KASHMIR

This chapter assesses Indian counterinsurgency policy in the state of Jammu and Kashmir. It examines first the domestic political context of policymaking on Kashmir and in particular the impact upon the present Congress-I government's Kashmir policy of differences within the ruling party itself as well as between the government and the political opposition. The second part of this chapter focuses directly on the counterinsurgency policy of the P. V. Narasimha Rao government, elected in July 1991, in particular on the set of initiatives in regard to Kashmir undertaken by Rajesh Pilot since his appointment to the post of minister of state for internal security in January 1993. Last, it weighs the prospects for the government's policy to succeed in Kashmir, specifically (1) to curb the insurgency and (2) to restore democracy.

KASHMIR ISSUE IN INDIAN POLITICS

One of the most notable developments in Indian politics in recent years has been the increasingly overt and violent display of hatred between Muslims and Hindus. This development surfaced in spectacular fashion in early December 1992, when a huge and frenzied Hindu mob attacked and dismantled a controversial Muslim religious shrine (Babri Masjid) in the north Indian town of Ayodhya, and again in the early months of 1993 when communal (mainly anti-Muslim) rioting, especially in Bombay, resulted in over 2,000 brutal killings. Many commentators connect these events to fundamental trends in Indian society, one of them a sharp decline in the ideal of secularism, another an equally sharp rise in the ideal of Hindu nationalism.[1] They may equally well be related, of course, to global trends—to an emerging, world-encompassing *Kulturkampf,* or "clash of civilizations," perhaps, as has been suggested recently by a highly regarded American academic.[2]

However they are explained, these events seem to foreshadow a political future for India, certainly in the near term and perhaps in the longer term as well, dominated to no small extent by intense rivalry between the Hindu majority and the huge (over 100 million) Muslim minority. The separatist movement in Kashmir, India's only Muslim-majority state and an inevitable testing ground of its commitment to secularism, is symptomatic of this rivalry and inevitably contributes to it.

Now in progress in India, in fact, is the potentially momentous conversion of the Kashmir issue from what had been for over four decades primarily a boundary or territorial dispute between India and Pakistan—in large measure an *international* dispute, in other words, with mainly international ramifications —into an *international-cum-domestic* dispute, whose domestic political ramifications are already proving more than mildly troublesome to New Delhi. Just how far the conversion has gone is a matter of widespread conjecture. The leadership of the right-wing, Hindu-nationalist Bharatiya Janata Party (BJP) clearly was gambling that progress in this direction was already substantial when it organized a nationwide "unity caravan" (*ekta yatra*) in late 1991 to publicize the Kashmiri separatist threat to India. Moving by slow stages from Kanniyakumari near the southern tip of India all the way to Srinagar between 11 December 1991 and 26 January 1992, the caravan, with the symbols and paraphernalia of popular Hindu epics on conspicuous display, was widely ridiculed in the national press and, in most respects, was a spectacular fiasco. The gamble obviously didn't pay off. Emboldened before the year was out by its sudden spurt in popularity in the wake of the Ayodhya incident, however, the BJP was ready to try again—albeit with altered tactics.

At the Bangalore session of the party's National Council in early July 1993, plans for combating the government's Kashmir policy—including stepped-up attacks both on Article 370 of the Constitution, which grants formal autonomy to the state of Jammu and Kashmir, and on the government's "soft" policy toward the Kashmiri rebels—were announced; and, in a gesture surely designed for its appeal to Hindu hard-liners on the Kashmir issue, Jagmohan, the state's ex-governor and embattled champion of its total and final constitutional integration into India, was conspicuous among the special invitees at the session.[3] Within weeks of the Bangalore meeting, the BJP began a public drive to recruit retired Hindu soldiers to a private militia designed to protect the Hindu-majority Jammu region of the state from guerrilla attacks by Kashmiri militants operating from the Muslim-dominated valley.[4]

How close was the BJP to capturing power at the center? The meteoric rise in its electoral showing in successive national elections—from winning two seats in the parliament (Lok Sabha) a decade ago in the 1984 general elections, to 86 in 1989, and to 119 in 1991, at that point becoming the principal opposition group in a legislature of 545 seats—was clearly a factor in its favor. Standing against it were the facts that it had yet to bring in better than 20 percent of the vote in nationwide polling, that its political strength was concentrated largely in the northern and northwestern states, that it held little charm for the country's large religious minorities (and not much for its huge and socio-economically backward Scheduled Caste and Scheduled Tribe population), and that its essentially conservative ideology made it unattractive as an alliance partner to most of the other opposition parties (especially those on the left). On top of this, it had, at least in the view of many observers, rather unsavory organizational allies—the Bajarang Dal (a Hindu paramilitary organization), the Vishwa Hindu Parishad (VHP, or World Hindu Council), and the Rashtriya Swayamsewak Sangh (RSS, or National Volunteer Corps).[5] The BJP's potential for expanding its electoral base sufficiently to oust its Congress-I rival thus seemed to depend as much on the party's ability to change its radical and Hindu extremist image as on the national "mood."

As for the mood, there is no doubt that in recent years it has been buffeted by Hindu nationalist feelings that worked to the advantage of BJP political strategists. These feelings included (1) strong resentment against what many felt was the government's "pampering" of Muslims; (2) the conviction that Muslims were polygamous, bred faster, and in general were culturally inferior to Hindus; (3) the strong suspicion that Muslims were basically loyal to Pakistan; and (4) the equally strong suspicion that foreigners (and not just Pakistanis) were meddling in India on behalf of the Muslim minority. By no means were these feelings wholly in conformity with the extremist rhetoric of some BJP sympathizers, such as the RSS notable who told the author that "Islamism is a greater threat to the world, to humanist values, than Communism. . . . Islam is Arab colonialism."[6] Overt and unashamed anti-Muslim prejudice is nowadays fairly commonplace in India, however, even among some of the educated middle class.

This seemingly pervasive Hindu nationalist and anti-Muslim mood has made serious compromise with the Kashmiris an unappealing proposition apparently even to many liberal Hindu intellectuals. When asked how many of these—*of those whose views really counted in policymaking circles in India*—would support a grant of genuine autonomy to the Kashmiri Muslims, one of New Delhi's best-known and most perceptive political analysts replied (seemingly in dead earnest) that the number—*counting all of India* (a land, we might note, nearing 900 million)—would come to no more than 10 or 20 individuals! He estimated that fully 90 percent of India's Hindus would today back the BJP's election pledge to abolish Article 370, to bring all of India's states, finally, equally under the Indian constitutional umbrella, and would also back the party's demand to amend civil law to compel Muslims to adhere to a single civil code. Pointing to a table full of his equally well-known colleagues and fellow intellectuals seated nearby in the fashionable dining room of the India International Centre, he declared that all of them—including a few civil rights advocates among them—were of this nationalist mentality.[7]

This same intellectual argued that the BJP's appeal was no longer really to communalism, the perennial rivalry between Muslims and Hindus. That, he insisted, no longer correctly described the Indian reality; its appeal now was to Hindu nationalism. The BJP, he said, no longer could or would rely on the Ayodhya "card": That issue played well enough, perhaps, with the lumpen element in the BJP ranks, with its greater appetite for crude rabble-rousing and violence, but it wouldn't go far with the politically vital Indian middle classes. Much more salient for them, he said, was the *Kashmir* issue, which had the same strong, essentially *patriotic* appeal in the south of India as in the north. He expected the BJP increasingly to depict Kashmir to Indian voters as "the unfinished business" of the independence struggle—and perhaps to capture power in part on the basis of that.[8]

The results of state legislative elections held across northern India in late November 1993 clearly did not confirm the thesis of an unstoppable BJP wave. Of the six elections held, the BJP won a majority of seats in only one (the National Capital Territory of Delhi). It formed the government in one other (Rajasthan), but only with the aid of independents. The Congress-I party won clear majorities in two states (Madhya Pradesh and Himachal Pradesh) and, with the aid of an allied party, was easily able to form the government in a third (Mizoram). In what was by far the most important contest (Uttar Pradesh), the BJP managed to squeak out a one-seat edge (177 to 176) over its closest opponent, a coalition of leftist parties; but this was far from enough for it to form the government. Congress-I did much worse in Uttar Pradesh, however, winning fewer than 30 of 425 seats. In the judgment of most political observers, neither the Congress-I nor the BJP had much to crow about: In Uttar Pradesh, India's most populous state and the one generally considered to be a vital springboard to national power, both had been soundly defeated. It was the BJP, however, for whose leaders the lessons of these elections were harshest. In 1991, its candidates had swept the polls in Uttar Pradesh, Madhya Pradesh, Himachal Pradesh, and Rajasthan, states containing about 25 percent of India's population. This feat had added immeasurably to the party's steamroller image. On grounds they had failed to prevent the widespread violence that followed the destruction of Babri Masjid by Hindu zealots, Prime Minister Rao had subsequently dismissed the BJP governments in all four of these states and placed them under direct federal rule. Therefore, the elections in November 1993 may well have been a greater psychological setback for the BJP than they were for the ruling party.[9]

If the BJP is able to overcome its present difficulties and to stage a comeback strong enough to take control of the central government in India, what difference would it make to Kashmir? Can the BJP mount a credible argument that it would be able to tackle the Kashmir problem more effectively than the ruling Congress-I party? Asked this question in July 1993, Jaswant Singh, currently a BJP member of parliament, one of a handful of non-RSS "liberals" among its top leaders, a likely cabinet choice in the event of a BJP electoral victory, and one of the party's most articulate spokesmen, answered that a BJP-led government most certainly would make a very big, and positive, difference.[10] "Paradoxes," he said, after reflecting for a moment, "resolve contradictions." The BJP, he said, is caricatured by the Congress-I party as a reactionary, fascist monster, its leaders as potential "Hindu Khomeinis." In truth, he argued, the BJP in power would retain maximum free choice of options in regard to Kashmir. This, he emphasized, partially clarifying the paradox, was because the starting point of the BJP's Kashmir policy—the protection of the national interest—would not be doubted by anyone. That, he offered, was a great strength.

The "critical event" in the valley, Singh suggested, was the kidnapping of Dr. Rubaiya Sayeed, the home minister's daughter, and the Janata government's mishandling of it. In the interest of the nation, he said, the home minister should have stepped down to free the government's hand in dealing with the militants. The BJP was allied then with the government, he conceded, and went along with its Kashmir policy. Nevertheless, caving in to the militants' demands was a serious mistake. It was, he observed dryly, the political opposition's *only* major error.

According to Singh, releasing the captive militants at that time sent entirely the wrong message to Kashmiris. The breakup of the USSR was then in progress; and the Baltic states were securing independence. These were inspiring events bound to be taken notice of in the valley. Disarray was already surfacing there; the situation was volatile and called for government firmness and a clear policy. The government's capitulation in the Rubaiya case at that explosive moment, he suggested, drained it of moral authority.

The government of Narasimha Rao inherited the mess in Kashmir, Singh conceded, it did not create it. In the two years since Rao came to power, however, his Kashmir policy, according to Singh, has been characterized by "drift, ad hocism and reaction to situations on a day-to-day basis." Girish Saxena, governor of Kashmir until March 1993, dutifully sent in his reports describing the problem; but Rao's government was entirely preoccupied with its own "incestuous" problems, as though only its own political survival were all that mattered in India. The Rao government, he said, speaks of the need to restore law and order to Kashmir, but for this government this is only a catch phrase. Law and order, properly understood, derives from the moral authority of the state—something which the Congress government, in Singh's opinion, was busily destroying.

What about Pakistan? It has to be understood, Singh observed, that Pakistan Occupied Kashmir was a part of the reality of Kashmir, that Pakistan had *locus standi* in Kashmir, and that it therefore had a clear interest in troubling India there. "I incline to the view," he said, "that if I were a Pakistani, I would fish in troubled waters [of Kashmir]. . . . I am of the view that it is *not* in Pakistan's national interest to permit resolution. . . . When India bleeds, Pakistan's interests are served. This is simply realpolitik." What this meant, he added, was "that the BJP will have to understand and then exercise enormous effectiveness via *unilateralism* in Kashmir." It could not afford to wait for bilateral or tripartite approaches.

The BJP would have no difficulties with human rights, he said with assurance. India's *economic liberalization* had to go hand in hand with its *political decentralization.* Neither, he said, could prosper without the other. Of course, he cautioned, in promoting decentralization one should not become a captive of words such as autonomy and self-determination. If you do become their captive, he said, it becomes difficult to know where to stop with them. Greater political decentralization, though a good thing in itself, should not be a license for lawlessness.

By addressing itself directly to the problems of the Kashmiri militants, said Singh, the BJP would restore the government's moral authority to Kashmir, and the militants would abjure violence on their own. They didn't really want to join Pakistan; and, in any event, the constant remaking of the map of South Asia had to end.

Jaswant Singh's apparent reasonableness, according to more than one close observer of Indian politics, was simply camouflage for a party that has made an assault upon Indian Islam a centerpiece of its political strategy. A New Delhi–based Western correspondent with lengthy experience in India maintained unequivocally, for example, that a BJP-dominated India would resemble Nazi Germany—and India's Muslims would be treated about like the Jews. RSS men, he said, openly spoke of wholesale "relocation" of the Muslims of Kashmir.[11] Similarly, a well-known American academic has argued recently that there was real danger that fascism "might come to India wrapped in a saffron robe, as some kind of cultural authoritarianism which ordains that anything that cannot be Hinduised cannot be tolerated."[12]

Whatever one's ultimate judgment about the BJP's credentials for ruling India, there can be no doubt that in the Kashmiri separatist uprising of recent years it has found an issue that could *conceivably* be turned to its considerable advantage in the years ahead. This fact is perfectly apparent to the leadership of the Congress-I party, whose potential political vulnerability over Kashmir is a matter of deep concern to party strategists.

The vulnerability stems from four separate political circumstances currently bedeviling Congress-I:

1. The Congress-I government of Prime Minister P. V. Narasimha Rao recently edged into place as a majority government. In December 1993, ten members of the Uttar Pradesh–based Ajit Singh faction of the Janata Dal party joined the Congress-I, giving it 266 seats in parliament against 262 for the opposition.[13] Until then, however, it had been a minority government whose political survival depended on fragile alliances with a number of small regional parties. The Congress-I's electoral victory in May 1991 lifted it from 196 to 220 seats in the Lok Sabha, a figure which, when its allies' seats were added, left it just short of a simple majority. The engineering of defections and recruitment of additional allies by midsummer 1993 had improved the Congress-I position somewhat, but not quite enough to overcome its minority status.[14] Three times in the first 25 months of rule, Rao faced no-confidence motions brought against his government by the opposition. On the third occasion (late July 1993) the government again won, but this time by the narrowest margin yet—14 votes (265 to 251)—and not before it was abandoned by a number of its former allies.[15] Defection at the time to Congress-I of seven members of the same Ajit Singh faction did bring the Congress-I total of elected deputies to 257, injecting some new life into it; but that still left the Rao government short of a majority.[16]

Its new majority standing undoubtedly gave the Congress-I a needed political and psychological boost. The boost was modest, however, and could easily prove temporary. The defectors' loyalties were hardly above suspicion. In any event, barring a more radical change in the allocation of seats in the parliament, Congress-I seemed permanently hobbled politically, deterred from taking unpopular or risky steps, as in regard to Kashmir, lest its still shaky grip on power be placed in yet further jeopardy.

2. In the 1991 elections, Congress-I voting strength in the northern part of the country dipped severely, while in the south, traditionally a bastion of support for strong regional opposition parties, Congress-I strength grew appreciably. This major reversal in party support patterns created a dilemma for the party, which ever since independence had drawn heavily on the votes of underprivileged minorities (not least the *Muslim* minority) in the northern states to push it to electoral victory. The dilemma was particularly apparent in Uttar Pradesh, the country's most populous state and the core of its Hindi-speaking heartland. There the BJP swept Congress-I from power following a campaign that deliberately targeted Hindu religious sensibilities and in which anti-Muslim sentiments were openly paraded. Trumpeting a party's secular credentials appeared to have lost some of its charm; appealing to Muslims too openly or too emphatically—a step easily interpreted as such if it involved even a hint of concession to Kashmiri Muslim separatist demands—might only deepen the antagonism of the Hindus that seemed to surface in 1991. Yet attempting to reclaim ground lost to the BJP by trading Muslim for Hindu voters, apart from its likely destruction of the Congress-I's inherited Nehruvian ideology, would scuttle the party's most reliable anti-BJP vote bank while at the same time alienating the leftist parties whose support could at any time prove vital to the Congress-I government's survival in parliament.[17] Congress-I's dismal showing in the legislative assembly election in Uttar Pradesh in 1993 obviously worsens the party's dilemma.[18]

3. Prime Minister Rao's problems were certainly not limited either to political opposition parties or to the capriciousness of Indian voters. They arose very clearly from within the ranks of his own party's leadership. They were traceable, on the one hand, to 73-year-old Rao's limitations as a leader as well as to the existence of powerful and ambitious rivals, such as Sharad Pawar, in 1993 chief minister of Maharashtra, and Madhya Pradesh strongman Arjun Singh, then human resources minister, who seemed prepared to seize upon almost any sign of slippage in Rao's popularity to unseat him. Arjun Singh, for instance, Rao's main cabinet rival, reportedly unleashed a volley of public criticism at his chief—unabashedly accusing him of being uncharismatic and suggesting that allegations of corruption leveled against him by the accused stockbroker Harshad Mehta had to be taken seriously—only days after Rao had narrowly escaped defeat at the hands of the political opposition in the no-confidence motion.[19]

Rao's problems were also traceable, however, to mounting divisions within the Congress-I party over the best way to tackle the BJP challenge and to the belief of some senior party tacticians that the official Congress-I position on Kashmir—which expresses commitment to Kashmir's special constitutional status, viewing it as a natural outgrowth of the unique circumstances surrounding Kashmir's accession to India, and which espouses, in particular, the retention in the Indian Constitution of Article 370—is out-of-date and a major political albatross. Just such a belief seems to have motivated Beant Singh, the

Congress-I chief minister of Punjab, who is said to have stunned a closed meeting of senior civil servants in Punjab in the early months of 1993 with a declaration of clear political heresy. "Why," he asked, without apology and in direct defiance of his party's official position, "can't we [Punjabis] buy land in Kashmir? The Kashmiris can buy land in Punjab!"[20]

4. Last but possibly most important of the circumstances bedeviling the Congress-I party in regard to Kashmir is the very deeply entrenched strength of political conservatives, of individuals with strongly held views opposed to serious concessions of any kind to the Kashmiri separatists, in the country's civil and military bureaucracy. This point was made again and again in the author's interviews in India. A sampling follows:

- The bureaucracy, said a spokesman for the National Conference party and ex-member of parliament from Kashmir, holds the key to *any* plan for Kashmir. The joint secretaries, the second-echelon of bureaucrats, he said, constitute the real decision-making level in the bureaucracy: They have a stranglehold on policy. The Ministry of Home Affairs, in particular, he said, had been infiltrated by people who toed the BJP line on Kashmir. Prime Minister Rao was indecisive, a weak leader, and not likely to take on the bureaucrats over Kashmir.[21]

- A very senior general at Indian army headquarters in New Delhi complained that Kashmir had over the years received far more federal aid than any other state. Kashmiris, he said, could buy property anywhere in India, but no one else in the country could buy property in Kashmir. Educated Kashmiris knew that they had been, in fact, *beneficiaries* of the Indian system; it was the lumpen element—especially the "religious" Kashmiris, who were easily subverted and misled.[22]

- A third-country diplomat remarked that large sections of the central bureaucracy (especially in home affairs, defense, and the intelligence groups) were opposed to extending *any* autonomy to Kashmir on the logical grounds that this would carry inherent long-term risks for India. Autonomy would be a "time bomb" ticking away and bound to go off at some time. "There is *tremendous* resistance to an autonomy offer," he said, "within the government itself." And were the prime minister minded to move in that direction, he would be unable to carry even his own bureaucrats along with him. On this issue there were strong divisions, too, within the armed forces, and the government naturally hesitates to risk alienating them.[23]

■ The real source of the Kashmir problem, a senior Indian civil servant in Srinagar observed, lay in India's domestic political situation. Hindu fundamentalism was gaining strength. Both the army and civil bureaucracy were affected by it. Hardcore conservatives now occupied key positions in the bureaucracy. Their strength explains why a clear Kashmir policy has not yet emerged in New Delhi. They are opposed to compromise. They are indifferent, even hostile to the idea even of talking to the Kashmiris, who mainly want a dignified way out of the insurgency. These hard-liners, according to him, are not overly upset about the complaints of international human rights organizations. They will argue: International pressure? Who cares! Let them pressure us! They can't hurt us.[24]

Many of the things said about the Indian government, certainly by its critics, are mere *caricatures* of it, of course, and cannot be taken as accurate representations either of its capabilities or actual performance. This author doubts, for instance, that in the political tests ahead that the Congress-I will prove quite as politically feeble—or the BJP as politically muscular—as some observers appear to think.[25] Its scarcely secure position in parliament does unquestionably handicap it; but in attempting to cross the political space between 20 percent of the national vote (roughly what the BJP got in 1991) and 38 percent (what the Congress-I received), the BJP—or the Hindu nationalist right wing in general—faces a few handicaps of its own. The Congress-I is down, no doubt, but not out.

Nevertheless, it is apparent to practically any careful observer that the Indian government's "elasticity of decision"—its ability to select rationally from a full array of options in regard to Kashmir state—is today sharply restricted. With only little room for maneuver, it should cause surprise to no one that the prime minister, while his government attempts to cope with the baffling circumstances of Kashmir, appears occupied equally with guarding his political flanks. Surely, this largely explains the content of his 1993 Independence Day speech, made in the midst of bloody attacks in Jammu and Kashmir state both upon Hindu civilians and army troops. In it Rao dwelt at some length on the Kashmir problem. He denounced Pakistan-sponsored terrorist violence and vowed that India would never loosen its grip on the state. "Let Pakistan do anything," he said, "Kashmir is a part of India. Nothing can take it away from us." He said that normalization of relations between India and the new Pakistani government that would take power after elections there the following October required Pakistan to accept that "Kashmir is an inalienable part of India." He also excoriated human rights activists. "They talk of the rights of militants," he said. "What about the rights of the unfortunate victims of militant violence?"[26] In rhetoric, at least, there was little to distinguish between Rao and his right-wing critics.

THE RAJESH PILOT INITIATIVES

As noted earlier in this chapter, Rajesh Pilot was appointed Minister of State for Home (Internal Security) in January 1993. This assignment gave him responsibility for overall supervision and coordination of the government's efforts, on both the civil and military sides, to quell separatist violence in Kashmir. Named to Rao's cabinet (as Minister of Communications) in 1991, and soon recognized as a troubleshooter for the prime minister's forces in problem states, Pilot, at one time an officer in the Indian air force, came to the new job with a reputation for being able, pragmatic, and energetic.

Notwithstanding this reputation, Pilot was described to this author by various Indians (some of them, admittedly, with large axes to grind) as "a damn fool," "a political nothing [who] doesn't count in Delhi," "ambitious but with no obvious talents for the job," "indiscreet and impetuous on occasion, but with some new good ideas," and as being "sincere, but not a mature, seasoned politician." He has taken plenty of flack from the Indian media, some of it almost hysterically hypercritical. For example, after labeling the Congress-I government's policy in Kashmir one of "suicidal drift" and an "unmitigated disaster," a recent issue of the popular newsmagazine *Surya India* placed the blame for it all squarely on Pilot's "blundering personal ambition." The continuing violence in Kashmir, it said, was "not the failure of the security forces, or the consequences of their excesses; it is the unmitigated folly of one man: Minister of State for Home, Rajesh Pilot, that has stoked the fire into a raging inferno [by making ill-considered concessions to the militants], escalating violence, washing away the gains of three years in a veritable river of blood."[27]

Though accompanied on his rounds about New Delhi by a heavy security detail, including a contingent of specially trained antiterrorist commandos (locally known as Black Cats), Pilot in person gives the impression neither of arrogance nor of power-madness. On the contrary, he appears approachable, mild-mannered, open to suggestion, and equipped with a sly wit.[28] His public remarks inevitably contain a hefty dose of sword waving: It was the government's intention, he said at a press conference in June 1993, "to fight the militants with very strong hands." And they are peppered with frequent (and equally inevitable) formulaic references to the government's unequivocal and unalterable intention to retain Kashmir in India. Nevertheless, it is quite clear that Pilot's appointment, which came in the immediate wake of an apparent massacre by security forces of over 40 civilians in downtown Sopore on 5 January 1993,[29] reflected the government's increasing dissatisfaction with the progress of counterinsurgency operations, that it heralded a shift in policy (albeit of uncertain magnitude), and that it was designed primarily to regain the political initiative in Kashmir.

This shift in policy—what we will call the Pilot initiatives (not meaning to credit him personally with their inspiration or, for that matter, to hold him alone responsible for them)—has to date taken shape mainly in: (1) an administrative shakeup in Kashmir, focused in particular on the replacement of key personnel in both civil and military positions in Srinagar; (2) formation of a so-called Unified Command to improve coordination of counterinsurgency operations among the security forces and between them and the civil administration; (3) installation of new routines for the processing, protection, and rehabilitation of detained militants; (4) launching of a variety of schemes (employment, educational, economic development) designed primarily to soak up unemployed Kashmiri youths in the valley; and (5) opening lines of communication to Kashmiri political leaders and to the militants themselves.

Here we need to take a quick look at how each of these five major initiatives was initially implemented and, insofar as is possible after such a short period, to make a preliminary assessment of them.

Administrative shakeup. Pilot's January 1993 appointment as junior minister in the Ministry of Home Affairs, part of a cabinet reshuffle in New Delhi, was followed rather quickly by a series of local administrative changeovers in Srinagar that were obviously meant to put a fresh, politically more conciliatory, face on the civil government. These included appointment of a new governor; reshuffling of the governor's small advisory staff (a de facto cabinet), in particular the appointments of Ashok Jaitley,[30] a senior Indian Administrative Service officer and political liberal with a well-established reputation for espousing soft-line policies on Kashmir, as political adviser and of retired Lieutenant General Mohammad A. Zaki,[31] the ex-commandant of 15th Corp in Srinagar, as military adviser; and replacement of a number of senior commanders of the Border Security Force in the state.

The most important of these moves was the change of governors. Girish Saxena, a former intelligence bureaucrat who had taken over as governor from Jagmohan in May 1990, was replaced in March 1993 by a retired general, the former Chief of Army Staff Lieutenant General (Rtd.) K. V. Krishna Rao. In sharp contrast to Saxena, an undoubted hard-liner with a reputation for tactful sophistication mixed with ruthless professionalism, Rao was a "thinking man's general," the author of a substantial work on Indian security, and a man who mixed an illustrious military career that began in 1942 with practical exposure to the problems of counterinsurgency during his earlier tours (1984–89) as governor of India's troubled northeastern states of Nagaland, Manipur, Tripura, and Mizoram, as well as in his earlier stint (1989–90) as governor of Jammu and Kashmir state.

In a lengthy chapter on counterinsurgency in his book, *Prepare or Perish,* published in 1991, Rao had given fairly clear expression to his views on the appropriate mix of political and military ingredients that ought to go into Indian counterinsurgent strategy. "Insurgency," he wrote, "is basically a political struggle, and needs political actions to eliminate it. The use of force or military means on their own, will not solve the problem. Force is essential, is early necessary to bring the situation under control." Nevertheless, it is essential, he said,

> that the insurgents are isolated and that the bulk of the population is not alienated. Concurrently, political, economic and sociological measures will have to be taken to deal with the main causes of insurgency. Thus, it is a combination of the requisite force and political efforts, that would bring insurgency under control and restore normalcy. It is vital that there is great understanding, cooperation and coordination between the civil and military, for success to be achieved in counter insurgency operations.

The Constitution should be scrupulously observed, he argued, and, whenever possible, problems should be resolved through the democratic process. "All possible assistance," he said,

> should be given to the State in the way of the requisite forces, development of the area, solving unemployment problem, giving good administration, removal of poverty and illiteracy and so on. The efforts should be to educate the people about the futility of carrying out insurgency and to win them over by resolving their problems.[32]

In an interview, Rao (then scarcely five months in office) outlined a four-part "plan of attack" on the Kashmir insurgency that obviously drew upon both his book and his experiences in India's Northeast.[33] First, he said, the security forces in the state, while they had certainly achieved some successes in countering the insurgents, had clearly alienated the public as well—with torture, custodial deaths, molestation, and rape. Military operations against the militants naturally had to be *relentlessly* pursued; but this had to be done without alienating the public any further. The security forces had to win back the public. This meant genuine efforts to meet with the common people, following up on their complaints, taking action against offenders, in addition to better discipline of—and better coordination among—the security forces. Second, the state administration had to be made more honest, effective, and responsive. This, he conceded, "will take some time." It called for unconventional approaches. In fact, it would be harder to accomplish, he conceded, than to change attitudes and practices in the security forces. The malaise afflicting the state administration ran very deep; corruption was rampant.

Third, democratic politics had to be revived. The older parties had to be reactivated; yet the militants would be free either to join them or to form their own. All would be free to fight the elections; whoever won would form the government. *Democracy was to be achieved before the end of the year* (1993).

And fourth, the public had to be won over to the government's side. In a year or so, said the governor, the present heavily military phase of the counterinsurgency would be over. In the meantime, cordon and search operations, whenever possible, had to be targeted strictly against the militants, leaving the innocent population alone. The public had to be told: Expel the militants from your villages; if they fail to leave, report them to the security forces. This appeal, he said, had worked with the Naga tribals in the Northeast, who finally stood up to the militants among them.

The governor's prescriptions for insurgency (whether read or listened to) are, without doubt, optimistic, rationalistic, not to say doctrinaire. As even one of his close associates said, they were far easier for him to articulate than to activate. Outside the tiny circle of the governor's close advisers, the stubborn fact persisted that there were many in the state administration who did not share the views of these "fresh faces" and would prove an extremely stubborn obstacle to change. Moreover, this fact, as we have seen throughout this discussion, was only one of several major such obstacles confronting the governor.

Nevertheless, the administrative shakeup by New Delhi was clearly not just a case of tokenism. The new appointees (Krishna Rao, Jaitley, and Zaki, among others), by Indian standards political moderates at least, coupled with some existing officeholders (such as the present state chief secretary Sheikh Ghulam Rasool, a locally resident Kashmiri Muslim appointed to the post in 1992), unquestionably gave the top echelon of civil government in the state an accommodative look. This look certainly did not warrant the comment in *Surya India* that "the bureaucracy, in its entirety, is riddled with sympathisers for the extremist cause, and is almost completely beyond the scope of discipline"—that many bureaucrats, in other words, were running with the hare and hunting with the hounds.[34] It did imply, however, that New Delhi had extended an olive branch of some size through the Kashmiri gate. It did not alter the fact, of course, that the problem of restoring to Kashmir what both the governor and Pilot liked to call "normalcy" was not going to be one simply of replacing personnel.

Unified Command. The Unified Command was introduced in May 1993. According to retired Lieutenant General Zaki, who in his capacity as military adviser to the governor (having been brought back to Srinagar from retirement in May) also serves as chairman of the Unified Command, its purpose was to institutionalize the coordination of counterinsurgency operations among the several security forces (police, paramilitary, and regular army), both to formalize the informal cooperation already going on and to aid in reducing duplication of functions.[35] The army remained, as pointed out in the last chapter, wholly responsible for defense of the external border, but with expanded responsibilities now for internal security. The paramilitary forces retained primary responsibility for internal security, although there was now reassignment of specific tasks. In particular, the CRPF, as noted earlier, had been removed entirely from active counterinsurgency operations.

The Unified Command, which takes form on a daily basis in early morning meetings of the senior commanders of the various security forces, left overall charge of internal security in the state to the Ministry of Home Affairs, with New Delhi's direction extending through the governor to Zaki. The army's role in internal security was expanded, but not its authority. Nowhere in the state, Zaki explained, did the army exercise exclusive responsibility for internal security.

Notwithstanding the statements of Pilot, Zaki, and the governor that the Unified Command was working very well, many informants took a fairly discouraging view of its performance potential. One, a well-known defense correspondent with extensive military background, argued that the Unified Command, while a good idea in principle, was simply unworkable on the ground. Total distrust, he said, prevailed among the security forces, especially between the regular army and the paramilitary forces. Whatever might be written on paper, he stated, these organizations would not share important intelligence information with one another; in fact, they would spare no effort to mislead and sabotage one another.[36] Another, a former senior (Hindu) bureaucrat, with intimate knowledge of the situation at the senior level of decision making in Srinagar, commented that Zaki, although unquestionably a good soldier, was hardly likely to transform the situation. After all, he said, it was Zaki himself who was in command *and physically present* on 21 January 1990 when his troops opened fire indiscriminately on Kashmiri crowds gathered in Srinagar to protest Indian rule. Zaki, he said, is resented by all of the security forces he is supposed to coordinate and will be unable to compel them to do much against their will.[37]

A third informant, a professional consultant to the Indian army on counterinsurgency, expressed strong support for the idea of a Unified Command, but complained that what the government had created was, in fact, a *disunified* command, with no one really in control and with each security service pitted against the others in order to control its turf. Zaki, he said, had not been given real authority over anything—not the local police, not the paramilitary forces, not the army. Nothing had been accomplished. The government, he suggested, seemed *extremely* reluctant to bite the bullet—to take on the several security bureaucracies and to *force* their cooperation. The Indian army, he said, of all available organizations was the best prepared to compel the changes that were needed in the state. It should be placed in command not only of border defense but of internal security. The latter needed to be yanked from the stifling embrace of the Ministry of Home Affairs. Indeed, a year or so of martial law in the state, with the Ministry of Defense in charge, might very well be the best tonic. The government's half measures, he said, wouldn't work.[38]

Treatment of detainees. Also introduced by the government in May 1993 was a package of preventive procedural rules, designed to curb excessive brutality against the militants by the security forces while at the same time helping to ward off the criticisms of the security forces by human rights groups. The package included (1) beefed-up counterinsurgency training of security troops, including instruction in the special circumstances of insurgency and the enhanced requirement for troop discipline; (2) assignment of local magistrates and JKAP personnel as observers with BSF or army columns on cordon and search operations to prevent abuses and to provide local language assistance; (3) required routine for prompt notification of families in event of arrests; (4) formal, once-monthly screening of detainees by a committee chaired by the director general of police to expedite release of the innocent; and (5) establishment of a mandatory procedure—via so-called speaking orders explaining the circumstances—for reporting custodial deaths to the Ministry of Home Affairs.

A prominent Kashmiri Muslim politician expressed the view that Pilot's package of rules for curbing atrocities, torture, and custodial deaths, while unquestionably well intentioned, was extremely unlikely to have any significant effect. Pilot's assertion, for instance, that he would receive daily reports on security force apprehensions in order to avoid deaths in custody would have no good effect in Kashmir because the very people locally charged with implementing this rule were not motivated to observe it faithfully and Pilot himself was much too far from the scene to superintend personally. The few "soft-liners" he had moved into Srinagar would not be able to control the situation. He pointed out that even he, a politician of no small reputation, was likely to be pushed around by even the lowliest member of a security detail.

In fact, he said, the proliferation of rules, rather than aiding in swift release of detainees, might prolong their agony by interfering with the profitable local business of arranging bribes for their release—the one effective way Kashmiri families still possessed to free their captive menfolk![39]

Employment schemes. Announced on 9 June in New Delhi by the Rajesh Pilot–led Kashmir Cell of the Ministry of Home Affairs was a potpourri of initiatives for Kashmir that included expansion of higher educational facilities, public works projects (repair and construction of roads and bridges), the opening of rehabilitation centers to provide retraining and indoctrination of softcore militants currently under detention, planned reactivation of the governor's Advisory Council, plus the reopening of the Srinagar Passport Office and the Srinagar stations of the radio (All India Radio) and television (Doordarshan) networks. The package drew immediate fire from the Indian press, some of which considered the package heavy on gimmicks and light on resources;[40] and it clearly disappointed the state's administrators in Srinagar, who saw nothing much in it that addressed the state's acute unemployment problem—estimated by the governor at about 80,000,[41] its shrunken revenues, or staggering deficit. Missing, in particular, was a specific reply to the state's public request for allocation of up to 10,000 new slots in the public services, in particular in the *security* forces, to help soak up the valley's army of unemployed—the pool from which the militant organizations presumably drew many of their recruits.

Later in June and in early July, Pilot held a number of interministerial meetings in New Delhi to review these programs and to draw up specific plans. Then in mid-July he led an interministerial group to Srinagar, where these plans were further thrashed out on the ground. While in Srinagar, Pilot reportedly sweetened the package with the announcement that the government's plans included "jobs for 10,000 Kashmiri youth in the state police department." The reply he received was far from encouraging. Some 500 women, who defied a militant-imposed ban on any meetings with Pilot, met him on 15 July on the lawns of a state guest house in Srinagar; but when he tried to talk of the government's plans, the women reportedly insisted upon turning the focus of the gathering to the abuses of Indian security forces. One of them is said to have complained: "We don't want our children put in the government service to fix roads. We want our children who have been taken into custody and tortured by security forces released."[42] Five days later, the JKLF and HMJK jointly called a general strike to protest against the entire government package. According to press reports, the strike paralyzed much of the valley; and even in Doda district in Jammu shops and business establishments were said to have closed. The militants objected to what they said was an effort by the government to pave the way for elections. In a joint statement, the militants registered "their outright rejection of any political process aimed at the settlement of the Kashmir dispute within the framework of Indian constitution."[43] Pilot's efforts had similar results when he made another stab at people-to-people diplomacy in Kashmir about two months later. According to news accounts, a massive strike again paralyzed the valley when Pilot sought contact with Kashmiris during a week-long visit in September.[44]

Talks with rebels. The last of the Pilot initiatives has been a two-track effort to regenerate a democratic political process in the state (1) by opening a dialogue with the Kashmiri militants—at least with the more moderate elements among them—and (2) by encouraging the state's erstwhile political leaders to resume normal political activity. We examine the first of these two tracks here, the second later in this chapter.

In February, then Governor Saxena reportedly arranged for secret meetings in Srinagar between Pilot and a number of militant leaders. There are indications that Pilot also met secretly with a number of imprisoned militants at a maximum security facility near Delhi. Pilot and other government officials have maintained publicly that the channels created then remain open. The pro-Pakistan organizations and more extremist elements in the valley are obviously dead-set against this government initiative; and the risks to more moderate elements of taking the government up on its offer are potentially severe.

Exploiting divisions in the ranks of the militants is an attractive tactic for the government; but in practice it has rarely proved rewarding. Release from prison, for instance, in April 1992 of five Kashmiri political leaders (Syed Ali Shah Geelani of Jama'at-i-Islami; Abdul Gani Lone of People's Conference; and Maulana Abbas Ansari, Qazi Nissar, and Abdul Gani Bhat of the defunct Muslim United Front) has yet to yield any visible benefits for the government; and the killing by assassins unknown on 31 March 1993 of the highly respected cardiologist Dr. Abdul Ahad Guru—a moderate Kashmiri political leader said by some, as we observed earlier, to be acting as a conduit between Pilot and the JKLF[45]—surely was a cold reminder that breaking ranks with the militants was likely to be swiftly punished. The assessment of India's prospects for successful dialogue with the rebels made in June 1993 by a senior official in Pakistan's Ministry of Foreign Affairs seems not far off the mark. Six months earlier, he said, the initiative appeared to be moving along well. Its chances were cut short, however, by the wider implications of the police revolt that year (1993) in Srinagar, by the continued refusal to participate in it by the Kashmiri moderates released from jail, as well as by the unabated demand by Kashmiris for complete independence.[46]

PROSPECTS

Curbing Insurgency

Governor Krishna Rao's confident assertions, noted earlier, that the situation in Kashmir would be significantly improved in a matter of months and that within a year or so the present military phase of the counterinsurgency would be over clearly bear little relationship with reality. So, too, the statements of a senior police official in Srinagar denigrating the militants as nothing but fanatic religious fundamentalists and foreign mercenaries in the employ of Pakistan, and the separatist movement itself as having been utterly criminalized, no longer deserving to be called a movement at all, just as clearly belong in the realm of fantasy.[47] The separatists' tenacity, ingenuity, and ability to foil the government's designs, and the deep sense of alienation from India that seems to be felt by many, if not most, Kashmiri Muslims, have been put on public display too often to be so easily dismissed.

Nevertheless, military professionals *on both sides* of the LOC seem generally agreed that the Indian army is far from nearing exhaustion, that it is learning valuable lessons in counterinsurgency from experience, and that—in due time, for the short term at least, and provided it is not unduly hobbled by political constraints—it is likely to prevail over the militants.

International support of the militants is an obviously important variable in this equation. As for Pakistan, there is no question that Islamabad practically at will can turn the temperature of rebellion either up or down in the valley. But few observers believe—and Kashmiri Muslims least of all among them—that Pakistan's commitment to the Kashmiri separatist cause is great enough either to risk placing Pakistan's own interests in excessive jeopardy of Indian retaliation or to guarantee the militants' survival. *Direct* intervention in Kashmir by Pakistani forces seems extremely unlikely. According to a very senior civil official in Srinagar, the Pakistani military's supervisory activity in the valley was done almost entirely from afar. He said that to date (July 1993) the Indian military was certain of having killed only one known ISI agent since the uprising began, and his killing had occurred only very recently (in May 1993) at a place near Srinagar. The official speculated that Pakistan's army, fearing that its proven direct involvement in Kashmir, quite unlike its involvement in Afghanistan, would only lend weight to the charges of terrorism being leveled against it, prudently conducted most of its business in Kashmir from Pakistan and via proxy agents.[48]

As for the Kashmiris' other putative Muslim allies, here too the potential for support appeared to be considerably greater than its probable delivery. One indication of this was given in Karachi in April 1993 at the twenty first meeting of the 45-member Organization of the Islamic Conference (OIC). The delegates to this meeting listened to a blistering OIC-commissioned fact-finding report on Kashmir that took India to task for brutal violation of the Kashmiris' human rights and that asked member-states to apply pressure on India to end its repression. But while the meeting's final resolutions used unusually harsh language in describing India's actions in Kashmir and included a call to member states to take "all necessary steps" to bring India to stop the abuses, they fell well short of slapping India with real diplomatic and economic sanctions. Instead they urged peaceful negotiation of the problem between India and Pakistan and called upon both countries to redeploy their forces to peacetime locations.[49] The bitter (and rather indiscreet) comment of one separatist leader made to the author in June not long after the OIC's meeting concluded—that the governments of the Muslim countries were "a rotten lot," concerned solely with their own political survival—may have captured the sentiments at the time of most of the militant groups.[50]

Muslim fighters from outside Kashmir, it is true, were reportedly turning up in greater numbers in 1993 than before to fight side by side with their Kashmiri coreligionists. A government official in New Delhi in late August, for instance, put the total of foreigners then fighting in Kashmir at up to 400 and said that since 1991 the security forces had killed 28 Afghans, 22 Pakistanis, a Sudanese, a Bahraini, and 3 other unidentified foreign nationals. At least 18 other foreign nationals had been captured, he claimed, and between 50 and 60 others had been identified by name in interrogations of captive militants.[51] Afghan fighters, in particular, have been officially reported in fairly large numbers in the valley. Among them, apparently, were some close associates of Afghanistan's notoriously combative new prime minister Gulbuddin Hekmatyar, ever since 1990 a vocal supporter of the Kashmiri militants.[52] A BSF estimate at about the same time (August 1993) claimed that the number of Afghans involved in the Kashmir insurgency had climbed to about 300; and the Indian government by then was apparently sufficiently aroused by this development to indicate its intention to take the matter up with Kabul.[53] Senior Indian civil and police officials in Srinagar acknowledged to the author in July that some foreign Muslim volunteers were being funneled into Kashmir. Both the governor and his security adviser, Lieutenant General Zaki, scoffed, however, at the larger figures describing the magnitude of this assistance being reported in the Indian press.[54] The possibility that the figures were being cooked by some officials in the Indian government to extract maximum propaganda advantage could not be dismissed. In any event, the Indian army was far from being overwhelmed by a rush of foreign fighters. For the moment, the direct involvement in the insurgency by Muslim volunteers was clearly more token than anything else.

The Kashmiris were still essentially on their own, with all that that implied for the future of their movement.

Restoring Democracy

The emergency provisions of the Indian Constitution give the central government extremely broad discretion both in regard to the *conditions* warranting the imposition of emergency and in regard to its *extension*. Provided the government suitably amends its proclamation and secures the consent of both houses of parliament (annually according to the Constitution, every six months in practice), the emergency that was first imposed in Kashmir on 5 July 1990—and the direct federal rule of the state (Presidential Rule) stemming from it—could continue indefinitely.[55] There are ample reasons, of course, to avoid an indefinite emergency, including the implication that the government in power lacks the capability to remove the conditions that brought on the president's proclamation of emergency in the first place.

The Congress-I government's publicly expressed priorities in regard to ending the emergency are somewhat ambiguous. At his June 1993 press conference, cited earlier, Pilot, responding to a question as to whether a time frame had been set for elections in Kashmir, replied: "No, there is no time frame. Normalcy is the first priority." When normalcy was restored, he said, without defining the term, the government would turn its attention to resurrecting the political process. And quite in line with this thinking, in late August the emergency was quietly extended for another six months.[56] Pilot's remark—and the government's action—appeared to contradict, however, the repeated and public commitments, already noted, made by the governor to the prompt restoration of democracy in the state.

There was little doubt, in fact, that the government was attempting to move in both directions, albeit far more energetically in the direction of law and order than toward resumption of normal political activity. Pilot's announcement on 9 June of the government's plan to reactivate the governor's Advisory Council, an appointive body that would consist at least in part of local political leaders and that could function as a quasi-legislature plus the government's quiet efforts to reintroduce National Conference leaders back into the valley were clear evidence that the government was at least thinking about resurrecting the political process.

Equally clear, however, were the huge barriers to any such resurrection. Establishment parties were conspicuous by their absence from the valley. The Congress-I had never been a significant factor in valley politics, and any latent support remaining for it, for obvious reasons, was kept either underground or under guard. No senior leaders of the former ruling party, the National Conference, continued to reside in the valley. All had removed themselves, and often their families, to Jammu or entirely out of the state. The topmost leaders, even in distant New Delhi, enjoyed round-the-clock police protection; and none of those who still visited Srinagar from time to time dared to venture beyond the heavily guarded precincts of the secure zone unless under heavy police guard.

One very senior National Conference leader, visiting Srinagar while the author was there, described himself as having been on the militants' "hit list" ever since 1990, when he had fled the valley with his family. The Indian government, he said, clearly wanted an elected government in place in the state; but just as clear, he said, was the fact that it wasn't prepared to take steps *essential* for that to happen. In his opinion, *maximum autonomy* of a *united* Jammu and Kashmir state, embracing all the areas included in the last maharaja's realm in 1947, had to be the government's objective—its *explicit* objective—before any National Conference leader could step foot safely in the valley and take a role in the restoration of the democratic political process. Taken together with his expansive concept of the state's necessary borders, this leader's definition of "maximum autonomy" as the reversion of the state's constitutional status to that held in 1947—that is, to the strong limits on central powers spelled out in the instrument of accession itself—left little room for bargaining and none at all, one can be certain, for resurrecting democracy.[57]

But if a key player in the administrative apparatus set up by the state government to foster political activity in the valley is correct, then even this politician's definition of requirements is too optimistic. According to the bureaucrat, the state's "political healing," if it came at all, would not come in a neat package; it would be very untidy. The political leader was wrong, he said, to think that a specific set of bold promises—an "autonomy package"—would end the insurgency. To this insurgency, he said, there would be no neat terminal point. More government officials—*and more politicians,* he said—were bound to be killed before it ended. One could not just turn off an insurgency. The militants, he observed, were themselves a real political force in the valley, with their own goals and with a degree of commitment. That particular politician, he suggested, might *never* get to walk freely again in the valley.[58]

It is essential, Governor Krishna Rao observed, that the politicians who fled the state come back, meet with the people, and regain their confidence. Like it or not, he said, they will have to take some risks.[59] His is a tall order, however, and there are likely to be very few takers.

It is difficult to avoid the impression that the government's efforts so far to restore democracy in Kashmir, apart from being minuscule in comparison with its military efforts, are, under prevailing circumstances, bound to be futile. The massive counterinsurgency operations themselves, as we have seen, each day inevitably generate additional hostility toward the government. Their suspension—or even reduction—does not appear in the cards; yet unless they are suspended, ridding the political atmosphere of its present deadly threats seems entirely improbable. The cruel fact seems to be that, in Kashmir at least and in spite of any good intentions to the contrary, political democracy and counterinsurgency do not mix.

Part III

The Problem of Settlement

In Part III, *we turn to the problem of "settling" the Kashmir dispute, that is, of resolving, reducing, or at least better managing it. Our task is twofold: first, to examine alternative formats—the bilateral, multilateral, and third-party means or instruments that are available as vehicles for the settlement process; and second, to examine alternative formulas—the specific rules, principles, and desired outcomes that are to govern its conduct and define its objectives. Under the heading of format (Chapter 7), we inspect with particular care the recent record of bilateral diplomacy over Kashmir between India and Pakistan (the Siachen talks). Under the heading of formula (Chapter 8), we undertake a survey and critical assessment of the various models that have been proposed for settling the Kashmir dispute and that might guide the negotiating process. Our purpose remains in large part diagnostic, but it borders now increasingly on the prescriptive.*

CHAPTER

·7·

Dilemmas of Format: The Instruments of Negotiation

There have been numerous efforts since 1947 to ameliorate conflict between India and Pakistan over Kashmir. (For a listing, see Appendix I.) Obviously, none of these efforts led to a full settlement of the conflict; not all of them, however, were complete failures. Our discussion of them is necessarily brief, selective, and largely current in focus. This suits our purpose, which is not one of chronicling the entire history of these developments but rather of attempting to understand the limitations inherent in the institutional formats themselves, that is, in the multilateral, third-party, and bilateral instruments or methods that India and Pakistan have resorted to in the past and are most likely to adopt again in any new round of efforts at settlement. Knowing what the Indian and Pakistani participants in earlier exercises learned of the reasons for the failures or for the occasional successes or partial successes may not make the job of producing agreement between them now any easier; but it should at least help us to appreciate the obstacles along the way.

In this chapter, we assess (1) the overall record of multilateral, third-party, and bilateral (India-Pakistan) efforts to settle the Kashmir dispute, and (2) the particular barriers that have impeded progress in the six rounds of the bilateral Siachen Glacier talks that began in 1986.

MULTILATERAL, THIRD-PARTY, AND BILATERAL OPTIONS: THE RECORD

The record of international (multilateral or third-party) mediative interventions in regard to the Kashmir dispute is clearly mixed: These interventions achieved both some successes and some failures. Among the successes were the cease-fire and truce agreements, discussed earlier in this study, arranged by the UNCIP in 1948 and 1949. The cease-fire agreement didn't hold for long, and the peacekeeping operation that emerged from it failed in large measure to keep the peace. But that failure can hardly be charged exclusively against the United Nations. Among the UN's failures were the several attempts to mediate the Kashmir dispute by UN representatives between 1950 and 1958.[1] Since the latter date, in no case has mediation been applied specifically and explicitly to the Kashmir dispute. British mediation of the 1965 Rann of Kutch crisis between India and Pakistan brought about a cease-fire agreement on 30 June 1965. However, that agreement, which was followed in February 1968 by the successful international arbitration of the Sind-Kutch boundary, applied only to a disputed stretch of the *international* border between India and Pakistan.[2] In January 1966, the Soviet Union successfully mediated an Indo-Pakistan agreement (the Tashkent Declaration) on cease-fire and restoration of peaceful relations, thus providing a formal ending to the 1965 war. This agreement provided for little more, however, than restoration of the territorial status quo ante. It stated that the Kashmir dispute had been discussed and that each side had set forth its respective position in regard to this dispute; but there were no provisions for its amelioration.[3]

From the beginning of the Kashmir conflict, international involvement has been looked upon with a certain amount of suspicion by both India and Pakistan. Both sides have been acutely conscious of the dangers inherent in mediation exercises, among them the mediator's own (and not necessarily compatible) political agenda; and both sides have also been painfully aware that even successful mediation, if it exposed them to charges of a sellout, could lead to domestic political disaster. Neither side's direct experience so far of mediation would in any way have altered those perceptions. Few Indians or Pakistanis, for example, would dispute former diplomat Thomas Thornton's conclusion in regard to the Tashkent mediation that "the only clear winner . . . was the Soviet Union."[4]

Pakistanis, in particular, had very little to show for their reliance on world sympathies save for a rather diluted and ambiguous international commitment to the "self-determination" of Kashmiris. Nevertheless, it has long been clear that the Pakistan government, the holder of the weaker hand in the Kashmir conflict, has been far more willing than its Indian counterpart to gamble on international involvement. Pakistanis have clung tenaciously, of course, to the Security Council resolutions that initially defined the UN's responsibilities in regard to Kashmir, and in particular have given unequivocal support to prospective UN supervision of a plebiscite in Kashmir. Moreover, when India, acting in the spirit of the bilateral Simla Agreement of 1972, barred UNMOGIP officers from investigating reports of violations on the CFL-turned-LOC, Pakistanis, giving the Simla Agreement their own reading, carried on as before as though there had been no change at all in the UN's responsibilities on the LOC.

In recent years, Pakistan's "internationalism" has been growing even more conspicuous. Its policymakers were showing very little hesitation, in fact, in appealing for mediation and for other forms of international intervention to protect the human rights of Kashmiris.[5] Transparent in these appeals was the belief, frequently voiced in Pakistan, that India had never before been quite so vulnerable to them.

Motivating this belief, no doubt, was the fact that Kashmiri self-determination, for the first time since 1947, had acquired an overt, incontrovertible, and deeply anti-Indian content. As noted in Chapter 4, Indians themselves generally conceded at least some Indian responsibility for the onset of the current Kashmir crisis; and they held nearly universally, furthermore, that Kashmiri alienation from India was far advanced. This meant that Kashmiri self-determination was no longer simply an attractive slogan for Pakistan to dangle before the international community, but a legitimate political issue driving an explosive mass movement.

Notwithstanding Pakistani beliefs about India's dilating vulnerabilities, through 1993 there were no clear signs that official Indian views on the issue of international mediation in the Kashmir conflict had undergone any softening. On the contrary, the Indian government seemed as fully opposed as before to any further dilution of the commitment to bilateralism wrung from Pakistan at Simla in 1972. Indians continued to view direct involvement of the international community in Kashmir as degrading India's independence while at the same time jeopardizing its integrity; and Pakistan's efforts to reintroduce it in the region, pretenses to the contrary notwithstanding, were aimed, Indians believed, solely at acquiring international support for territorial claims that Pakistan had not the power to realize on its own.

Any plan for international intervention that envisioned a major expansion in UN activity in Kashmir was thus caught between two strongly opposed points of view. When asked whether they would support an enlarged role for the United Nations in Kashmir, for instance, Pakistanis were almost invariably enthusiastic. "Certainly," responded a Pakistani diplomat to the author in summer 1993. "Why not stretch the role of UNMOGIP on the LOC to cover the Siachen?" Asked the same question, Indians, however, were infinitely more reticent. "We will not like UN intervention," said Foreign Secretary Jyotinder Nath Dixit to the author. Indeed, he stated flatly, the Indian government is firmly opposed to it. Recalling that it was the Indian government itself that had appealed for Security Council intervention in January 1948, Dixit said that had New Delhi delayed its appeal at that time for just one more week, the Pakistani forces would have been pushed out of Kashmir by the Indian army, sparing India years of grief. India had made a serious mistake then, he observed (echoing the sentiments of innumerable other Indians), and it would not make such a mistake again.[6]

If the United Nations would urge Pakistan's noninterference in Kashmir, said Dixit, that would be helpful. Indeed, if it confined itself to *urging* India to seek a settlement, Dixit stated, that too would be all right. But U.S. envoy John Malott's suggestion, made during his visit to New Delhi in May 1993, that thought be given to *reinforcing* the UNMOGIP mandate in Kashmir was, in Dixit's view, "maladroit." The fact is, he said, that UNMOGIP is generally viewed in India as being partial to Pakistan. "We have to fight," he said, "to retain [the military observers] here."

Dixit didn't say so, but an even more basic fact, of course, was that the UN's presence in Kashmir symbolized for Indians their continuing failure to win full international support for their official position, namely that Jammu and Kashmir state, at least that part of it under India's direct control, was an integral part of India and that there no longer *was* a valid dispute over its possession. For the Pakistanis, in contrast, the UN's presence in Kashmir was physical testimony to the basic legality of their territorial claim—to the very existence of the dispute. No wonder, then, that proposals to "beef up" the UN's presence got such divided reviews from South Asian audiences.

There was no question that the UN's organizational role in Kashmir could stand some beefing up. By the 1990s, its peacekeeping mission there, even in the judgment of the military observers themselves, was little more than a silent spectator of events. Ways to strengthen it were easy to imagine. Possibilities included:

1. Improved transport facilities (e.g., helicopters)
2. More observers
3. Deployment of the military observers directly on the LOC, to enable routine patrol, rather than in distant field posts
4. Concrete response by UN headquarters to authenticated reports of major violations of the LOC rather than squirreling them away in UN files

But to glance at these suggestions was to recognize that implementing them meant political intrusion in the dispute and the likely imposition, on one side or the other, of a potentially stiff political price. The option of *forcing* measures like these on India and Pakistan (using the Somalia model of international intervention, in other words) seemed wholly out of the question; and the likelihood of securing their mutual consent to them, given current Indian sensitivities alone, seemed exceptionally remote. Hence, an "activist" model of UN intervention or role expansion in Kashmir had to be judged impractical. By the same token, however, downgrading the UN mandate there, for instance by withdrawing all or part of the observer team, unless it were done as part of a negotiated package to which Pakistan gave its consent, would inevitably appear anti-Pakistani. So a "deactivist" model of UN intervention hardly seemed appropriate either. Unfortunately, as one member of the UN team in Srinagar put it, the present was apparently just not the time for a major UN initiative of *any* kind over Kashmir.[7] Whether this left room for any UN initiative at all in Kashmir is an issue to which we return in Chapter 8.

Turning now to the bilateral approach, we see that, on the subject of Kashmir, it too has been made recourse to by India and Pakistan rather infrequently. True, the Kashmir dispute has been discussed in bilateral talks between India and Pakistan in many different forums, more or less formally, and by officials of widely differing rank and importance, on countless occasions. Since the 1949 cease-fire ending the first India-Pakistan war, however, settlement of the Kashmir dispute has been the explicit, primary objective in direct, formal, and substantive bilateral talks between them on only three occasions—the series of talks held between the prime ministers of India and Pakistan in July-August 1953, the talks held at the same level in May 1955, and the six rounds of ministerial-level talks held between December 1962 and May 1963. (See Appendix I.)

The series of talks held in 1962–63 was the most intensive and long-lasting. In large measure, it was the brainchild of the United States and Great Britain, which appear to have believed that the time was ripe for nudging the two rivals toward a settlement of the Kashmir problem. The Indian side had just experienced military defeat and humiliation at the hands of the Chinese Communist army in the border war of October–November 1962; and its pressing need for arms provided the West with an obvious opening. Unlike the earlier encounters, therefore, this one took place with India, in particular, clearly under some duress and, seemingly, more willing than usual to modify the CFL in a way advantageous to Pakistan. One Indian account of these negotiations claims that the Indian team, led by then Minister for Railways Sardar Swaran Singh, was prepared to concede up to 1,500 square miles of Indian-held territory in Kashmir in return for Pakistan's acceptance of the modified line as a permanent international boundary.[8] According to this account, the chief Pakistani negotiator, then Foreign Minister Zulfikar Ali Bhutto, flatly rejected the offer, telling Swaran Singh that the Kashmir Valley was indivisible and that Pakistan had to have the whole of it.[9] Another Indian participant in these talks maintained in an interview with the author that Swaran Singh, eager to achieve a breakthrough over Kashmir, actually included in his territorial offer to Bhutto a toehold in the coveted Valley of Kashmir itself. According to him, the territorial offer made by India in these negotiations was the maximum offer it ever made on Kashmir.[10] In any event, this series of talks, like its two predecessors, ended in complete failure.

Since then, India and Pakistan have shown little inclination to engage again in direct bilateral talks over Kashmir. On the contrary, they appear in large part to have deliberately steered away from the subject. In fact, apart from the Siachen negotiations, which were quite narrowly focused on issues arising in the last decade over a relatively small, remote, and uninhabited corner of Kashmir, India and Pakistan have made only two more-or-less serious attempts since 1963 even to *initiate* direct, substantive talks between them focused on the Kashmir conflict. And both of these attempts ended in failure.

The first stemmed from the 1966 Tashkent negotiations. As pointed out earlier, those negotiations were focused largely on troop withdrawals and restoration of the prewar status quo. In accord with the Tashkent Declaration's provisions calling for direct talks between the two signatories in regard to their common problems, meetings were held subsequently in Rawalpindi between the foreign ministers of India and Pakistan on 1–2 March 1966. The two sides failed to agree on Kashmir's inclusion on the formal agenda of this meeting, however, and the talks were abruptly terminated.[11]

The second and very recent attempt was in early January 1994 at a meeting of the foreign secretaries of India and Pakistan in Islamabad. Their meeting, the first since August 1992, when worsening relations between the two countries over Kashmir had resulted in the suspension of further talks, was the seventh round of foreign secretary–level discussions held since they were launched as a confidence-building activity in 1990. Indian Prime Minister Rao had suggested resumption of the talks in a letter of congratulations to Benazir Bhutto when she became prime minister of Pakistan for the second time in October. In an unprecedented gesture, his letter had offered a comprehensive dialogue on Kashmir—apparently without preconditions. Kashmir's inclusion on the agenda was itself an accomplishment; but gloomy predictions by observers in the weeks preceding the meeting that it would accomplish little or nothing proved prophetic. Over two days, the two sides spent less than three hours in formal discussions. No progress was reported, and no further talks were scheduled. Neither side made an effort to conceal its disappointment over the results.[12]

These failures are especially disconcerting because India and Pakistan have not availed themselves of the alternative multilateral or third-party options for settling the dispute since the failure of UN mediation efforts in 1958; and, as we have seen, there were no signs recently that these options were gaining in favor on the Indian side.

In recent years, India and Pakistan have, of course, taken a number of steps indicating interest in and, perhaps, increasing capacity for security cooperation at the bilateral level. These steps have included the signing and formal ratification of the nuclear nonattack agreement, as well as a number of agreements on confidence-building measures.[13] Hardly any observers, however, whether Indian, Pakistani, or foreign, have judged these steps to be solid guardrails against the outbreak of war; and many, in fact, have suggested they were designed as much for consumption by public opinion in the West as for conflict management in the subcontinent. None of them, in any event, was focused specifically on Kashmir; and taken all together they most certainly did not supply an adequate measure of the region's "ripeness" for more substantive agreements in regard to conflict management in Kashmir. A more reliable guide to that, perhaps, was to be found in the Siachen negotiations, the most recent major series of bilateral talks between India and Pakistan relating to the boundary in Kashmir, and in the debate that has gone on in both countries since the talks commenced in 1986 over their potential for bringing the two rivals closer to an agreement on Kashmir. We turn to these topics now.

SIACHEN TALKS: THE PERILS OF BILATERALISM[14]

The Siachen Glacier dispute has persisted for almost a decade. In dispute, as we saw in Chapter 2, was a wedge-shaped piece of territory, about 1,000 square miles in size, bounded on the north by the Sino-Pakistan border agreed to in 1963, on the east by the Pakistan-claimed line reaching from map coordinate NJ 9842 (the northern extremity of the LOC) to the Karakoram Pass, and on the west by the jagged peaks of the Saltoro Range. Both India and Pakistan have committed substantial forces to defend their claims to this territory; and so far neither side has given any unambiguous signs of relenting from the struggle. Bilateral negotiations in regard to Siachen were begun in January 1986, some 21 months following the outbreak of fighting on the glacier, and, after six rounds, were suspended without agreement in November 1992.

By the time these talks began, the military situation on and around the glacier itself had settled into a fairly routine pattern of artillery exchanges and local skirmishing. Combat, in any conventional sense, was barely conceivable; and neither side, in fact, seemed anxious either to risk an all-out assault to drive the other from the glacier or to escalate the conflict beyond it. Incentives to end the conflict weren't hard to find. Clearly, continued fighting put considerable pressure on resources and, of greater importance, threatened to taint all efforts to normalize India-Pakistan relations. With no military solution in sight, diplomacy was an obvious alternative.

The talks were held in an environment of political turbulence and upheaval that was extraordinary even by South Asian standards. When they began, Soviet armed forces were still in occupation of Afghanistan, Rajiv Gandhi was in power on the Indian side, and Zia ul-Haq seemed firmly in the saddle on the Pakistani side. When they terminated, the Soviet forces were gone from Afghanistan, the Soviet Union itself had been disbanded, the Cold War was over, and both Rajiv and Zia were dead—the first of them definitely, the second very likely, at the hands of assassins.

The talks were launched with considerable fanfare in both countries and, at least in the popular media, with more than merely perfunctory expressions of optimism. They were formally announced on 17 December 1985 at the close of a dramatic six-hour visit to New Delhi by President Zia—the last stop on his self-styled "journey of reconciliation" to several countries in the region. The visit, Zia's sixth face-to-face encounter with Indian Prime Minister Rajiv Gandhi, was remarkably productive.[15] After only two hours of formal talks, the two leaders adjourned to the airport, where they jointly announced a galaxy of six normalization initiatives. Most notable of these was the agreement—widely hailed as the region's first nuclear confidence-building measure—not to attack one another's nuclear installations. Hardly less notable was Rajiv's acceptance of Zia's proposal that during the first six months of 1986 he make a visit to Islamabad—a visit which, if actually made, would be the first by an Indian political leader to Pakistan since the Indus Waters Treaty was signed in 1960. The announced package also included the decision by the two leaders to initiate formal discussions on the Siachen issue. Signaling the elevated status of this issue on the agenda of India-Pakistan relations, the defense secretaries of the two countries were designated to lead the discussions.[16]

The first round of the Siachen talks was held in Rawalpindi early in January 1986, less than a month following the Delhi Summit and within days of the lifting of martial law in Pakistan. Defence Secretary Syed Ijlal Haider Zaidi led the ten-member Pakistani delegation; his Indian counterpart S. K. Bhatnagar led a six-member delegation from India. As in subsequent rounds, army officers and Defence Ministry civilians were predominant on both teams. The discussions, spread over two days, were devoted largely to the formal statement of the two sides' respective positions on the dispute.[17] Pakistan's basic argument was that India's military action in the Saltoro Range was a direct violation of the provision in the Simla accords barring the threat or use of force to bring change in the LOC resulting from the cease-fire of

17 December 1971. In support of this argument, the Pakistani team produced a large wall map with the LOC shown running northeastward in a straight line from NJ 9842 to the Karakoram Pass on the border with China. This extension of the LOC, they insisted, along with Pakistan's right to administer all territory lying westward of it, was implicit in the 1963 Sino-Pakistani Border Agreement. India's tacit acceptance of Pakistan's authority in this territory, they said, was a matter of record. (See Chapter 2.) The Indians responded that Pakistan was itself in violation of the Simla accords, which barred not only the threat or use of force but any attempt at *unilateral* alteration of the LOC. At the close of these discussions, on 12 January, the conferees issued a brief joint statement expressing their resolve to seek a negotiated settlement in accordance with the spirit of the Simla agreement and promising to meet for a second round in New Delhi in March or April.[18]

The second round was postponed until June. Zaidi and Bhatnagar again led their delegations. The talks were reportedly held in a "cordial and friendly atmosphere," and it was agreed, upon their conclusion, that the dialogue should be continued at a later date. There were no signs of any material progress, however, and, according to a Pakistani diplomat, the second round was highly repetitious, a "pantomime," he said, of the first.[19]

Long before the second round began, however, it had already become quite apparent that the Delhi Summit, notwithstanding the flurry of agreements reached, had made practically no dent in the traditional enmity of India and Pakistan. The agreements had been entirely verbal; and within two months of the summit, in fact, most of them were seen to be unraveling, some of them with astonishing rapidity. The only substantive progress was a trade promotion accord reached by the Indian and Pakistani finance ministers in early January; but the follow-up meetings intended to implement this accord failed to materialize.[20] Meetings in the early months of 1986 of the Indian and Pakistani foreign secretaries were unable to reconcile differences in the draft treaties of nonaggression, peace, and friendship; and the nuclear nonattack commitment languished until after Zia's death.[21] In regard to Rajiv's proposed visit to Pakistan, impediments began surfacing in the press in late February; and in May—about a month before the Siachen discussions were set to resume—New Delhi announced its indefinite postponement.[22]

Distrust of one another's intentions seemed greater than usual. Indians, for their part, suspected that Zia's "peace offensive" had more to do with coaxing a renewed security assistance package out of Washington, an item then under negotiation, than with fostering improved relations with India. And Pakistanis, for their part, were equally suspicious that New Delhi's burst of enthusiasm for regional reconciliation stemmed more from its need for U.S.

technology transfers, also under negotiation at the time, than from sincere interest in good-neighborly relations.[23]

The moment, in any event, was hardly ripe in South Asia for negotiating an issue as delicate as Siachen. Indeed, far from witnessing speeded-up normalization, in 1986 the number of angry charges and countercharges exchanged between the political leaders and media of India and Pakistan reached a near-record level. To note merely some of them is to recognize the scale of the problem faced then and later by the region's advocates of subcontinental detente. Indians, on the one hand, accused Pakistan of backing Sikh terrorist activities in East Punjab; of provoking a conventional arms race in the region with the import of sophisticated offensive weapons from the United States; of threatening a nuclear arms race; of undermining the Simla accords by harping insistently on the Kashmir issue in international forums; of blocking the expansion of regional trade; of supplying arms to Sri Lanka for use against ethnic Tamils; of failing to seek justice in the trial of five Sikh extremists involved in the 1981 hijacking of an Indian aircraft to Pakistan; of mishandling the hijacking by Sikhs of a Pan Am airliner at Karachi airport; and even of involvement in an abortive assassination plot against Prime Minister Rajiv Gandhi. Pakistanis, on the other hand, accused India of instigating Hindu-Muslim communalism and of mistreating the Muslim minority of India; of supplying military assistance to the Soviet-backed regime in Kabul; of physical assault on a Pakistani diplomat in New Delhi; of flagrant interference in Sri Lanka and of propagating a sinister Indian version of the Monroe Doctrine; of denying the right of Kashmiri Muslims to self-determination; and of threatening war by massing Indian troops near the Pakistan border during the Indian army's Operation Brass Tacks military exercises in the latter part of the year.

The Brass Tacks exercises had an especially chilling effect on India-Pakistan relations. Launched in late autumn 1986 in the border state of Rajasthan adjacent to Pakistan's politically troubled Sind province, they involved hundreds of thousands of troops and were the largest in India's history. They prompted Pakistan, whose forces were also engaged in autumn exercises, to order a countermobilization of its own. In January 1987, when both sides massed troops and armored formations along the Punjab border, India and Pakistan seemed perilously close to war. The Pakistanis accused India of masquerading as war games a planned attack on the lightly defended Sind border; the Indians, in turn, accused Pakistan of concocting the threat of war to gain propaganda advantage over India. To many observers, Operation Brass Tacks seemed clearly intended to intimidate Pakistan, perhaps "to remind Islamabad of India's regional primacy, to persuade Pakistan to terminate alleged support for Sikh terrorists, or simply to provide a foreign distraction for domestic political purposes."[24] In the view of at least one Indian defense analyst, it was not an "exercise" at all, in fact, but a calculated attempt to provoke Pakistan into war with India.[25] Whatever the truth, it dealt a major setback to the normalization process, in general, and to the Siachen talks in particular.

India and Pakistan moved swiftly to defuse the Brass Tacks crisis. On 4 February 1987, they reached agreement to begin withdrawing newly deployed troops from their border.[26] Existing distrust had, however, been substantially reinforced. Hence, it was not until November 1987, by which time the atmosphere had improved considerably between India and Pakistan, that the decision was taken to resurrect the talks over Siachen.

After a lapse of just under two years, the third round was held in Rawalpindi in May 1988. Both sides seemed this time to take a more serious view of the negotiations. The atmosphere was more relaxed than in earlier rounds; and discussion, especially in the informal and intensive sessions that developed among some of the participants, moved away from restatement of formal positions and toward specific proposals for bringing about disengagement of military forces. At this point, however, both sides were clearly sensitive to the fact that disengagement, quite apart from purely military considerations, could entail heavy domestic political costs. The Siachen situation had in the long interval between the second and third rounds developed into a troublesome issue in the tussle for power in progress between President Zia and Benazir Bhutto; and it was more than likely that India's compliance with Pakistan's demand for a unilateral withdrawal of Indian forces from Siachen would unleash similar difficulties for the Indian political leadership. Face-saving formulas of disengagement were evidently explored. According to a Pakistani participant, the Pakistani delegation expressed its willingness, for example, to spare India embarrassment by reformulating in more neutral terms its proposal for military disengagement—that is, to substitute *redeployment* of (both) forces to pre-Simla positions in place of *withdrawal* of (Indian) forces.[27] Notwithstanding such efforts, these talks too ended inconclusively with, however, a promise to meet again for a fourth round.

The fourth round had been set for New Delhi in September. Zia's death occurred in August. Pakistan's interim government then announced that it would hold elections the following November to choose a new civilian leadership. These surprising developments obviously placed the Siachen negotiations in a new, and rather uncertain, political context. The Pakistanis moved, nevertheless, to carry on with the talks as planned. This step, according to a Pakistani delegate, was meant to assure India's recognition that Pakistan intended to maintain continuity in its India policy.[28] Once again, the talks provided a forum for candid informal exchanges in regard to specific issues. As expected, however, this round too had few concrete results.

The fifth round of the Siachen talks was held nine months later, in June 1989, this time in Rawalpindi. This round followed Benazir Bhutto's accession to the office of prime minister of Pakistan. Bhutto was widely felt to be less encumbered with anti-Indian stereotypes than the older generation of Pakistani leaders. With Rajiv Gandhi she seemed to share not only youth but a progressive view of the need for regional cooperation. These factors, along with others, stimulated some observers to suggest that the setting was more propitious for settlement than before and that a breakthrough in India-Pakistan relations was possible.[29] To be sure, that optimism was not based on evidence of solid progress in the four preceding rounds. On the contrary, about all that the previous Siachen negotiations appeared to have produced was a fairly clear definition of the two sides' *formal* negotiating positions and of the substantial gap that remained between them.

Indian and Pakistani participants in the fifth round of discussions described the two sides' initial positions in this round in nearly identical language. The Indian terms, as given to the author in a briefing at Indian army headquarters in New Delhi on 12 June 1990, were six in number:[30]

1. *Cessation* of "cartographic aggression" by Pakistan (that is, of its unilateral attempts to extend the LOC from its agreed terminus at map reference point NJ 9842 to the Karakoram Pass on the border with China).[31]
2. *Establishment* of a demilitarized zone (DMZ) at the Siachen glacier.
3. *Exchange* between India and Pakistan of authenticated maps showing present military dispositions on the ground.
4. *Delimitation* by India and Pakistan of a line from map reference point NJ 9842 northward to the border with China "based on ground realities."
5. *Formulation* of ground rules to govern future military operations in the area.
6. *Redeployment* of Indian and Pakistani forces to mutually agreed positions. This was "the last step" to be taken.

Pakistan's terms by the opening of the fifth round of talks, in contrast, were fewer in number. As identified for the author by members of the Pakistani delegation, they contained only two essential points:

1. *Redeployment* of Indian and Pakistani forces to mutually agreed positions held at the time the cease-fire was declared in 1971 (i.e., pre-Simla positions). And only then

2. *Delimitation* of an extension of the LOC beyond map reference point NJ 9842.

These two sets of terms appeared to be almost diametrically opposed. India was insisting on the primary importance of coming to agreement first on fixed, legitimate *boundaries* (whether of a DMZ, present military dispositions, or the actual delimitation of an extended LOC); Pakistan, on the other hand, was insisting that *military withdrawal* from the contested area (reestablishment, in other words, of the vague territorial status quo ante) had to precede everything else. True, the language was ambiguous and there was plenty of room for interpretation. No one, for example, could be certain of the precise location of pre-Simla military deployments; and a delimitation "based on ground realities," while obviously favoring India, did not rule out compromise in regard to the alignment of an extended LOC. Nevertheless, there was a fundamental antilogy in the *sequence* of steps to be taken. Given the circumstances each side faced in the Siachen conflict, these positions were hardly unexpected. The question, of course, was whether they were at all negotiable.

The fifth round of talks, still at the defense secretary–level, began on 15 June 1989. Surprisingly, as this round progressed the difficulties seemed to give ground. The first sign of this came in the joint statement issued in Rawalpindi on 17 June upon the conclusion of the talks. The statement revealed few details; but it clearly gave the impression that agreement on some fundamental matters had been reached. According to press accounts, the statement said that the two delegations had discussed specific proposals aimed at an early settlement of the Siachen issue in accordance with the Simla Agreement. There was agreement by both sides, it said, to work toward a comprehensive settlement based on redeployment of forces to reduce chances of conflict, avoidance of the use of force, and the determination of future positions on the ground so as to conform with the Simla Agreement and to ensure durable peace in the Siachen area. Army authorities of the two sides were to determine future positions. The next round of talks between the defense secretaries was to be held at New Delhi in the near future.[32]

The joint statement's phrasing, in particular its affirmation that the two countries sought "a comprehensive settlement based on redeployment of forces," was interpreted by Pakistanis to mean that military withdrawal from the Siachen had been agreed in principle and that, in the sequence of steps envisioned in the settlement, it would have priority—precisely what their negotiating team had been demanding all along. Interpreting the statement as a potentially significant shift in the Indian position and an important gain for Pakistan, Pakistanis appeared elated.[33] Indians reacted more guardedly to the results of the fifth round, stressing that the agreement had only laid down broad principles for follow-on negotiations. But even sections of the Indian press allowed that the agreement spelled a major concession to Pakistan.[34]

Reinforcement of the impression that Pakistan had indeed wrung a major concession from India in the talks came the day following release of the joint statement. On that day, separate talks between Foreign Secretary Dr. Humayun Khan of Pakistan and his Indian counterpart, S. K. Singh, had concluded. The Indian foreign secretary had flown to Islamabad in the midst of the fifth round of Siachen talks to hold what was announced as a comprehensive review of bilateral relations between India and Pakistan. S. K. Singh, who had been India's ambassador to Pakistan from 1985 to 1989, had a reputation for being friendly to Pakistan, for having built unusually close rapport with President Zia, and for favoring reconciliation. Dr. Khan, who had recently been Pakistan's envoy to India, enjoyed a similar reputation among Indians. Neither of the foreign secretaries had attended any of the defense secretary–level talks going on in Rawalpindi. On 16 June, they had, however, joined the leaders of the two delegations to the Siachen talks in a roughly two-hour discussion with Prime Minister Benazir Bhutto. Also in attendance at this meeting were General Mirza Aslam Beg, chief of the Pakistan Army Staff, and several members of the prime minister's advisory staff. It was on this occasion, it seems, that the decision was taken to proceed with the Siachen talks on the basis of the principles contained in the joint statement announced on the following day.[35]

The foreign secretary–level discussions concluded on 18 June with a joint press conference at Islamabad airport. About what was said by the two foreign secretaries at this press conference, there is not much disagreement. About the meaning of what was said, however, there is considerable controversy.

Dr. Humayun Khan began the session by outlining in general terms the progress of recent bilateral talks between India and Pakistan, including those over the Siachen Glacier. In response to a question, he expressed his understanding of the essence of the agreement reached in the Siachen negotiations. His explanation furnished a crucial detail absent from the joint statement. What he said, according to virtually all reports, was that both sides had agreed to withdraw their forces *to positions held at the time of the Simla accord* (July 1972) and that senior army officers from both countries would now meet to identify these positions.[36] When called upon for his reaction, S. K. Singh—whether in response to Dr. Khan's general statements or to his more specific comments on the Siachen agreement is disputed—expressed his agreement with what had been said. If the Indian foreign secretary had any reservations about Dr. Humayun Khan's comments, he did not utter them at the time.[37] Hardly had news reports of these developments gone out over the local and international airways, however, when the agreement over Siachen—to the extent there was any—began to unravel.

The next morning, in fact, the press was summoned to South Block in New Delhi to be informed by Aftab Seth, a joint secretary in the Ministry of Information and Broadcasting, that no agreement had been reached with Pakistan in regard to the withdrawal of forces from the disputed glacier to pre-Simla positions.[38] Then and in later encounters with the press, Indian spokesmen were at pains to point out that the Indian foreign secretary had not intended to endorse Dr. Khan's specific observations on the Siachen talks, that the wording in the joint statement in regard to redeployment had been misinterpreted,[39] that there had been no more than an agreement on approach in the defense secretary–led negotiations, and that the agreement's principal accomplishment, in fact, had been to get Pakistan to join India in renouncing the use of force to settle the issue. They emphasized that, while there had not yet been agreement on an extension of the LOC, a "major step forward" had been the decision to show the positions of the two armies in the area. When that was done (and only then), the two countries could move to consider the problem of force redeployment.[40]

Spokesmen for the Pakistani government maintained, in reply, that the statement's wording was unambiguous, that it clearly implied that the glacier—all of it—would soon be vacated of Indian troops, and that only after that was done were all other matters to be sorted out.[41]

Pakistani officials involved in the negotiations insisted in interviews with the author that the fifth round had been conducted in "real earnest," that the joint statement issued on 17 June had, in fact, been a signal achievement, and that the agreement reached had been, in the words of one senior diplomat, a "thrilling outcome." The Pakistani delegates were convinced, they said, on the basis of their informal discussions with their Indian counterparts, that there *was* an agreement, even if informal, and that the agreement was that redeployment (simply a euphemism for withdrawal from Siachen) would occur first, delimitation afterward. They had explained to their Indian counterparts, they said, that there was no urgent need for either India or Pakistan to mount a hasty delimitation of the LOC in the Siachen area. This area held no population, no minerals, and no strategic interest. What was urgent, the Pakistanis had argued, was clearing the Siachen Glacier of troops—a reversion, in other words, to pre-Simla conditions—leaving both sides' claims to the territory intact pending the outcome of negotiations.

Discussion of the territorial question during the fifth round brought into full view the fundamentally antinomic relationship between the Indian and Pakistani positions on the Kashmir boundary problem. Indian delegates to the talks argued from the premise that the Indian army's *control* of key passes in the Saltoro Range warranted recognition of Indian territorial *rights* to the

Siachen Glacier. In particular, they insisted that any steps toward demilitarization of the glacier (that is, the withdrawal of Indian and Pakistani troops from forward positions in its vicinity) would have to follow agreement on the extension of the LOC to the Chinese border. This extension, they suggested, should follow the high crest of the Saltoro Range and run in a generally northeasterly direction. They designated this extension the Actual Ground Position Line (AGPL), distinguishing it in name but not in function from the LOC. The Indians, according to Pakistani sources, kept trying to introduce a more complicated package. They talked about a "limited" disengagement, about a "thinning out" of forces on the glacier. They tried hard, said the Pakistanis, to get the Pakistani delegation to commit itself to practically any kind of mutually agreed boundary in the Siachen area, at one point indicating that they would be content to do without a precise line identifying present force positions if only the Pakistanis would consent to rows of dots! For the Pakistanis, however, fixing a precise boundary in Kashmir was in principle not negotiable, not at least until certain political prerequisites had been satisfied. Pakistani negotiators conceded that the LOC might eventually be extended to the Chinese border; but they clung tenaciously to the view that its extension could come only *following* demilitarization of the glacier and its immediate vicinity. For them, in other words, a complete and unequivocal pullout of Indian forces—India's tacit relinquishment of title to the glacier—was the sine qua non of an agreement. Without it, Pakistan's already paper-thin "custodial" claim to the glacier, from the Pakistani viewpoint, seemed very likely to be shredded.

By the end of the fifth round, in the Pakistani view, there existed a clear understanding on both sides on the order of precedence to be given redeployment, that there was "no immediate urgency to undertake delimitation"; as one Pakistani diplomat put it, "it can take years."[42] The Pakistanis insisted, furthermore, that their public statements at the time were part of a calculated effort to make their position clear and explicit, and that Dr. Humayun Khan's comments at Islamabad airport, in particular, had been fully rehearsed with (and approved by) the Indian delegation. Nevertheless, the spare and convoluted language of the joint statement issued on the conclusion of the defense secretary–led talks on 17 June lent itself to virtually any interpretation; and even if Dr. Humayun Khan's press conference amplification of the agreement's specific contents was wholly accurate, as even some Indians claimed, his disclosure of them may well have been premature.[43]

A senior Indian diplomat involved in the negotiations agreed that toward the end of the fifth round of the Siachen talks, the two sides seemed on the verge of settlement. Both sides, he said, were agreed on the need to redeploy their forces and to demilitarize the glacier. Both sides were agreed, moreover, on jointly conducted weekly or biweekly helicopter patrols of the glacier to keep the peace. The Pakistani civilians involved in the negotiations, including Prime Minister Benazir Bhutto, seemed, in the opinion of this official, to want to deescalate the conflict and supported redeployment. So also, he said, did Chief of Army Staff General Beg. Others among the Pakistani delegation, however, in particular certain military members, took a very hard line, resisting settlement. The Indians, he insisted, were *not* trying to drive a hard bargain. They wanted a settlement of the Siachen problem, he emphasized, and they did *not* insist on extending the LOC at that time. The Indians, in fact, according to this individual, did not insist on any boundaries at all in the negotiations, only on mutual withdrawal or redeployment of forces and joint policing of the glacier.[44]

A senior Indian military participant in the negotiations echoed his diplomatic colleague's emphasis on the crippling effect on the talks exercised by serious divisions of opinion within the Pakistani delegation. "Their military," he said, "wanted a solution when Zia was still in power." But when Benazir took power, he observed, the Pakistan army changed its tune and wouldn't "allow Benazir to get a settlement." The Pakistan army's insistence on mutual withdrawal of forces to pre-Simla positions, the real location of which no one really knew, he said, was a deliberate effort to scuttle the talks. Assuring the failure of the talks, in fact, was the real motivation, he insisted, behind Pakistani opposition to taking the essential initial step toward redeployment—the joint recording of *present* military deployments. This commentator insisted that confusion had marked the Pakistani side in the negotiations from the beginning, and that "confusion compounded" had marked the fifth round. No one on the Pakistani delegation, he said, possessed complete authority to negotiate. Chaos reigned and contradictory statements were commonplace. Pakistani confusion made the talks difficult and "inconvenient." The Pakistanis, he averred, held no clear range of options, no clear brief. They constantly had to clear matters with higher-ups.[45]

Pakistanis were as quick as the Indians to blame the other side's military hard-liners for obstructing a settlement. The breakdown in the negotiating process that came hard on the heels of the fifth round of talks, said a Pakistani member of the negotiating team, was basically the result of disagreement between the Indian army and the civil government. The civil government, he argued, was more inclined to pursue a settlement; the military—which was in a position to embarrass the central government if it did not get its way—was less inclined. It was not, he emphasized, India's imminent elections or domestic political opposition to the redeployment idea that explained Indian resistance to a settlement. Indeed, to accommodate the Indians in this regard, he clarified, the Pakistanis had offered to delay implementing redeployment until after the elections were over. "We were cheated of the settlement," he said.

In spite of the controversy over the fifth round of talks, consultations over Siachen continued between the two countries for another two months following the altercations in June. Pursuant to the June agreement, military commanders' talks on Siachen were held in New Delhi between 9 and 10 July. These talks, led by senior army officers of each country, were described as preliminary to the setting up of a joint military commission whose task would be to mark ground positions on the Siachen. They reportedly focused on draft proposals for demilitarizing the Siachen, that is, for operationalizing the provision on force redeployment agreed to in the fifth round.[46] On their conclusion, no joint communiqué was issued. Each side later accused the other of deliberately undermining these discussions.

A member of the Pakistani negotiating team in these discussions argued, for instance, that it was already clear by the July meetings that New Delhi was not serious about a settlement. The Indian team's proposals, he said, were "so absurd that they must have been ashamed to put them across." For one thing, he said, the Indians insisted on maintaining a supposedly civilian base camp on the Siachen, seriously diluting the principle of troop withdrawal. The base camp was to be located on a small "connecting" glacier in the vicinity of Bilafond Pass. The Indians, he said, claimed that the base would be strictly for civilian use and that its facilities, including a helipad, would support foreign mountaineering expeditions to the glacier. To the Pakistanis, this officer observed, this proposal was simply ridiculous. The Indians, he averred, were insisting in the same breath that the Pakistanis vacate entirely all military positions they had taken in the vicinity of the Siachen since 1972. In practice, he observed, this meant Pakistani withdrawal from its militarily vital posts on adjacent Baltoro Glacier, including those at Conway Saddle, the International Himalayan Expeditionary Camp, and so on. This too, the Pakistanis felt, was "absolutely absurd," since it would position the Pakistani military scores of miles distant from the Siachen Glacier itself. The Indians, he pointed out, were demanding that their own forces redeploy only so far as their main base camp at Dzingrulma at the eastern end of the glacier. That, he said, would leave them with a full military presence at the glacier's snout and with a quasi-military presence (in the form of a "civilian" mountaineering camp) at its center.[47]

To his claims, senior Indian diplomats retorted that by "redeployment" the Pakistanis apparently meant only *Indian* withdrawal, and that it was the Pakistanis, in fact, who were insisting on maintaining in the immediate vicinity of the Siachen threatening military outposts that were clearly post-Simla in origin.[48]

A week following the meeting of the army delegations in New Delhi, Prime Ministers Rajiv Gandhi and Benazir Bhutto met for a two-day summit conference in Islamabad. Gandhi's trip was heralded as the first state visit to Pakistan by an Indian leader in nearly 20 years. There had been reports that a Siachen treaty might be signed during his visit. By the time of his arrival in Islamabad, however, expectations that the meeting would produce a major breakthrough in India-Pakistan relations had dimmed considerably.[49] The joint communiqué issued at the end of the summit meeting reported that the two leaders had endorsed the results of the fifth round of talks on Siachen and had directed their defense secretaries to continue working toward an agreement based on the principals expressed in the June joint statement.[50] It was apparent from their remarks at a joint press conference concluding the summit, however, that such an agreement was far from imminent. Both went to some lengths to stress that the Siachen issue was very complicated and that there could be no quick-fix answers to it.[51] A London publication headlined its dispatch on the meeting "Cold War Ends" and opined that "the amiable exchanges between the two prime ministers during Mr. Gandhi's visit . . . suggest that things are proceeding smoothly."[52] Closer to the mark, it seems, was an editorial in a Pakistani newspaper that described the joint communiqué as a "damp squib" and hinted at deep underlying differences.[53]

On 17 August, military teams representing the two armies gathered in Rawalpindi for one last effort to breathe life back into the Siachen talks. Revised proposals for implementing redeployment were again reviewed. The talks concluded on 20 August without any visible signs of progress. Both sides offered reassurances that there had been no collapse in the negotiations and that the agreement to redeploy their forces still stood.[54] For the moment, however, further discussion appeared pointless. After the August round, the talks were indefinitely suspended.

Just how close India and Pakistan actually came in June 1989 to an agreement over Siachen is obviously debatable. There is no doubt, however, that the explosion of separatist violence only months later in the Valley of Kashmir dealt a nearly lethal blow to the entire idea. Whatever momentum had been gathering between the two governments for a settlement of Siachen vanished almost overnight, to be replaced by steady volleys of angry charges and countercharges, menacing troop buildups and maneuvers along both the international and Kashmir borders, and—at least in the judgment of some observers—even the threat of a nuclear exchange.[55] Debate over Siachen persisted into the new decade, however, especially among Indians, and in some ways grew even more robust.

Public debate at this time focused on the question of whether the strategic or other benefits to be gained by either country from control of the glacier could conceivably warrant the heavy human and material costs involved in protracted struggle. The argument on one side in this debate was that the Indian army's seizure of the glacier in 1984 was a serious blunder that was only compounded by the continuing refusal to reach a settlement over it with Pakistan. Clearly contributing to this school of thought were the widely publicized comments of a retired lieutenant general, M. L. Chibber, who headed the Indian army's Northern Command when India seized the Siachen in 1984. Chibber, who retired from the army in 1985, has acknowledged that he was one of a small group of influential senior officers who began lobbying in the late 1970s for a more aggressive Indian policy toward the disputed Siachen territory. There is some irony in the fact, therefore, that his was the first authoritative military or political voice in India to call publicly for negotiated withdrawal from the glacier. Indeed, few in India put the case for compromise over Siachen more strongly than he.[56]

In an interview with the author, Chibber declared flatly that the Indian and Pakistani armies had "stumbled" into the Siachen dispute. The Pakistanis, he said, had no grand strategic design on the glacier and were not acting in collusion with the Chinese. That idea, he observed, was a post facto concoction of Indian bureaucrats. Pakistan's protests over Indian "incursions" onto Siachen in 1982 and 1983, he noted, simply hadn't attracted much attention in India. They were easily overlooked, he said, against the background of constant provocations and firings along the lengthy LOC. India's military occupation of the Saltoro passes in spring 1984, he pointed out, was meant only to deter the Pakistanis from getting to them first; the Indian army had no plans for permanent occupation. At bottom, he said, the Siachen conflict was a mistake.[57]

Chibber was not the only member of the Indian military elite at this time to have expressed such views. Seated in spring 1991 in the offices in New Delhi of the *Indian Defence Review,* one of India's leading defense journals, the author listened, for example, as two well known and widely published defense analysts—both of them, like Chibber, very senior retired army officers—declared the Siachen glacier to have no military value to either side. Neither country, said one of them, a retired major general, ever anticipated the scale of the struggle into which the Siachen dispute would grow. It was now a "monster," he said, and was out of control.[58]

Voices fueling the other side in this debate were just as emphatic that India's Siachen venture was not only readily manageable but, far from being a blunder, was paying India rich dividends. Briefings given Indian newsmen by Indian army spokesmen at the Siachen battlefront in late August 1989, for instance, appear to have laid particular emphasis on the ease of continuing to hold the glacier against the Pakistani challenge. The general officer in command of the Siachen sector, according to one account,

> was at pains to assert that the Indian hold on the glacier was not tenuous as made out by some sections of the media and that in fact over the years the logistical infrastructure as well as the combat positions [of the Indian forces] had been strengthened. In fact, the experience gained over the years had given the Indian side considerable confidence and the deployments had become much stronger. He went as far as to say that from the point of view of combat the Indian side had an "easy, confident, laid-back style" with considerable support available to the troops in terms of artillery fire, equipment and logistics.[59]

The most arresting manifestation of dissension over Siachen in the Indian army to have been experienced by the author, however, occurred during the question-and-answer session that followed his lecture "The Siachen Dispute" in the Ministry of Defence in New Delhi on 31 May 1991. The lecture, in building a case for a negotiated settlement, had emphasized the point that the Siachen had no apparent military or strategic value. Responding to the author's remarks, retired Lieutenant General M. N. Kaul, who, like Chibber, had at one time commanded the Indian army's Northern Command, identified himself as the one who had pushed hardest for the Indian army's moves to secure control of the Siachen Glacier. It was he, he said, who had supervised planning and organizing of the army's early scouting expeditions to the Siachen in the late 1970s. The Indian army's interest in the area had developed quite early, he insisted, aroused by Pakistan's own developing interest in it. The "taking" of Siachen, he stated, was a long-term, systematic effort, made in response to strategic compulsions, in particular the need to avoid a repetition of the disastrous events that had befallen India in the late 1950s in the Aksai Chin region of Ladakh. There was, in other words, much interest in and considerable activity on and around the glacier by the Indian army long before fighting actually broke out there in 1984. The point, he said, was that the Siachen *had* military and strategic importance. India could not afford to leave the LOC unfinished. Even if the glacier's strategic value were minimal today, he said, the probability was strong that it would acquire such value in the future.

Chairing this meeting was Lieutenant General Z. C. Bakshi, a much-decorated and well-known officer who had retired in 1979 after serving as director general of military operations and as commander of Northern Command. Himself a Kashmiri with many years of service in Kashmir, Bakshi chose to conclude the two-hour gathering with a pair of anecdotes, both of them obviously chosen to illustrate the point that *at no time* prior to the 1980s, in his knowledge, had anyone in the Indian army high command ever given any serious thought whatsoever to the Siachen. In fact, he said, the high command, with every member of which, he pointed out, he was on close terms, had on a number of occasions categorically declared the area to be of no military or strategic importance. Whether intended or not, it was a clear rebuff of Kaul. How many in the audience, which consisted of several score active and retired senior officers from the various services, agreed with Bakshi was impossible to determine.[60] That there was at least *some* dissent in the Indian army over this issue had, however, been clearly established.

Inevitably, the dissent over Siachen apparent in the upper ranks of the Indian army began surfacing with some regularity in the Indian press. Commentaries focusing on the extravagant costs, high casualty rates, and pointlessness of the Siachen operation replaced those that had boasted of the bravery, endurance, and exploits of the Indian troops dug in at such spectacular and forbidding elevations. Typical was the assessment in May 1992 of one of India's leading newsmagazines, in which India's Siachen adventure was described as "a diplomatic and military disaster, a waste of such magnitude that it should be graded as a crime against humanity."[61] The Indian and Pakistani governments, it claimed, were together spending about $1.2 million per day maintaining their forces at Siachen. "Since April 13, 1984," when the Siachen fighting began, it said, the two countries together "have spent over Rs 15,000 crore [$6 billion] here, almost equal to India's entire annual defence budget." Pleading for a negotiated solution of this "ridiculous war," it declared that "Siachen veterans [were] unanimous that India, which dominates the heights and has proved its military supremacy in the region can afford an unilateral withdrawal. In all probability, the Pakistanis will follow suit."[62]

Opinion in Pakistan in the early 1990s in regard to the Siachen dispute seemed less divided than in India and considerably more positive. The Pakistan army, in particular, had given no indication of serious ambivalence over Siachen. On the contrary, its spokesmen had gone to great lengths, presumably not without effect on public opinion, to convey the impression that its military situation at the glacier, in terms of supply, transport, casualties, and overall costs, was superior to that of the Indian army and that the continuing military stalemate there, in fact, worked to Pakistan's advantage. Notwithstanding the military's apparent optimism, Pakistan's civilian leaders, perhaps with an eye on the country's defense budget, committed themselves publicly on a number of occasions in this period to resumption of the negotiations suspended in 1989.[63]

In late summer 1992, three years after the fifth round had collapsed in failure, the subject of resuming talks cropped up in discussions between Indian and Pakistani diplomats. The occasion was the sixth round of the formally scheduled foreign secretaries' talks that took place in New Delhi in August of that year. In these talks, India's foreign secretary, Dixit, according to the Pakistanis, appeared "upbeat" and declared India's willingness to talk with Pakistan about Kashmir. Dixit, they said, had suggested: Let's start by discussing Siachen, then take up the Sir Creek issue, and then, "down the line" perhaps even Kashmir. Since relations between India and Pakistan at the time were far from friendly, the Pakistanis were naturally skeptical; but the temptation to go ahead with talks, they said, was strong. If Kashmir was put on the agenda at some point in the process of dialogue, it would be the first time official talks were held on the subject since 1963. Pakistan's prime minister Nawaz Sharif, subsequently wrote to Indian prime minister P. V. Narasimha Rao proposing bilateral talks on Kashmir under Article Six of the Simla Agreement (which committed the two sides to further discussion of "a final settlement of Jammu and Kashmir"). In the meantime, the two sides resumed talks on the Siachen Glacier and on the Sir Creek (involving a fairly minor boundary question at the southern end of the international border between India and Pakistan).[64] The sixth round of the Siachen talks and the fifth round of the Sir Creek talks were held simultaneously in New Delhi in early November 1992. Results of both, on the surface at least, seemed very meager.[65]

Indian and Pakistani diplomats interviewed by the author in regard to the sixth round of talks on Siachen agreed that the matter of troop disengagement and redeployment, which had generated considerable heat in earlier rounds, was no longer at issue: The Pakistanis had dropped their insistence on withdrawal to pre-Simla (1972) positions, accepting that the two forces would simply withdraw to tacitly understood positions—the Indians to Dzingrulma (the eastern snout of the glacier), the Pakistanis to Goma (a point at the foot of the Saltoro Range roughly 12 miles above Dansam). The Indians, in turn, had dropped their insistence on maintenance of a "mountaineering camp"—with helipad—midway up the glacier itself. The sticking point, both sides agreed, was their inability to agree on a formula for marking *current* deployments that did not do injustice to either side's territorial claim.

The Pakistani diplomats said that the Indians still wanted, one way or another, to mark present deployments on a map—to give formal acknowledgment, in other words, to "existing ground realities." This, the Pakistanis felt, would enable the Indians at some later point to claim a legal right to *restore* troops to that position; and, in any event, it would give the Indians a *locus standi* on the glacier itself, since they now dominated virtually the whole of the feature, a condition that Pakistan was being denied. The Pakistanis claimed that they did finally agree in the talks to *initial* maps showing current force dispositions, a concession to the Indians, but that they had insisted that wording be added that the initialing should not prejudice either side's present territorial claim.

Pakistani reluctance to yield to the Indians in this regard, as explained by one Pakistani diplomat, arose from the fact that they viewed India's seizure of the Siachen in 1984 as "the single most serious violation [ever] of the Simla agreement." The Pakistan government could not just hand the glacier to India, he explained; it had to be able to explain and justify the redeployment, in effect a withdrawal, to the Pakistani people.

The Indian team in the sixth round, he said, proposed to rename the AGPL—the line in the Saltoro Range now held by Indian troops and given its present name by them—the Line of Contact and to designate a three-mile wide stretch in the Saltoro Range a demilitarized security belt, or "zone of disengagement." The Pakistani team, he said, took the view: If we accept this new line or zone, the Indians will be in a position to form out of the disputed Siachen territory not a *belt* but a vast *triangle* (its three points: map coordinate NJ 9842, the Karakoram Pass, and Indra Col)—an area in which only Indian troops would be permanently based (at Dzingrulma, or what the Indians call Base Camp), thus undermining Pakistan's own territorial claim to the glacier based on the NJ 9842–Karakoram Pass axis. The Indian team responded to their complaints, according to this Pakistani diplomat, by saying: Okay, we'll draw a line *perpendicular* from NJ 9842 to the China border; and for purposes of inspection and verification of compliance with the accord, Pakistan will be authorized access up to that line. This proposal, however, from the Pakistani perspective, still meant Pakistan's entire exclusion from the territory *eastward* of the perpendicular line and left Indian troops the only forces on permanent deployed status *anywhere* in the triangle—situations threatening, this diplomat argued, to Pakistan's already tenuous territorial claim. The Pakistani team, he said, attempted to argue that the Indian proposal would simply freeze, without solving, the Siachen problem. Better, the Pakistanis said, to leave the matter of territorial claims to later, working up a Siachen agreement now as a confidence-building measure, a place to begin the process of settling the basic issue of the LOC.

In an interview with the author, Indian Foreign Secretary Dixit agreed with the Pakistanis that redeployment was no longer a problem.[66] However, the two sides were still stuck, he said, on two points: (1) Disagreeing with the author's Pakistani informants, Dixit said that the Pakistanis refused to commit themselves to *existing* deployments; that is, they refused either (a) to initial maps showing these deployments or (b) even to initial a *verbal* description of them. (2) India, he said, accepts the Siachen as a no-man's-land. India says: Let's just redeploy, leaving the question of the LOC's extension alone for the time being. In principle, he observed, the Pakistanis too accept that the Siachen is a no-man's-land; but they insist that *notionally* India must concede Pakistan's claim to a line running northeastward to the Karakoram Pass from map coordinate NJ 9842.

Did the sixth round of bilateral talks over Siachen move India and Pakistan any closer to a settlement? According to a Pakistani diplomat-participant in this round, interviewed by the author in summer 1993, the answer was no. He argued, in fact, that this round of talks appeared doomed even before it got under way and that, at least in some ways, it marked a retreat from the earlier rounds. When it came time for the joint statement concluding the talks, he said, the Indian team refused to include the word "agreement" to describe the talks, though the joint statement ending the fifth round in 1989 had said that an *agreement in principle* had been reached. This, he said, appeared to be a deliberate Indian attempt to dilute even the earlier accord.

Even if we write his observation off as obligatory diplomatic fencing, the fact remains that the Indians in this round, as in the preceding ones, seemed in no great haste (and to be under no great compulsion) to vacate the glacier. They appeared as adamant as ever that a settlement of Siachen must take account of and—in one way or another—explicitly recognize the Indian army's successful "capture" of the glacier and, thereby, its de facto extension of the LOC to the China border along an axis distinctly favorable to India. Indian diplomats have proposed a number of artful disguises to conceal what was being done; and they have shown willingness to modify—or even scrap—the more egregiously lopsided of these proposals in the face of Pakistani objections. So far as one could tell, however, the Indian position on this most central issue in the Siachen dispute remained essentially as hard-and-fast as ever: The Indians continued to maintain that they had taken nothing that belonged to Pakistan, that it was for the Pakistanis to face up to the "ground realities," and that the Indians were not going to agree to demilitarization of the glacier without forcing the Pakistanis to pay a stiff political price. The Indians were simply not interested in demilitarization—in the re-creation of a no-man's-land at Siachen—just for its own sake. In return for any Indian territorial concession, in other words, there had to be a clear quid pro quo.

No one put this position more unequivocally than the recently retired chief of the Indian army, General Sunith F. Rodrigues. The Siachen issue, he told the author in 1991, was essentially a closed matter. The "ground reality," he said, was that the Indian army controlled virtually the whole of the area east of the Saltoro Range. He explained this, he said, to all foreign envoys, including those from Pakistan. He has offered to take them to the glacier, he said, and to examine with them the disposition of forces. "What is there to negotiate?" he asked. The Indian army has lost lives on the glacier, shown much bravery, and endured terrible hardship. "This I have to bear in mind," he observed. "The LOC was acquired by force," he pointed out, "not by negotiation. The Siachen is the same. What more is there to say?" The Indian army, he said, was prepared to stay on the Siachen indefinitely. Siachen was a relatively minor issue, he added; it had already been settled by force of arms. It was no longer negotiable. The new AGPL was now a de facto extension of the LOC. These facts, he said, he had communicated directly to the Pakistanis.[67]

The author's discussions with very senior officers of the Indian army in New Delhi in summer 1993 turned up no greater sense of urgency over Siachen than had been found two years earlier. The situation there, said one well-placed Indian general, had changed remarkably during the intervening two years. Environmental casualties, he said, were down dramatically—*by 90 percent*—to a rate *less,* he said, than that of an ordinary military unit elsewhere in the country. Artillery firing had ceased. Nowadays there were *no* fighting-related casualties at least on the Indian side. India, he said, was big enough to adapt itself to the situation: It was able to absorb the costs of Siachen without any significant adverse impact on the country at large. The economic costs of Siachen, he argued, were routinely inflated by the media; India, he said, could bear them indefinitely.[68]

The sixth round of talks over Siachen was obviously a victim, at least in part, of the Kashmiri insurgency and of the deepening hostility it has generated in India-Pakistan relations. This hostility did not preclude an agreement over Siachen, but it rendered less likely any significant softening by either side of its principal demands. The Pakistanis were naturally reluctant to agree to anything at Siachen that, by adding legitimacy to the Indian claim that *title* to territory derived primarily from *actual control* over it, might be used against them in the high-stakes struggle for Kashmir as a whole. The Indians were no less reluctant, of course, to consider a settlement of Siachen that was not in some way linked to Pakistan's covert intervention both in Kashmir and in Punjab. Hence, their interest not only in completing the LOC but in getting Pakistan to reconfirm, in a bilateral treaty, its international legality.

For Indian policymakers, the Siachen negotiations were thus mainly a forum in which to nudge Pakistani negotiators closer to acceptance of the unofficial, but actual, Indian position on the LOC, namely that it was the de facto international boundary between India and Pakistan. This position required

Pakistani acknowledgment of India's superior military might, of Pakistan's inability, in other words, to alter the situation in Kashmir through force of arms. These thoughts seem to have been implicit in the remarks made to the author in July 1993 by the Indian Foreign Secretary Dixit. The Indian government, he observed, was willing to talk to Pakistan on the issues. The 1972 Simla agreement, in two sections, provided a proper framework for such talks. Pakistan, unfortunately, rejected the first section (stressing the need for bilateralism and for attention to a whole range of issues between the two countries), insisting on going straight to the second—the future status of Kashmir. India's formulation of the problem, the insistence on "taking ground realities into account," he said, was not meaningless. There were two ways to talk, he suggested: You can go back to partition and try to begin all over again, but this is unrealistic; or you can discuss Kashmir subject to the demographic, political, and other changes that have taken place over the decades. This, he observed, was India's preference. Pakistan, rejecting this approach, had instead chosen to nurture its client—Pakistan Occupied Kashmir—and to ignore the changes. India won't say so publicly, he noted, but it is not averse to conversion of the LOC into the permanent boundary.

Following collapse of the sixth round of Siachen talks in November 1992, India-Pakistan relations appeared to sink even further, with Pakistan complaining that members of the Pakistan embassy in New Delhi were being increasingly harassed and even beaten. The Pakistan government announced on 17 August 1993 that it was recalling High Commissioner Riaz Khokar from New Delhi following what it claimed were renewed attacks on embassy staff.[69] Indian frustration and impatience with Pakistan's continued spoiler role in Kashmir were plain to see. Asked in July 1993 if India had any plans for further negotiations with Pakistan, Rajesh Pilot responded: How can India trust Pakistani intentions? The government is *open* to discussions with Pakistan, but Pakistani attitudes make it impossible. "Yesterday," he said,

> I met with the Pakistani High Commissioner Riaz Khokar. I brought to his attention facts about training camps and infiltration. Pakistan's credibility in this connection must first improve; the Simla agreement must be observed. We have abundant proof of Pakistan's involvement in Kashmir. No, I am not saying that this [i.e., Pakistan's cessation of this activity] is a *precondition* for talks, but *some* advance in credibility is required. The government is prepared to name the villages, to name even the Pakistani officers who are training the infiltrators.[70]

Within a few months of this observation, India had, as we noted earlier, relaxed its position enough to permit the prime minister to invite resumption of the foreign secretary–level talks—and, most surprisingly, to concede the necessity for Kashmir's inclusion on the agenda. The Indian government's expectations of these talks could not, however, have been very great.

India, as a third-country envoy commented to the author in July 1993, was in no hurry for negotiations. No serious dialogue would begin until the Indians felt their position much strengthened in Kashmir. Moreover, since India viewed the LOC as the de facto international border, Pakistan would have to reconcile itself to the LOC's permanence. To do that, Pakistan, of course, would have to have an Indian commitment at hand to some kind of autonomy package for Jammu and Kashmir so that it could proclaim victory at home. Any such package, he said, would be opposed tooth-and-nail by the Indian bureaucracy; and since the Pakistanis were quite convinced that the Indians wouldn't concede autonomy in the first place, they would not help to move the game in that direction. The Pakistani game, he suggested, which was essentially to keep the pot boiling in Kashmir, was *eventually* a losing one: India's determination to hold Kashmir, he observed, was very great, greater in any event than Pakistan's desire to acquire it. In such circumstances, he said, it might appear rational for Pakistanis to engage in meaningful dialogue with India; but for their own reasons they obviously didn't agree.[71]

We are driven to conclude that bilateralism provides a relatively frail scaffolding on which to place the burden of settling the Kashmir dispute. Unhappily, this presents us with a cruel dilemma. On the one hand, we obviously can't just discard bilateralism. The alternatives to it, as we have seen, are not very promising themselves. We will argue later on, in fact, that the impetus for ending, or in any event for better managing, the Kashmir dispute *must* come from India and Pakistan. On the other hand, leaving the task of settlement entirely or even largely in their hands, if the record of bilateralism just reviewed has any lesson for us, is almost bound to result in their continued failure to accomplish it.

For the moment, we set this problem of format aside. We will return to it in Part IV. We need now to examine an equally nettlesome problem—that of formula.

CHAPTER

·8·

DILEMMAS OF FORMULA: THE AIMS OF NEGOTIATION

The discussion moves now to an examination of issues pertaining to the rules, principles, and desired outcomes that are to govern the conduct and define the objectives of the settlement process. Assuming that the parties to the Kashmir dispute could identify a mutually agreeable *format* for the conduct of negotiations, we ask, how would each define an acceptable negotiating *formula*? What subjects are to be included or excluded from discussion? In what sequence and in accord with which principles are these subjects to be considered? And what are the acceptable contours of an interim or of a final settlement? What are to be the terms of negotiation, in other words, and at what should negotiation be aimed?

The focus of discussion is an array of models, frameworks, or "solutions" that have been proposed in recent years for settling the Kashmir dispute. These models are categorized, compared, and critically evaluated (for acceptability mainly).

MENDING KASHMIR: ALTERNATIVE MODELS

Side by side with most of the planet's major territorial disputes have grown up virtual cottage industries crafting proposed solutions to them. The Kashmir dispute is no exception. Before the recent surge of Kashmiri separatism broke out in open rebellion at the start of the present decade, many scores of more-or-less serious such proposals (with greater or lesser amounts of official involvement) had already been produced by Indians, Pakistanis, and others; and in the last few years the existing stock was being rapidly replenished by dozens of new proposals. By now, these proposals present a rather extensive, not to say bewildering, array of possibilities. An essential initial task, then, is to reduce this array to a manageable set of broad categories.[1]

Part of the reduction can be accomplished simply by excising a number of possibilities from consideration. These include (1) maintaining the status quo in Kashmir (accepting the situation as irremediable, in other words, at least for the time being);[2] (2) eliminating India's separatist problem in Kashmir through application of increasingly draconian measures of violent repression against the separatists and/or through stepped-up warfare against the separatists' chief ally, Pakistan; and (3) eliminating India's separatist problem in Kashmir through demographic maneuvers, that is, through fundamental alteration of Kashmir's ethnic composition either by (a) driving Kashmiri Muslims across the LOC into Pakistan ("ethnic cleansing," in other words) or (b) resettling non-Muslims (Hindus and Sikhs) in large numbers in currently Muslim-majority areas of the state ("ethnic dilution"). However repugnant, dangerous, or costly these possibilities may be, all of them are, of course, conceivable developments. Some of them have no doubt been given serious consideration.[3] One might argue, in fact, that at least some are more *likely* developments—some would even argue more *preferable* developments—than those we will be considering. The first of the three is not aimed at settlement of the dispute at all, however; and both of the other two would settle it via unilateral (and more-or-less forceful) imposition of a solution, not via negotiation. In fact, the single-minded pursuit of any one of them would automatically block a negotiated settlement between India and Pakistan and would likely expand or at least prolong the conflict, not mend it.

When these options are removed, we are left with four main categories of proposals premised basically on (1) territorial partition, (2) modification of political sovereignty, (3) political autonomy, or (4) political independence. These are broad categories, often overlapping and with great possibility for varying their specific contents. Each has both attractive and unattractive features. A *negotiated* settlement of the Kashmir dispute, it is apparent, would have to be cobbled together from the elements of one or, more likely, of a combination of them.

Partition

In its application to the Kashmir dispute, the partition solution has been defined as both temporary and permanent. *Temporary* territorial partition formed the basis of the UNCIP-brokered cease-fire agreement reached between India and Pakistan in 1949. That agreement, as we observed in Part I of this study, designated the whole of the former princely state of Jammu and Kashmir disputed territory. It granted both signatories interim administrative authority, pending final resolution of the dispute, over the parts of this territory in their hands at the time military hostilities ended. Not built into the agreement, however, was an enforcement mechanism to preclude India and Pakistan on their own from extending claims to sovereignty over all or at least part of the state. The determination of both states since then to assert precisely such claims has created in present-day Kashmir, as we have already seen, a confused amalgam of partial and overlapping sovereignties.

Permanent territorial partition, in turn, formed the core of virtually every proposal laid before India and Pakistan over the next decade either by UNCIP or by the several special representatives deputed by the United Nations to the task of mediating a peaceful settlement. These proposals spelled out a fairly broad range of possible territorial outcomes: Depending on the partitioning principle adopted, either side could get all, some, or none of Kashmir. These proposals also allowed for some variation in procedure: There was to be a plebiscite to assure formal Kashmiri consent to the territorial outcome; but the plebiscite could either blanket the entire state or, as suggested in the scheme offered to India and Pakistan in September 1950 by UN mediator Sir Owen Dixon, be limited or "regional"—confined, that is, primarily to the politically most uncertain area of the state, the Valley of Kashmir.[4] No variation was permitted, however, in regard to the number of potential beneficiaries of partition; there were only two—India and Pakistan. There was no provision at that time, in other words, for a third—independent Kashmir—alternative.

Permanent partition remains today, of course, the formal or declared objective of both India and Pakistan, though each obviously defines the matter in very different terms. Pakistan still demands that the UN resolutions of 1948 and 1949 pertaining to Kashmir, including the stipulation of a popular plebiscite to determine the state's final accession to either India or Pakistan, be honored; India responds that the state's accession to India is final and that Pakistan's vacation of its aggression in Kashmir (its withdrawal from Azad Kashmir and the Northern Areas) is all that is required to end the dispute. As much as before, these definitions of the objective are unmindful of Kashmiri aspirations for either autonomy or independence. They also appear to be almost wholly unamenable to compromise between India and Pakistan. Their endless invocation by these two countries, however, has long had the look not of actual expectation but of ritual incantation. If the truth be told, privately expressed disbelief in the likelihood of a UN-supervised plebiscite has been common for many years on the Pakistan side; and observers have long suspected that the Indian position, laying claim at times even to territories *adjacent* to Kashmir in Pakistan proper, was adopted largely as an expedient counterweight to Pakistan's own more extreme demands—in particular, to pressure Pakistan to pull back from its demand for a plebiscite.[5] We have observed at a number of points in this study, in fact, that the Indian government, already in possession of the larger and most prized section of the state and aware of the difficulty that would face any effort to pry Pakistan loose from the rest, has made no secret of its willingness to settle for considerably less than the whole of Kashmir—to accept conversion of the LOC, in other words, into a permanent international boundary.

Conversion of the LOC could be accomplished in a number of ways. It could, for example, include relatively minor *territorial adjustments* or *exchanges* to rectify irrationalities in the border. As we saw in Chapter 7, modifications to the LOC of this kind were offered by India to Pakistan in the 1962–63 negotiations; and from time to time there have been indications that the Indian government continues to think along these lines.[6] Conversion could also include *boundary control* provisions, such as for the opening of transit points at regular intervals, or for the maintenance of a "soft" (customs-free) border for trade, travel, and binational employment. Or it could itself form part of a larger, multifeatured *autonomy* package embracing more than territorial partition. This last possibility we explore in some detail when we examine the alternatives under political autonomy. For now, however, it is essential to note that conversion of the LOC into a permanent international boundary, however accomplished and whether embellished with incentives or not, inevitably acts to bestow legitimacy on the territorial status quo, on the outcome, that is, of the three wars that India and Pakistan have fought since independence. By asserting the primacy of actual military *control* over putative legal *entitlement,* it tacitly acknowledges India's dominant political standing in the region. By requiring Pakistan to relinquish its claims to the coveted Valley of Kashmir and the Kashmiri separatists their claims to independence, while at the same time entailing little or no detachment from India of territories now in its possession, it leaves existing political and economic arrangements essentially undisturbed. Thus, of the several conceivable forms of partition, it is clearly among the most generous to India. That helps to explain, no doubt, the widespread opposition to the conversion option one encounters in Pakistan and, conversely, the very broad support this option has always gotten from practically all points on the Indian political compass.[7] For this very reason, however, conversion of the LOC, at least in its relatively plain or unembellished forms, must be classed among the least promising of negotiating principles.

Much more radical than the LOC conversion option are proposals to negotiate anew—and on a basis other than the already drawn LOC—the state's territorial division between India and Pakistan. A number of possibilities present themselves, but by far the most common proposal has been that all or most of the Valley of Kashmir be transferred to Pakistan, with India retaining the larger but less populated Ladakh and Jammu regions of the state.

This proposal obviously collides with the aspirations of Kashmiri Muslims either for independence or for retention of the state in its pre-1947 form. It would leave a substantial share of the state's territory and, unless a plan for mass resettlement were included, of its Muslim population too still in Indian hands. It also runs up against the fact that the population targeted for division is ethnically mixed, ecologically interdependent, and economically integrated. As impartial scholarship on the subject of secession has often demonstrated, surgical removal of one part of such a population via territorial partition cannot be done without pain to the other parts.[8] Partition, moreover, usually merely *repositions* ethnic heterogeneity without eliminating it; and it rarely if ever does away entirely either with political exploitation of ethnic minorities or with grounds for continued conflict.[9]

From another angle, however, adoption of this option, by placing under Muslim-dominant Pakistan's control the majority of the state's Muslims and the overwhelming majority of its Kashmiri-speaking Muslims, would largely rid India of at least one—*ethnic Kashmiri*—minority problem while at the same time eliminating the core of the grievance that Pakistan has been nursing since the state's accession to India in 1947. It would eliminate too the constitutional anachronism (and the political quicksand surrounding it) of having a maverick Muslim-majority state in Hindu-majority India. Were the repartition to be modeled after the so-called Trieste solution, the 1954 agreement that divided the disputed city of Trieste between Italy and Yugoslavia but with the assurance that the city's inhabitants had free access to both sides of the partition line, it might overcome at least some of the usual disabilities of partition while at the same time laying the foundations for cooperation—perhaps even of demilitarization—between India and Pakistan that is difficult to imagine under the present partition arrangement.

Negotiating a new inner boundary in Kashmir along the lines just suggested would clearly represent a profound change in policy, especially in India. A massive effort to marshal public support behind it would be required. This could prove extremely difficult. Overt support for any such plan is practically nonexistent in India today, and it is not hard to see why. The 1947 partition plan, as we have observed, was itself hardly popular with Indians; and neither in the manner in which it was conducted nor in its longer-range consequences, we need hardly remind ourselves, was it likely to breed confidence in partition as a conflict-reducing mechanism. Turning the valley over to Pakistan under pressure would look to practically all Indians, and indeed would be, a spectacular political defeat for India. Turning it over under any conditions, however, would tempt the political opposition in India to *represent* it to the Indian electorate as a defeat, whether it deserved that description or not. One has only to recognize the great reluctance the Indian government has shown to yield on its claims to the Siachen Glacier or the Aksai Chin in the entirely uninhabited, remote, and unfamiliar northern parts of Kashmir to sense the difficulty that would attend transfer to Pakistan of the symbolically, politically, and psychologically vital Valley of Kashmir.

Now it is possible, of course, as Raju Thomas has suggested, that "although this solution may not please any of the three main parties to the dispute, eventually, it may prove to be the minimum compromise choice acceptable to all three."[10] This solution most certainly would not displease all three parties equally, however, and it is hard to see how it could ever be successfully held up to Indians, in particular, as a compromise. Unless presented as part of a broader settlement package containing far more tangible, compensatory benefit to India than Pakistan seems now likely to grant, this option too must be judged highly improbable.

Modification of Sovereignty

Common nowadays is the notion that the traditional sovereignty of nation-states is in decline. Many attribute this decline largely to the economic "dysfunctionality" of the nation-state system.[11] But many others hold it to be just as much a sign of the failure of nation-states to adjust to demands by "submerged" ethnic minorities for self-determination.[12] In this changed atmosphere, with sovereignty seemingly at bay, proposals calling for the modification of sovereignty to resolve ethnic strife no longer seem so radical or so unwelcome as in the past. As a result, they are rapidly proliferating.

Broadly speaking, proposals calling for modified sovereignty in regard to Kashmir have fallen into three categories: (1) *multilateral (global)*—those built upon direct control over Kashmir by the international community, primarily via the United Nations; (2) *multilateral (regional)*—those built upon a *confederal* arrangement consisting of the states of the South Asian region; and (3) *bilateral/joint*—those built upon a shared, cooperative, or *condominium* arrangement between India and Pakistan.

Direct UN control of Kashmir has always been proposed as a transitional mechanism (a temporary *suspension* of state sovereignty, in other words), one that would provide interim international administration, whether over the valley alone or over the entire state, for a period of five or ten years, or even longer, pending conduct of a plebiscite or until a settlement of some kind was reached.[13] Some students of the United Nations argue that its charter, without amendment, could readily accommodate such "oversight" activity. One suggested approach, for instance, would revive the Trusteeship Council, turning it "into a modern international clearinghouse for self-determination." The trust territory, in this scheme,

> would be that part of a member state voluntarily placed into trusteeship by the government of that state for the purpose of resolving a self-determination claim under U.N. supervision. The Charter provides that the administering authority of the trust territory "may be one or more states or the Organization itself." Thus the United Nations acting through the Trusteeship Council could administer the trust territory in the manner agreed upon by the concerned parties, including the ruling government. A trusteeship agreement would lock in the cooperation or acquiescence of the ruling government.[14]

Entrusting sovereignty to an impartial international body in this way has intrinsic appeal, of course. It could remove the conditions underlying the state's *internal* crisis, defuse a militarily dangerous situation on its *external* border with Pakistan, at the same time that it supplied a neutral institutional mechanism to preside over a peaceful and unhurried search for a permanent settlement. We have said enough in this study already, however, to indicate that the Indian government, for one, is extremely unlikely to subscribe to this proposal voluntarily; and one may wonder too whether Pakistan, whose appeals in the past for international support over Kashmir have earned it little more than lip service, could ever be persuaded to entrust its own stake in Kashmir so fully to any international body. Neither state, in the face of the dispute's evident complexities, could be at all certain that it would be any closer to settlement when the period of "international trust" ended than when it began. Moreover, even in the unlikely event that India and Pakistan were both persuaded fully of the merits of the approach, its feasibility would still have to be strongly doubted. Gaining concerted UN involvement in Somalia and the former Yugoslavia has proven a daunting—and far from wholly successful—task. Arranging it in the by far more remote area of Kashmir, contested between two states of more than ordinary political and military muscle, and where the dispute, in fact, directly involves the veto-bearing (and Muslim minority–troubled) Chinese might well tax the capacities of the United Nations far beyond what it now seems able to bear.

Condominium and confederal proposals, in contrast, prescribe far more basic and permanent modifications of sovereignty—the former establishing a species of Indian and Pakistani "cosovereignty" over Kashmir, the latter conferring a degree of political autonomy on Kashmir but within a confederation of equal and autonomous states that joins Kashmir with India, Pakistan, and (at least in some formulations) the rest of the states of the South Asian region.

The specific content of these proposals naturally varies. As sketched in by Thomas, for instance, the condominium arrangement would mean joint Indo-Pakistani control over an undivided Jammu and Kashmir state, full withdrawal from it of Indian and Pakistani forces, a ban on both Indian and Pakistani settlement or ownership of land in it, along with open borders (for trade, transit and employment) for the state's residents. This arrangement, he observes, could act as a "bridge of friendship" between India and Pakistan and over time lead up to implementation of a single, decentralized, and democratic confederation of several autonomous South Asian republics. In that confederal arrangement, he suggests, political and cultural matters would remain largely the responsibility of the component units, while the confederation's central government "would only deal with defense, foreign affairs, communications and currency."[15] Much the same formulation, including the phasing in over time of a regional confederation, is spelled out in the plan of a "South Asia house" advanced recently by a joint U.S.-Russian study mission.[16]

Often pointed out by Indian students of the Kashmir dispute is the fact that in the twilight of his life, Prime Minister Jawaharlal Nehru himself expressed serious interest in the confederal idea. Talking to a *Washington Post* correspondent in New Delhi at the end of 1962, Nehru suggested that a confederation between India and Kashmir could lead by stages to a similar arrangement linking the eastern and western halves of Pakistan and then to a large confederation joining all the states of the South Asian region. This, he said, would open Kashmir to Pakistan, pacify East Bengali feelings, overcome communalism, and create opportunities for peaceful cooperation between India and Pakistan. "Confederation," he is reported to have said, "remains our ultimate goal. Look at Europe, at the Common Market. This is the urge everywhere. There are no two peoples anywhere nearer than those of India and Pakistan, though if we say it, they are alarmed and think we want to swallow them."[17]

Within a few years of Nehru's death, however, India's most renowned student of the Kashmir conflict, Sisir Gupta, dismissed all such proposals as impractical. Confederation had to precede condominium over Kashmir, he argued, and confederation itself required a long gestation period. "A powerful section of public opinion in Pakistan," he said, "would regard any such suggestion as a clever and subtle manoeuvre to undo Partition."[18] The idea is occasionally resurrected by Indian writers yet today, but rarely without strong reservations.[19] The fact is that there is very little *serious* support for any of these sovereignty-modifying proposals in *either* India or Pakistan. For Pakistanis, in particular, confederalism, as Nehru recognized, is a codeword for Indian reannexation of territories lost in 1947—for the absorption of Kashmir and Pakistan *by* India, in other words, not for the wholly unlikely grant to them of equal status in the region *with* India. Modifying sovereignty, for both Pakistanis and Kashmiris, runs the risk of forfeiting it entirely.

While this category of proposals is not without its attractions, the probability of its negotiated acceptance and implementation at any point in the near future has got to be judged extremely meager.

Political Autonomy

Of the four alternatives we are considering, devolutionist, decentralizing, or *autonomy*-inclined solutions without doubt have had the strongest support in Western studies of ethnopolitical conflict. One evident reason for this is that they have often appeared to work. "The recent historical record," according to one of the latest and most systematic such studies, "shows that, on balance, autonomy agreements can be an effective means for managing regional conflicts." Of the 11 instances of autonomy solutions to ethnic rebellion that were studied, the author noted, seven (including two in India, one in Bangladesh) led to deescalation of rebellion. Of the four that did not (including one in Pakistan), two failed because of the central government's defection from the autonomy agreement, not because of any flaw in the autonomy arrangement itself. Implementation of another (in Sri Lanka) was pending, leaving only one (Indian Punjab) where the autonomy agreement itself seemed flawed and was followed by yet greater violence.[20]

The prominence of four South Asian countries (Bangladesh, India, Pakistan, and Sri Lanka) in the survey of political autonomy agreements just cited is remarkable. Among other things, it would appear to suggest that solutions of this kind are considered worthy of serious discussion, indeed of practical application, throughout that entire region. And this is generally true. Also true, however, is that when it comes to Kashmir, autonomy has been the focus of discussion—at least of *public* discussion—mainly among Indians and their sympathizers. It has never found much favor among Pakistanis; and its appeal to Kashmiris, whose quest for either independence or union with Pakistan it would permanently deny, seems to have lost ground in recent years. Thus, designing an autonomy proposal that appeals, more or less equally, to all three of the principal actors in Kashmir—and appeals to them strongly enough to justify their setting aside the alternatives—poses an extraordinary challenge to the region's statecraft.

Most of the problems found in the autonomy proposals that have surfaced in recent years are evident in the proposal put forth by an ex-foreign secretary of India, Jagat S. Mehta. In an article entitled "Resolving Kashmir in the International Context of the 1990s," Mehta spelled out the following requirements:[21]

1. *Pacification of the Valley.* A necessary precondition of settlement with Pakistan is termination of the insurgency, including the ferreting out of hard-core militants and plugging of infiltration from Pakistan. Specifically, "to quarantine Kashmir against militancy, until a political solution is reached, a 20 kilometer belt could be created along the line of control from which all non-residents would be barred, and all residents required to carry laminated identity cards."[22]

2. *Restoration of an autonomous Kashmiriyat.* Democracy should be wholly restored; Article 370 of the Indian Constitution, with its express guarantee of the state's "autonomous personality," should be retained; and "a national policy of constitutional decentralization for the whole of India" should be set as a long-term objective. The separate identities of the Jammu and Ladakh sub-divisions of the state should be accommodated "in the promise of general decentralization and not in the special vivisection of the old boundaries of Jammu and Kashmir."[23]

3. *Conversion of the LOC into a "soft border permitting free movement and facilitating economic exchanges . . ."*

4. *Immediate demilitarization of the LOC to a depth of five to ten miles with agreed methods of verifying compliance.*

5. *Conduct of parallel democratic elections in both Pakistani and Indian sectors of Kashmir.* Subsequently, the "elected governments of the two halves should be permitted to have contact with each other and promote cultural and economic exchanges between these parts of old Kashmir."[24]

6. *Final settlement of the territorial dispute between India and Pakistan can be suspended (kept in "a cold freeze") for an agreed period.*

7. *Pending final settlement, there must be no continuing insistence by Pakistan "on internationalization, and for the implementation of a partial or state-wide plebiscite to be imposed under the peacekeeping auspices of the United Nations."*[25]

Stripped of some of its verbal coating, this proposal—which Mehta sanguineously termed "a potential catalyst towards South Asian cooperation"—amounts to little more than a cosmetic enhancement of territorial partition, a sort of "conversion-plus" formula that offers Pakistan and the Kashmiris an incentive to accept the LOC as the de facto international boundary between India and Pakistan without, however, serious disturbance to either the territorial or the political status quo. In most respects, it is what New Delhi has apparently been willing to accept all along. As far as autonomy settlements go, it doesn't go very far at all. Pakistani (and Kashmiri) objections would likely take the following form:

1. The requirement that a military solution (crushing of the insurgency and quarantine of the state against infiltration from Pakistan) precede a political settlement with Pakistan would appear to rule out an immediate dialogue either with the hardcore separatists or Pakistan, while at the same time implying that Pakistan had no locus standi in the dispute.

2. There is nothing in the history of Article 370 to reassure the Kashmiris or Pakistanis that, having already failed once to protect Kashmir's autonomy, it would not fail again. Its retention in the constitution, in the absence of stronger guarantees than now exist against its dilution, is no guarantee at all of Kashmiri autonomy. National decentralization is offered as a *long-term* guarantee; but all recognize that decentralizing India does not now have a powerful constituency to back it and that its achievement at any time in the near future is bleak at best. Mehta's plan does nothing, moreover, to address the autonomy aspirations of Jammu and Ladakh.

3. Similarly, the "soft border" element of Mehta's proposal simply normalizes commerce and transit across the LOC, laying the foundation for its ultimate conversion into a de facto "regular" border at least as well as for its ultimate disappearance.

4. Immediate demilitarization of the LOC, when settlement itself is postponed to a future date, may put the military cart before the political horse. In the absence of Pakistan's sustained military pressure on the LOC, what incentive would there be for India faithfully to carry through with its political promises?

5. Holding democratic elections in Kashmir poses no insuperable obstacles; but the proposed subsequent "contact" between the elected governments in the two halves of Kashmir is too informal, insubstantial, and easily suspended to provide a reliable framework for the routinization of crossborder cooperation.

6. Putting final settlement into a "cold freeze" has the seeming merit of allowing tempers to cool and "confidence-building measures" to take effect, thereby easing the task of reaching agreement. Unfortunately, India may be more inclined to use the interval provided to fortify itself *against* future accommodation than to prepare itself and its citizens for any requisite future concessions.

7. Likely to promote just such an eventuality is Mehta's final stipulation that Pakistan, pending final settlement, abdicate entirely its demand for a UN-supervised plebiscite and that it accept an exclusively bilateral negotiating format.

Other autonomy proposals that have been advanced have sought to overcome some of these objections. The well-known Indian writer A. G. Noorani, for example, has argued that it was "sheer escapism" for Indians to think that Pakistan could ever accept demarcation of the border simply on the basis of the existing LOC. For settlement to work, he said, there had to be something in it for Pakistan. India's restoration of Article 370 "to its original strength," he suggested, should be the subject of a bilateral accord with Pakistan, which would simultaneously extend the same degree of autonomy to Pakistan-controlled Kashmir. That way, he said, India's compact with its Kashmiri population, and Pakistan's with its Kashmiris, would legally be guaranteed by the other side. Each side would then have the right to protest if the other's guarantees of autonomy were in any way violated. Pakistan would still be barred from taking Kashmir away from India, "but it could be of some satisfaction to Pakistan that the Union's powers over the State are restricted under a compact with it as well as with the people of the State."[26]

In most respects, however, there is little to distinguish the components of Noorani's autonomy package from Mehta's. Indeed, in his insistence that the bilateral accord include each side's formal acceptance of the other's sovereignty over lands now held in Kashmir and, accordingly, that the LOC as a part of this agreement be formally converted into a permanent international boundary, he departs even less than Mehta from India's conventional demands.

Much the same can be said of the autonomy proposal outlined by Selig S. Harrison, a senior associate of the Carnegie Endowment for International Peace in Washington, D.C. Unlike Mehta's plan, Harrison's allows for no "cold freeze" or suspension of final settlement between India and Pakistan. Like Noorani's, his calls for immediate conversion of the LOC into a permanent international border as part of a bilateral accord between India and Pakistan. Unlike both Noorani's and Mehta's schemes, Harrison's does explicitly take into account the ethnic divisions within Kashmir. He recommends, in particular, that the state be divided on religious lines, that most of mainly Hindu Jammu and mainly Buddhist Ladakh be split off and fully integrated into the Indian Union, and that the rest—the predominantly Muslim valley plus Muslim-majority areas of

Ladakh and Jammu—be made a new and entirely separate state of Kashmir with special autonomous status along the lines of the Trieste settlement. For the most part, however, Harrison's plan, like those of Mehta and Noorani, amounts to a "conversion-plus" formula with Kashmir's autonomy contingent upon Pakistan's acceptance of the state's permanent division at the LOC.[27]

One of the more complicated of these autonomy formulas is that of B. G. Verghese, a well-known Indian policy analyst and former editor of *The Hindustan Times*. Distinguishing his proposal as the Fourth Option (the first three being maintenance of the status quo, detachment of part or all of Kashmir from India and its reattachment to Pakistan, and independence for part or all of the state), Verghese advocates a solution that he labels "co-confederalism." Co-confederalism, as he describes it,

> would leave existing sovereignties intact but confer a large measure of autonomy (self-determination, azadi) on either side of J&K through negotiations between the two metropolitan states and the J&K units on either side. . . . On the Indian side this might well entail federalisation of Kashmir, Jammu and Ladakh, with regional autonomy for each and further devolution to sub-units. . . . The degree of central devolution [to Jammu, Ladakh and the valley] could even vary. . . . Pakistan would need to work out similar arrangements on its side.[28]

Verghese's plan, like most autonomy proposals, calls for conversion of the LOC, following "suitable adjustments in order to secure a rational border," into a permanent, demilitarized, and "soft" international border. Additionally, however, it calls "for some kind of overarching structure, maybe an informal council, meeting periodically on either side to consider matters of common concern such as trade, exchange, economic cooperation, tourism, the environment, harnessing the potential of the Indus system and trans-border crime."[29] Verghese's tantalizing hint of some kind of overarching, transborder governance is left entirely undeveloped, however, far too sketchy in its present form to convey anything concrete. This leaves his co-confederalism formula, like the other autonomy proposals, still essentially in the category of a "conversion-plus" plan—and as little likely as the others to wean Pakistanis from their traditional skepticism.

This discussion does not exhaust the existing stock of autonomy proposals. Neither does it preclude the appearance of new and more imaginative proposals describing autonomy configurations that go beyond the "conversion-plus" approach that has dominated efforts so far. It does suggest, however, that the autonomy option, like the others we have already considered, is neither an uncomplicated nor a very certain route to settlement of the Kashmir dispute.

Political Independence

The independence solution to ethnic conflict, in sharp contrast with autonomy, gets very little unqualified support from Western analysts. For many of them, the dangers implicit in "the breakup of nations"—in an increasingly fragmented world order, in other words—appear in most cases to outweigh whatever benefits independence might bring.[30] Even those among them more favorably inclined toward the independence option usually describe it, in fact, as the choice of last resort, valid when all else fails, perhaps, but not an especially good choice in and of itself.[31]

Indian writers, for their part, have almost always taken an unequivocally dim view of the independence option for Kashmir. An independent Kashmir, they say, far from developing into an Asian Switzerland, would be politically weak, vulnerable to exploitation by its more powerful neighbors, and economically unviable. And even if these heavy liabilities could somehow be overcome, they say, independence would still be an undesirable objective. It would, Gupta observed in his 1966 study, "encourage sub-national tendencies in other parts of the subcontinent. . . . If a precedent were to be set in Kashmir, a process of balkanization would eventually spread throughout the subcontinent, whether it is India or Pakistan."[32]

In one form or another, this precedential theme, which makes Kashmiri independence hostage to the subcontinent's volatile mix of ethnic and religious identities, is echoed over and over again in more recent studies by Indian authors. A sampling of their arguments follows:

- If Pakistan tries to liberate Kashmir, or if Kashmir breaks away with its help, Pakistan runs the risk of endangering the welfare of 100 million Muslims in India. . . . Willynilly, because of the way Pakistan was carved out of India to represent a Muslim homeland, Indian Muslims became implicated in Pakistan's actions. . . . In a very real sense there is no place left for India's Muslims in Pakistan. Kashmir thus threatens to make 100 million Muslims politically and emotionally homeless.[33]

- But—here's the rub—if permitting greater autonomy and decentralization is to be effective and peaceful, it must realistically stop short of the option of secession of Kashmir from the Indian Union. . . . Pakistan, in self-interest, must not risk arousing, much less provoking, the monsters of secession and communalism in India. With three million unassimilated Afghans, Pakistan cannot accommodate another massive wave of refugees.[34]

- Independence, either for part or all of J&K, is equally unrealistic. Although an artificial product of war, the Line of Control does follow a rough and ready ethnocultural divide in some measure. Further, "self-determination" within the two parts of J&K could result in the balkanisation of a mosaic put together by history, with every new "self-determined" minority being assailed for a newly created majoritarianism which lesser minorities refuse to accept. Such an unraveling would be a recipe for strife, insecurity and destabilization of the region. Encouraging new religious divides would have repercussions in India and Pakistan and even in Bangladesh. . . . Undoing the sub-continent by seeking to promote unviable solutions in J&K would be folly.[35]

Indian distaste for Kashmir's independence is nearly matched by that of Pakistanis. Decades of struggle with India over Kashmir, from their perspective, would have been wasted were Kashmir to emerge independent of both India and Pakistan. Even worse, an independent Kashmir, tempted to extract whatever it could from the rivalry among its much more powerful neighbors, might well pursue a foreign policy no more accommodating of Pakistan's interests than has been India's. Kashmiri self-determination, as we have observed before in this study, has never meant for Pakistanis that Kashmiris had a right to any more than a bifold choice of destinies.

The seeming unpopularity of the independence option among both Indians and Pakistanis leaves the Kashmiri Muslims as its only consistent advocate. And even they, as we have seen, are divided on the issue, some appearing to favor union with Pakistan over independence. Whether this pro-Pakistani sentiment represents substantially more than politically expedient appeasement of the Kashmiri militants' principal and indispensable ally could be settled, of course, by conducting a free, impartial, and internationally supervised plebiscite in Kashmir as called for long ago in UN resolutions. The plebiscite instrument has been used successfully in a number of instances elsewhere in the world in the last several years; and, once the insurgency in Kashmir were ended, there is in principal nothing to bar its successful employment there.[36] The likelihood of its adoption in the Kashmir case appears, however, extremely slender. Of this, there can be no reasonable doubt. India has set itself resolutely against it; and the Kashmiris' insistence on a trifold definition of possible outcomes, so far as one can tell, is unlikely to win Pakistani support.[37] For the time being at least, neither a plebiscite nor Kashmir's independence, we must conclude, appear to be in the cards.

BROADENING THE STATE SYSTEM: DECONSTRUCTING SOVEREIGNTY

The negotiating formulas we have considered thus far have in very large measure taken as starting assumptions (1) that the mitigation of conflict in Kashmir is best sought by introducing change of one sort or another in the *territorial* arrangement of Kashmir and (2) that an arrangement of this kind requires no more than the *peripheral* involvement of the international community. These assumptions, our discussion has made clear, present rather formidable limitations. Despairing of this fact, some scholars have begun to think seriously about alternatives that would move the focus of negotiation both away from territory and toward the international community. One of the most imaginative products of this thinking was outlined recently in a book by the international legal scholar Gidon Gottlieb.[38]

World order, Gottlieb contends, demands that something be done to respond to the mounting clamor for ethnic or national self-determination. International efforts of a juridical character, he says, whether providing for international protection of human rights or for creation of special minority rights regimes, are not an adequate response. But neither, he says, are territorial approaches. Creating new sovereign states, in particular, is no answer to the problem. On the contrary, the multiplication of new states "is a recipe for an even more dangerous and anarchic world."[39] Territorial approaches, according to Gottlieb, have been based on the wrong mindset. "From Bosnia to Azerbaijan," he says, "the stakes for the warring sides are expressed in terms of independence, of statehood, of homeland, of boundaries, of autonomy, and of sovereignty. These notions need to be deconstructed, taken apart and reassembled in a different way for a better fit to the national and ethnic problems that flourish in the post-Cold War world."[40]

A better fitting alternative to either the juridical or territorial approaches, Gottlieb argues, would be something that took advantage of the fundamental transformations of the international system now in progress—namely, the decline in the sovereignty of states and the corresponding increase in the scope for collective intervention by the international community. This third alternative he calls "states plus nations."

Central to the states-plus-nations approach is the "deconstruction of sovereignty" into its two basic components—"sovereignty as power over people and sovereignty as power over territory." The first kind Gottlieb designates a "new space" in the international system. This new space, he says, involves the conscious enlargement or "extension of the formal system of states to include alongside it a system of nations and peoples *that are not organized territorially into independent states.*"[41] This can be accomplished, he claims, without undermining the integrity of existing states. It does require, however, constructing an integrated set of arrangements at the international as well as domestic level. "The international legal community can be broadened beyond states and international organizations," he suggests,

> to formally include peoples and nations. Nations and peoples that have no state of their own can be recognized as such and endowed with an international legal status. Those that are politically organized could be given the right to be a party to different types of treaties and to take part in the work of international organizations. . . . What is required is for the international community to grant peoples organized on a nonterritorial basis a status similar to that of states, albeit limited to nonterritorial concerns.[42]

Arrangements tailored to this approach might include issuance to the inhabitants of a country of two passports—one recognizing membership of a "national home" (which might reach across state boundaries), the other recognizing citizenship of a state; the creation of territorial arrangements that allow for multiple and functionally specific "layers" of boundaries (one for security, another for access to water and natural resources, for example); or even codification of collective security guarantees to peoples and nations having no state of their own.[43]

Gottlieb's states-plus-nations concept is unabashedly futurist: It obviously departs in very fundamental ways from conventional notions of the etiquette of state-society relations in multiethnic countries. Elements of it, however, as he suggests, are appearing even now in the practice of at least some Western countries; and one should be prepared, moreover, for those countries to act increasingly as global advocates of something like this concept. Insofar as India and Pakistan are concerned, however, it is without a doubt ahead of its time. Questions of national identity and territorial integrity are for these two states matters not of abstract theorizing but of the utmost practical, indeed daily, urgency. They are matters, to put it bluntly, of national survival. What may sound progressive and enlightened in the West seems altogether irrelevant and even dangerous to them. Proposals entailing even very minor changes in the status of Kashmir, as we have seen, meet stiff resistance. Proposals as radical and far-reaching as Gottlieb's are not likely to be seriously considered at all. More likely than not, they will be condemned as part of a sinister plot, hatched in the capitals of the rich and powerful Western world, to prevent these countries from ever reaching their true national potential.

Whatever the future may hold, what are needed now in South Asia are more modest measures for reducing conflict than are represented by the concept of states-plus-nations. It is to consideration of these that we turn in Part IV.

Part IV

Recommendations

So far, this book has examined the Kashmir dispute as a boundary problem, as a separatist problem, and as a problem of settlement. In this final part, we take up a rather different task, that of policy recommendation. We turn first to current U.S. policy (Chapter 9). Acknowledging the inevitable importance of the U.S. role in the Kashmir dispute, a number of specific suggestions in regard to focus, strategy, and objectives are made. Turning then to India and Pakistan (Chapter 10), we suggest a number of steps that seem essential to break these two countries loose from their present condition of political deadlock. Consistent with the purposes of this book set forth in the introduction, no detailed, step-by-step recipe is drawn up to guide Indian and Pakistani statesmen to a settlement. That is the task of diplomacy. Our objective, instead, is to help clear away the clutter of almost a half century of argument so that the matrix of fundamental choices confronting Indian and Pakistani policymakers, once they have summoned the political will to move in the direction of settlement, can be more readily perceived. Our purpose at this stage of the discussion is almost wholly prescriptive.

CHAPTER

·9·

The U.S. Role in Kashmir: Toward Constructive Engagement

This chapter examines the Kashmir dispute from the standpoint of the U.S. policymaker. It asks: At what kind of settlement of the Kashmir dispute should U.S. government policy be aimed? And what is the best way for the U.S. government to move the settlement process in that direction? The author's own preferences in this regard are here identified and a number of specific policy recommendations made.

The Kashmir conflict has had a powerful impact on the relationship of both India and Pakistan with the United States. Most conspicuous over the years, perhaps, has been its impact on Washington's decisions in regard to arms transfers to the region, which from 1947 onward could not be made without factoring in their probable consequences for the region's most bitter territorial rivalry. The conflict has had equally broad impact, however, on a whole range of long-term U.S. policy efforts in the region, including nuclear nonproliferation, promotion of economic development, and the protection of human rights. It has constantly threatened, moreover, to escalate into a full-scale war that could force the unwilling involvement of the United States. Like its Indian and Pakistani clients, the United States was thus in some respects held hostage to the Kashmir problem. This problem could be neglected, perhaps, but it couldn't be avoided.

While a substantial and prolonged American interest in Kashmir was thus not to be doubted, it has generally been understood in both India and Pakistan that Washington's stake in the dispute had never been sufficient for it to mount a major and sustained attempt aimed at settlement of it. U.S. involvement in the region during most of the post–World War II era, Indians and Pakistanis well knew, was largely derivative of the global strategic struggle between the superpowers. The region itself, apart from the role it played in this struggle, had little to interest the United States. The end of the Cold War, seen from either New Delhi or Islamabad, thus seemed far more likely to reduce than to increase U.S. involvement in the region.

That perception—of nearly unavoidable decline in active American involvement in the region—has of late been especially widespread in Pakistan. Frequently articulated there in recent years, in fact, has been the view that post–Cold War U.S. policy toward South Asia had already shifted not to a more neutral position, but to one tilted conspicuously against Pakistan; that Pakistan, in fact, had abruptly, quite unceremoniously, and through no particular fault of its own been stripped of the favored position it enjoyed in the galaxy of U.S. client states in the Zia period; and that in regard to Kashmir, in particular, Washington now actually leaned toward a policy that favored India.

There was an element of exaggeration, not to say self-exculpation, in this view. Nevertheless, the belief that a basic shift in U.S. policy was under way in regard to Kashmir and that this shift, together with other developments, indicated a major post–Cold War change in Washington's perception of the U.S. interest in the region, was certainly not unfounded. Less than subtle hints of a shift on Kashmir were apparent, for example, in the testimony in congressional hearings on South Asia on 6 March 1990 of a high-level Bush administration diplomat, John H. Kelly, who was then assistant secretary of state for Near Eastern and South Asian Affairs.

In his written statement to the Subcommittee on Asian and Pacific Affairs, Kelly employed formulaic prose of the sort that would not have raised eyebrows very much in either India or Pakistan. "The United States," he said, "thinks that the best framework for a resolution of this dispute can be found in the 1972 Simla Agreement, in which both India and Pakistan agreed to resolve their dispute over Kashmir peacefully and in bilateral channels, without prejudice to their positions on the status of Kashmir."[1] This wording was sensitive to India's position on bilateralism; but it was also protective of the escape clause—"without prejudice to their positions on the status of Kashmir"—Zulfikar Ali Bhutto had insisted upon at Simla as a shield for the original UN resolutions on Kashmir.[2] Written replies to subcommittee questions on Kashmir submitted by the State Department soon after the hearing elicited similar, and equally inoffensive, wording. In his oral testimony in reply to Congressman Stephen Solarz's persistent questioning, however, Kelly enunciated positions that appeared to most observers to take leave of conventional U.S. policy as well as to issue a not-so-subtle rebuke to Pakistan. The critical part of the exchange between Solarz and Kelly focused on the matter of holding a plebiscite in Kashmir. It went as follows:

Mr. Solarz: What is the position of the United States with respect to whether there should be a plebiscite?

Mr. Kelly: Well, first of all, we believe that Kashmir is disputed territory, and we believe that since the two countries—India and Pakistan—agreed in Simla in 1972 to try to resolve the issue between the two of them, we would endorse efforts for them to try to resolve it between themselves.

Mr. Solarz: Well, how did we vote upon that resolution at the U.N. back in 1949?

Mr. Kelly: In favor, Mr. Chairman.

Mr. Solarz: Right. So at that time we favored a plebiscite. Do we still favor a plebiscite, or not? Or is it our position now that whether or not there should be a plebiscite is a matter which should be determined bilaterally between India and Pakistan?

Mr. Kelly: Basically, that's right, Mr. Chairman.

Mr. Solarz: So we are no longer urging a plebiscite be held?

Mr. Kelly: That's right.

Mr. Solarz: But we would accept whatever India and Pakistan agreed to?

Mr. Kelly: That's right, Mr. Chairman.

Mr. Solarz: And if there were a plebiscite, do we have any position as to what the question in the plebiscite should be?

Mr. Kelly: The exact text of the question was never formulated in 1949. Admiral Chester Nimitz was appointed as the supervisor of the plebiscite, but the actual text was never formulated.

Mr. Solarz: But I have the impression the resolution said the choice should be between becoming part of Pakistan or India. Is that correct?

Mr. Kelly: Yes, sir.

Mr. Solarz: So, at that point, the plebiscite implicitly precluded independence?

Mr. Kelly: That's right, sir.

Mr. Solarz: And I gather we have no position on whether independence should be an option in the plebiscite, provided both countries were to agree on a plebiscite?

Mr. Kelly: We haven't spoken to that position.[3]

Kelly's responses were fully in harmony with long-standing U.S. efforts—articulated by Congressman Solarz in his opening statement to the 6 March hearing—to avoid deep entanglement in the Kashmir issue.[4] Considering the past record and present prospects of the plebiscite option, moreover, they were not unrealistic.

In his clear public admission that the United States no longer favored a UN-supervised plebiscite in Kashmir, however, Kelly—holding forth on a manifestly controversial issue in a closely watched congressional meeting, barely one year after the last Soviet trooper had quit Afghanistan—unquestionably handed a political setback to Pakistan. And further, in acknowledging the possibility that a bilateral settlement of the Kashmir issue might not include a plebiscite (or, if it did, that the United States might not object if the plebiscite precluded the option of Kashmir's independence of both India and Pakistan), he handed a setback also to the Kashmiris.

The plebiscite option, we need to understand, remains an important factor in the Kashmir dispute *no matter how slender its chances of being activated.* Notwithstanding its ritualized invocation by Pakistanis, it retains for them not only symbolic but political importance: It was at the outset of the Kashmir dispute, and it has never ceased to be, the legal hinge on which much of the Pakistani position on Kashmir depended. Recall here that it was India's repeatedly reaffirmed commitment to an internationally supervised plebiscite that gave the Kashmiri maharaja's accession to India its *provisional* character in the first place and, further, that it was this provisional character of the accession that warranted designation of Kashmir by the international community as *disputed* territory. Ironically, the plebiscite option, in view of the political strength Kashmiri separatism has demonstrated in the last several years, would seem to have acquired an even more powerful logic recently than it possessed when Washington was giving the idea its unqualified support in the early 1950s. Kelly possibly intended no more than to discourage false hopes of more direct American involvement; but what he may have accomplished, instead, was, on the one hand, to encourage New Delhi's determination to settle the Kashmir problem strictly on its own terms and, on the other, to broaden the Pakistanis' already substantial doubts about American evenhandedness. In disavowing the multilateral element of the plebiscite arrangements drawn up in the UN's authorizing resolutions, he may also have cut some of the ground from under their other—peacekeeping—components. The United States, suggested one UNMOGIP officer to the author, wrongly arrogated to itself the world's policy on plebiscite without any consultation with the United Nations. "Washington," he said, "should have kept its mouth shut."[5]

Needless to say, Kelly's remarks on Kashmir got a very different response in India. There appreciation was openly and warmly expressed for Washington's apparent efforts to move toward what seemed to Indians a less Pakistan-centered policy on Kashmir. A senior editorialist with *The Times of India,* for example, reflecting an attitude manifested over and over again among Indian government officials and intellectuals, in 1991 declared the Bush administration's apparently changed view of Kashmir "stunning," for Pakistan "the most brutal stroke of all."[6]

Indian delight with this largely unexpected turn of events in U.S.-Pakistan relations was certainly understandable. It appeared to weaken Pakistan's long-standing position on Kashmir while at the same time offering some promise of improvement in U.S.-Indian relations. By no stretch of the imagination, however, did it eliminate Kashmir as an obstacle in the way of the latter. Indians, in fact, no less than Pakistanis harbor a very strong feeling of distrust over American policy toward Kashmir. In the last few years, this distrust has cropped up with particular frequency in expressions of Indian resentment over what many Indians considered to be U.S. "meddling" in Kashmir in regard to human rights. As pointed out earlier in the discussion, reports of human rights abuses and atrocities against Kashmiris were generally downplayed in India or dismissed as propaganda. On the Kashmir issue, as on so many others, the inviolability of Indian sovereignty was insisted upon as the measure of genuine American friendship with India. That Indian sovereignty was demonstrably neither absolute nor inviolate, and that in regard to the infringement of human rights and the matter of national self-determination it was possibly in decline, was accepted by some Indian intellectuals. But not by many.

Nothing so well illustrated Indian sensitivities of the sort just described as the somewhat frenzied outburst that occurred in India at the end of October 1993 in reaction to the unguarded remarks of yet another assistant secretary in the Department of State, this time an appointee of the Clinton administration. Following a briefing of South Asian correspondents called on the eve of her departure on an official visit to three of India's neighbors in the region (Bangladesh, Pakistan, and Afghanistan), Assistant Secretary of State for South Asia Robin Lynn Raphel was quoted in the Indian press as having responded to a journalist's question in regard to Kashmir with the comment: "We [the United States government] view Kashmir as a disputed territory and that means that we do not recognise that Instrument of Accession as meaning that Kashmir is forever more an integral part of India."[7]

Raphel's phrasing was certainly provocative. Though technically consistent with Washington's formal position on the Kashmir dispute, it was bound to strike Indians as being out of step with the more qualified position on the dispute's legal origins that the U.S. government had seemed to adopt in the wake of Kelly's earlier observations. Not surprisingly, therefore, it drew an instant and angry official protest from New Delhi, and for days thereafter the Indian press lambasted Washington, often in the most vitriolic prose (and with little regard for historical facts), for undermining Indian unity and for tilting back toward Pakistan on Kashmir.[8] Political circumstances in India at that moment did not exactly incline Indians to be tolerant of even the mildest of diplomatic blunders: In progress were both politically crucial elections in a number of northern states as well as the extremely tense confrontation between the Indian army and Kashmiri militants holed up in Srinagar's famed Hazratbal mosque. Raphel's timing was bad, in other words, even if her history was impeccable.

The damage done to Indo-U.S. relations by the incident, in any event, was vastly less than claimed. Washington bureaucrats had all been given a very useful reminder, however, that the road through the treacherous semantic thicket of the Kashmir dispute was not clearly marked.

Since the end of the Cold War, Washington has thus been faced with the not inconsiderable task of designing an approach to Kashmir that took account both of its own diminished interest in the South Asian region and, at the same time, of the need to find the middle ground among the politically very prickly issues of which the Kashmir dispute was made. The insistence that India and Pakistan must themselves initiate the process of détente between them was clearly consistent with Washington's diminished interest. As expressed by Deputy Assistant Secretary of State for South Asia John Malott in an informal address in New Delhi in May 1993, the U.S. position was governed by three basic principles. The third of them, he said, was that "the United States is prepared to be helpful in this process, if that is desired by both sides. . . . [T]he primary role must be yours. We cannot want peace more than you do."[9] Deciding what was consistent with the middle ground was likely to be a lot harder: As we have seen, "evenhandedness" did not have the same meaning on the two sides of the LOC.

Complicating Washington's task in this connection were the inevitable calls to take immediate, dramatic, and "forceful" action in Kashmir—calls, to put it very simply, to "do something about it" that came from special interest lobbies, the media, Congress, public opinion, not to mention activist-minded individuals in the foreign policymaking establishment itself. I would include here proposals to blacklist or in some other way to sanction India and/or Pakistan, whether for acts of terrorism or for violations of human rights. Such action, in this author's judgment, is very little likely to produce the desired results. This is, of course, a highly controversial matter. It deserves some explanation.

First, the terrorism issue. This issue, which gained increasing prominence in Washington policy circles in the last year of the Bush administration, sprung from the widely held belief that Pakistan's assistance to both the Kashmiri and Sikh militants in India extended well beyond the moral, political, and diplomatic support freely acknowledged by the government of Pakistan, and that Pakistan in fact was giving them military training and weapons. Toward the end of 1992, the Department of State seemed on the brink of designating Pakistan a sponsor of international terrorism, an act that would add Pakistan to the U.S. terrorism list. Addition to that list would be costly for Pakistan: Countries on it are barred from getting American aid and from purchasing U.S.-made weapons; trade benefits are withdrawn; and access to international lending institutions is curtailed. Already under an aid cutoff since October 1990 due to U.S. nonproliferation legislation, Pakistan could hardly afford the additional blow. No decision had been reached by the end of the Bush administration, however, and the problem was passed along to the new Clinton administration.

Once elected, Clinton moved swiftly on the issue. Even before his inauguration, he sent a message to the Pakistan government with the warning that Pakistan was being placed on a "watch list" of nations suspected of giving support to international terrorism, and that it would be given from four to six months to refute Indian charges that it was backing separatist insurgencies in Punjab and Kashmir.[10] During that period, Pakistan took a number of steps, allegedly including the shutting down of training camps, to convince Washington that it was not guilty of the terrorism charges. Its efforts ultimately paid off. At the end of April 1993, the State Department's annual report *Patterns of Global Terrorism* made little mention of Pakistan.[11] And in mid-July, Secretary of State Warren Christopher announced the U.S. government's decision to remove Pakistan from the list of suspected terrorist states.

Though Pakistan's innocence of India's charges was still in doubt, Washington's decision was clearly sensible. The terrorism list, while it has unquestionable political appeal at home, is simply too blunt an instrument for the complex environment of India-Pakistan relations. As applied to Pakistan, it was wholly one-sided; absent of any mechanism to induce positive behavior by India; and, to boot, derived from a most unsatisfactory characterization of the Kashmir problem.

Now, there can be no reasonable doubt, as this study has taken pains to point out, that Pakistan's contribution to the uprising of Kashmiri Muslims during the past four years has extended beyond its officially conceded limits. Just how far (or for just how long) it has extended in this manner we may debate; but we cannot plausibly deny that Pakistan has supported the uprising militarily. For a number of reasons, however, branding this support "international sponsorship of terrorism" is glaringly inappropriate. Among these reasons two stand out:

1. The actions of Indian security forces both in the valley, where these forces have the look of an army of occupation, and on the LOC, where small arms firing on innocent civilians on the Pakistan side of the line is routine, themselves can easily fit standard definitions of terrorist behavior. In these circumstances, to apply the terrorist designation to Pakistan but not to India flies in the face of logic and, besides, is obviously discriminatory. Instead of defusing the Kashmir conflict, it would likely complicate it by handing New Delhi a convenient and readily exploitable issue with which to flail its long-time adversary.

One could apply the terrorist designation to both India and Pakistan, of course, and in that way overcome discrimination; but that would mean placing under severe sanctions countries containing about one billion people (nearly 20 percent of humanity), a step that ought to give pause to even the most ardent counterterrorism advocate in Washington.

2. The uprising in Kashmir is not, by any fair standard of comparison, a *terrorist* movement. It includes terrorist activities, no doubt, along with a fair amount of corruption and criminality. But it is primarily a *separatist* or *independence* movement, whose origins, as we have seen, are certainly to be found to some extent in the political mishandling of the state by India ever since independence in 1947. Pakistan's material support of this movement—given Pakistan's obvious and enormous strategic, political, and economic stake in its success; given the international community's (including America's) acceptance of Kashmir as disputed territory; and given the movement's certain failure in the *absence* of Pakistan's material aid—is for all practical purposes inevitable, and only to the most obtuse mind to be understood simply as "terrorism."

Official U.S. government characterizations of the problem in Kashmir have consistently sought to portray it in terms inclusive both of the terrorist element and of human rights violations, and in that way to strike a balance in criticism of Pakistan and India. In congressional testimony at the end of April 1993, for instance, John Malott declared that Washington's fundamental objectives in South Asia embraced both an end to terrorism and the strengthening of human rights. "In Jammu and Kashmir," he explained,

> militants have launched an insurgency and are resorting to terrorist attacks, Indian security forces commit human rights abuses, and the political dialogue between Kashmiris and the GOI [Government of India] remains stalled. We believe that outside support for the militants and the cycle of violence between the militants and government security forces must end. In addition, India should safeguard human rights fully, grant genuine access to Kashmir for international human rights groups, and pursue a meaningful political dialogue with the

> Kashmiris. . . . We have been particularly concerned about continuing reports of official Pakistani support for militants who commit acts of terrorism in India. We are keeping this situation under active, continuous review, and have raised this issue continuously with the Pakistani government at the highest level.[12]

In at least one sense, the assistant secretary's description was unobjectionable; the points of view of India, Pakistan, and the Kashmiris were all reflected in it. Apart from that, however, it took a rather narrow view of the Kashmir problem. Nowhere in his prepared comments, for instance, did he try to put terrorism, or Pakistan's alleged support for it, in any kind of political or historical perspective. There was no hint that the militants might be *more* than terrorists, or that the Indians might be as guilty (or even guiltier) of terrorism, or that the Kashmiri people's views might not get a hearing at all in India were they not backed up with guns. Surely, Washington's definition of the Kashmir conflict should be faithful both to its complexity *and to the legitimate stake in its outcome of all parties to it.* Only in that way could U.S. policy avoid the appearance either of partiality or (even worse) naivete. Only in that way, moreover, could there be any realistic hope that U.S. policy might help unravel the dispute.

Second, the human rights issue. The argument of James Goldston and Patricia Gossman, appearing in the 25 May 1993 issue of *The Washington Post,* that the United States and its allies, if India did not end its abuse of human rights in Kashmir, "should suspend all military assistance and military sales to India," should consider a resolution appointing a special UN rapporteur on Kashmir, and should bring to bear against India the leverage of multilateral lending institutions, betrays the same narrow perspective of the problem of Kashmir that we already saw in connection with the terrorist label.[13]

Here again, there is no doubt at all that Indian security forces have upon numerous occasions committed gross violations of human rights in Kashmir and that the emergency powers handed to these forces, as we have seen, emasculate the local courts and deprive Kashmiris of even the most elementary protections from arbitrary arrest, torture, and prolonged detention without trial.

But these abuses are not peculiar to Kashmir, and India is hardly the only party guilty of them in the region. India is, after all, battling a secessionist movement that, whether it achieves its announced goal of independence or accession to Pakistan or not, obviously threatens (in an area of considerable strategic importance) India's territorial integrity; and it is battling a movement that unquestionably has the strong backing of India's principal rival Pakistan, which is, by its own admission, a fledgling nuclear weapon power. It is battling a movement, also, whose own methods and objectives are hardly above reproach.[14] Few governments would deal with such a situation with kid gloves.

Further complicating the situation for India is the political vulnerability to charges of a sellout of Kashmir of the present politically wobbly Congress government. As we observed, Kashmiri separatism, even in its mild autonomy-seeking form, has little support in India. The ruling Congress-I party is itself divided on the issue, and the prime minister—faced with a formidable right-wing Hindu nationalist challenge to his rule—is understandably reluctant to risk his party's future by taking unpopular steps in regard to Kashmir. The Indian prime minister, frankly speaking, doesn't have much policy leeway in regard to Kashmir. He has taken a position in support of Kashmir's present "special standing" under Article 370 in the Indian constitution. But even that standing, so diluted by the central government's legislation over the years that it is practically meaningless, seems increasingly radical (and political vulnerable) amid the Hindu nationalist (anti-Pakistan and anti-Muslim) fervor that grips today some sections of the Indian people.

The Indian government, we observed earlier, appears determined to crush the Kashmiri insurgency. There is little doubt that its security forces have the ability to do that, albeit in doing so they are virtually bound to deepen the now nearly universal alienation from Indian rule that has set in among the Kashmiri people. No amount of moral or material pressure by the rest of the world is likely to dissuade India from this course.

This is an undeniably tragic situation. One struggles to identify some course of action to relieve it. This author does not believe, however, that adoption by the U.S. government of a punitive policy toward India over human rights—certainly not if that is the core of the policy—will yield the desired results. On the contrary, it might well have consequences that are better avoided. One of these would be to place in even greater jeopardy than now the possibility that the United States could ever play a mediatory role in the Kashmir dispute.

We have seen that Assistant Secretary Kelly's remarks to a congressional subcommittee in March 1990, endorsing the Simla Agreement and seeming to disassociate the United States from Security Council resolutions calling for an internationally supervised plebiscite, struck a powerful blow at Pakistan's traditional position. And the first and second of Malott's "basic principles"—stating that the U.S. government considers all of Kashmir to be disputed territory, on both sides of the LOC, and that the issue of Kashmir was best settled by India *and* Pakistan, taking into account *also* the views of both Muslim and non-Muslim Kashmiris—were hardly designed to accord with India's well-known position. They are, in fact, in direct opposition to it. Now, it is possible, of course, that these U.S. stands will somehow strike everyone—since they strike *at* everyone—as remarkably neutral. They may; but this assumption, one suspects, may be overly sanguine.

The separatist problem in Kashmir is only one part—and a relatively small part—of the entire canvass of U.S.-India relations. It should remain that. U.S. policy toward India, a country of great importance in Asia and from which the United States should avoid becoming estranged, should not be made contingent to any great extent upon New Delhi's adoption of a "gentler" strategy in Kashmir than has thus far been pursued. The United States should, of course, continue to press India to seek more energetically a political solution there; and it should continue, as well, to urge upon it, and *vigorously,* higher priority to the observance of basic human rights. But this is best done in full sight of the entire context of human rights violations; and it should be done with the expectation that the Indian government will give highest priority by far to its territorial integrity, to the security of its frontiers, and—by no means least—to the political survival of its present incumbents.

So far, we have concentrated our attention mainly on what the U.S. government ought *not* do about the Kashmir dispute. It is necessary now to ask ourselves what it *ought* to do. In this regard, this author has no hesitation in suggesting that Washington, provided that its efforts are deliberately focused on the step-by-step achievement of carefully identified and limited objectives, provided also that it is both patient and persevering, could play a constructive role in Kashmir. The probability of success, it seems likely, will be significantly heightened to the extent (1) that the *focus* of U.S. efforts is fixed primarily on the international dimension of the dispute, in particular on the international boundary problem (the LOC), and that it specifically targets the need to bring about a deescalation of military hostilities on that boundary; (2) that the *strategies* employed by the United States exploit to the maximum existing conflict management structures in the region, foremost among them being the suspended talks over Siachen; and (3) that of three particularly important policy *objectives* (demilitarization of the boundary, renegotiation of the boundary, and reconstitution of peacekeeping machinery on the boundary), demilitarization is given the greatest urgency. These recommendations naturally require some explanation. This explanation we present here, with some unavoidable repetition of the foregoing arguments, in fairly systematic form.

I. Focus

1.1 U.S. policy in regard to the Kashmir dispute between India and Pakistan should be held to a limited set of relatively modest objectives focused first and foremost on the boundary problem between India and Pakistan, specifically on the deescalation of military hostilities on the LOC. As we have seen, this problem branches off into a number of highly complicated issues involving inadequacies not only in the LOC's delimitation but in its vulnerability to hostile cross-border penetration and reprisal. These are obviously major issues, and they are not likely to yield easily to settlement. They will certainly not yield unless they are successfully detached from the larger and profoundly perplexing questions of territorial possession that the Kashmir conflict is primarily about. On their face, however, they do not seem wholly intractable and might well reward patient and dogged diplomacy. They are certainly a dangerous bundle of issues, deserving of U.S. policymakers' serious attention.

1.2 Apart from its greater promise of success, a focus held rather tightly to reduction and eventual elimination of armed hostilities on the LOC holds a number of additional advantages for the United States. One is that it bolsters, or at least does not undermine, the claim of the U.S. government to impartiality in this dispute. It does not require, for example, that the United States give prominence to positions on the Kashmir dispute (in regard to human rights abuses, for instance, or in regard to the status of past UN resolutions on the matter) that would inevitably be construed as partisan by one side or the other. A second advantage is that its prospects for gaining broad support from the international community are brightened to the extent that incendiary political and ideological issues imbedded in the Kashmir dispute (the right of national self-determination, secular versus sectarian principles of statehood, the limits of sovereignty) are kept at bay. In 1972, India and Pakistan committed themselves at Simla to the peaceful settlement of all disputes between them. Both countries routinely reiterate their support of this commitment. For the United States to encourage more determined efforts in this direction can hardly be faulted.

1.3 While they should not be the primary focus of U.S. policy in regard to Kashmir, human rights problems stemming from the Kashmir conflict, including violations committed by Indian security forces, are inescapable and should be straightforwardly addressed. Their fundamental nonresolvability in the face of continued failure of *both* India and Pakistan to maintain a peaceful boundary between them should, however, be conceded. Their roots in the *international* dispute over Kashmir, in other words, should be emphasized in

U.S. policy. Accordingly, it is as important for the United States to question the nature and extent of Pakistan's support to the Kashmiri uprising as it is to question the manner in which India puts it down.

1.4 The relatively narrow focus recommended here should not be understood as support for U.S. retreat in any manner from its traditional position that Kashmir is a disputed territory. That position is both technically correct and politically vital to maintain. No doubt, the temptation is strong to jettison it; and, as the reported comments in New Delhi recently of the British foreign secretary, Douglas Hurd, suggest, some in the Western camp are more than willing to oblige.[15] Such an action should, however, be resisted.

II. Strategy

2.1 U.S. policy in regard to the Kashmir dispute should continue to emphasize the practical and urgent necessity for *bilateral* negotiations between India and Pakistan. Without them, one can hardly imagine progress of any kind. This fact should not be allowed to act as a barrier, however, to alternative U.S. strategic choices in regard to Kashmir. Rigid adherence to bilateralism would be, in fact, a serious mistake. For one thing, bilateralism, for Pakistanis, is often simply a codeword expressing support for the Indian position. The Simla Agreement was the direct consequence of Pakistan's military defeat; and an emphasis on bilateral measures of conflict management (that is, when they are expressed without simultaneous invocation of the multilateral obligations incurred over four decades ago) implies to Pakistanis their continuing political subordination. For another, bilateral institutions for conflict management are not well developed in the region and cannot be counted upon to withstand the sorts of pressures that may be brought against them. There is, after all, a staggering (and quite unavoidable) asymmetry in the power relationship between India and Pakistan; and along with that there are assumptions about what constitutes an "appropriate" regional role and status for each of them that are fundamentally incompatible. Trust in the other side's good intentions is extremely meager in India-Pakistan relations; and the ability of confidence-building measures to build trust is not viewed in South Asia with nearly the same degree of optimism as in the West. Official rhetoric aside, knowledgeable Indians and Pakistanis expect very little to come of bilateral negotiations between them, certainly not of *unassisted* bilateral negotiations. Hence, essential for the United States is to maintain flexibility in its approach to the problem and to rule out in advance none of the strategic alternatives (or combinations of them).

2.2 Having greatest potential, perhaps, are those strategies that take advantage of (without necessarily being limited to) *existing* conflict management structures in the region. Foremost among these are the suspended bilateral talks over the Siachen Glacier. Pressure ought to be brought to bear on India and Pakistan to continue with these talks until a settlement is reached. (See below, 3.2b.) Less promising but worth investigating, however, is modification of the role of UNMOGIP. Few Indians or Pakistanis interviewed by the author in recent years expressed support for this. Few, however, appear to have given much serious thought to it. UNMOGIP's role can be modified, perhaps usefully, without necessarily elevating it. Some of the limits on its operations are self-imposed. There is almost no publicity given to its operations, for instance, and the reports of its investigations continue to be squirreled away without any apparent UN action taken. Augmentation of its numbers, reassertion of its responsibilities on the Indian side of the LOC, and possibly even extension of its responsibilities to the Siachen area are among the more radical modifications that could be considered.[16] Complete replacement of UNMOGIP by something more effective should not be ruled out. (See below, 3.3a.)

2.3 The potential for multilateral or third-party mediation of the boundary problem is fairly slender but should also be considered among the "live" alternatives. The United Nations, the South Asian Association for Regional Cooperation (SAARC), and the United States itself, among other possibilities, are all potential candidates for the role of mediator. Indians, in particular, will scoff at the suggestion: New Delhi has expressed its unequivocal opposition to any form of mediation on countless occasions. As we have seen, however, India and Pakistan have submitted before to third-party mediation of boundary differences between them and in one instance to international adjudication. Mediation can be confined to the prenegotiation phase, if necessary, focused on bringing the parties to the negotiating table. Or it can be limited to a minor segment of the boundary problem—the Siachen dispute, for instance. Mediation is likely to *follow* successful bilateral negotiation between India and Pakistan, not precede it.

III. Objectives

3.1 *Demilitarization of the boundary*

3.1a The primary objective of U.S. policy in regard to Kashmir should be demilitarization of the boundary (LOC). Demilitarization refers to the limitation, reduction, or elimination (1) of all forms of armed violation of the boundary and (2) of forces and fortifications adjacent to the boundary. Its introduction may occur in discrete stages or all at once. Its implementation should not be understood to imply any change in the legal status of the boundary.

3.1b An essential initial step toward demilitarization is joint Indo-Pakistani acceptance of full restoration of a cease-fire on the LOC. Both countries have flagrantly violated their own bilateral agreements in this regard. Neither has any grounds for complaint against external efforts to encourage a cease-fire. A hopeful development to take into account in this regard, of course, is the success that India and Pakistan have had in the recent past in imposing, informally, a partial (heavy-weapons) cease-fire on the LOC. Needed now, and a very practical focus for U.S. diplomats, is an agreed ban on small arms fire—*especially that which is directed at civilian targets along the LOC.*

3.1c A second essential initial step is sealing of the LOC against infiltration. The infiltration question is of extreme political sensitivity to Pakistan, which does not accept the Indian claim to ownership of Jammu and Kashmir, and which considers its political and moral support (at least) of the Kashmiri uprising a matter of national right. No doubt, it will be extremely difficult to secure an agreement on it. It is absolutely essential, therefore, that U.S. encouragement of this step be accomplished evenhandedly via diplomacy, without fanfare and not through provision of technical assistance (surveillance equipment) to the Indian army or through threat of sanction against Pakistan for engaging in support of terrorism. A formal bilateral agreement between India and Pakistan on infiltration is almost certainly impossible, at least in early stages of negotiation. Provided that concessions by India (at Siachen?) are adequate, Pakistan's informal consent to *suspend* infiltration activities may, however, lie within reach.

3.1d A third essential initial step is the broadening of the cease-fire to the Siachen fighting. At Siachen there is no formally agreed LOC; hence, there is no formally agreed cease-fire. For most of the last ten years, heavy shelling there has been even more routine than on the LOC. The Indians have introduced their most sophisticated heavy artillery (Bofors 155 mm) to the Siachen theater; and a renewal of serious hostilities there is well within the realm of possibility. It might be procedurally advisable to seek a formal cease-fire agreement first at Siachen and to extend it from there to the LOC. (See 3.2b.)

3.1e Definitely more difficult and probably second-stage steps toward demilitarization of the LOC might include joint agreements on (a) mutual and balanced force reductions in Kashmir, (b) dismantling of bunkers and fortifications adjacent to the LOC, and (c) creation of a formal demilitarized zone (DMZ) on the LOC. Steps akin to these were provided for in the Karachi Agreement of 1949. Their failure then to be implemented should certainly temper optimism in regard to their likely acceptability now. They should not be discarded, however, since they offer the best guarantee for continued observance of any initial agreement on cease-fire. Once again, their adoption first in the Siachen theater, where provisions of this kind *in principle* have already been informally agreed, may be a useful precedent for the rest of the LOC.

3.2 *Renegotiation of the boundary*

3.2a A secondary but still critically important objective of U.S. policy in Kashmir should be the renegotiation of the boundary dividing Indian- and Pakistan-administered sections of the state. Renegotiation of the boundary should be aimed at its pacification, however, not at its hardening, which, at the moment, would be totally unacceptable to Pakistan. *Primary attention should be given to the reform of existing rules for policing the boundary, in other words, not to the redelimitation of the LOC or, in the case of Siachen, to its extension.*

3.2b Highest priority under the heading of boundary renegotiation should be given to resumption of direct bilateral talks over the Siachen Glacier dispute. These talks should be based on the results of the sixth round of negotiations ended in November 1992. They should focus exclusively on the Siachen sector. They should be understood, however, as potentially preliminary to more extensive negotiations over the LOC. In particular, they should be utilized to formulate ground rules (in regard to joint patrolling of the boundary, for instance, or in regard to phased force disengagement) applicable at later stages to the LOC. Especially advisable is the creation of a demilitarized zone at Siachen. Mediation of the Siachen talks by the United Nations or another third party, including the United States, should be given serious consideration. The failure of the sixth round of Siachen talks to reach agreement has, of course, impaired Washington's ability to exploit "existing conflict management structures." Observe, however (1) that India and Pakistan have held six rounds of intensive talks on the Siachen over a period of seven years, a fairly good sign that they recognize the negotiability of that dispute, (2) that most remaining technical issues were agreed between them in the most recent (sixth) round, and (3) that they appear very reluctant to talk (formally) about anything else. *Dogged, detailed, U.S.-led consultations with these two governments in regard to expediting a further and* ***successful*** *round of talks might yet bear fruit.*

3.2c The Siachen negotiations, apart from accomplishing the disengagement of forces on the glacier, should be used to win Indian and Pakistani acceptance of practical norms to govern conduct of military activities on or in the vicinity of the LOC. Such rules should include, for instance, strict bans on indiscriminate cross-border firing or firing on unarmed helicopters.

3.2d Redelimitation of the LOC, if attempted, should be focused on the elimination of those points on the LOC where civilian transportation routes and areas of civilian habitation lie within easy range of enemy artillery and mortar fire (Neelam-Kishanganga Valley, for instance). Such changes would work largely to the disadvantage of the Indian army, however, and should not be given undue importance.

3.2e At later stages, renegotiation could include (a) provision of one or more open transit points on the LOC; (b) renaming of the LOC to rid it of the negative connotations of Simla; and (c) creation of a Joint Indo-Pakistan Boundary Commission to oversee joint management of the LOC and to provide a permanent institutional framework for the continued negotiation of boundary questions.

3.2f U.S. impartiality in regard to renegotiation of the LOC, in particular in connection with the Siachen sector, can be displayed most quickly and easily by providing full public clarification of erroneous and controversial changes in some official maps of northern Kashmir issued beginning in the late 1960s by cartographic agencies of the U.S. government.

3.3 ***Reconstitution of peacekeeping machinery on the boundary***

3.3a Another secondary and yet critically important objective of U.S. policy in Kashmir should be the reconstitution of peacekeeping machinery on the LOC. Always commonplace, violations of the LOC in recent years have been rampant. None of the other objectives recommended above can be secured without parallel improvements in peacekeeping. We have taken note of UNMOGIP's inadequacies in this regard. Modification of its composition, size, and mission should be carefully considered. As observed above, however, revocation of its mandate should also be considered.

3.3b The potential for constituting *bilateral* (joint) Indo-Pakistan patrolling of the LOC should be seriously weighed. Success in this endeavor would obviate the necessity for reinvigorating the existing multilateral mechanism, UNMOGIP, a step that India is likely to reject anyway, while at the same time it would significantly upgrade security cooperation between India and Pakistan. Joint patrolling of the Siachen was apparently discussed by India and Pakistan in the fifth round of the Siachen talks in 1989; there is no apparent reason why this device could not be applied to the LOC. U.S. technical or other support for such an undertaking should be offered.

CHAPTER

·10·

INDIA AND PAKISTAN: BREAKING THE DEADLOCK

October 1993 marked the forty-sixth anniversary of Jammu and Kashmir's accession to India and thus of the formal onset of the Kashmir dispute. When it began, this dispute was fundamentally an international conflict over territory, a boundary dispute, in other words. It had a large domestic component even then, of course, to which the autonomy-conferring Article 370 of the Indian constitution and the obstreperous Sheikh Abdullah's eventual incarceration by Jawaharlal Nehru testify. It was *mainly* an international conflict, however, because its domestic side was—rather arbitrarily and only temporarily we now know, but successfully—swept under the rug.

Even with its domestic side more or less tamed, however, the Kashmir dispute very quickly acquired a reputation as one of the world's most perplexing international conflicts over boundary. This it achieved not only by virtue of the disputed territory's large size, politically sensitive demography, and strategically important location, but because of the extremely controversial circumstances of the state's accession to India, the immediate outbreak of war between India and Pakistan because of this controversy, and—not least important and nearly as immediate—the largely fortuitous involvement of the United Nations. Over time, these early complications over the boundary were augmented by India's war with China and the latter's successful retention of a fairly large corner of the disputed territory, another war with Pakistan (also over Kashmir), and then, to cap them all off, a decade-long armed struggle between India and Pakistan over the undefined boundary in the spectacular terrain of the Siachen Glacier at the northernmost edge of Kashmir.

Recent reemergence on the Indian side of the LOC of the long-dormant Kashmiri separatist movement has added yet another twist to the Kashmir dispute. As we have seen, the separatists, in the face of a massive deployment of armed strength against them, have determinedly resisted the effort to crush them. So the Kashmir dispute today, to India's discomfort and to Pakistan's gratification, houses once again, albeit this time much less manageably, a serious domestic conflict. In the short run, this new internal layering in the dispute may not hold up under the weight of Indian repressive measures. Nevertheless, the major redefinition its appearance has already superimposed upon this dispute—in particular, the addition to it of a major new actor with a set of demands not easily reconciled with those of either India or Pakistan—has most certainly rendered the dispute's solution still more complicated.

Pressed nowadays by the challenges issuing simultaneously from the overlapping but far from identical revisionist demands of both Pakistanis and Kashmiris, the South Asian region's slender stock of indigenous conflict management and resolving machinery has proven almost wholly inadequate for the task at hand. A number of confidence-building agreements, providing for nonattack of nuclear installations, exchange of lists of these installations, advance notification of military maneuvers in border regions, periodic field commander meetings, establishment of safeguarded (hot line) communication links between army headquarters, and nonviolation of air space, have been reached between India and Pakistan in recent years; but, in the absence of well-established and legitimated bilateral institutions to monitor, enforce, update, and augment them, they could inspire very little confidence in times of crisis. To be sure, the primacy of bilateral negotiations was formally recognized in the Simla Agreement; but very little has been done since then to bring the promise of that agreement to realization.

Not much relief from current pressures appeared to be available, either, from the international community. Resort to multilateral mediation was, of course, not entirely without success in the early years of the dispute; but its acceptability, especially to the Indians, had declined precipitously even before the first decade of the dispute was ended. Still less impressive has been the record in Kashmir of third-party mediation. Indeed, there has been only one major instance of that (the Tashkent Declaration, 1966) over the entire history of the dispute, and its results, we have already taken note, were hardly remarkable.

Surrounded by these devilishly complex and interlocking boundary, separatist, and settlement problems, India and Pakistan seem to have reached an impasse over Kashmir. The impasse is made especially difficult to overcome by the seeming unwillingness of many leaders in either country even to try. Indians, on the one hand, have shown very little inclination to offer any significant concessions to Pakistan. Indeed, not a few of them have seemed reluctant to extend to it even the most rudimentary respect for its national existence. As one of the most senior members of the Indian foreign policy bureaucracy put it, Pakistanis, though their country is hardly the equivalent of even one of India's larger states, still harbor the outrageous aspiration to dominate India. They are willing to do anything to achieve that objective, he said, even to convert to Islamic fundamentalism, for instance, if that appeared necessary to secure the support of the Islamic states, as well as to take assistance shamelessly from the United States, China, or any other source. Pakistan, he declared, is not a viable state. It has no common purpose, no unity. It has to be anti-Indian simply in order to survive as a country.[1]

Pakistan's rulers, on the other hand, have seemed no more inclined than the Indians to rush to settle the Kashmir dispute. They can recall no prior instances of serious Indian compromise over Kashmir; and they almost all appear persuaded that the Indian government will volunteer none in the future. They freely admit, therefore, that at least for now chances of a settlement over Kashmir are extremely slight. This bleak prognosis does not necessarily induce fatalism in them, however, or a desire to strike a quick bargain with India. In recent years, in fact, Pakistanis have often seemed more optimistic about their own country's future—and contemptuous of India's, by the way—than ever in the past. History seemed somehow to be marching with them. The Pakistani government, said one ex-foreign ministry bureaucrat in Islamabad, was presently—and in sharp contrast with the mood in Pakistan in the early 1980s—in a confident mood, confident, that is, that India was likely, sooner or later, to collapse politically and, potentially, to fall apart. This, he said, was the *strongly* held view of most Pakistanis who mattered in foreign policy affairs. They did not feel an overwhelming need, for other than immediate and tactical reasons, to yield to either Indian or Western pressures. As they assessed the situation in Kashmir, he said, they believed it was necessary for the uprising to continue, to go on bleeding India, to allow time for there to develop in India a pro-settlement lobby with which Pakistanis, finally, could bargain on equal terms. Kashmir's independence, he added, was not an acceptable option to the Pakistan government. In fact, the government viewed it as *worse* than the status quo for *both* India and Pakistan. Pakistanis, he said, continued to feel that they were robbed of Kashmir in 1947; and only accession to Pakistan could overcome that feeling.[2]

This regional impasse between India and Pakistan obviously subverts the capacity of the international community to intervene effectively in regard to the Kashmir dispute. Both sides, of course, regularly demand immediate international action to resolve the dispute, yet the action each demands is more often than not patently self-serving, not to mention neglectful of the contradictions in its own position. Pakistan, for instance, seeks international action against India on grounds of human rights violations; yet Pakistan also seeks international conduct of a plebiscite in Kashmir, the terms of which should exclude the choice of Kashmir's independence.[3] India, for its part, seeks international action against Pakistan on grounds of terrorism, conveniently discarding Pakistan's internationally validated claim to the territory of Kashmir not to mention the Kashmiris' allegations against India of state-sponsored terrorism in Kashmir. India also seeks international curbs on military assistance to Pakistan, arguing that sophisticated weapons imports embolden Pakistan's reckless adventurism in Kashmir; yet in practically the same breath India asks for increased U.S. military assistance to itself.[4] The international actions sought, in other words, are almost entirely punitive and retaliatory, not mediative and conciliatory. The situation's volatility invites international attention; yet openings for impartial and mitigative international intervention are hard to spot.

It is tempting in these circumstances, and by no means not without justification, simply to classify the India-Pakistan dispute over Kashmir among the world's "conflicts unending" and to conclude, as did the author of a book by that name, that "the South Asian problem is unripe for solution."[5] In choosing to do that, however, one would be failing to notice that since that book's publication in 1990 two of the five cases examined by its author—the problem of White rule in South Africa and the Arab-Israeli dispute in the Middle East—have undergone profound changes and may not any longer fit the category of unending regional conflict; and the change that has come over them has come about, by the way, through a process of internationally promoted negotiation (among domestic disputants, in South Africa's case), which almost no one thought possible right up until it happened. One would also be giving insufficient importance, in this author's judgment, to a number of signs, including the partial (heavy weapons) cease-fire installed on the LOC during 1992, that Indian and Pakistani policymakers are themselves apprehensive about the dangers of escalating conflict inherent in the continuing deadlock between them over Kashmir.

But can this deadlock be broken? It can, I think, provided that Indian and Pakistani leaders can be persuaded to make *that* their goal in Kashmir and, thus, to abandon for now the dreary, counterproductive, and almost certainly hopeless quest for a *solution* to it. There is a vast difference between these two goals. Breaking deadlock, on the one hand, requires only that the adversaries reach agreement that the status quo in Kashmir is, for both of them, intolerably dangerous and costly, and that they should, therefore, develop specific and durable rules and institutions to govern their disagreement in less dangerous and costly ways. Notice, however, that from this standpoint they accept that the dispute is a more-or-less permanent fixture of the political equation between them. Seeking a solution, on the other hand, requires not only that they agree on the intolerability of the status quo but that they agree, also, on the desirability of the new circumstances that are to replace it. Breaking deadlock is itself obviously a formidable undertaking. Insisting that it be considered inseparable from a solution, for all practical purposes, renders it impossible.

A major premise of the discussion throughout this book, until now only implicit, has been that there does not exist, in fact, a *right* solution to this dispute—not one, in other words, that would seem morally superior to any other, that would eliminate or neutralize the contradictions now imbedded in the dispute sufficiently to end it, or that would be likely to surmount enough of the objections to it to win the support of all the main protagonists. Our discussion has shown, for instance, that Pakistan's claim to Kashmir on grounds that its accession to India in 1947 was provisional, in view of all the historical circumstances existing at that time, clearly has merit. But India's claim that Pakistan's intervention in Kashmir, both before and after the act of accession, was not innocent of aggression also has merit. And so, indeed, does the Kashmiri claim, emerging now after nearly a half century of political exploitation by *both* India and Pakistan, that they ought to rule themselves. Our discussion has also shown that these claims can not realistically be reconciled with one another. No matter how hard we try, we cannot fabricate a formula that allocates equally among the claimants possession of the irremediably finite territory of Kashmir.

Even if the merits of these claims could somehow be scientifically weighed and the claims themselves reconciled, however, it would make little difference to our argument. The fact of the matter is that India wields a terribly disproportionate share of power in the South Asian region and, when it comes to a settlement in Kashmir, cannot be treated as the equal of Pakistan, much less of Kashmir. Pakistani and Kashmiri claims, it bears repeating, unquestionably have merit; but merit is not the only (or most important) variable to be reckoned with. We simply cannot escape the harsh logic implied in the ranking of probable outcomes in the Kashmir struggle given to the author by a senior Pakistani diplomat, who suggested that the *least likely* outcome was Kashmir's accession to Pakistan, that its *next least likely* outcome was Kashmir's achievement of independence, and that the *most likely* outcome was crushing of the separatist movement by India and the continuation of the territorial status quo.[6] Unless its power is accommodated, in other words, India will surely be tempted to forgo entirely all talk of negotiations and, instead, without equivocation to apply in Kashmir the model of counterinsurgency perfected in the course of fighting Sikh secessionists in the Punjab (a model, by the way, extensively instructed by India's very lengthy, varied, and bloody experiences with secessionist insurgency in its Northeast). Central to this model has been heavy reliance on the military muscle embodied in the security forces, the relentless and merciless hunting down of hardcore militants, the complete rejection of serious political compromise with them, imposition of severe sanctions against potential sympathizers among the noncombatant population, and suspension of civil rights. This model appears to have brought India a victory of sorts over the Sikh militants in Punjab. It was applied there, one should note, with the acquiescence, if not active support, of a large segment of the Sikh population, many of whom were fed up with the corruption, factional feuds, and ruthless tactics of the militants. Its full adoption in Kashmir, we observed earlier in this study, would likely require some modification of its components. Whether modified or not, however, this model has undeniable appeal to those engaged in counterinsurgency operations there. In contemplating what to do about Kashmir, this blunt fact—the inescapable requirement that Indian power be recognized and, in significant measure, accommodated—has got to be taken fully into account.

Yet there is another angle to the region's power equation that also needs to be taken into account. This is that Pakistan, while clearly in no position to wrench Kashmir from Indian hands, is fully capable of playing a skillful spoiler role there. Of this capability, the record of the last four years speaks rather plainly: India's power has failed conspicuously to overcome its vulnerability to costly retaliation by its foes in Kashmir. Indian leaders themselves are under no illusions about this. Describing the official Indian view of the Kashmir dispute, the Indian foreign secretary Jyotinder Nath Dixit, for instance, listed the following points:

1. We accept that there is alienation in the valley.
2. We accept that the government of India must explore the roots of this alienation.
3. We understand that this alienation cannot be dealt with solely by India's security forces (i.e., that the problem is also political).
4. We understand also that the responsibility for the problem cannot be placed wholly on Pakistan.
5. However, we believe that Pakistan plays a very key role.

Elaborating on the last point, he drew a verbal portrait of India's conflict with Pakistan that went something like this: India, he said, is very large and ethnically polyglot while Pakistan is smaller and ethnically more coherent. These two countries, he explained, are members, so to speak, of a joint family. Now, if one member of this family (India) has its house set on fire, the other (Pakistan) could choose either to help put the fire out or it could add to the fire by pouring gasoline on it. The second, he said—to pour gasoline on the fire in India's house—was Pakistan's choice.[7] India's weaknesses, obviously, were

Pakistan's strengths. Any arrangement in Kashmir not also taking *this* blunt fact into account, we might add, will just as surely fail.

Assuming for the moment that the deadlock can be broken, what exactly does that mean? It means, as has just been pointed out, that the notion that there exists a right solution must be discarded *in its entirety* and *by both India and Pakistan.* It means, second, that these two countries must give clear indication, largely with symbolic gestures that we consider later, that they have, in fact, set this notion aside. It means, third, that both sides must commit themselves to a process of substantive negotiation about Kashmir that is aimed at demilitarization—that is, at a reduction in the military threat each poses to the other in Kashmir. It means, fourth, that solving the Kashmir dispute, while remaining a distant possibility, is replaced by the more immediate and pragmatic purposes of preventing war between India and Pakistan as well as creating an environment congenial to the progressive realization of a more stable and secure relationship between them. It means, finally, that the solution to the dispute, if it ever comes within reach, will be sought without preconditions and primarily for the purposes just stated.

Concretely, what might India and Pakistan do *now* to set in motion the process of breaking deadlock? There are a number of possibilities. We examine three, the first two largely symbolic, the third substantive:

1. *Pakistan's position on the achievement of settlement in Kashmir should be formally amended to allow for alternatives to the current bifold version of plebiscite.* It is both contradictory and unrealistic for Pakistanis to demand of the Indian government that it concede the right of self-determination to the people of Kashmir while at the same time insisting upon a definition of self-determination that is transparently self-serving. It is not required that the plebiscitary instrument itself be formally repudiated; neither would this concession require that Pakistan consent to the scrapping of the UN resolutions that authorized the plebiscite in the first place. What would be required is that Pakistan concede that the plebiscite might allow for other than accession to either India or Pakistan.

Taking such a step would admittedly require a fairly basic amendment of Pakistan's traditional stance. It would not, it bears repeating, represent a retreat from Pakistan's demand that there *be* a plebiscite; and it would thus not in any way mean Pakistan's abandonment of the position that ownership of Kashmir *is in dispute.* It would, however, imply that the *future* of Kashmir was considerably more open-ended than Pakistan's present formal position can accommodate.

The original plebiscite proposal could not, in any event, be implemented today in its original form.[8] The desirability of converting to a limited (partial or regional) plebiscite, as we have seen, was already recognized in 1950 by Sir Owen Dixon; and the passage of over four decades since then obviously would require still greater modification of the instrument to take account of the major demographic and political changes that have occurred in the state. It is virtually inconceivable nowadays, for instance, and it would certainly not be considered just by many were sovereignty over the non-Muslim regions of the state—Jammu and Ladakh—to be transferred to Muslim Pakistan via majority vote of the state's predominantly Muslim population.

No doubt, Pakistan's leaders would pay a political price at home for making a gesture of this kind. There is no better way, however, for Pakistan to convey the message to India of its willingness to discard the futilitarian quest for a right solution. Neither is there a better way to convey to both the Muslims and non-Muslims of Jammu and Kashmir—and, for that matter, to the international community—Pakistan's recognition of the enlarged meaning of self-determination in today's world. Nevertheless, a gesture as bold as this would clearly deserve an equivalent gesture from the Indian side.

2. *India's position on the achievement of settlement in Kashmir should be formally amended to eliminate any Indian claim to sovereignty over that part of Kashmir currently in Pakistan's possession (i.e., Azad Kashmir and the Northern Areas).* This measure, by vacating, on the one hand, India's claim to the whole of the state of Jammu and Kashmir and by recognizing, on the other, the validity of Pakistan's possession of a part of it, would give Pakistan immediate and uncontested legal standing in Kashmir. It would not concede that that part of Kashmir in *Indian* hands was in dispute (or that Indian sovereignty over it was in any way limited or provisional); but, in striking from the Indian claim any entitlement to the territory presently in Pakistani hands, it would clearly compensate Pakistan for its relinquishment of insistence on a bifold plebiscite.

Taking this step would, of course, not be entirely painless for India. Pakistan would be gaining Indian recognition of Pakistan's sovereignty over its portion of Kashmir without having to extend the same benefit to India: That part of Kashmir in Indian hands would, in Pakistani eyes *and in the eyes of the international community,* still be disputed. It would not bring into question the legality of accession, however, and it would be entirely consistent with, even if it did not exactly fulfill, what all along has been the apparent aim of Indian policy in Kashmir—the permanent division of the state via conversion of the LOC into the international boundary.

3. *Pakistan and India should negotiate an agreement providing for the mutual, complete, and unconditional withdrawal of their armed forces from* *the Siachen Glacier.* The military and strategic importance of the Siachen Glacier is, of course, debatable; but a strong undercurrent of skepticism about its importance exists in decision-making circles (military and civilian) on the Indian side, which now holds the glacier, a fact that should vastly ease arranging for the Indian army's exit. The Pakistan army may relish its role in keeping the Indian army tied down at Siachen; but it would relish even more the Indian army's withdrawal. The waste of resources and environmental damage stemming from nearly a decade of fighting at Siachen have been spectacular. Few would contest that. Both sides would benefit from cessation of the fighting. There is nothing very vital at stake.

The Siachen dispute, as we have seen, is the one fragment of the Kashmir dispute about which Indians and Pakistanis have been able to sustain serious negotiations. These negotiations cannot succeed, however, if agreement is made contingent upon Pakistan's acquiescence, in one way or another, to the territorial status quo—India's de facto control of the glacier, in other words. It is time to admit that the question of ownership needs to be set aside and that the Siachen territory must revert to the status of a no-man's-land that it held up to 1984. The LOC, for now, should be left unfinished. This is an untidy solution; and, judged exclusively in terms of square miles that would have to be turned loose of military control, it is weighted against the Indians. The compensation for this is great, however, if it leads to the deescalation of tensions between India and Pakistan and to the demilitarization not only of the Siachen but of the LOC. Moreover, existing territorial claims to the glacier—the Indian claim to the AGPL in the Saltoro Range, on the one hand, the Pakistani claim to a line running from gridpoint NJ 9842 to the Karakoram Pass, on the other—would not be jettisoned in the agreement, merely set aside.

The end of the Cold War has not transformed the traditional enmity of India and Pakistan into a relationship premised upon peace and cooperation. It appears unlikely to do so. If there is to be such a relationship, it will have to be secured mainly through the dogged efforts of the leaders of these two countries. Among their efforts, settling the Kashmir dispute will necessarily demand high priority. Their first step should be to break the current deadlock. One hopes they succeed.

APPENDICES

APPENDIX I

Chronological listing of major bilateral negotiations, international peacekeeping, and mediation efforts relating to India-Pakistan disputes over Kashmir and Siachen Glacier, 1947 through January 1994

UNITED NATIONS MEDIATION: KASHMIR

A. UN Commission on India and Pakistan (UNCIP), 1948–50

1 Jan 1948 Letter of Indian representative to president of UN Security Council. Security Council action to restore peace in Kashmir requested. Conditional commitment made to Kashmiri self-determination "by the recognized method of a plebiscite or referendum . . . under international auspices."

20 Jan 1948 Security Council resolution S/654. UN Commission on India and Pakistan (UNCIP) established. Indian and Pakistani representatives to UN agreed, in talks held under president of Security Council, to appointment of a three-member Commission of Mediation to go to Kashmir to investigate facts and exercise a mediatory influence. Plebiscite and other issues not specified.

21 Apr 1948 Security Council resolution S/726. UNCIP expanded to five members. Immediate departure for subcontinent to restore peace and arrange for plebiscite authorized. Establishment of UN observer group in Kashmir authorized.

7 Jul 1948 Arrival in subcontinent of expanded UNCIP.

13 Aug 1948 UNCIP cease-fire and truce agreement. Requirement reaffirmed that future status of the state of Jammu and Kashmir to be determined by reference to "the will of the people." Cease-fire ordered by India and Pakistan, to take effect 1 January 1949.

1 Jan 1949 Cease-fire implemented.

5 Jan 1949 UNCIP resolution on demilitarization. Plebiscite reaffirmed.

28 Apr 1949 UNCIP submission of new truce proposals to India and Pakistan. Rejected by both India and Pakistan.

Apr 1949 Appointment of Fleet Admiral Chester W. Nimitz as plebiscite administrator by UN secretary general.

27 Jul 1949 Agreement between military representatives of India and Pakistan regarding the establishment of a cease-fire line in the state of Jammu and Kashmir [Karachi Agreement]. UN military observers authorized. Agreement followed joint military meetings in Karachi under Truce Subcommittee of UNCIP, 18–27 July.

26 Aug 1949 UNCIP submission of arbitration proposal to India and Pakistan. Rejected by both India and Pakistan.

22 Dec 1949 Proposals on demilitarization and plebiscite submitted by General A. G. L. McNaughton, president of the Security Council, to India and Pakistan. No agreement reached.

14 Mar 1950 Security Council replacement of UNCIP with a UN representative.

B. UN Representative, 1950–58

12 Apr 1950 Security Council appointment of Sir Owen Dixon as UN representative for India and Pakistan.

15 Sep 1950 Report of the UN representative for India and Pakistan, Sir Owen Dixon, to the Security Council. No progress reported in mediation efforts. Partition and partial (regional) plebiscite recommended.

Apr 1951 Security Council appointment of Dr. Frank P. Graham as UN representative for India and Pakistan.

Dec 1951–Feb 1953 Revised draft proposals on demilitarization submitted by Dr. Frank P. Graham, UN representative for India and Pakistan, to India and Pakistan. Agreement on certain key proposals not reached.

21 Feb 1957 Security Council authorization of Mr. Gunnar Jarring, president of the Security Council, to hold talks with India and Pakistan in regard to proposals on demilitarization and plebiscite.

29 Apr 1957 Report of the president of the Security Council, Mr. Gunnar Jarring, to the Security Council. Proposal to arbitrate dispute rejected by India.

2 Dec 1957 Security Council authorization of Dr. Frank P. Graham, UN representative for India and Pakistan, to renew mediation efforts.

28 Mar 1958 Report of Dr. Frank P. Graham, UN representative for India and Pakistan, to the Security Council. Proposals, including proposal to arbitrate dispute, rejected by India.

THIRD-PARTY MEDIATION: KASHMIR

10 Jan 1966 Tashkent Declaration. Agreement between India and Pakistan on cease-fire and restoration of peaceful relations, reached following mediation by Soviet Union, 3–10 January.

UNITED NATIONS PEACEKEEPING: KASHMIR

24 Jan 1949 First UN military observers arrived in subcontinent to supervise cease-fire.

27 Jul 1949 Karachi Agreement. UN Military Observer Group in India and Pakistan (UNMOGIP) authorized.

5 Aug 1965 Infiltration across CFL into Indian Kashmir by Pakistani irregular forces. Rapid breakdown of cease-fire.

1 Sep 1965 Outbreak of second Indo-Pakistan war. Attack across CFL into Jammu by Pakistani regular armed forces.

4 Sep 1965 Security Council resolution S/6661. Immediate cease-fire, respect for cease-fire line, and full cooperation with UNMOGIP called for.

6 Sep 1965 Attack on Pakistan across international border by Indian armed forces.

6 Sep 1965 Security Council resolution S/Res/210(1965). Immediate cease-fire and prompt withdrawal of all armed personnel to positions held before 5 August called for. Strengthening of UNMOGIP by UN secretary general requested.

20 Sep 1965 Security Council resolution S/Res/211(1965). Cease-fire deadline of 22 September and subsequent withdrawal of all armed personnel to positions held before 5 August demanded.

23 Sep 1965 Establishment of UN India-Pakistan Observation Mission (UNIPOM) by UN secretary general. Supervision of cease-fire and withdrawal of armed personnel on international frontier outside of Kashmir mandated. UNMOGIP responsibility confined to CFL in Kashmir.

1 Mar 1966 UNIPOM functions terminated and the organization dissolved.

3 Dec 1971 Spread of third Indo-Pakistan war to western border. Pakistani air strikes against Indian targets in western sector, including Srinagar, followed by Indian retaliatory attacks along international border and CFL.

8 Dec 1971 General Assembly resolution. Immediate cease-fire and withdrawal of all forces by both sides from one another's territory called for.

16 Dec 1971 Fall of Dacca and surrender of Pakistani forces in East Pakistan.

17 Dec 1971 Unilateral Indian declaration of cease-fire in West Pakistan, acceptance by Pakistan, and end of fighting.

21 Dec 1971 Security Council resolution S/307. Withdrawal of all forces by both sides from one another's territory, including Kashmir, called for.

19 Feb 1972 Indian announcement to United Nations of willingness to negotiate settlement with Pakistan without preconditions.

3 Jul 1972 Simla Agreement. New line of control (LOC) established in Jammu and Kashmir, and commitment made to bilateral negotiation of disputes. Peacekeeping function of UNMOGIP tacitly diminished.

DIRECT BILATERAL NEGOTIATIONS: KASHMIR

30 Oct–8 Dec 1947 Meetings between representatives of India and Pakistan over Kashmir at Lahore and New Delhi. Auspices of Joint [Inter-Dominion] Defence Council. No agreement reached. Abandoned in favor of UN intercession.

25–27 Jul 1953 Meetings between prime ministers of India and Pakistan at Karachi. Preliminary discussions, including Kashmir, held.

17–20 Aug 1953 Meetings between prime ministers of India and Pakistan at New Delhi. Expert committees to deal with specific issues proposed, plebiscite to ascertain the wishes of the Kashmiri people endorsed, and deadline for appointment of plebiscite administrator by end of April 1954 agreed. (Subsequent correspondence in regard to Kashmir between the prime ministers of India and Pakistan, 27 August 1953–21 September 1954, resulted in no agreement.)

14–18 May 1955 Meetings between prime ministers of India and Pakistan on Kashmir at New Delhi. No agreement reached. Continuation of talks called for.

19–23 Sep 1960 Meetings between prime ministers of India and Pakistan at Karachi. Indus Waters Treaty signed. Major issues in Indo-Pakistan relations, including Kashmir, considered. No progress reported on Kashmir.

27–29 Dec 1962 Ministerial talks on Kashmir. First round at Rawalpindi.

16–19 Jan 1963 Ministerial talks on Kashmir. Second round at New Delhi.

8–10 Feb 1963 Ministerial talks on Kashmir. Third round at Karachi.

12–14 Mar 1963 Ministerial talks on Kashmir. Fourth round at Calcutta.

21–25 Apr 1963 Ministerial talks on Kashmir. Fifth round at Karachi.

14–16 May 1963 Ministerial talks on Kashmir. Sixth round at New Delhi. Joint communiqué ending talks reported no agreement reached on settlement of Kashmir dispute.

1–2 Mar 1966 Post-Tashkent meeting between Indian and Pakistani foreign ministers at Rawalpindi. Terminated upon failure to agree on inclusion of Kashmir on formal agenda.

28 Jun–2 Jul 1972 Simla peace talks between prime ministers of India and Pakistan. Kashmir excluded from formal agenda. New line of control (LOC) established in Jammu and Kashmir. Formal commitment made to final settlement of Jammu and Kashmir.

19 Oct 1993 Prime Minister P. V. Narasimha Rao's call for "comprehensive dialogue" with Pakistan, to include issues relating to Kashmir dispute, in letter to Benazir Bhutto, newly elected prime minister of Pakistan.

2–3 Jan 1994 Foreign secretary talks. Seventh round at Islamabad. Kashmir included on agenda. No progress reported. No further meetings scheduled.

DIRECT BILATERAL NEGOTIATIONS: SIACHEN

17 Dec 1985 Meeting between prime minister of India and president of Pakistan at New Delhi. Agreement reached to hold talks at defense secretary level on Siachen issue.

10–12 Jan 1986 Defense secretary talks on Siachen. First round at Rawalpindi. Resolved to seek negotiated settlement in accordance with spirit of Simla agreement.

10–12 Jun 1986 Defense secretary talks on Siachen. Second round at New Delhi.

4 Nov 1987 Meeting of Indian and Pakistani prime ministers at conference of South Asian Association of Regional Cooperation (SAARC) in Kathmandu. Agreement to revive suspended meetings of defense secretaries on Siachen issue.

19–20 May 1988 Defense secretary talks on Siachen. Third round at Islamabad.

23–24 Sep 1988 Defense secretary talks on Siachen. Fourth round at New Delhi.

15–17 Jun 1989 Defense secretary talks on Siachen. Fifth round at Rawalpindi. Agreement reached to work towards a comprehensive settlement of the Siachen issue based on redeployment of forces. Army authorities would determine further positions of forces on the ground. Next round scheduled at New Delhi following in-depth examination of specific proposals.

16–18 Jun 1989 Foreign secretary (collateral) talks on Siachen at Islamabad. Pakistani foreign secretary reported in Pakistani press to have declared fifth round agreement on withdrawal of forces from Siachen. Report subsequently denied by India.

9–10 Jul 1989 Military commanders talks on Siachen at New Delhi.

16–17 Jul 1989 Meetings between prime ministers of India and Pakistan at Islamabad. Results of fifth round of defense secretary talks approved. Defense secretaries directed to work toward a comprehensive settlement in accordance with Simla agreement and based on redeployment of forces. Military authorities directed to continue discussions to determine future positions on the ground to which redeployment would take place.

18–20 Aug 1989 Military commanders talks on Siachen at Rawalpindi. No progress reported. Siachen talks suspended.

16–19 Aug 1992 Sixth round of regular talks between foreign secretaries of India and Pakistan at New Delhi. Resumption of Siachen talks proposed.

4–6 Nov 1992 Defense secretary talks on Siachen. Sixth round at New Delhi. No progress reported. No further round scheduled.

APPENDIX II

Map: Indian Security Forces in Indian-Held Kashmir

Source: This map was supplied to the author in June 1993 by Pakistan military intelligence. Accuracy of Indian army deployments depicted on this map has not been independently verified.

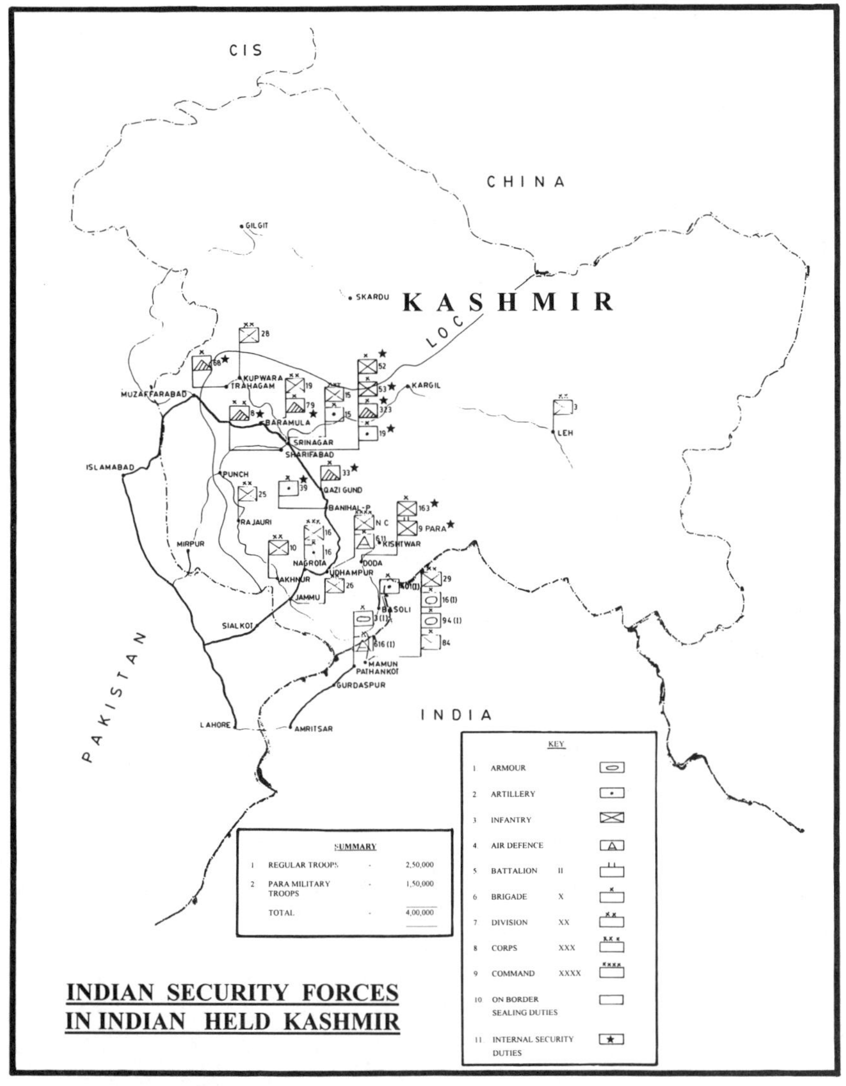

APPENDIX III

Interviews

Listing of interviews includes name, position at the time of first interview, and year(s) of interview(s). In cases of multiple interviews in different years, more than one position may be indicated. Dates of interviews are given by year only to prevent identification of sources quoted in the text in those cases where anonymity was requested. Official briefings are included here as interviews. A number of politically sensitive interviews have been omitted from this listing.

PAKISTAN (including Azad Kashmir)

Ahmad, Chaudhary Khurshid. Section Officer, General Services, Secretariat, Azad Kashmir. 1986.

Ahmad, Mushtaq. Major General, Director General, Military Intelligence Directorate. 1993.

Ahmed, Bashir. Brigadier (Rtd.), and political-defense affairs writer. 1991, 1993.

Ahmed, Bashir. Brigadier (Rtd.), and Senior Research Officer, Institute of Regional Studies. 1989, 1990, 1991.

Ali, Mohammad Imtiaz. Major General (Rtd.), Special Advisor to the Prime Minister on Defense. 1990.

Awan, Ayub Baksch. Former Director, Directorate Intelligence Bureau (DIB), and former Secretary, Ministry of Home Affairs. 1986, 1987, 1989.

Aziz, Mir Abdul. Kashmiri expatriate publicist and newspaper editor. 1986, 1989, 1990, 1991, 1993.

Bashir, Khalid. Major General, Director General, Inter-Services Public Relations Directorate. 1993.

Bukhari, Syed Asif Riaz. Brigadier, Chief of Staff, 10th Corps (Chaklala). 1989.

Choudhary, Dr. M. Khairat. Chairman, Department of Economics, University of Azad Jammu and Kashmir. 1986.

Dani, Dr. Ahmed Hasan. Historian, Professor emeritus, Quaid-i-Azam University, and Director, Centre for the Study of the Civilization of Central Asia. 1985, 1987.

Dogar, Yasub Ali. Brigadier, CO, 323rd Brigade, Force Command Northern Areas (Dansam), 10th Corps. 1989.

Hayat, Sikander. Bureau Chief, *The Frontier Post*, and Senior Editor, *The Pakistan Observer.* 1990, 1991, 1993.

Husain, Begum Syeda Abida. Former Ambassador to the United States. 1993.

Husain, Noor. Brigadier (Rtd.), and Director General, Institute of Strategic Studies. 1986, 1993.

Jabbar, Mohammad Abdul. Additional Chief Secretary for Development, Azad Kashmir. 1986.

Khan, Amanullah. Chairman, Jammu and Kashmir Liberation Front (JKLF). 1993.

Khan, Aziz Ahmad. Director General for South Asia, Ministry of Foreign Affairs. 1990.

Khan, Mansha. Colonel (Rtd.), Vice President, Azad Kashmir branch, People's Party of Pakistan (PPP), and former Speaker, Azad Kashmir Assembly. 1986.

Khan, Mohammad Ilyas. Brigadier, CO, 2nd Azad Kashmir Brigade. 1993.

Khan, Noor. Air Chief Marshal (Rtd.), Pakistan Air Force. 1986.

Khan, Sardar Abdul Qayyum. President, and Prime Minister of Azad Jammu and Kashmir. 1986, 1993.

Khan, Sardar Muhammad Ibrahim. President, Azad Kashmir branch, People's Party of Pakistan (PPP), and former President, Azad Kashmir. 1986.

Khan, Shaharyar. Foreign Secretary. 1993.

Khan, Shujaat Ali. Brigadier, CO, 62nd Brigade, Force Command Northern Areas (Skardu), 10th Corps. 1989.

Khurshid, K. H. President, Kashmir Liberation League (KLL), and former President, Azad Kashmir. 1986.

Matinuddin, Kamal. Lieutenant General (Rtd.), Director General, Institute of Strategic Studies. 1987.

Meer, Khurshid Hasan. President, Awami Jamhoori Party, and former member of federal cabinet. 1986.

Mirza, Professor Khan Zaman. Director, Institute of Kashmir Studies, University of Azad Jammu and Kashmir. 1986.

Qayyum, Afzar. Lieutenant Colonel, CO, Mujahid Force (paramilitary) Battalion (Athmuqam, Neelam Valley). 1991.

Qureshi, Khalil Ahmed. Secretary for (Refugee) Rehabilitation, Government of Azad Kashmir. 1991.

Shahi, Agha. Former Minister of Foreign Affairs. 1993.

Siddiqi, A. R. Brigadier (Rtd.), and Editor-in-Chief, *Defence Journal.* 1990.

Suharwardy, A. H. Author, and former Chief Secretary, Government of Azad Kashmir. 1991.

Syed, Anis Ali. Major General, Surveyor General, Survey of Pakistan. 1989.

Ullah, Riaz. Major General, Director General, Inter Services Public Relations. 1991.

Vardag, Asaf F. Senator; Vice President, Pakistan Muslim League; Additional Secretary General, Islamic Democratic Alliance (IDA); and Chairman, Defence Committee of the Senate. 1991.

Walid, Abdul. Major, CO, 1st Battalion, 2nd Azad Kashmir Brigade. 1993.

Zaidi, Syed Ijlal Haider. Former Secretary of Defence. 1990.

Zakir, Mohammad. Brigadier, CO, 6th Azad Kashmir Brigade. 1993.

Zaman, Zahid. Brigadier, CO, 5th Azad Kashmir Brigade. 1991.

INDIA (including Jammu and Kashmir)

Ahmed, Dr. Bashiruddin. Research Associate, Centre for Policy Research. 1991.

Anderson, Walter. Political Section, U.S. Embassy. 1991.

Baid, Samuel. Senior correspondent (Pakistan desk), United News of India (UNI). 1990, 1991.

Banerjee, David. Major General, and Deputy Director, Institute of Defence Studies and Analyses (IDSA). 1990, 1993.

Baweja, Harinder. Correspondent, *India Today*. 1993.

Bedi, B. S. Director General of Police, Jammu and Kashmir State. 1993.

Bernicat, Marcia S. B. Political Section, U.S. Embassy. 1993.

Bhargava, G. S. Political and security affairs author, and former Principal Information Officer, Government of India. 1990, 1991, 1993.

Blakeman, Chat. Political Section, U.S. Embassy. 1993.

Blowria, Sudhir S. Principal Secretary to the Governor of Jammu and Kashmir (IAS). 1993.

Chibber, Dr. Manohar Lal. Lieutenant General (Rtd.), former GOC, Northern Command. 1990.

Chopra, Dr. Pran. Senior Associate, Centre for Policy Research. 1990.

Chopra, Pushpindar Singh. Author and defense analyst. 1990.

Cretz, Gene. Political Section, U.S. Embassy. 1991.

Damodaran, A. K. Secretary, Policy Planning Committee, Ministry of External Affairs. 1986.

Dersingkar, Dr. Giri. Director, Centre for the Study of Developing Societies. 1990, 1991.

Desmond, Edward. Bureau Chief, *Time International*. 1991.

Dewan, Parvez. Secretary of Information and Tourism, Jammu and Kashmir. 1993.

Dixit, Jyotinder Nath. Foreign Secretary. 1993.

D'Suza, Kevin. Major General, GOC, 19th Infantry Division (Baramulla). 1991.

Farooqi, Naeem. Lieutenant Colonel, Public Relations Officer, 15th Corps (Srinagar). 1991.

Galarza, Ricardo. Major General, Chief Military Observer (CMO), United Nations Military Observer Group in India and Pakistan (UNMOGIP). 1993.

Gonsalves, Eric. Director, India International Centre, and former Director General for East Asia, Ministry of External Affairs. 1991.

Gupta, Arvind. Joint Secretary, on deputation from Ministry of External Affairs to Institute of Defence Studies and Analyses. 1990.

Gupta, Madhukar. Director, Kashmir Desk, Ministry of Home Affairs. 1993.

Gupta, Shekhar. Features Editor, *India Today.* 1990, 1991.

Itoo, Wali Mohammad. Former Speaker, Kashmir Assembly (National Conference). 1993.

Jagmohan, Malhotra. Former Governor, Jammu and Kashmir. 1991.

Jaitley, Ashok. Political Advisor to the Governor, Jammu and Kashmir, and former Chief Secretary, Planning and Development, Jammu and Kashmir. 1991, 1993.

Johnsen, Thor A. Brigadier General, Chief Military Observer (CMO), United Nations Military Observer Group in India and Pakistan (UNMOGIP). 1986.

Joshi, Dr. Manoj. Senior correspondent, *The Hindu.* 1990, 1991.

Kapoor, Amar. Additional Director General of Police (Criminal Investigation Division/CID), Jammu and Kashmir. 1993.

Karim, Afsir. Major General (Rtd.), and defense writer. 1991.

Khokar, Riaz. High Commissioner of Pakistan in India. 1993.

Kumar, D. Colonel, CO, Headquarters Battalion, 7th Assam Rifles (Chokibal). 1991.

Lasrado, George M. Brigadier, CO, Headquarters Brigade, 15th Corps (Srinagar). 1991.

Madhok, Balraj. Professor, author, and former Member of Parliament (Bharatiya Jana Sangh). 1993.

Malik, Nazir Ahmed. Member, Jammu and Kashmir Forum for Human Rights and Civil Liberties. 1993.

Mann, H. R. S. Major General, GOC, 28th Division (Kupwara). 1993.

Marwah, Ved P. Senior Research Associate, Centre for Policy Research, and former Police Advisor to the Government of Jammu and Kashmir. 1993.

McCollough, Dundes. Political Section, U.S. Embassy. 1991.

Mir, Iqbal. Assistant Director for Protocol, Kashmir Division, Government of Jammu and Kashmir. 1993.

Mosina, Dan. Political Section, U.S. Embassy. 1991.

Mukerjee, Dileep. Senior Editor, *The Times of India*. 1991.

Nanavatty, R. K. Brigadier, CO, 102nd Brigade (Ladakh). 1990.

Nath, Surinder. General, Vice Chief of Army Staff (VCOAS), and former GOC, 15th Corps (Srinagar). 1993.

Noorani, Abdul Ghafoor. Attorney, and author. 1993.

Palit, D. K. Major General (Rtd.), author, and former Director General of Military Operations. 1990.

Panaj, C. S. Director of Military Intelligence, 15th Corps (Srinagar). 1991.

Pilot, Rajesh. Minister of State for Internal Security, Ministry of Home Affairs. 1993.

Qasim, Mir. Former Chief Minister of Jammu and Kashmir. 1990.

Qayyum, Abdul. Attorney and President, Bar Association of Jammu and Kashmir. 1993.

Raghavan, V. R. Lieutenant General, Director General of Military Operations, and former GOC, 28th Infantry Division (Ladakh). 1990, 1993.

Rao, K. V. Krishna. Lieutenant General (Rtd.), and Governor, Jammu and Kashmir State. 1993.

Rao, P. V. Narasimha. Prime Minister. 1993.

Rasgotra, M. K. Former Foreign Secretary, and former Ambassador to the United States. 1986.

Rasool, Sheikh Ghulam. Chief Secretary, Jammu and Kashmir. 1993.

Rikhye, Ravi. Author, defense analyst, and Member, Institute of Defence Studies and Analyses (IDSA). 1986, 1990.

Rodrigues, S. F. General, Chief of Army Staff (COAS). 1991.

Sachar, Rajendra. Supreme Court Justice (Rtd.), and President, People's Union for Civil Liberties (PUCL). 1993.

Sareen, Rajendra. Political affairs author, and Manager, Public Opinion Trends and Analysis (POT). 1990, 1991.

Sawhney, Pravin. Defense correspondent, *Observer,* and *Indian Express.* 1991, 1993.

Sen Gupta, Dr. Bhabani. Senior Associate, Centre for Policy Research. 1986, 1993.

Seth, Aftab. Joint Secretary, External Publicity, Ministry of Information and Broadcasting. 1990.

Sidhva, Shiraz. Correspondent, *Sunday,* and *Financial Times* (London). 1991, 1993.

Singh, Dinesh. Minister of External Affairs. 1993.

Singh, Jaswant. Member of Parliament (Bharatiya Janata Party). 1993.

Singh, Kewal. Former Foreign Secretary, and former Ambassador to the United States. 1986.

Singh, S. K. Former Foreign Secretary. 1990.

Soz, Saifuddin. Professor, and former Member of Parliament from Kashmir (National Conference). 1991, 1993.

Sturgeon, William. Lieutenant Colonel, CO, HQ Battalion (Rustom picket/LOC). 1991.

Tarkunde, V. M. Supreme Court Justice (Rtd.), and former President, People's Union for Civil Liberties (PUCL) and Citizens for Democracy. 1993.

Thomas, Mathew. Lieutenant General (Rtd.), and Editor, *Indian Defence Review.* 1991.

Vaida, G. H. Member, Jammu and Kashmir Forum for Human Rights & Civil Liberties. 1993.

Van Biesebroeck, Ides. Captain, Military Observer (MO), UNMOGIP. 1991.

Venkateswaran, A. P. Senior Associate, Centre for Policy Research, and former Foreign Secretary. 1990, 1991.

Verghese, George. Senior Associate, Centre for Policy Research. 1990, 1991.

Zaki, Mohammad A. Lieutenant General (Rtd.), Military Advisor to the Governor, Jammu and Kashmir, Chairman of the Unified Command, and former GOC, 15th Corps (Srinagar). 1991, 1993.

NOTES

Introduction

1. A. Siegfried (1938), quoted in J. R. V. Prescott, *Political Frontiers and Boundaries* (London: Allen & Unwin, 1987), p. 131.

2. For an earlier elaboration of this thesis, see Robert Wirsing, "Kashmir Conflict: The New Phase," in Charles H. Kennedy (ed.), *Pakistan 1992* (Boulder, CO: Westview Press, 1993), pp. 133–65.

Chapter 1

1. According to a leading student of boundary disputes, the geographer J. R. V. Prescott, the concept of boundary dispute refers to four distinct types of disagreements between countries: (1) *territorial* boundary disputes, in which the dispute is basically about the rights to possession of a borderland territory; (2) *positional* boundary disputes, in which it is the actual location of the boundary that is the primary focus of contention; (3) *functional* boundary disputes, in which conflicts "arise because states are unreasonably diligent in applying regulations or because they are negligent in enforcing rules"; and (4) *resource development* boundary disputes, in which the focus is largely on transboundary resources such as rivers. These types are obviously not mutually exclusive, and it is equally obvious that the Kashmir dispute overlaps all of them. *Political Frontiers and Boundaries* (London: Allen & Unwin, 1987), p. 98.

2. For discussion, see *ibid.,* pp. 103–14.

3. See Golam W. Choudhury, *Pakistan's Relations with India* (New Delhi: Meenakshi Prakashan, 1971), p. 68.

4. On the latter point, see Government of India, *White Paper on Jammu and Kashmir* (New Delhi, 1948), p. 2. This paper presents an excellent summary of India's formal positions on Kashmir at an early stage in the conflict's evolution.

5. According to Prescott, "territorial disputes based solely on legal arguments . . . are comparatively rare," and "the largest number of territorial disputes lack any significant legal component . . ." *Political Frontiers and Boundaries,* p. 103.

6. Government of India, *White Paper on Jammu and Kashmir,* p. 80.

7. *Ibid,* p. 82.

8. The decision to divide British Punjab and Bengal between the two new successor states was made over the objection of Muslim League leader Mohammad Ali Jinnah, who had long demanded that these two Muslim-majority provinces be ceded intact to Pakistan. Dividing them proved a much harder task than did drawing the new international boundary between

India and Pakistan that lay between the southern border of Punjab, where the Punjab Boundary Commission's jurisdiction ended, and the Arabian Sea. That stretch followed existing princely state or, in the case of Sind, provincial borders. Generally speaking, the religious mixtures found in these areas presented fewer difficulties than were found in Punjab and Bengal. The number of Sikhs, in particular, thinned out rapidly south of Punjab. Later on a boundary dispute did surface between India and Pakistan over the Rann of Kutch, a stretch of coastal swampland lying between Sind province of Pakistan and Gujarat province of India, at the southern end of the international border. The Rann was largely uninhabited, however, and the dispute over it did not entail issues of religious composition.

9. The specific terms of reference of the Punjab Boundary Commission, as contained in the instructions to the commission of 30 June 1947, were: "The Boundary Commission is instructed to demarcate the boundaries of the two parts of the Punjab on the basis of ascertaining the contiguous majority areas of Muslims and non-Muslims. In doing so it will also take into account other factors." Nicholas Mansergh, et al. (eds.), *Constitutional Relations Between Britain and India: The Transfer of Power 1942-47,* Vol. XI (London: Her Majesty's Stationery Office, 1982), Document No. 415. This and companion volumes in this series will be cited hereafter as *TP,* followed by volume and document number. For a detailed and excellent study of the work of the Punjab Boundary Commission, see Kirpal Singh, *The Partition of the Punjab* (Patiala: Punjabi University, 1972).

10. *TP,* XI, 45.

11. *TP,* XII, 164.

12. Quoted in Chaudhri Muhammad Ali, *The Emergence of Pakistan* (New York: Columbia University Press, 1967), p. 221.

13. The issue of whether the princely states actually recovered sovereignty with the lapse of British paramountcy and thus had the right to choose independence is considered later in this chapter in the section on the aggression issue.

14. Lord Birdwood, *A Continent Decides* (London: Robert Hale Limited, 1953), p. 303.

15. In Bengal's case, Pakistan was awarded the non–Muslim-majority (largely Buddhist) Chittagong Hill Tracts. At the same time, however, a number of Muslim-majority districts or *tehsils* in Calcutta's hinterland were awarded to India's West Bengal. On the Bengal awards, see Ali, *The Emergence of Pakistan,* pp. 205-10.

16. *TP,* XII, 488.

17. *TP,* XII, 488.

18. Radcliffe's comment was recorded in a memorandum prepared for Under-Secretary of State for India Arthur Henderson, dated 20 August 1947, cited in Hugh Tinker, "Pressure, Persuasion, Decision: Factors in the Partition of the Punjab, August 1947," *Journal of Asian Studies* 36:4 (August 1977), p. 702. Concerning Gurdaspur, the memorandum stated: "The reason for this change [from the notional boundary] is understood to be that the headwaters of the canals which irrigate the Amritsar District lie in the Gurdaspur District and it is important to keep as much as possible of these canals under one administration."

19. Birdwood, *A Continent Decides,* p. 36. According to Kirpal Singh's account, the two Muslim members of the commission had no doubt that Gurdaspur would go to India. He

quotes a newspaper report stating that Justice Mohammad Munir had claimed in a Lahore speech in April 1960 that he had "no hesitation in disclosing [that] it was clear to both Mr. Din Mohammed and myself from the very beginning of the discussions with Mr. Radcliffe that Gurdaspur was going to India and our apprehensions were communicated at a very early stage to those who had been deputed by the Muslim League to help us." *The Partition of the Punjab*, pp. 78–79. Professor Hugh Tinker points out that no provisions at all had been made for the Sikh community in Mountbatten's 3 June plan. The word *Sikh* did not appear in the plan. Neither did it appear anywhere in Radcliffe's award. In spite of these omissions, however, Tinker concludes that

> underlying Radcliffe's report seems to be an awareness that the Sikhs could not with justice be totally dispossessed. After all, the Muslims were to have their homeland, comprising three entire provinces and extensive portions of three other provinces. The non-Muslim majority of Indians would have three-quarters of undivided India as their own. But the Sikhs had only the central districts of Punjab—the Manjha—as their home. . . . [U]nder the Independence Act, the Sikhs would find the districts that were their main centers of population divided—six to India, seven to Pakistan. To a considerable degree, Radcliffe acquiesced in the necessity for a Solomon-like award which would divide the community in two. But he did reflect carefully upon the problem of preserving intact the Sikh heartland, Amritsar and the Manjha.
>
> Tinker, "Pressure, Persuasion, Decision," pp. 697–98.

20. V. P. Menon, *The Transfer of Power in India* (Princeton, NJ: Princeton University Press, 1957), p. 403.

21. Birdwood, *A Continent Decides*, p. 36. Later in this volume (p. 236) Birdwood observed that "it was Radcliffe's award to India of the Gurdaspur and Batala *tehsils*, with Moslem majorities, which rendered possible the maintenance of an Indian force at Jammu based on Pathankot as railhead, and which enabled India to consolidate her defences southwards all the way from Uri to the Pakistan border." For Lord Birdwood's more comprehensive discussion of Kashmir, see *Two Nations and Kashmir* (London: Robert Hale, 1956).

22. H. V. Hodson, *The Great Divide: Britain—India—Pakistan* (London: Hutchinson, 1969), p. 354.

23. Alan Campbell-Johnson, *Mission With Mountbatten* (New York: E. P. Dutton & Co., 1953), p. 152.

24. Michael Brecher, *Nehru: A Political Biography* (London: Oxford University Press, 1959), p. 360.

25. *Ibid.*, p. 361. In his earlier book focused directly on Kashmir, Michael Brecher had been similarly dismissive of Pakistani claims of a conspiracy underlying the accession of Kashmir to India. Curiously, in that work, originally Brecher's Ph.D. dissertation, there was no reference at all to the Gurdaspur issue, Radcliffe, or the boundary awards. *The Struggle for Kashmir* (Toronto: Ryerson Press, 1953), see especially pp. 33–39.

26. Birdwood, *A Continent Decides*, p. 36.

27. Hodson, *The Great Divide*, pp. 353–34.

28. Ian Stephens, *Pakistan* (London: Ernest Benn Limited, 1963), p. 177.

29. Alastair Lamb, *The Kashmir Problem: A Historical Survey* (New York: Praeger, 1966), p. 42. Lamb went on to say that the Radcliffe award nevertheless "aroused much suspicion in Pakistan as to the disinterestedness of the British; and, if nothing else, it shows the scant preparation which the British made for partition and the little thought they appear to have given to its consequences." Skepticism about Pakistani claims in regard to the Radcliffe award is also apparent in the classic study of the Kashmir conflict by Josef Korbel, the Czech diplomat named to the United Nations Commission for India and Pakistan at its establishment in 1948. See *Danger in Kashmir* (Princeton, NJ: Princeton University Press, 2nd ed., 1966), pp. 57–63.

30. Ali, *The Emergence of Pakistan,* pp. 218–19.

31. *Ibid.,* p. 216.

32. Aloys A. Michel, *The Indus Rivers: A Study of the Effects of Partition* (New Haven, CT: Yale University Press, 1967), p. 189.

33. *Ibid.,* p. 193. Radcliffe's boundary award in the Punjab created a number of anomalies in regard to irrigation canals and their headworks. For comment, see Penderel Moon, *Divide and Quit* (Berkeley: University of California Press, 1962), pp. 186, 226.

34. Sardar Vallabhbhai Patel, Durga Das (ed.), *Sardar Patel's Correspondence 1945–50. Volume I. New Light on Kashmir* (Ahmedabad: Navajivan Publishing House, 1971). Hereafter cited as Das, I, followed by the document number. Mountbatten's papers had been made available years earlier (1962) to H. V. Hodson, whose study, *The Great Divide,* was published in 1969. It was not until another decade had passed, however, before access was granted to other scholars.

35. For full citation of the *Transfer of Power* series, see note 9 above.

36. Representative of revisionist accounts exploiting these new resources was the much-discussed book by Ayesha Jalal, *The Sole Spokesman: Jinnah, the Muslim League and the Demand for Pakistan* (London: Cambridge University Press, 1985).

37. See, for example, Latif Ahmed Sherwani, *The Partition of India and Mountbatten* (Karachi: Council for Pakistan Studies, 1986); and Y. Krishan, "Mountbatten and the Partition of India," *History* 68:222 (February 1983), pp. 22–38.

38. Professor Tinker conceded that Radcliffe

> did at first intend to allot a substantial portion of Ferozepore District to Pakistan, . . . [d]oubtless . . . as compensation for the allocation of Muslim-majority areas in Gurdaspur to India. Perhaps his subsequent withdrawal of the boundary to the line of the Sutlej River was to make a less irregular frontier, perhaps it was to lessen the possibility of immediate friction between the new India and Pakistan. [However,] the alternative explanation—that Lord Mountbatten exercised his powers of persuasion over Lord Radcliffe to induce him to modify one relatively small sector of his Punjab award in order to give the new Governor-General [Mountbatten] a better start in office, or to make India look with more favor upon a continuing Commonwealth relationship, or to bring about some other happening—cannot be entertained on the basis of the correspondence included with the "Transfer of Power" Papers, preserved by the Commonwealth Relations Office.

Tinker, "Pressure, Persuasion, Decision," p. 704.

39. R. J. Moore, *Making the New Commonwealth* (Oxford: Clarendon Press, 1987), p. 30.

40. *Ibid.*, p. 31.

41. "There is justice in Hugh Tinker's observation," he says, "that Radcliffe was, in effect, obliged to fashion a 'para-political solution' to the Sikh problem, of which the plan for the transfer of power and partition had taken no account. His award is consistent with that obligation above all others." *Ibid.*, p. 37.

42. Philip Ziegler, *Mountbatten* (New York: Alfred A. Knopf, 1985), p. 402.

43. *Ibid.*, p. 420.

44. *Ibid.*, p. 421.

45. *Ibid.*, p. 421. Ziegler quotes a 9 August diary entry of John Christie, a joint private secretary to the viceroy, recording a comment of George Abell, the viceroy's private secretary: "'George tells me H.E. [Mountbatten] is in a tired flap and is having to be strenuously dissuaded from asking Radcliffe to alter his awards.'"

46. *Ibid.*, p. 422.

47. Simon Scott Plummer, "How Mountbatten Bent the Rules and the Indian Border," *The Daily Telegraph* (London), 24 February 1992. The author is indebted to Alastair Lamb for bringing this item to his attention.

48. The Punjab award had apparently been completed by 8 August, which was the date on which the secretary to the Radcliffe Commission, Beaumont, provided the viceroy's private secretary, George Abell, with advance information about the new Punjab boundary for secret transmission to the Punjab governor, Sir Evan Jenkins. News of the new boundary was quickly leaked, however. Among those learning of it was Kanwar Sain, who at the time of the transfer of power was chief irrigation engineer of the state of Bikaner, in which Ferozepore *tehsil* was located. Sain wrote in his autobiography, published in 1978, that he persuaded the maharaja of Bikaner first to dispatch a telegram to Mountbatten outlining his objections to the "rumored" boundary award and then to send Sain and the state's prime minister, Sardar Panikkar, by air to New Delhi to present Bikaner's case for retaining within India the headworks of the Bikaner Gang Canal (located in Ferozepore *tehsil*) directly to the viceroy, with whom the maharaja was personally acquainted. Sain and Sardar Panikkar apparently succeeded in getting a brief meeting with Mountbatten on 11 August. Sain claims that Mountbatten declined to intervene and bluntly informed the maharaja's emissaries that "the Viceroy had nothing to do with the Radcliffe Commission. That Commission has been appointed by His Majesty's Government. Radcliffe is not to report to me." That same evening Sain and Panikkar heard on the radio that announcement of the Punjab boundary award had been delayed by a few days. Kanwar Sain, *Reminiscences of an Engineer* (New Delhi: Young Asia Publications, 1978), pp. 90–124. Mountbatten kept no record of the meeting with Sain and Panikkar. The maharaja's telegram and Mountbatten's reply to it, in which he declined to meet with the maharaja's delegation, are reproduced in *TP*, XII, 405, 427. In his biography of Mountbatten, Ziegler concedes only that Sain's remarks offer "some tenuous support" to the allegations of impropriety charged against Mountbatten. Ziegler, *Mountbatten*, p. 420.

49. Beaumont's statement also contained the observation that a serious error had been made in appointing a Hindu, Rao Sahib V. D. Ayer, to the sensitive position of assistant

secretary to the Radcliffe Commission. According to Beaumont, only he, Radcliffe, and Ayer knew the details of the awards as they were chalked out and that Ayer had undoubtedly kept Nehru and V. P. Menon, who from 5 July was secretary of the States Department and the man chiefly responsible for managing the accession of the princely states to India, fully informed of progress.

50. Alastair Lamb, *Kashmir: A Disputed Legacy, 1846–1990* (Hertingfordbury, U.K.: Roxford Books, 1991). The earlier and more narrowly focused work was originally published in the United Kingdom as *Crisis in Kashmir, 1947–1966* (London: Routledge & Kegan Paul, 1966) and in the United States as *The Kashmir Problem.* Lamb has subsequently published yet another volume on Kashmir—*Birth of a Tragedy: Kashmir 1947* (Hertingfordbury, U.K.: Roxford Books, 1994). This book was received by the author too late for its often extremely illuminating commentary to be taken into account in this study. In it, Lamb offers fresh evidence in support of his arguments and explores a number of provocative theses, including the intriguing possibility that Maharaja Hari Singh never actually executed an instrument of accession, that were only glimpsed in his 1991 volume.

51. As evidence, Lamb cites the official record of an interview on 4 August 1947 between Mountbatten and the nawab of Bhopal and the maharaja of Indore, in the course of which Mountbatten observed that Kashmir "was so placed geographically that it could join either Dominion, provided part of Gurdaspur were put into East Punjab by the Boundary Commission." For the document, see *TP,* XII, 335.

52. Lamb, *Kashmir: A Disputed Legacy,* p. 107.

53. *Ibid.,* pp. 108-9. The letter and note are reprinted in *TP,* XI, 201, 229.

54. Lamb, *Kashmir: A Disputed Legacy,* pp. 109–10. The record of interview is reprinted in *TP,* XI, 294.

55. Lamb, *Kashmir: A Disputed Legacy,* p. 111.

56. *Ibid.,* p. 112. "This Sikh component," Lamb admitted, "has complicated greatly the interpretation of the records by those in quest of answer to the mysteries of the origins of the Kashmir dispute."

57. *Ibid.,* pp. 115–16.

58. Lamb's relatively benign view of Mountbatten appeared at a number of points in his earlier work, in which Mountbatten's occasional lapses are described more often to be the result of ignorance or unpreparedness than of conspiratorial planning. For examples, see Lamb, *The Kashmir Problem,* pp. 44–46, 48–49.

59. Among the best of such efforts is Sherwani, *The Partition of India and Mountbatten.* See also S. Hashim Raza (ed.), *Mountbatten and Pakistan* (Karachi: Quaid-i-Azam Academy, 1982).

60. M. J. Akbar, *Nehru: The Making of India* (London: Viking, 1988), p. 411.

61. *Ibid.,* pp. 411, 438.

62. *Ibid.,* p. 438. Akbar enlarges upon these arguments in his later book, *Kashmir: Behind the Vale* (New Delhi: Viking, 1991). Set against the frequently moralistic tone of his fellow countrymen's writings on Kashmir, the very deliberate realism of Akbar's books is

unquestionably refreshing. His scholarship is less than painstaking, on the other hand, so that one is bound to take the refreshment with a grain of salt.

63. Michel, *The Indus Rivers,* p. 184.

64. *Ibid.,* p. 173.

65. Government of Pakistan, Ministry of Foreign Affairs, *White Paper on the Jammu and Kashmir Dispute* (Islamabad, January 1977), p. 4.

66. Lamb, *Kashmir: A Disputed Legacy,* p. 152.

67. On this, see the revealing correspondence carried on between Mountbatten and some of his Pakistani critics in Raza (ed.), *Mountbatten and Pakistan.*

68. Lamb, *Kashmir: A Disputed Legacy,* p. 116. "The most serious charge against the last Viceroy's handling of the accession of the State of Jammu and Kashmir in the final weeks of the British Raj," Lamb wrote in concluding his chapter on partition, "is the degree to which Mountbatten (or his advisers) seem to have accepted Jawaharlal Nehru's views about Kashmiri politics and to have failed to explore the Muslim dimension."

69. *TP,* XI, 229.

70. Ziegler, *Mountbatten,* p. 701.

71. *Ibid.,* pp. 393–94. Brecher commented that "Mountbatten's most notable triumph in the sphere of personal relations was an intimate bond of friendship with Nehru. . . . [W]ith Nehru there developed a relationship of mutual trust, respect, admiration and affection which is rare among statesmen and unprecedented in the annals of the British *Raj.*" *Nehru: A Political Biography,* pp. 410–11.

72. Ziegler, *Mountbatten,* p. 701. According to Brecher, Mountbatten "had a shrewd insight into men and affairs and possessed formidable powers of persuasion. His mind was quick and he was able to remember all manner of detail." *Nehru: A Political Biography,* p. 410.

73. *TP,* XII, 456. Italics added. In his discussion of partition, Lamb cites this telegram but only to document Kak's resignation. One could argue that the telegram, which reached Mountbatten the day following Radcliffe's submission of the boundary awards, came too late to influence his judgment. But such an argument would rest on the very dubious propositions that Webb had been the first of Mountbatten's subordinates to recognize the reality of Kashmir's politics and that the views of Kashmir state officials on this subject had to this point been entirely ignored.

74. According to a Kashmir bibliographer, records relating to Kashmir of the Indian ministries of Home Affairs and External Affairs, for example, are closed back to 1913 except by special permission. Jammu and Kashmir State Archives are open to Indian and foreign scholars only up to 1925. Ramesh Chander Dogra, *Jammu and Kashmir: A Select and Annotated Bibliography* (New Delhi: Ajanta Publications, 1986), pp. 88–94.

75. In the immediate postindependence period, about 700 British officers were serving in the Pakistan army, about 300 in the Indian army. David W. Wainhouse et al., *International Peacekeeping at the Crossroads* (Baltimore: The Johns Hopkins University Press, 1973), p. 67.

76. On Mountbatten's role in India following the transfer of power, see Hodson, *The Great Divide*, pp. 401–519.

77. The argument continues to be made that had Lord Mountbatten agreed to serve as a "super" governor-general over both the new dominions or, alternatively, had Jinnah deferred to Mountbatten's proposal that he serve as common governor-general of both dominions, this problem of a missing impartial referee might not have arisen. For one view on this question, see Sherwani, *The Partition of India and Mountbatten*, pp. 83–99.

78. *TP*, XI, 45.

79. V. P. Menon, *The Integration of the Indian States* (Calcutta: Orient Longmans, 1956), p. 66. For the document, see *TP*, VII, 262.

80. Hodson remarks that "the main object of Muslim policy in this sphere was, on the face of it, to secure leverage for Pakistan and embarrass India." *The Great Divide*, p. 360. He might have added that the Congress, since it stood to gain quite disproportionately from a policy espousing the transfer rather than lapse of paramountcy, was also guided mainly by self-interest.

81. Ziegler comments that Mountbatten "devoted himself to bullying or cajoling the rulers into accession. . . . To [him] accession was so self-evidently to the benefit of the rulers and so important for the future of India that he would have believed any measure of persuasion justified." *Mountbatten*, p. 409. See also Campbell-Johnson, *Mission with Mountbatten*, pp. 140–43.

82. None of the ten states that acceded to Pakistan had done so by 15 August. Ali, *The Emergence of Pakistan*, p. 235.

83. For a Pakistani account of the Junagadh episode, see *ibid.*, pp. 276–78. For an Indian view, see Menon, *The Integration of the Indian States*, pp. 124–50.

84. Menon, *The Integration of the Indian States*, p. 344.

85. See *ibid.*, pp. 314–89; Ali, *The Emergence of Pakistan*, pp. 278–81; and Hodson, *The Great Divide*, pp. 475–93.

86. Pakistan's leadership was no doubt influenced in part by the nizam's prompt authorization of a huge loan to the new, and virtually bankrupt, government of Pakistan. Menon, *The Integration of the Indian States*, pp. 339–40, 370–71; and Stanley Wolpert, *Jinnah of Pakistan* (New York: Oxford University Press, 1984), pp. 358–59.

87. In a statement released to the press on 13 July 1947, about a month prior to the transfer of power, Mohammad Ali Jinnah seemed to give maximum freedom to the princes to choose between India and Pakistan, or to choose independence from both of them, in deciding the accession question. Speaking specifically of Kashmir, he made it clear, however, that this question should not be settled without regard to the feelings and sentiments of the people. *TP*, XII, 87. There is evidence that Pakistan's leaders, thinking that a concession in regard to Kashmir might be obtained in return for their agreement to a plebiscite in Junagadh, gave some thought to the latter in the weeks just prior to the accession of Kashmir to India. See Lamb, *Kashmir: A Disputed Legacy*, pp. 127–28; and Ziegler, *Mountbatten*, p. 444.

88. Ziegler, *Mountbatten,* p. 444.

89. Menon, *The Integration of the Indian States,* p. 108. For Mountbatten's address to the princes, see K. Sarwar Hasan (ed.), *The Kashmir Question: Documents on the Foreign Relations of Pakistan* (Karachi: Pakistan Institute of International Affairs, 1966), pp. 11–16.

90. Government of India, *White Paper on Jammu and Kashmir,* p. 23.

91. Menon, *The Integration of the Indian States,* p. 395.

92. *Ibid.,* pp. 413–14.

93. Hodson, *The Great Divide,* pp. 441–44. According to Mountbatten's press secretary, New Delhi's policy since the transfer of power had "been to refrain from inducing Kashmir to accede. Indeed, the States Ministry, under [Sardar Vallabhbhai] Patel's direction, went out of its way to take no action which could be interpreted as forcing Kashmir's hand and to give assurances that accession to Pakistan would not be taken amiss by India." Campbell-Johnson, *Mission with Mountbatten,* p. 223. Much the same point was made in a 1968 work by Russell Brines. "[T]he evidence," he suggested,

> discounts the persistent Pakistani claim that the efficiency of the October 27 airlift proved that the Indians had prepared beforehand for an invasion of Kashmir and that the preceding events, including the Maharajah's clumsy intrigues, were designed to justify it. . . . There is no reason to reject V. P. Menon's testimony that India could and would have let Kashmir go to Pakistan before the start of the raids. . . . [D]espite Muslim suspicions and Nehru's affection for Kashmir, there is no clear evidence of Indian political manoeuvring to control the state before the fighting began.

The Indo-Pakistani Conflict (London: Pall Mall Press, 1968), pp. 73, 80. No one, however, has pushed the "reactive intervention" argument further than Mehr Chand Mahajan, who was prime minister of the state of Jammu and Kashmir at the time of accession. In his autobiography, published in the early 1960s, he pictures the Indian government even in the midst of the tribal invasion as seemingly paralyzed, and says that the Kashmir government in the last moments before accession to India was considering, if India failed to act, surrender to Pakistan or even to turn for assistance to Afghanistan. "See in contrast [to Pakistan's coercive and aggressive acts] India's attitude," he wrote, "hesitating to sign a standstill agreement, giving small help here and there by air on humanitarian grounds, indifferent to accession, no response and no reply [to Srinagar's appeals for aid] on 24th or 25th even when armed attacks on innocent people were on and loot, arson and butchery were going on. Raiders were approaching Baramula." *Looking Back* (New York: Asia Publishing House, 1963), p. 276.

94. Government of India, *White Paper on Jammu and Kashmir,* p. 33.

95. Menon, *The Integration of the Indian States,* p. 414.

96. Brines, *The Indo-Pakistani Conflict,* p. 72.

97. Birdwood, *A Continent Decides,* p. 223. R. J. Moore's judgment, published about 35 years later, was not much different. According to him, evidence had established "beyond reasonable doubt that the scheme of invasion originally emerged spontaneously among the tribes as a response to outrages against Muslims in East Punjab and the Maharaja's

territories. However, though the central government of Pakistan did not organize the invasion it condoned the active assistance that the provincial government [of NWFP] gave to it." *Making the New Commonwealth,* p. 52.

98. Akbar Khan, *Raiders in Kashmir* (Karachi: Pak Publishers Limited, 1970), p. 11.

99. *Ibid.,* pp. 13–14.

100. *Ibid.,* pp. 16, 22–23.

101. Questioned in 1985 in regard to the tribal invasion, Akbar Khan offered no new details to his earlier narrative. See Abdul Rahman Siddiqi, "Of Pakistan's First War and Coup," *Defence Journal* (Karachi) 11:6–7 (June–July 1985), pp. 1–28.

102. Birdwood, *A Continent Decides,* p. 223.

103. Sardar Mohammad Ibrahim Khan, *The Kashmir Saga* (Lahore: Ripon Printing Press, 1965), pp. 79–82.

104. *Ibid.,* p. 17.

105. *Ibid.,* p. 95.

106. A. H. Suharwardy, *Tragedy in Kashmir* (Lahore: Wajidalis, 1983), pp. 113–14.

107. *Ibid.,* p. 123.

108. *Ibid.,* p. 126. Italics added.

109. *Ibid.,* pp. 201, 203.

110. *Ibid.,* p. 209. The Government of Pakistan admitted to the United Nations mediation team that arrived in the area in July 1948 that its regular armed forces had been directly involved in the fighting in Kashmir since the preceding May. The admission obviously left the government's role in Kashmir during the preceding six months unaccounted for. Suharwardy's criticism of the government's duplicity was voiced years ago by Lord Birdwood, who said that "the Pakistan case would not have suffered by a frank admission of [its military involvement in the tribal invasion]. It was in its denial that heated controversy was engendered." *A Continent Decides,* p. 223.

111. Major A. S. B. Shah, then a joint secretary in Pakistan's Ministry of Foreign Affairs, apparently was the only Pakistani official openly sent to Srinagar between partition and accession to negotiate directly with Kashmir state officials. From all accounts it proved fruitless. See Lamb, *Kashmir: A Disputed Legacy,* p. 126. It is hard to disagree with Birdwood's assessment that the Government of Pakistan's Kashmir policy, in the months preceding accession, was largely self-defeating. "In these critical days before and after partition," he wrote,

> the objective seeker of truth is impressed with the apparent absence of any higher-level attempt at negotiation with Kashmir on the part of the Pakistan Government. Had there been merely a negative absence of inquiry as to the Maharaja's intention, it could have been regarded as a constitutional and correct attitude in a refusal to exert pressure. But in fact evidence is to the effect that in so far as a Pakistan Government then

> existed, it was attempting to force the Maharaja's hand by economic pressures on the State, which could only have the effect of damaging her own interests.
>
> *Two Nations and Kashmir* (London: Robert Hale Limited, 1956), p. 46.

112. A retired Pakistan army officer and well-known figure in the politics of Azad Kashmir told the author flatly and with apparent sincerity a few years ago that the Kashmir problem had been precipitated in the first place by the "foolishness" of Pakistan's leaders, not by the maharaja and not by India. Claiming to have been posted to Srinagar by Pakistani military intelligence in the months immediately following partition, he says that the government of Pakistan authorized a whole string of self-defeating activities in Kashmir—including clandestine operations in the valley, the interdiction of crucial supplies, and the deliberate expulsion of Hindu and Sikh refugees from Pakistan across the border into Kashmir—that had "prematurely forced the issue of Kashmir" and led directly to India's successful military intervention. My informant, who was a participant in Pakistan's ill-fated 1965 effort to infiltrate a guerrilla force into Kashmir Valley and who says that he remains today a stout supporter of continued military confrontation with India over Kashmir, argued nevertheless that the government of India would not have interfered militarily in Kashmir had Pakistan not provoked it. Interview with the author, Rawalpindi, June 1986.

113. Lamb, *Kashmir: A Disputed Legacy*, pp. 121–41; and Moore, *Making the New Commonwealth*, pp. 62–71. My comments here are heavily dependent on these two authors.

114. *TP*, XII, 129, 149, 259, 260, 269, 302, and 385.

115. In mid-September, Patel had written to Baldev Singh, India's minister of defense:

> You know the difficulties of the State, and I feel that at this juncture it would be most useful to have an officer of our own Army as Commander-in-Chief of the Kashmir Forces. . . . It is possible that . . . you might find it difficult to spare Col. Kashmir Singh Katoch. While it is possible for us to find substitutes, I am doubtful whether Kashmir could get a more suitable person. I would, therefore, request that any such reasons should give way to the overriding consideration of having our own man as Commander-in-Chief of the Kashmir State Forces.

Das, I, 39. Patel did note that, were the government of Kashmir to decide to join "the other Dominion," Katoch would revert to India.

116. Lamb, *Kashmir: A Disputed Legacy*, p. 129.

117. On a visit to New Delhi in mid-October, Mahajan had extensive consultations with a gallery of India's greatest leaders, including Sardar Patel, Nehru, Gandhi, Mountbatten, Baldev Singh, and V. P. Menon. Mahajan, *Looking Back*, pp. 126–28.

118. Das, I, 57.

119. See Das, I, 42, 43, 47, 48, 50–54, 59–64, 66, 67.

120. Das, I, 59.

121. Das, I, 49.

122. Lamb, *Kashmir: A Disputed Legacy,* p. 130.

123. Presidential adviser McGeorge Bundy, in explaining that the Viet Cong assault on Pleiku had affected only the timing of the American bombing campaign launched in its wake against North Vietnam, said that "Pleikus are streetcars." Quoted in Robert Jervis, *Perception and Misperception in International Politics* (Princeton, NJ: Princeton University Press, 1976), p. 14.

124. Government of India, *White Paper on Jammu and Kashmir,* p. 4. The date of the Uri encounter was 26 October. The *Dawn* article incorrectly gives the date as 26 November.

125. Lamb, *Kashmir: A Disputed Legacy,* pp. 154–55.

126. *Ibid.,* p. 157. At an earlier point in his discussion, Lamb appeared to confuse the date of the accession of Patiala to India, which occurred in August 1947, with the date on which the covenant was signed creating the Patiala and East Punjab States Union (PEPSU), which was 5 May 1948. By the date he gives for its accession—5 May 1947—there still was no agreement on independence, much less a PEPSU, in existence.

127. Menon, *The Integration of the Indian States,* p. 449. One could argue, of course, that if Patiala's armed forces did not fall under New Delhi's authority in the category of defense, they did so in the category of foreign affairs. That argument, though perhaps tenable, would itself quickly run up against the stark reality that no agreement was ever reached between India and Pakistan in regard to the precise political status of the princely states upon the lapse of British paramountcy. From the Indian perspective, the government of Kashmir never did recover full independence; hence, there would be no question here of "foreign affairs" being involved.

128. *Ibid.,* p. 450.

129. *Ibid.,* p. 451.

130. Lamb, *Kashmir: A Disputed Legacy,* pp. 140–41.

131. Stephens, *Pakistan,* p. 205. Stephens goes on to say, however, in complete conformity with Lamb's view, that his comment about the military side of India's intervention

> by no means says that scheming of a *political* kind, for Kashmir's accession to India, had not been started in Delhi by leading Hindus long before, indeed as far back as June. The pointers towards this seem altogether too solid and many to ignore. And Indian politicians and civilian officials, doubtless, would have been at least as good as Pakistanis at concealing from temporary British superiors things undesirable for them to know.

132. It has been argued, for example, that in contrast with India's "systematic preparations, through fraud and conspiracy, for the incorporation of Jammu and Kashmir into the Indian Union, there were no counter-moves from Pakistan. The approach of the Founder of the State, Quaid-i-Azam Muhammad Ali Jinnah, was based on the principles of honour and fair-play which had been the sheet-anchor of the movement for Pakistan." Government of Pakistan, *White Paper on the Jammu and Kashmir Dispute,* p. 14.

133. Government of India, *White Paper on Jammu and Kashmir,* p. 45.

134. *Ibid.*, p. 47.

135. Akbar, *Nehru: The Making of India*, pp. 448–49.

136. Menon, *The Integration of the Indian States*, p. 405.

137. Government of India, *White Paper on Jammu and Kashmir*, pp. 52–55.

138. *Ibid.*, p. 71.

139. Menon, *The Integration of the Indian States*, pp. 407–8.

140. Government of India, *White Paper on Jammu and Kashmir*, pp. 75-79.

141. Brecher, *The Struggle for Kashmir*, pp. 63–66. Brecher was certainly not alone in his negative appraisal of Ayyengar's performance at the United Nations. See, for example, Akbar, *Kashmir: Behind the Vale*, pp. 127–29; Kuldip Nayar, *Distant Neighbours* (New Delhi: Vikas, 1972), p. 70; and Campbell-Johnson, *Mission With Mountbatten*, pp. 287, 290.

142. Jinnah was apparently quite cool to the idea when Mountbatten first proposed it at their meeting in Lahore on 1 November. Hodson, *The Great Divide*, p. 459.

143. Government of India, *White Paper on Jammu and Kashmir*, p. 75.

144. See, in particular, the discussion of plebiscite in H. S. Gururaj Rao, *Legal Aspects of the Kashmir Problem* (Bombay: Asia Publishing House, 1967), pp. 86–113. See also H. O. Agarwal, *Kashmir Problem—Its Legal Aspects* (Allahabad: Kitab Mahal, 1979).

145. Hasan (ed.), *The Kashmir Question*, p. 212.

146. Rao, *Legal Aspects of the Kashmir Problem*, p. 113.

147. Lamb, *Kashmir: A Disputed Legacy*, p. 151.

148. Pakistan's representative, Sir Zafrullah Khan, prefaced his remarks on the Kashmir conflict to the Security Council in mid-January 1948 with a vivid description of the oppressiveness of the Dogra rulers. "What is not fully known," he said,

> is the depths of misery to which [the people of Kashmir] have been reduced by a century of unmitigated tyranny and oppression under Dogra rule until it is difficult to say which is the greater tragedy to a Kashmiri: his life or his death. Death often provides release from the unbroken chain of suffering, misery and privation which begins in the cradle and ends only in the grave.
> Hasan (ed.), *The Kashmir Question*, p. 145.

149. Hodson, *The Great Divide*, p. 454.

150. Akbar, *Nehru*, p. 448.

Chapter 2

1. We adopt here the customary distinction between delimitation, the delineation of boundaries on maps, and demarcation, the actual physical marking off of boundaries on the ground.

2. The Karachi Agreement, formally the "Agreement Between Military Representatives of India and Pakistan Regarding the Establishment of a Cease-Fire Line in the State of Jammu and Kashmir," is reproduced in K. Sarwar Hasan (ed.), *The Kashmir Question: Documents on the Foreign Relations of Pakistan* (Karachi: Institute of International Affairs, 1966), pp. 226–30.

3. V. D. Chopra, *Genesis of Indo-Pakistan Conflict on Kashmir* (New Delhi: Patriot Publishers, 1990), p. 86.

4. During the abortive 1962–63 negotiations with Pakistan over the Kashmir boundary, Indian acceptance of the CFL as the permanent international border appears, according to one author, to have been virtually unqualified. Y. D. Gundevia, *Outside the Archives* (Hyderabad: Sangam Books, 1984), pp. 243–48. There are recurring reports that New Delhi retains interest in this option. See, for example, Aziz Haniffa, "A Deal with Pakistan on Kashmir?" *India Abroad* (New York), 4 September 1992.

5. This distinction is also manifest in the titles of the White Papers on the Kashmir conflict produced by the two governments: India's is called the *White Paper on Jammu and Kashmir,* Pakistan's the *White Paper on the Jammu and Kashmir Dispute.*

6. For background on Azad Kashmir, see Leo E. Rose, "The Politics of Azad Kashmir," in Raju G. C. Thomas (ed.), *Perspectives on Kashmir: The Roots of Conflict in South Asia* (Boulder, CO: Westview Press, 1992), pp. 235–53.

7. According to one source, Bhutto's proposal was made in autumn 1973 at public meetings in the Azad Kashmiri cities of Mirpur and Muzaffarabad. Khan Zaman Mirza, director of the Institute of Kashmir Studies, University of Azad Jammu and Kashmir, interview with the author, Muzaffarabad, 23 June 1986. Mirza claims to have been present at the Muzaffarabad meeting.

8. Khurshid Hasan Meer, interview with the author, Islamabad, 5 February 1986. Toward the end of his rule, Bhutto organized a unit of the Pakistan People's Party in Azad Kashmir, departing from the convention that Azad Kashmir was for Kashmiri parties only and, thus, further diluting the proposition that Azad Kashmir was a separate political entity. Bhutto's clear intent in all of these efforts, according to Sardar Muhammad Ibrahim Khan, three-time president of Azad Kashmir, was to merge the Northern Areas into the North West Frontier province and to make Azad Kashmir a "unit" of Pakistan with representation in the National Assembly. According to Ibrahim Khan, Bhutto considered a number of ad hoc arrangements to move the country in that direction but took no concrete steps. His motive was "to make Pakistan's jurisdictional hold on the area legal and constitutional." Ibrahim Khan contends that Bhutto wanted Pakistan to be a factor to be reckoned with in international affairs. For that reason, he sought closer relations with China. That, he knew, risked placing the Northern Areas in greater jeopardy from the Soviet Union and India. Hence, the legitimacy of Pakistan's claim to that area had to be strengthened. Interview with the author, Islamabad, 9 January 1986.

9. *The Muslim* (Islamabad), 21 July 1986.

10. See, for example, the Government of Pakistan publication, *Kashmir in Maps* (Rawalpindi: Public Relations Directorate, Ministry of Kashmir Affairs, 1955).

11. Robert C. Mayfield, "A Geographic Study of the Kashmir Issue," *The Geographical Review* 45:2 (April 1955), p. 196. A 1963 map issued by the Information Division of the Pakistan

Embassy in Washington, D.C., was titled "Map of Jammu and Kashmir State and Gilgit Agency." However, it depicted all boundaries—those separating Gilgit Agency from Pakistan, Gilgit Agency from Jammu and Kashmir, and Jammu and Kashmir from India—as *provincial* boundaries, leaving quite vague the matter of political affiliation. See the file "India, Kashmir & Jammu," Geography and Map Reading Room, Library of Congress.

12. Government of Pakistan, *Atlas of Pakistan,* 1st ed. (Rawalpindi: Director of Map Publications, Survey of Pakistan, 1985).

13. Chaudhri Muhammad Ali, *The Emergence of Pakistan* (New York: Columbia University Press, 1967), pp. 297–98.

14. Hassnain describes the provisional government set up at Gilgit following the governor's arrest as "purely a military junta and the people had no choice but to submit." F. M. Hassnain, *Gilgit: The Northern Gate of India* (New Delhi: Sterling Publishers, 1978), p. 157.

15. J. Korbel, *Danger in Kashmir* (Princeton, NJ: Princeton University Press, 2nd ed., 1966), p. 92.

16. Azad Kashmiri views on the Gilgit question are surveyed briefly in Robert Wirsing, *Pakistan's Security Under Zia, 1977–1988* (New York: St. Martin's Press, 1991), pp. 150–53. Azad Kashmir's political leadership, almost without exception, has held out over the years for a more expansive definition of Jammu and Kashmir—one that includes Gilgit Agency—than the central government has been inclined to support. For a Pakistani (but non-Kashmiri) version of the Gilgit uprising, see A. H. Dani, *History of Northern Areas of Pakistan* (Islamabad: National Institute of Historical and Cultural Research, 1989), pp. 326–407. For a detailed Indian account, see Hassnain, *Gilgit: The Northern Gate of India,* pp. 122-58. See also V. P. Menon, *The Integration of the Indian States* (Calcutta: Orient Longmans, 1956), pp. 393, 404–5.

17. *Atlas of Pakistan,* p. vi.

18. Prime Minister Nehru himself reportedly stated in the Lok Sabha on 26 May 1956 that Chitral was a part of Jammu and Kashmir state and that Pakistan's sovereignty over that area would no longer be recognized. Sisir Gupta, *Kashmir: A Study in India-Pakistan Relations* (Bombay: Asia Publishing House, 1966), pp. 305–6. See also the White Paper, *Statement of Facts on Gilgit, Hunza, Nagar, Yasin, Ponial, Chitral and Skardu,* produced in Srinagar by the Government of Jammu and Kashmir state (1983?).

19. In his early work on Kashmir, Alastair Lamb speculated that in laying claim to Chitral, Prime Minister Nehru may have been "hoping to make the plebiscite less attractive in Karachi. After all, if Chitral really was a part of Kashmir, and if Pakistan did lose the plebiscite as it was then envisaged by the United Nations, then the consequences would be even more disastrous. It is possible that here was another Indian argument for the recognition, at any rate tacitly, of the cease-fire line as the legal boundary." *The Kashmir Problem: A Historical Survey* (New York: Praeger, 1966), pp. 90–91.

20. It also makes it practically impossible for scholars to fix upon a single figure either for the physical size of the state or for the proportion of it in the hands of either side. Pakistan's official *Atlas,* for instance, gives 81,085 square miles as the size of the disputed territory of Jammu and Kashmir, and 95,818 square miles if Gilgit Agency is included. These figures are at odds with those given on an inside-cover map of Jammu and Kashmir reproduced in a recent and widely read book by Malhotra Jagmohan, a former Indian governor of the

state. According to his figures (which appear taken from official 1991 Indian statistics), the total area of the state equals about 85,809 square miles. This includes the territories (1) "illegally handed over by Pakistan to China" in 1963 (2,000 square miles), (2) "under illegal occupation of China" (14,500 square miles), and (3) "under illegal occupation of Pakistan" (30,161 square miles). Considering those parts directly under Indian and Pakistani control (69,309 square miles), the Indian share is 56.5 percent, the Pakistani share 43.5 percent. Jagmohan, *My Frozen Turbulence in Kashmir,* 2nd ed. (New Delhi: Allied Publishers Ltd., 1992). The standard—but inevitably arbitrary—figure given by many for the disputed territory is 84,471 square miles. On this, see Korbel, *Danger in Kashmir,* p. 6; and A. Lamb, *Kashmir: A Disputed Legacy,* 1846–1990 (Hertingfordbury, U.K.: Roxford Books, 1991), n. 3, pp. 14–15. Lamb maintains that Kashmir is split roughly in half between India and Pakistan. Wainhouse, in contrast, states that the cease-fire of 1949 left India in possession of 73 percent of the land. David Wainhouse et al., *International Peacekeeping at the Crossroads* (Baltimore: The Johns Hopkins University Press, 1973), p. 70. A very rough but popular rule-of-thumb to apply in regard to respective shares, adjusted to include the Chinese-held portion of the state, is: India—45 percent, Pakistan—35 percent, and China—20 percent.

21. At the time of the cease-fire order on 1 January 1949, total Indian armed strength in Kashmir, excluding Kashmir state forces and militia, was the equivalent of about three divisions; regular Pakistani troops in Kashmir numbered about half that, but they were substantially augmented by about 32 battalions of local, Azad Kashmiri, irregulars. Sylvain Lourie, "The United Nations Military Observer Group in India and Pakistan," *International Organization* 9:1 (February 1955), n. 4, p. 20.

22. UN Document S/726.

23. Upon arrival of the UNCIP mission in the subcontinent in July 1948, it was informed officially by the government of Pakistan that regular troops of the Pakistan army had been directly involved in the fighting in Kashmir since the preceding May. This compelled UNCIP to shift its endeavors from bringing about the withdrawal of "tribal invaders" to bringing about a cease-fire in what had become an international war between two UN members.

24. UN Document S/1100.

25. UN Document S/1430, Annex 26.

26. See Kuldip Nayar, *Distant Neighbours* (New Delhi: Vikas, 1972), pp. 231–40; and Imtiaz H. Bokhari and Thomas Perry Thornton, *The 1972 Simla Agreement: An Asymmetrical Negotiation,* FPI Case Studies Number 11 (Washington, D.C.: Foreign Policy Institute, The Johns Hopkins University, 1988), pp. 19–21, 28–40.

27. Alan James, *Peacekeeping in International Politics* (New York: St. Martin's Press, 1990), p. 161.

28. Handout, "United Nations Military Observer Group in India and Pakistan," UNMOGIP Headquarters, Rawalpindi, dated January 1985.

29. Rosalyn Higgins, *United Nations Peacekeeping, 1946–1967, Documents and Commentary, vol. II: Asia* (London: Oxford University Press, 1970), pp. 357–60.

30. Lourie, "The United Nations Military Observer Group in India and Pakistan," pp. 30–31.

31. UNMOGIP's peacekeeping peers around the world today all outstrip it substantially—in most cases very substantially—in size. As of 27 September 1993, there had been a total of 28 UN peacekeeping missions deployed since 1948. Of these, 15 were currently deployed. One of these (in Cambodia) was winding down. Their locations, dates begun, and currently assigned personnel (estimated, in some cases) were as follows:

1. Middle East (1948)	234
2. India-Pakistan (1949)	38
3. Cyprus (1964)	1,524
4. Golan Heights (1974)	1,129
5. Lebanon (1978)	5,300
6. Iraq-Kuwait (1991)	300
7. Angola (1991)	100
8. El Salvador (1991)	527
9. Western Sahara (1991)	328
10. Former Yugoslavia (1992)	25,000
11. Cambodia (1992)	19,500
12. Somalia (1992)	24,000
13. Mozambique (1992)	6,500
14. Liberia (1993)	500
15. Haiti (1993)	1,600

Figures for the Mozambique, Liberia, and Haiti missions were *authorized* (not yet deployed) strengths. "U.N. Peacekeeping Operations to Date," Reuters wire-service, 29 September 1993 [CompuServe Mail]. The peacekeeping mission in Cyprus, with over 1,500 members, patrols a no-man's-land extending 118 miles across the island between the quarreling Turks and Greeks. This is about one-fifth the length of the CFL/LOC in Kashmir. Current trends apparently favor larger missions. Up until 1992, the largest peacekeeping team ever authorized was the force of 20,000 sent by the United Nations to the former Belgian Congo in 1960.

32. UNMOGIP's original functions have been identified as (1) the investigation of complaints, (2) the collection of order of battle and general troop information, and (3) some responsibility for the control of civilians. Lourie, "The United Nations Military Observer Group in India and Pakistan," p. 28. The second of these, which meant routine access to extremely sensitive order-of-battle information, was essential if UNMOGIP was to monitor the two commands' adherence to the ban on reinforcements contained in the 1949 ceasefire agreement. "So far as is known," observes one study, "no other peace-observation group has ever been furnished with this information—a testimony to the confidence of both armies in the United Nations military observers." This function placed an unusually heavy premium on impartiality in the conduct of peacekeeping duties. No doubt, it helped to account for the sparseness of published reports on UNMOGIP operations. David W. Wainhouse et al., *International Peace Observation: History and Forecast* (Baltimore: The Johns Hopkins University Press, 1966), p. 367.

33. *Ibid.*, p. 372. The procedure no doubt acted at times to escalate the number of complaints, since both sides would seek to paint the other as the worst offender. The usefulness of the procedure is certainly questionable. Many have wondered, along with the general who commanded Indian forces on the western front in the 1971 war, "what the UN did in New York with the millions of 'violations' they received." Lieutenant General K. P. Candeth, *The Western Front: The Indo-Pakistan War 1971* (New Delhi: Allied Publishers, 1984), p. 37.

34. Wainhouse et al., *International Peace Observation,* p. 368. According to the authors:

> the increase in incidents between 1954 and 1961 stemmed from the policy of Krishna Menon, then the Indian Defense Minister, that the cease-fire line should become a fixed international boundary. Apparently, he had concluded that neither a plebiscite, nor an international agreement for partition, nor any other alternative would assure Indian control of the vale [of Kashmir]. He therefore evacuated civilians from the 500-yard demilitarized zone on the Indian side of the cease-fire line and encouraged the Kashmir police to use force to prevent the Pakistanis from crossing the border. The Pakistanis did not follow a similar policy and continued civilian activities within the 500-yard demilitarized zone on their side of the line, since they have always contended that the cease-fire line is not a boundary. Most of the incidents arose when Pakistani civilians approached or crossed the line.

35. One of these three crossing points, according to a member of the UNMOGIP team in India, has been closed for four years due to a jurisdictional dispute between India and Pakistan. Interview with the author, New Delhi, May 1991.

36. In 1985, for instance, Pakistan reported about 150 Indian violations of the CFL/LOC to UNMOGIP. All were investigated, and in nearly all cases (95 percent) awards were made—that India had, indeed, committed the violation. Member of the UN observer team, interview with the author, Rawalpindi, January 1986.

37. Wainhouse et al., *International Peacekeeping at the Crossroads,* p. 74.

38. Interview, New Delhi, May 1991.

39. Interview, Rawalpindi, January 1986. Another UNMOGIP officer compared the situation on the CFL/LOC to the Western Front in World War I, where trench lines often seemed to have no logical pattern and where forward pickets were often within shouting distance of one another.

40. As one author put it, UNMOGIP "no longer formally checks on the levels of forces and armaments in Pakistan-held Kashmir. But on the basis that one party cannot unilaterally abrogate an ongoing agreement, Unmogip continues to respond, to the best of its ability, to Pakistan's frequent complaints about cease-fire infringements. Investigations are conducted—but on the Pakistan side only; judgements are made as to whether or not a violation has taken place, or stating that the investigation was inconclusive; each result is passed on to Pakistan; and periodically they are also transmitted to India—who studiously ignores them. Thus the Observers on the Pakistan side lead an active and challenging life, but their postings to the Indian side entail a lot of inaction and a corresponding amount of boredom." James, *Peacekeeping in International Politics,* pp. 161–62.

41. Interview with the author, Rawalpindi, January 1986.

42. Member of the UNMOGIP observer team, interview with the author, Rawalpindi, January 1986.

43. Lourie, "The United Nations Military Observer Group in India and Pakistan," p. 30. Lourie offers as characteristic the case of an observer who, witnessing the outbreak of firing between Indian and Pakistani patrols in July 1950, "jumped in his official jeep . . . and drove into the path of fire with the United Nations flag flying from his vehicle. Both patrols

withheld fire for the time necessary for other observers to rush to them and request a suspension of the firing."

44. Higgins, *United Nations Peacekeeping 1946–1947,* p. 373.

45. Wainhouse et al., *International Peace Observation,* p. 371.

46. Korbel, *Danger in Kashmir,* p. 163.

47. James, *Peacekeeping in International Politics,* p. 160.

48. *Ibid.,* p. 162.

49. *Ibid.,* p. 163. Yet more equivocal in their outlook were the writers who concluded their 1974 assessment of UNMOGIP with the comment: "It is difficult to assess the extent of UNMOGIP's achievement and whether its presence has prevented the complete destruction of a state—or has preserved a status quo that has been harmful rather than beneficial. But when a settlement is reached and UNMOGIP leaves, it is likely to be remembered for its longevity of stay rather than for its positive accomplishments." Indar Jit Rikhye, Michael Harbottle, and Bjorn Egge, *The Thin Blue Line: International Peacekeeping and Its Future* (New Haven, CT: Yale University Press, 1974), p. 133.

50. See, for example, B. L. Kak, "Peace-keepers Turn Spies?" *Sunday* (Calcutta), 30 June 1985; "Snooping in Peace: UN Observers in Kashmir Accused of Spying," *The Week* (Cochin), 12 August 1990; and Rakesh Kumar Datta, "The Insecurity Issue in J & K," *The Tribune* (Chandigarh), 13 August 1990.

51. Janak Singh, "India May Seek Recall of UN Group," *The Times of India,* 7 July 1990.

52. Wainhouse et al., *International Peacekeeping at the Crossroads,* p. 89.

53. Portions of the material in this section appeared in Charles H. Kennedy (ed.), *Pakistan 1992* (Boulder, CO: Westview, 1993). Reprinted by permission of the publisher.

54. Higgins, *United Nations Peacekeeping, 1946–1967,* p. 348.

55. For a detailed discussion of the background and development of the Siachen Glacier dispute, see Wirsing, *Pakistan's Security Under Zia, 1977–1988,* pp. 143–94.

56. For an illuminating discussion of the geostrategic significance of the Karakoram Highway, see Mahnaz Z. Ispahani, *Roads and Rivals: The Political Uses of Access in the Borderlands of Asia* (Ithaca, NY: Cornell University Press, 1989), pp. 185–213.

57. *The American Alpine Journal 1981,* p. 298. The author of a popular American trekking guide book wrote in 1982 that "just to the north [of Rimo Glacier] is the Karakoram Pass, now the official meeting point of Pakistan, India, and China." Hugh Swift, *The Trekker's Guide to the Himalaya and Karakoram* (San Francisco: Sierra Club Books, 1982), p. 157. See also the comments on Pakistan's administrative control of access routes to Mount K-2 by Galen Rowell, a member of a 1975 American expedition, in *In the Throne Room of the Gods* (San Francisco: Sierra Club Books, 1977), pp. 16–23.

58. National Geographic Society, *Atlas of the World,* 5th ed. (Washington, D.C.: National Geographic Society, 1981), pp. 184–85; Joseph E. Schwartzberg (ed.), *A Historical Atlas of South Asia* (Chicago: The University of Chicago Press, 1978), pp. 87–88; and *The Times Atlas of the World,* 6th ed. (London: Times Books, 1980), plate 31.

59. See, for example, the series of UN maps of Kashmir published in 1949 (Series 188), filed under "India, Kashmir & Jammu," Geography and Map Reading Room, Library of Congress.

60. The CFL was freely depicted on official Pakistani maps until 1965. See, for example, "Map of Jammu and Kashmir State and Gilgit Agency," published by the Information Division, Embassy of Pakistan, Washington, D.C., 1963, filed under "India, Kashmir & Jammu," Geography and Map Reading Room, Library of Congress. Since then, both official and commercial Pakistani maps, including the country's first and only official atlas, simply label the entire Kashmir area (minus, of course, Gilgit Agency) as "disputed territory," omitting any depiction of the CFL/LOC. See *Atlas of Pakistan,* pp. 44–45. Indian commercial maps produced in the early postpartition years sometimes displayed the CFL. See, for example, "New Map of Kashmir with Cease-Fire Line by U.N.O." (New Delhi: Pustak Mandir, 1949?), filed under "India, Kashmir & Jammu," Geography and Map Reading Room, Library of Congress. Indian practice since then has been to depict the entire state of Jammu and Kashmir—devoid of a CFL or LOC—as unconditionally forming part of the Indian union.

61. *The Times Atlas of the World,* comprehensive ed. (London: Times Books, 1977), plate 31.

62. For this and other illuminating cartographic information, I am much indebted to Professor Joseph E. Schwartzberg of the University of Minnesota.

63. None of the atlases gave any reason for the extension of the CFL/LOC from NJ 9842 to the Karakoram pass. The 1978 *Historical Atlas of South Asia,* for example, describes it simply as an "undelimited extension of cease-fire line as depicted on many maps" (plate IX.C.2, p. 87).

64. See, for instance, "Kashmir: Where Three Powers Compete," published in 1964 by the Civic Education Service in Washington, DC., for schoolroom use. Possibly the first U.S. map to do so, this map shows the CFL extending clearly all the way to the Karakoram Pass.

65. See the map insert titled "Southern Asia" (Sheet 7, Series 1106) in *South Asia and the Strategic Indian Ocean: A Bibliographic Survey of Literature,* DA Pamphlet 550-15 (Washington, D.C.: Headquarters, Department of the Army, 1973). This map appears to have been produced by the U.S. Army Topographic Command as early as April 1969.

66. See, for example, Operational Navigation Chart (ONC) G-7 (Washington, D.C.: Defense Mapping Agency, revised December 1987). This map was compiled in July 1974. The 1987 revision affected aeronautical information only.

67. According to retired Lieutenant General M. L. Chibber, who headed the Indian army's Northern Command in 1984 when the armed confrontation over Siachen first began, the Indian army first became aware of U.S. "cartographic misrepresentation" of the Siachen area in January 1978 when he was shown a commercial tourist map of Northern Kashmir printed in the United States. "Siachen—The Untold Story (A Personal Account)," *Indian Defence Review* (January 1990), pp. 146–47.

68. Letter to the author from William B. Wood, The Geographer, U.S. Department of State, dated 31 January 1992.

69. A copy of the guidance was supplied to the author by the Office of the Geographer, Department of State. In 1988, the Defense Mapping Agency circulated a *Chart Updating Manual* to users of its maps indicating that the Kashmir boundary was portrayed incorrectly on its Operational Navigation Chart of the area (ONC G-7). Its Tactical Pilotage Chart of the area (TPC G-7D), which had been fully revised in 1986, had already eliminated the international boundary linking the CFL/LOC with the China border.

70. "Agreement Between Military Representatives of India and Pakistan Regarding the Establishment of a Cease-Fire Line in the State of Jammu and Kashmir, 27 July 1949 (S/AC.12/TC.4)," in Hasan (ed.), *The Kashmir Question,* p. 229.

71. See, for example, K. Subrahmanyam, "Kashmir," *Strategic Analysis* 13:2 (May 1990), pp. 135–36.

72. National Geographic Society, *Atlas of the World,* 6th ed. (Washington, D.C.: National Geographic Society, 1990), p. 78. In its map of Southern Asia, this edition shows a straight-line extension of the CFL/LOC from map coordinate NJ 9842 to the Karakoram Pass. Note, however, that the newest edition of *A Historical Atlas of South Asia* (New York: Oxford University Press, 1992) correctly depicts the LOC on its administrative overlay map.

73. Indians freely concede that the 1972 LOC delimitation agreement entirely ignores the territory beyond map coordinate NJ 9842. What many Indians have argued, however, is that the agreement of 1949 establishing the original CFL did *not* ignore it and that that agreement should, therefore, be given precedence. See, for example, Manoj Joshi, "Siachen: India for Peaceful Solution," *The Hindu* (international ed.), week ending 19 March 1988. (Joshi, a respected journalist and close observer of the Siachen dispute, was given permission by Indian military authorities to inspect the 1972, but not the 1949, delimitation documents.) Apart from the questionable legality of this position, given the obvious legal precedence of the re-delimitation exercise in 1972, there is, in fact, no evidence to back it up. A senior Indian diplomat intimately familiar with the Siachen issue confided to this author in summer 1990 that there was absolutely nothing in the documentary record of the 1949 delimitation exercise to support Indian claims in this regard. His statement was confirmed by a senior member of the UNMOGIP observer team in Kashmir, interviewed by this author in summer 1991. Thus far, this author has not been given permission personally to inspect the full delimitation documents of either the 1949 or 1972 delimitation exercise.

74. "Boundary Agreement Between the Governments of the People's Republic of China and Pakistan, 2 March 1963," in Hasan (ed.), *The Kashmir Question,* p. 384.

75. Pakistanis took some comfort from the fact that a widely acclaimed book written in the early 1980s by one of India's best-known defense analysts showed the CFL/LOC running northeastward from map coordinate NJ 9842 to the Karakoram Pass on the Chinese border, in effect ceding the contested area of the Siachen Glacier to Pakistan with room to spare. Ravi Rikhye, *The Fourth Round: Indo-Pak War 1984* (New Delhi: ABC Publishing House, 1982), map facing p. 68. Potentially even more upsetting to Indians were the maps of Jammu and Kashmir shown in a book published in India in 1984 by retired Lieutenant General K. P. Candeth, *The Western Front: The Indo-Pakistan War 1971*. In the 1971 war, Candeth commanded the Indian army's Western Command, which then included all of

Kashmir. His two maps, including a close-up of the Nubra River valley immediately east of the Siachen Glacier, both showed the Siachen comfortably to the west of the CFL/LOC.

76. Jasjit Singh, "Siachen Glaciers: Facts and Fiction," *Strategic Analysis* 12:7 (October 1989), pp. 703–4.

Chapter 3

1. Mahnaz Z. Ispahani, *Roads and Rivals: The Political Uses of Access in the Borderlands of Asia* (Ithaca, NY: Cornell University Press, 1989), p. 153.

2. Alastair Lamb, *Kashmir: A Disputed Legacy 1846–1990* (Hertingfordbury, U.K.: Roxford Books, 1991), p. 17.

3. Josef Korbel's judgment of Kashmir's strategic importance was typical of foreign observers in the early decades of the Cold War. "It would be difficult," he said, "to exaggerate the strategic importance of the State of Jammu and Kashmir to the security of the Subcontinent, lying as it does so near the precarious borders of the Soviet Union and China." *Danger in Kashmir* (Princeton, NJ: Princeton University Press, 2nd ed., 1966), p. 9.

4. *TP*, XI, 229.

5. Government of India, *White Paper on Jammu and Kashmir* (New Delhi, 1948), pp. 45–46.

6. K. Sarwar Hasan (ed.), *The Kashmir Question: Documents on the Foreign Relations of Pakistan* (Karachi: Pakistan Institute of International Affairs, 1966), p. 80.

7. *Ibid.*, p. 98.

8. Quoted in Michael Brecher, *The Struggle for Kashmir* (Toronto: Ryerson Press, 1953), p. 47.

9. Ispahani, *Roads and Rivals*, p. 184.

10. Ayesha Jalal, *The State of Martial Rule: The Origins of Pakistan's Political Economy of Defence* (Cambridge: Cambridge University Press, 1990), p. 64.

11. *Ibid.*, p. 50.

12. *Ibid.*, p. 44.

13. Raju G. C. Thomas, "India: Balancing Great-Power Intrusions and Regional-Security Interests," in R. G. C. Thomas (ed.), *The Great-Power Triangle and Asian Security* (Lexington, MA: Lexington Books, 1983), p. 66.

14. Cited in Jalal, *The State of Martial Rule*, p. 113.

15. Shirin Tahir-Kheli, *The United States and Pakistan* (New York: Praeger, 1982), pp. 12–13. At an early point in the Cold War, Pakistani leaders apparently nourished the hope that they could extract a guarantee of Pakistan's territorial frontiers, if not from the United States then from the Soviet Union. Jalal, *The State of Martial Rule*, pp. 111–12.

16. "All the members of the presidium were present [upon Nehru's arrival] at the airport in Moscow, and [President] Bulganin, for the first time in his career, drove with Nehru in an open car through the milling streets of the capital. It was clearly an effort both to outpace the reception in China a year earlier and to demonstrate to Nehru that the regard for him in the Soviet Union was in converse proportion to that in the United States." Sarvepalli Gopal, *Jawaharlal Nehru: A Biography*, vol. II: 1947–1956 (Cambridge, MA: Harvard University Press, 1979), p. 246.

17. S. Nihal Singh, *The Yogi and the Bear: A Study of Indo-Soviet Relations* (Riverdale, MD: Riverdale Publishers, 1986), p. 14. "The question of Kashmir as one of the states of the Republic of India," Khrushchev reportedly stated, "has already been decided by the people of Kashmir." Quoted in Sumit Ganguly, *The Origins of War in South Asia: Indo-Pakistani Conflicts Since 1947* (Boulder, CO: Westview Press, 1986), p. 69.

18. Gopal, *Jawaharlal Nehru*, II, p. 253.

19. Singh, *The Yogi and the Bear*, pp. 13–14. The Soviets' first intervention in the Security Council debate over Kashmir occurred in 1952. The Soviet spokesman attacked the proposals for settlement of Kashmir as an inspiration of Western imperialist powers. The Kashmiris' right to self-determination was supported. Implicitly, India's position was condemned. See Josef Korbel, *Danger in Kashmir* (Princeton, NJ: Princeton University Press, 2nd ed., 1966), pp. 259–65.

20. Shivaji Ganguly, *U.S. Policy Toward South Asia* (Boulder, CO: Westview Press, 1990), pp. 87–88.

21. *Ibid.*, p. 97.

22. In one of the more thoughtful discussions of this issue, Raju Thomas was careful to distinguish "between regional security issues that are primarily autonomous but that are affected by the nature of great-power relations, and problems of regional security that are primarily induced by great-power politics." He concluded that "with the exception of Afghanistan, the South Asian region indicates a condition where regional security problems tend to be independent of but affected by politics within the great-power [Soviet Union-United States-China] triangle. The situation here suggests the primacy of regional-security issues over great-power politics." "Introduction: The Great-Power Triangle and Asian Security," in Thomas (ed.), *The Great-Power Triangle and Asian Security*, pp. 7, 10.

23. Raju G. C. Thomas, "India," in Thomas (ed.), *The Great-Power Triangle and Asian Security*, p. 69.

24. According to a leading Indian biographer of Nehru, the evidence suggested that Nehru's August 1953 offer of a plebiscite in Kashmir to Pakistan's prime minister Mohammad Ali "had been genuine and would have held if the prospect of a military alliance between Pakistan and the United States had not impinged on it." Gopal, *Jawaharlal Nehru*, II, p. 185.

25. "A careful reading of the Pakistani record," observes Shirin Tahir-Kheli, "shows that President Ayub Khan moved against India [in 1965] not because he had acquired sophisticated weapons but because he feared that the United States was becoming less interested in Pakistani security and was preparing to downgrade the quality and the quantity of future arms transfers." "The Impact of Arms Transfers on Recipient Countries," in Alvin Z. Rubinstein (ed.), *The Great Game: Rivalry in the Persian Gulf and South Asia* (New York: Praeger, 1983), p. 193.

26. Margaret W. Fisher, Leo E. Rose, and Robert A. Huttenback, *Himalayan Battleground: Sino-Indian Rivalry in Ladakh* (New York: Praeger, 1963), p. 82. There is evidence that India's intelligence officials knew of Chinese use of the Aksai Chin as early as 1951. According to Steven A. Hoffmann,

> the [Indian] army had not regarded such activity as a security threat or as a matter that it could act on, given its meager resources and the geographical problems involved. Officials of the MEA [Ministry of External Affairs] did not want to disrupt relations with China over a physically unenforceable claim and were not certain of the usefulness of the Aksai Chin to India. Nor were they certain whether the Chinese had done anything more than improve an old existing international trade route. Therefore, they may not have brought the matter to Nehru's attention, or he may not have wanted to make an issue of it.

India and the China Crisis (Berkeley: University of California Press, 1990), p. 35.

27. *Ibid.*, p. 84. Various Chinese maps, including one published in a Chinese textbook in 1954, showed the Aksai Chin within Chinese boundaries. See John W. Garver, *Foreign Relations of the People's Republic of China* (New York: Prentice-Hall, 1993).

28. See Lamb, *Kashmir: A Disputed Legacy, 1846–1990,* pp. 71–72, 233–34; and Sarvepalli Gopal, *Jawaharlal Nehru: A Biography,* vol. III: 1956–1964 (Cambridge, MA: Harvard University Press, 1984), p. 303.

29. In UN voting on the Korean War, for instance, Pakistan voted to brand North Korea as the aggressor, but abstained from voting on the resolution labeling the PRC as an aggressor when Chinese forces crossed the Yalu. Yaacov Y. I. Vertzberger, *China's Southwestern Strategy: Encirclement and Counterencirclement* (New York: Praeger, 1985), p. 10.

30. *Ibid.*, p. 11.

31. *Security complex* has been defined as a regional security subsystem that is "substantially confined within some particular geographical area. The assumption is that local sets of states exist whose major security perceptions and concerns link together sufficiently closely that their national security problems cannot realistically be considered apart from one another. . . . [S]ecurity complexes rest, for the most part, on the interdependence of rivalry rather than on the interdependence of shared interests." Barry Buzan, "A Framework for Regional Security Analysis," in Barry Buzan and Gowher Rizvi (eds.), *South Asian Insecurity and the Great Powers* (New York: St. Martin's Press, 1986), pp. 7–8.

32. Among many excellent works on the Sino-Indian war and its origins, see Fisher, Rose, and Huttenback, *Himalayan Battleground*; Hoffmann, *India and the China Crisis*; Neville Maxwell, *India's China War* (New York: Doubleday, 1972); Alastair Lamb, *The China-India Border: The Origins of the Disputed Boundaries* (London: Oxford University Press, 1964); and Yaacov Y. I. Vertzberger, *Misperceptions in Foreign Policymaking: The Sino-Indian Conflict, 1959–1962* (Boulder, CO: Westview Press, 1984).

33. Hoffmann, *India and the China Crisis,* p. 3.

34. George N. Patterson, *Peking Versus Delhi* (New York: Praeger, 1964), p. 46; and U. S. Bajpai, *India's Security* (New Delhi: Lancers Publishers, 1983), pp. 84–86.

35. Fisher, Rose, and Huttenback, *Himalayan Battleground,* p. 145.

36. *Ibid.*, p. 128.

37. *Ibid.*, p. 306.

38. Gopal, *Jawaharlal Nehru,* III, p. 305. Gopal, who served as director of the Historical Division in the Indian government's Ministry of External Affairs from 1954 to 1966, played a major role in developing India's case in the border controversy with China. For the official Indian and Chinese presentations on the border question, see Government of India, *Report of the Officials of the Government of India and the People's Republic of China on the Boundary Question* (New Delhi: Ministry of External Affairs, 1961). For an astute comparison of these presentations from a pro-Indian perspective, see Fisher, Rose, and Huttenback, *Himalayan Battleground,* pp. 98–128. Other pro-Indian studies that examine the history of the Ladakh border question are B. N. Mullik, *My Years With Nehru: The Chinese Betrayal* (New Delhi: Allied Publishers, 1971), pp. 87–103; Gondker Narayana Rao, *The India-China Border: A Reappraisal* (Bombay: Asia Publishing House, 1968); and P. C. Chakravarti, *The Evolution of India's Northern Borders* (London: Asia Publishing House, 1971), pp. 104–52.

39. Lamb, *The China-India Border,* p. 169.

40. *Ibid.*, p. 175.

41. *Ibid.*, p. 174. Lamb argues that the Indian position on the boundary alignment in Aksai Chin is based on misquotation of an 1899 British note to the Chinese government. For detailed discussion of this and other cartographical arguments in regard to Ladakh and Aksai Chin, see Alastair Lamb, *The Sino-Indian Border in Ladakh* (Columbia: University of South Carolina Press, 1975).

42. Maxwell, *India's China War,* p. 11.

43. *Ibid.*, p. 175.

44. *Ibid.*, pp. 97–98.

45. *Ibid.*, p. 273.

46. *Ibid.*, p. 275.

47. Maxwell himself acknowledged an "unavoidable imbalance" in the book deriving from the acute difference between India and China in terms of access to sources. *Ibid.,* pp. 13–14.

48. Vertzberger, *Misperceptions in Foreign Policymaking,* pp. 108, 175. See also Yaacov Y. I. Vertzberger, "India's Strategic Posture and the Border War Defeat of 1962: A Case Study in Miscalculation," *The Journal of Strategic Studies* 5:3 (September 1982), pp. 370–92.

49. Hoffmann, *India and the China Crisis,* p. 113.

50. *Ibid.*, pp. 113–14.

51. *Ibid.*, p. 167.

52. John Lall, *Aksaichin and Sino-Indian Conflict* (New Delhi: Allied Publishers, 1989).

53. "The Chinese and the Indians fought over the *territory* of Aksaichin in 1962," Lall wrote, "but they fought *because* of the lack of responsible statesmanship at the turn of the century." *Ibid.*, p. 202.

54. *Ibid.*, 289–90; and John Lall, "Approaching India-China Boundary Dispute," *Mainstream* (New Delhi), 10 December 1988, pp. 5–7.

55. D. K. Palit, *War in High Himalaya: The Indian Army in Crisis, 1962* (New Delhi: Lancer International, 1991).

56. Intimately familiar with the Indian army's operations in Kashmir and Ladakh, Palit was picked immediately after the Sino-Indian war as military adviser to the Indian team selected to conduct talks with Pakistan over the Kashmir boundary. For Palit's illuminating account of these talks, see *ibid.*, pp. 368–407.

57. *Ibid.*, pp. 1–2.

58. *Ibid.*, pp. 34–36.

59. Vertzberger, *China's Southwestern Strategy*, p. 4.

60. *Ibid.*, p. 6.

61. Yaacov Y. I. Vertzberger, *The Enduring Entente: Sino-Pakistani Relations 1960–1980*, Washington Papers No. 95 (New York: Praeger, 1983). A similar point of view had been argued earlier by Anwar Hussein Syed, *China and Pakistan: Entente Cordiale* (Amherst: University of Massachusetts Press, 1974).

62. On China's contribution to Pakistan's nuclear plans, see Vertzberger, *China's Southwestern Strategy*, pp. 102–4; and Carnegie Endowment for International Peace, *Nuclear Weapons and South Asian Security*, Report of the Carnegie Task Force on Non-Proliferation and South Asian Security (Washington, D.C.: Carnegie Endowment, March 1988), pp. 40–42.

63. I am relying here on my own earlier account of the Border Agreement in Robert Wirsing, *Pakistan's Security Under Zia, 1977–1988* (New York: St. Martin's Press, 1991), p. 147.

64. Ispahani, *Roads and Rivals*, pp. 182–83. See my comments on these roads in Wirsing, *Pakistan's Security Under Zia, 1977–1988*, pp. 165–69.

65. John W. Garver, "The Indian Factor in Recent Sino-Soviet Relations," *The China Quarterly*, no. 125 (March 1991), pp. 55–56.

66. *Ibid.*, p. 56.

67. *Ibid.*, pp. 66–67. In a more recent article, Garver points out that within months of the outbreak of the Kashmiri insurgency, the Chinese took yet another step toward accommodating India on the Kashmir issue. Beginning in March 1990, public Chinese pronouncements on Kashmir dropped all but an oblique reference to the United Nations and, instead, cited exclusively the need for bilateral negotiations. John W. Garver, "China and South Asia," *The Annals of the American Academy of Political and Social Science* 519 (January 1992), pp. 83–84.

68. Samina Yasmeen, "The China Factor in the Kashmir Issue," in Raju G. C. Thomas (ed.), *Perspectives on Kashmir: The Roots of Conflict in South Asia* (Boulder, CO: Westview, 1992), p. 320.

69. Thomas, "Introduction: The Great-Power Triangle and Asian Security," pp. 16–17.

70. R. Jeffrey Smith, "China May Have Revived Germ Weapons Program, U.S. Officials Say," *The Washington Post* wire-service, 24 February 1993 [CompuServe Mail].

71. Gill Tudor, "Pakistan Mulls Response to U.S. Sanctions," Reuters wire-service, 26 August 1993 [CompuServe Mail].

72. Details in regard to the force reductions were left to be worked out through consultations, possibly a sign that the accords were more symbolic than substantive. Lena H. Sun, "China, India Sign Accord to Ease Border Dispute," *The Washington Post* wire-service, 8 September 1993 [CompuServe Mail].

73. David Shambaugh, "China's Security Policy in the Post-Cold War Era," *Survival* 34:2 (Summer 1992), p. 93.

74. Patrick E. Tyler, "China's Military Regards U.S. As Main Enemy in the Future," *The New York Times,* 16 November 1993, p. A5.

75. In contrast, the U.S. economy was expected to expand by only 2.7 percent in 1993. The predicted world economic growth rate for 1993, according to the International Monetary Fund, was 2.2 percent. "IMF: Asia Leading World Economies," United Press International wire-service, 22 September 1993 [CompuServe Mail].

76. Shambaugh, "China's Security Policy in the Post-Cold War Era," p. 100.

77. *Ibid.,* p. 103. "Two things are certain," says the author:

> China will only grow stronger, and its central geographic position in Asia will dictate that it has an interest and a role to play in almost every regional issue. If present trends continue, by the early twenty-first century, China will join the United States, Japan and the EC as one of the world's four leading economic powers. Its military machine, already powerful, will only gain strength. Its influence will increase accordingly. (P. 99)

78. "China's Military Program Said to Threaten India," United Press International wire-service, 27 November 1993 [CompuServe Mail].

79. *Ibid.,* p. 105. Other observers have drawn much the same conclusion. See, for example, Bonnie S. Glaser, "China's Security Perceptions: Interests and Ambitions," *Asian Survey* 33:3 (March 1993), p. 271. For a Chinese view, see Qimao Chen, "New Approaches in China's Foreign Policy," *Asian Survey* 33:3 (March 1993), pp. 237–51.

80. George Perkovich, "A Nuclear Third Way in South Asia," *Foreign Policy,* no. 91 (Summer 1993), p. 87.

81. Glaser, "China's Security Perceptions," p. 267.

82. See, for instance, "Hands Across the Himalayas," *The Economist,* 11 September 1993, p. 31.

83. Sandy Gordon, "Indian Defense Spending: Treading Water in the Fiscal Deep," *Asian Survey* 32:10 (October 1992), pp. 934, 950.

84. On this, see Gerald Segal, "China and the Disintegration of the Soviet Union," *Asian Survey* 32:9 (September 1992), pp. 848–68; and J. Richard Walsh, "China and the New Geopolitics of Central Asia," *Asian Survey* 33:3 (March 1993), pp. 272–84.

85. Garver, "China and South Asia," pp. 84–85. "What is more likely," says Garver, "is that there will be continual maneuvering between China and India for power and influence in South Asia, but with both sides attempting to keep this rivalry from taking the two countries back to the era of open confrontation."

86. "India Using Most of Army for Internal Security," United Press International wire-service, 30 August 1993 [CompuServe Mail].

87. Chinese attitudes toward Kashmir, we should note, are no more helpful to Pakistan than to India. Best described as the wish to avoid involvement of any kind in the dispute, these attitudes inhibit the Chinese from playing the moderating or mediating role much desired of them by Pakistan. Premier Li Peng, responding to an appeal by visiting Pakistani prime minister Benazir Bhutto in late December 1993 that China play a more active role in Kashmir, reportedly told her "that issues existing between Pakistan and India—including the Kashmir dispute—must in the end be resolved properly through patient bilateral dialogue." Jeffrey Parker, "China Says Kashmir Is Issue for Pakistan, India," Reuters wire-service, 28 December 1993 [CompuServe Mail].

Chapter 4

1. One such was K. Subrahmanyam, the erstwhile and well-known director of the Ministry of Defense–sponsored Institute for Defence Studies and Analyses (IDSA) in New Delhi, who described Op Topac in precisely these terms in the pages of IDSA's *Strategic Studies* (May 1990), then, noticing his error, apologized in print for it (insisting, however, that the "scenario" anyway had been fully vindicated by subsequent events in Kashmir). Another was Malhotra Jagmohan, former governor of the state of Jammu and Kashmir, who recounts the Op Topac story at length in a recent book on Kashmir, using it to drive home a major point of the volume—Pakistan's enormous role as precipitant of the insurgency. As for Topac's authenticity, Jagmohan concedes only that "a doubt has been expressed in certain quarters whether `Operation Topac' was at all formulated by the Pakistan authorities." He says that the plan's authorship is immaterial since Pakistan's massive subversion of Kashmir is a matter of record anyway. *My Frozen Turbulence in Kashmir,* rev. ed. (New Delhi: Allied Publishers, 1992), pp. 406–10. Even in Pakistan, by the way, some journalists and analysts took the Indian version as gospel.

2. For an unusually revealing glimpse of ISI activities in Afghanistan, see Mohammad Yousuf, *The Bear Trap: Afghanistan's Untold Story* (London: Leo Cooper, 1992).

3. Interview with the author, Islamabad, June 1993.

4. That Zia and his colleagues in ISI were giving more attention to Kashmir at the time Op Topac was allegedly being planned (spring–summer 1988) seems likely. The Soviets were on the eve of exiting from Afghanistan and Pakistan possessed incentives, assets, and expertise that made stepped-up intervention in Kashmir more attractive than it had been through all the years of the Afghanistan imbroglio. In a sense, then, Op Topac probably does describe a policy shift of sorts that was going on in Pakistan at the time. For one of

the better-argued Indian essays from this perspective, see A. G. Noorani, "Pakistan's Complicity in Terrorism in J & K: The Evidence and the Law," *Indian Defence Review* (January 1992), pp. 24–34. Most of Noorani's evidence is, nevertheless, circumstantial.

5. This is the argument, capsulized, of Afsir Karim, *Counter Terrorism: The Pakistan Factor* (New Delhi: Lancer International, 1991).

6. Lieutenant General (Rtd.) K. V. Krishna Rao, interview with the author, Srinagar, 3 July 1993. Rao, appointed to his second term as governor by Prime Minister Narasimha Rao (no relative) in March 1993, served earlier in the same capacity from July 1989 to January 1990. General Rao is the author of a sophisticated study of Indian security problems, *Prepare or Perish: A Study of National Security* (New Delhi: Lancer Publishers, 1991). In it he writes (p. 303) of Kashmir:

    > While the country [India] should be prepared in every respect to give a befitting reply to Pakistan, should she resort to any adventurist action, the situation in Jammu and Kashmir must be handled with great care. It has to be realized that the problem is basically political and requires a political solution, while maintaining control from the law and order point of view. The population must not be further alienated under any circumstances and every effort must be made to win them over. A way must be found for involvement of the people's representatives immediately. Legitimate grievances of the people must be remedied without loss of time. The Administration must be revamped and regional disparities removed. Irresponsible talk about abrogation of Article 370 [granting formal constitutional autonomy to Kashmir state], teaching the Kashmiris a lesson and so on must stop. On the other hand, every effort should be made to regain the confidence of the local population. They must be made to feel that the entire country is behind them, understands their problems and is prepared to do everything possible to alleviate them. For their part, the people should try and explain to the extremist elements the futility of indulging in violence at the behest of a foreign power (who could never be their well-wisher) and the need to adopt constitutional methods for the redressal of any of their legitimate grievances.

7. Interview with the author, New Delhi, June 1991.

8. Interviews with the author, New Delhi and Rawalpindi, June-July 1993.

9. Jagmohan, *My Frozen Turbulence in Kashmir.*

10. Interview with the author, New Delhi, 10 July 1993.

11. Reference here is strictly to the period *since* establishment of the CFL in 1949. There was, of course, a third major instance of infiltration in the Kashmir conflict, but it occurred in the period *prior* to formation of the CFL and was certainly not covert. It was India's complaint to the UN Security Council on 1 January 1948 that Pakistan was giving aid to tribal invaders of the state of Jammu and Kashmir that precipitated international intervention in the Kashmir conflict in the first place.

12. For one critical account, see Mohammad Musa, *My Version: India-Pakistan War 1965* (Lahore: Wajidalis, 1983), pp. 35-44. Musa was commander-in-chief of the Pakistan army at the time of Operation Gibraltar.

13. Robert Wirsing, "The Indo-Pakistan Boundary Dispute in Kashmir: The Potential for Conflict Management on the Line of Control and an Assessment of Policy Alternatives for the United States," unpublished contract research report prepared for the Office of Research, Bureau of Intelligence & Research, U.S. Department of State, Washington, D.C. (21 December 1991), pp. 35–47.

14. Indian army officers briefing the author on the infiltration problem in June 1991 at 15th Corps headquarters in Srinagar made no effort to conceal the fact that precise data, whether in regard to the number of Kashmiri trainees in Pakistan or the number, type or location of training camps, simply didn't exist. Many of the camps, they said, were quite small, very modestly outfitted, located in remote areas, and easily shifted.

15. The interviews were conducted at 15th Corps headquarters in Srinagar. A total of 34 captives were included, in two separate groups, for a period of two hours. Indian army officers were present and acted, when necessary, as translators. There is no question that the captives, whose future well-being was obviously at stake, "slanted" their testimony to suit their captors' interests. Most had little or no formal education, however, and their comments did not appear to have been rehearsed.

16. Interview with the author, June 1991. The quotation is abbreviated and paraphrased, but faithfully reflects the speaker's statement.

17. Apparently, the changeover by the government of Pakistan was quite swift. According to one (possibly inflated) report, by October 1990 "Pakistani intelligence was training as many as 4,000 JKHM [Hizb-ul Mujahideen] cadre against fewer than 1,500 of the JKLF." Prem Shankar Jha, "Irresponsible Brinkmanship," *The Hindu,* 18 December 1991.

18. Edward A. Gargan, "12 Are Killed as Pakistani Police Fire on Kashmiris Marching Toward Border," *The New York Times,* 13 February 1992, p. A3. Confrontations between the marchers and police occurred over several days at a number of different points along the border. Estimates of the total number of marchers ranged from 5,000 to 20,000. Following the most violent clashes, Pakistan's federal minister for Kashmir Affairs, Sardar Mehtab Ahmad Khan Abbasi, was reported to have denied categorically in the National Assembly in Islamabad that the marchers had been fired upon by law enforcing agencies. Aroosa Alam, "Police Firing on Marchers Denied," *The Muslim* (Islamabad), 14 February 1992. See also Shekhar Gupta, "Pakistan: Raising the Stakes," *India Today* (New Delhi), 29 February 1992, pp. 14–15; and Shakil Shaikh and A. Q. Ishrat, "15,000 Marchers Reach Chinari," *The Muslim,* 12 February 1992.

19. A number of the captive infiltrators interviewed by the author in June 1991 at the Indian army's 15th Corps Headquarters in Srinagar claimed to have participated in the March demonstration. One of them displayed what appeared to be torture marks on his body, according to him inflicted by Pakistani police interrogators after the demonstration was broken up.

20. The figure of 8.5 million includes 1.98 million in Pakistan-controlled Azad Jammu and Kashmir and an estimated 450,000 in Pakistan's so-called Northern Areas.

21. Amanullah Khan, chairman of the Rawalpindi-based wing of the JKLF, was born in Gilgit. Most of his JKLF associates in Pakistan are culturally Punjabi.

22. Interview with the author, Srinagar, July 1993.

23. Sikh militants from the Punjab have on occasion launched attacks on Hindus in Jammu; and a number of Buddhist militant groups are active in Leh district.

24. Estimated total strength of the militants then was 10,000 to 12,000, including 8,000 to 9,000 in the valley and 2,000 to 3,000 in Pakistan-controlled Kashmir.

25. Jagmohan, *My Frozen Turbulence in Kashmir,* pp. 703–4.

26. Interview with the author, Rawalpindi, 9 June 1993. An American diplomat interviewed by the author in New Delhi in May 1991 gave the figure 200 as the total of Kashmiri militant organizations then active in the state.

27. For details on Dr. Guru's assassination, see Asia Watch and Physicians for Human Rights, *The Human Rights Crisis in Kashmir: A Pattern of Impunity* (New York: Human Rights Watch, June 1993), pp. 141-46; "Prominent Doctor Slain in Kashmir," United Press International wire-service, 1 April 1993 [CompuServe Mail]; and Yusuf Jameel, "Kashmiri Militants Deny Killing Rebel Leader," Reuters wire-service, 2 April 1993 [CompuServe Mail].

28. By 1993, the THK included some 12 groups—Islamic Students League, Mehaz-i-Islami, Islamic Study Circle, Jamiat Ahle Hadith, Jama'at-i-Islami-i-Kashmir, Mahaz-i-Azadi, Muslim Conference, People's League, Tehreek Nifaz-i-Shariat-i-Islami, Dukhtaran-e-Millat, Jamiat Ulema-i-Islam, and Muslim League.

29. Arthur Max, "India-Kashmir's New Leaders," Assocated Press wire-service, 10 November 1993 [CompuServe Mail]; and "Kashmir: Led by a Saint," *The Economist,* 9 October 1993, pp. 36–40.

30. See the comments, for example, on "curriculum changes" in Pakistani training camps in the Government of India publication, *Facets of a Proxy War* (New Delhi, 1993), p. 25.

31. Interview with the author, New Delhi, June 1991.

32. Interview with the author, Srinagar, July 1993.

33. See Asia Watch, *Kashmir Under Siege: Human Rights in India,* (New York: Human Rights Watch, 1991), pp. 129–53; and Asia Watch and Physicians for Human Rights, *The Human Rights Crisis in Kashmir: A Pattern of Impunity,* pp. 168–71.

34. Said by police to have been the largest mass killing of Hindu civilians by Muslim rebels since the uprising began, the incident seemed bound to provoke increased demands for even sterner crackdowns on the militants by Indian security forces. For details, see Omesh Kumar, "35 Killed in Indian Kashmir, Premier Calls for Stepped-up Vigil," United Press International wire-service; "Kashmiri Militants Kill 15 Hindu Bus Passengers," Reuters wire-service; and Binoo Joshi, "India-Kashmir," Associated Press wire-service, 14 August 1993 [CompuServe Mail].

35. Briefing of the author, Ministry of Home Affairs, New Delhi, July 1993.

36. Interview with the author, Srinagar, July 1993.

37. Interview with the author, New Delhi, June 1993.

38. Interview with the author, Srinagar, July 1993.

39. Interview with the author, New Delhi, June 1993.

Chapter 5

1. Interview with a senior police official, Srinagar, July 1993. For details on the mutiny, see Qaiser Mirza, "India-Kashmir," Associated Press wire-service, 22 April 1993; "Kashmiri Police Fight Indian Paramilitary Forces," Reuters wire-service, 22 April 1993; "Police Revolt in Kashmir, Three Policemen Killed in Punjab," United Press International wire-service, 23 April 1993; Yusuf Jameel, "Kashmir Police Strike Over Colleague's Death," Reuters wire-service, 23 April 1993; Yusuf Jameel, "Army Poised for Showdown with Kashmir Policemen," Reuters wire-service, 27 April 1993; Yusuf Jameel, "Troops in Indian Kashmir Disarm Police, Take Over," Reuters wire-service, 28 April 1993; Qaiser Mirza, "India-Kashmir," Associated Press wire-service, 28 April 1993; and "Authorities Fire 79 Police for Fomenting Rebellion," United Press International, 5 May 1993 [CompuServe Mail]. Senior Superintendent of Police Rajendra Kumar, the Hindu police chief of Srinagar, whose arrest for failing to intervene to prevent the death of their colleague had been demanded by the mutineers, was himself transferred out of the state. The state government ordered an official inquiry into the incident.

2. Balwinder Singh Bedi, for instance, who in 1993 was director general of police and the seniormost police official in Jammu and Kashmir state, is a Uttar Pradesh–born Sikh with years of service fighting the Sikh insurgency in the Punjab; and Amar Kapoor, the additional director general of police, who headed the all-important Criminal Investigation Division, is a Hindu.

3. India maintains at least 11 different paramilitary forces. Some that are not mentioned in the text, including the Ladakh Scouts and National Security Guards, are also either permanently or transiently based in Kashmir.

4. The higher figure is more common; but a Pakistani brigade commander on the LOC gave an estimate to the author in June 1993 closer to 100,000. He said that there were presently 88 battalions of BSF and CRPF troops in Kashmir, and that each battalion had roughly 1,000 men, yielding a total of 80,000 to 90,000.

5. The present governor of Jammu and Kashmir state, Lieutenant General (Rtd.) K. V. Krishna Rao, told the author in an interview in Srinagar on 3 July 1993 that currently there were over 300 companies of BSF and CRPF troops stationed in Kashmir, in contrast with only 36 based there in 1989, when Rao was in his first term as governor. On 23 June, Minister of State for Home Affairs (Internal Security) Rajesh Pilot stated at a press conference in New Delhi that there were presently 30 to 35 battalions of paramilitary forces in Kashmir, each battalion having between 600 and 800 troops. Neither Rao nor Pilot made clear whether by "Kashmir" was meant merely the valley or the entire state. In any event, both these estimates fell well short of figures suggested by neutral observers.

6. Interview with the author, early July 1993. He did not say to which of the CPOs they had been recruited.

7. The most recently formed of the CPOs, with the smallest representation in Kashmir, is the Rashtriya Rifles. Consisting mainly of ex-army soldiers, it is deployed today in the valley in near brigade strength (about 5,000 troops). For background and discussion of the

paramilitary forces, see Khusro Rustamji, "The Paramilitary-Army Interface," *Indian Defence Review* (January 1991), pp. 91–95; and the articles by J. F. Ribeiro, Ved Marwah, H. S. Sodhi, and Manvendra Singh in *Indian Defence Review* 8:1 (January 1993).

8. Pakistan army officers claim that Indian army divisions in the Valley of Kashmir are all significantly oversized, each carrying four brigades (instead of three), with the brigades themselves being heavily reinforced, each carrying five or six battalions (instead of three).

9. A spokesman for the Pakistan government claimed on 21 July 1993 that one Indian army division was already in process of being inducted into Kashmir while another was being readied. "Pakistan Says More Indian Troops Going to Kashmir," Reuters wire-service, 21 July 1993 [CompuServe Mail]. A Pakistani brigade commander on the LOC told the author in mid-June 1993 that the 6th Mountain Division was to be deployed in Jammu in the Poonch-Rajauri sectors of the LOC and that the 39th Mountain Division would be deployed at Srinagar.

10. "Indian Troops on China Border May Go to Kashmir," Reuters wire-service, 22 September 1993 [CompuServe Mail].

11. Briefing, 19th Infantry Division headquarters, Baramulla, June 1991.

12. As many as 150 infiltrators were discovered attempting to cross on this occasion. The Indians claim to have killed 72 of the infiltrators in the encounter, called Operation Dudhi by the Indians, which lasted three days. The author was briefed on this encounter at battalion headquarters at Chokibal by Colonel D. Kumar, Commander, 7th Assam Rifles, in June 1991.

13. Interview with the author, New Delhi, June 1991.

14. What the Indian army calls its Forward Defended Area along the border consists of three or four tiers of defensive lines. According to an Indian army general in command of troops on the LOC, the paramilitary forces (the Border Security Force, in other words) are ordinarily deployed no farther forward than the third or fourth tier. Implied, perhaps, was that if the infiltrators could make it through the initial—regular army–defended—tiers, then perhaps bribery might facilitate passage the rest of the way.

15. At a press conference in June 1993, Minister of State Rajesh Pilot commented that "the geography [in Kashmir] is totally different . . . We cannot use the same policy [in regard to sealing the border] in Kashmir [as in Punjab]."

16. Interview with the author, Baramulla, June 1991.

17. The battalion tactical headquarters of the Indian army at Bulbir Outpost (what the Pakistanis call DAT Top) is only two to three miles from Athmuqam and enjoys a commanding view of that section of the Neelam Valley. Pakistanis claimed in a briefing at Athmuqam that the Indians, employing 54 guns, had fired anywhere from 10,000 to 15,000 rounds at eight to ten villages in the subdistrict in the weeklong period. The author's visit to Athmuqam confirmed that damage from the shelling was extremely heavy.

18. Interview with the author, Athmuqam, June 1991.

19. A member of the UNMOGIP observer team in India suggested in an intervew with the author (May 1991) that the shelling, which was not only heavy but extremely expensive, revealed India's anger and frustration over the infiltration problem. It could serve no other conceivable purpose, he observed, except to signal Indian displeasure to the Pakistanis. The area of heaviest shelling, he noted, was also the area of heaviest infiltration. The Indians, he said, shell Pakistani villages, and the Pakistanis retaliate by shelling Indian gun emplacements.

20. This was apparently one of the first occasions when the new Hot Line facility connecting the two headquarters was brought into play, according to one source on the initiative of the Indians.

21. Pakistani officials complained in late September 1993 of especially heavy civilian casualties resulting from what they said was the Indian troops' "indiscriminate firing on civilians" across the LOC. "Indians Reported Stepping Up Firing in Kashmir," Reuters wire-service, 27 September 1993 [CompuServe Mail].

22. The pattern of small arms firing on the LOC seemed to vary considerably from sector to sector. According to a Pakistani brigade commander facing the Indians in what the Indians call the Uri sector (north of the Pir Panjal range), small arms fire across the LOC in this sector was very rare, and civilians, in spite of the fact that many of them lived in sight of Indian guns, were almost never targeted. He accounted for the variation with the suggestion that over most of the LOC's length in this sector Pakistani military outposts had a clear advantage in elevation, hence the Indians were vulnerable to reprisal. Moreover, in this sector, he suggested, the Indians had the Valley of Kashmir, with its insurgency, to their backs. Having one problem already, they did not want two. South of the Pir Panjal range, he indicated, the Indians generally held the advantage in elevation on the LOC *and* they had a relatively secure area, in Jammu, to their rear. In his opinion, prudence governed India's policy in regard to firing across the LOC.
As for the level of command at which this policy was determined, one can only guess. Judging by standard rules of engagement, machine gun fire on the scale occurring in summer 1993 on the LOC would have to be authorized on a routine basis at least at battalion, more likely at brigade, level. Broad policy covering such fire, however, would be the prerogative of the area commander (Northern Command) acting on the advice of and in consultation with the army's general headquarters.
Pakistani officials claimed in December 1993 that in the preceding three years Indian border guards had killed at least 600 Pakistani civilians in random shootings across the LOC. Musfirah Altaf, "Pakistan-India," Associated Press wire-service, 16 December 1993 [CompuServe Mail].

23. This set of Home Ministry statistics appeared on a handout supplied to the author by a third-country diplomatic source.

24. Governor (retired Lieutenant General) K. V. Krishna Rao told the author on 3 July that the army estimated that there had been a total of 500 infiltrators from Pakistan into Kashmir so far that year, a figure, he said, less than the corresponding figure for the same period in 1992. An official report on 24 August said that from April through July 1993, 113 infiltrators had been killed and 27 captured in border clashes. Arthur Max, "India-Afghans," Associated Press wire-service, 24 August 1993 [CompuServe Mail].

25. Gill Tudor, "U.S. Forces Pakistan to Stop Arming Kashmir Rebels," Reuters wire-service, 25 August 1993 [CompuServe Mail].

26. Interviewed by the author in Srinagar in July 1993, the official maintained that cross-border smuggling operations were only a small part of the immense corruption and "commercialization" that had overtaken the insurgency in recent years, affecting both the militants and the security forces very deeply.

27. Indian army officers claim that the infiltrators are generally guided across the hazardous Indian forward-defended area by local inhabitants, frequently Gujjar Muslims who traditionally tend herds of goats or sheep in the hills rising on all sides of Kashmir Valley. The pay is apparently lucrative enough—currently a rifle or two plus as much as $100 per head—to overcome anxiety over the dangers obvious in such service.

28. A rocket attack by the militants in May 1993 on the state government's secretariat building in the heart of Srinagar's security zone killed two government employees and reminded the rest of their extreme vulnerability. George Joseph, "Muslim Guerrilla Attack Kills Two, Spreads Panic," United Press International wire-service, 12 May 1993 [CompuServe Mail]. In spite of particularly tight security measures to protect against attacks by the militants on Srinagar's airport, a powerful time bomb was somehow placed in an air-conditioning duct in the arrival terminal on 17 July 1993. It was defused, but it must have given the state police chief, who was a waiting passenger, second thoughts about existing security arrangements. "Bomb Defused at Kashmir's Srinagar Airport," Reuters wire-service, 18 July 1993 [CompuServe Mail]. When departing from that airport one week earlier, this author, though given VIP treatment, was frisked thoroughly (not counting electronic detection systems) *seven* times. Less fortunate mortals had to undergo at least *eight* physical friskings plus *two* thorough searches of their vehicles and luggage at police barriers set up on the approach road several hundred yards distant from the airport.

29. An unusually candid documentary film shown on Indian television in 1992, apparently intended to give a realistic portrayal of the difficulties faced by the BSF in the conduct of these cordon and search operations, had the opposite effect, on this viewer at least, of generating strong sympathy for their victims.

30. For a particularly interesting and energetic effort to justify them, by one who was most instrumental in installing them in the state, see Jagmohan, *My Frozen Turbulence in Kashmir,* pp. 518–49.

31. This description of TADA was given by a small group of Kashmiri Muslim attorneys, representing the state's Bar Association, interviewed by the author in Srinagar in July 1993. For additional details, see Amnesty International, *India: Torture, Rape & Deaths in Custody* (New York: Amnesty International, March 1992), pp. 18–19.

32. Jagmohan, *My Frozen Turbulence in Kashmir,* p. 527.

33. The press conference was held at the Foreign Correspondents Club in New Delhi on 23 June 1993.

34. The Home Ministry official, when the author pointed out far higher estimates given out by others (including this official's boss, Rajesh Pilot), refused to alter the 3,000 figure, insisting that this was indeed the absolute total of all Kashmiri militants then under detention or in jail under either TADA or the PSA. He said that 98 percent of these were held in prisons within Jammu and Kashmir state.

35. The 36,000 figure was given the author in a briefing by Pakistani military intelligence officials in Rawalpindi in June 1993. A small group of Kashmiri Muslim attorneys interviewed

by the author in Srinagar in early July 1993 argued, not unconvincingly, that the government's figures were absurdly low. They said that there were then 15,000 Kashmiri Muslims in jail under TADA and that an additional 5,000 were being held in preventive detention under the PSA. One of the attorneys, who had himself been held in various jails in Jammu and Kashmir state under both pieces of legislation for two years, insisted that in one jail alone—Kot Balwal jail in Jammu City—there were in summer 1993 about 1,400 Kashmiri Muslims being held under TADA or the PSA.

36. Useful reports on the human rights situation in Jammu and Kashmir state include:

1 Co-Ordination Committee on Kashmir, a consortium of Indian human rights groups, following team visits to Kashmir in 1990, 1992, and 1993: *Report on Kashmir Situation* (New Delhi, 22 April 1990), *Human Rights Situation in the Kashmir Valley* (New Delhi, 20 October 1992), *Kashmir: A Report to the Nation* (New Delhi, 1993).

2 Amnesty International: "Sopore: A Case Study of Extrajudicial Executions in Jammu and Kashmir," ASA 20/17/93 (April 1993); "Masoof Sultan: A Rare Survivor of Torture and Attempted Killing in Custody in Jammu and Kashmir," ASA 20/28/93 (June 1993); "India: Deaths and Torture at the Hands of the Security Forces on the Increase in Jammu and Kashmir, ASA 20/WU/05/93 (15 June 1993); and *India: Torture, Rape & Deaths in Custody.*

3 Asia Watch Committee: *Kashmir Under Siege: Human Rights in India* (New York: Human Rights Watch, May 1991).

4 Asia Watch Committee and Physicians for Human Rights: *The Human Rights Crisis in Kashmir: A Pattern of Impunity* (New York: Human Rights Watch, June 1993); "Rape in Kashmir: A Crime of War," vol. 5, no. 9 (9 May 1993); and *The Crackdown in Kashmir: Torture of Detainees and Assaults on the Medical Community* (March 1993).

37. The army's denigration of the police and paramilitary forces is apparently a deeply-ingrained tradition. See Rustamji, "The Paramilitary-Army Interface," p. 95.

38. Interview with the author, New Delhi, July 1993. As a consequence of these conditions, he noted, the troops' loyalty to the officers was somewhat lacking and so was the officers' ability to enforce the discipline that the job in Kashmir required.

39. Asia Watch and Physicians for Human Rights, *The Human Rights Crisis in Kashmir: A Pattern of Impunity,* pp. 86–90.

40. Interview with the author, New Delhi, June 1993. He confessed some admiration for the hardcore militants who were almost impossible to crack even under severe torture; but even they, he said, could usually be made to talk by threatening harm to their families.

41. In the face of the author's considerable skepticism, this source insisted that the security forces had raped no more than 15 women in Kashmir since the uprising began, while the Kashmiri militants, in the same period, had raped over 70.

42. In mid-December 1993, the Indian government o\fficially acknowledged having punished about 150 army personnel for violating human rights. At the same time, parliament approved setting up a National Human Rights Commission empowered to investigate future abuses. "India Punishes Troops on Rights Abuse," Reuters wire-service, 18 December 1993 [CompuServe Mail].

Chapter 6

1. See, for example, Khushwant Singh, "India, the Hindu State," *The New York Times,* 3 August 1993, p. A15; Edward A. Gargan, "Rising Tide of Hindu Hostility Is Worrying India's Muslims," *The New York Times,* 17 September 1993, p. A1; and "The Hindu Upsurge: The Road to Ayodhya," *The Economist,* 6 February 1993, pp. 21–23.

2. Samuel Huntington, "The Clash of Civilizations?" *Foreign Affairs* 72:3 (Summer 1993), pp. 22–49. For a number of critical replies to Huntington, see "Comments," *Foreign Affairs* 72:4 (September/October 1993), pp. 1–26.

3. Yubaraj Ghimire, "Looking Beyond Ayodhya," *India Today,* 15 July 1993, pp. 47–49.

4. "Opposition Party Begins Recruiting Ex-Soldiers to Private Militia," United Press International wire-service, 9 August 1993 [CompuServe Mail].

5. For background on the RSS and on Hindu revivalism in general, see Walter Andersen and Sridhar D. Damle, *Brotherhood in Saffron: Rashtriya Swayamsevak Sangh and Hindu Revivalism* (Boulder, CO: Westview Press, 1987).

6. Interview with the author, New Delhi, June 1993.

7. Dinner conversation with the author, New Delhi, July 1993.

8. The validity of my informant's thesis seemed to be questioned somewhat in a survey taken of Indians in the immediate wake of the Ayodhya episode. The results of the survey indicated that destruction of the mosque received fairly strong support from Hindus and (not surprisingly) very little from Muslims. Hindu support, as my informant had suggested, was far from uniform. Strongest Hindu support, however, came not from the lumpen element but from respondents who were older, male, upper caste, and middle class—especially traders, small businessmen, and white-collar workers. Weakest support came from students and labor. Pradeep K. Chhibber and Subhash Misra, "Hindus and the Babri Masjid: The Sectional Basis of Communal Attitudes," *Asian Survey* 33:7 (July 1993), pp. 665–72. For the view that the Ayodhya issue and rabble-rousing will, in fact, *remain* central to BJP strategy, see Amulya Ganguli, "Mr Advani's Return: BJP as a One-Man, One-Issue Party," *The Indian Express,* 29 June 1993.

9. For commentary on these elections, see "India-Elections," Associated Press wire-service, 27 November 1993 [CompuServe Mail]; Neelam Jain, "India's Ruling Party Suffers Setbacks in State Polls," United Press International wire-service, 28 November 1993 [CompuServe Mail]; Gill Tudor, "India's Ruling Congress Party Bolstered by Polls," Reuters wire-service, 30 November 1993 [CompuServe Mail]; and Molly Moore, "Hindu Militants Slip in Indian Elections," Washington Post wire-service, 30 November 1993 [CompuServe Mail].

10. Interview with the author, New Delhi, 10 July 1993. With one minor exclusion, Jaswant Singh offered the interview entirely on the record.

11. Interview with the author, New Delhi, May 1991.

12. Harold A. Gould, "Fascism Wrapped in Saffron Robe," *The Times of India,* 1 July 1993.

13. "India's Rao Wins Majority in Parliament," Reuters wire-service, 30 December 1993 [CompuServe Mail].

14. By January 1992, Congress-I held 231 seats in the Lok Sabha, which then had an effective strength of 521 seats. With its 18 allies, it required 12 more members of parliament for a simple majority and 30 to gain a majority on its own.

15. Sitting deputies at the time of the third no-confidence motion totaled about 534. Apart from the votes for and against Rao, there were eight abstentions and about ten absences. Kashmir's six seats were vacant since there had been no elections held there since 1987.

16. Within days, the Janata Dal defectors were absorbed fully into the Congress-I, occasioning charges of "vote-buying" by the opposition.

17. In the 1991 Lok Sabha elections, the Muslim vote was shared about equally by the Congress-I and the left-leaning parties gathered into the Janata Dal and Left Front. Muslim votes for the BJP were neglible. The pattern of Muslim voting seemed to indicate that whichever party was in the best position to defeat the BJP got the bulk of Muslim support. "How India Voted," *India Today,* 15 July 1991, pp. 34–35.

18. In the 1993 state electoral contest in Uttar Pradesh, a state in which Muslims are about 17 percent of the population, a substantial share of the Muslim vote seems to have been cast for the winning leftist coalition—not a very good omen for the Congress-I.

19. "Rao Rival Attacks Indian Leader Again," Reuters wire-service, 18 August 1993 [CompuServe Mail].

20. The chief minister was referring, of course, to provisions of the Jammu and Kashmir state constitution barring sale of land to nonresidents. His comments were reported to the author by a civil servant in attendance at the meeting.

21. Interview with the author, New Delhi, June 1993.

22. Interview with the author, New Delhi, July 1993.

23. Interview with the author, New Delhi, June 1993.

24. Interview with the author, Srinagar, July 1993.

25. For a strong argument that the results of recent national elections have fundamentally transformed the Indian party system—and in the BJP's favor, see Yogendra K. Malik and V. B. Singh, "Bharatiya Janata Party: An Alternative to the Congress (I)?" *Asian Survey* 32:4 (April 1992), pp. 318–36. "Without a doubt," the authors conclude, "the BJP's overall performance showed that the party has the potential to emerge as an alternative to the Congress (I)."

26. Vijay Joshi, "India-Kashmir," Associated Press wire-service, 15 August 1993 [CompuServe Mail]; "We Could Be Friends, India's Rao Tells Pakistan," Reuters wire-service, 15 August 1993 [CompuServe Mail]; "Indian Forces on Alert, General Strike in Muslim Kashmir," United Press International wire-service, 15 August 1993 [CompuServe Mail]; and "Indian Lawmakers Call for Tougher Action Against Kashmir," United Press International wire-service, 16 August 1993 [CompuServe Mail]. See also Jawed Naqvi, "India's Rao Cautions Pakistan on Aid to Militants," Reuters wire-service, 24 September 1993 [CompuServe Mail].

27. Ajai Sahni, "Kashmir: Cynical Gambit," *Surya India* (June 1993), pp. 4–14.

28. The author attended a press conference held for Pilot at the Foreign Correspondents Club in New Delhi on 23 June 1993. The author's interview with Pilot a few weeks later in the Ministry of Home Affairs was conducted off the record.

29. On the Sopore incident, see George Joseph, "Three Paramilitary Officers Suspended As Much of Kashmir Observes Strike," United Press International wire-service, 8 January 1993 [CompuServe Mail]; and George Joseph, "Federal Ministers Study Cause of Death and Destruction in Kashmir Town," United Press International wire-service, 9 January 1993 [CompuServe Mail].

30. Jaitley has since then been transferred out of Kashmir.

31. Zaki has since then been severely injured in an automobile accident in Srinagar.

32. K. V. Krishna Rao, *Prepare or Perish: A Study of National Security* (New Delhi: Lancer Publishers, 1990), p. 258.

33. Interview with the author, Srinagar, 3 July 1993.

34. Sahni, "Kashmir: Cynical Gambit," p. 6.

35. Interview with the author, Srinagar, 4 July 1993.

36. Interview with the author, New Delhi, June 1993.

37. Interview with the author, New Delhi, June 1993.

38. Interview with the author, New Delhi, July 1993.

39. Interview with the author, Srinagar, July 1993.

40. See, for instance, the editorial "Not Good Enough" in *The Times of India,* 11 June 1993.

41. Interview with the author, Srinagar, 3 July 1993.

42. Qaiser Mirza, "India-Kashmir," Associated Press wire-service, 15 July 1993 [CompuServe Mail]. Insofar as the 10,000 jobs in the "state police department" were concerned, Pilot, who presumably meant to include paramilitary forces as well, may have been misquoted.

43. Yusuf Jameel, "Kashmir Strike Rejects Indian Economic Package," Reuters wire-service, 20 July 1993 [CompuServe Mail].

44. "Strike to Snub Indian Minister Cripples Kashmir," Reuters wire-service, 10 September 1993 [CompuServe Mail].

45. Pilot publicly denies ever having met or in any way to have contacted or approached Dr. Guru.

46. Interview with the author, Islamabad, June 1993.

47. Interview with the author, Srinagar, July 1993.

48. Interview with the author, Srinagar, July 1993.

49. Michael Perry, "Islamic States Condemn Iraq Over Kuwait," Reuters wire-service, 28 April 1993 [CompuServe Mail]; and "Islamic Report Accuses India of Repression in Kashmir," Reuters wire-service, 27 April 1993 [CompuServe Mail].

50. Skepticism about the fidelity of Muslim states to their brother Kashmiris was expressed openly in Pakistan at the time by the Kashmiri expatriate leader Amanullah Khan and by Sardar Abdul Qayyum Khan, then prime minister of Azad Kashmir. "Kashmiri Leader Seeks Moslem Arms, Money to Fight," Reuters wire-service, 15 May 1993 [CompuServe Mail].

51. Arthur Max, "India-Afghans," Associated Press wire-service, 24 August 1993 [CompuServe Mail].

52. In August, Indian security forces reported killing an Afghan national, Akbar Bhai (or Akbar brother), said to have been a member of the Hezb-i-Islami militia of the Afghan prime minister Hekmatyar. "Afghan Killed by Security Men in India's Kashmir," Reuters wire-service, 8 August 1993 [CompuServe Mail]. And in July, Indian security forces allegedly killed one of Hekmatyar's former bodyguards, Mohammed Akbar Qureshi. Max, "India-Afghans."

53. Omesh Kumar, "India to Ask Afghanistan to Halt Mujahideen," United Press International wire-service, 8 August 1993 [CompuServe Mail].

54. Interviews with the author, Srinagar, July 1993.

55. The argument made by some Indians that there was an absolute constitutional bar against an extension beyond three years and that the government faced a constitutional crisis on 5 September 1993 (the three years plus a two-month grace period) unless it restored democracy to Kashmir in the meantime was based on a misreading (or nonreading) of the Constitution.

56. In late August, both houses of the Indian parliament reportedly approved the government's request for extension of direct rule in Kashmir. "Red Cross Officials Discuss Kashmir With India," Reuters wire-service, 26 August 1993 [CompuServe Mail]; and "Indian Parliament Extends Direct Rule in Troubled Kashmir," United Press International wire-service, 28 August 1993 [CompuServe Mail]. The state's elected chief minister, Farooq Abdullah, resigned his position in January 1990. Governor Jagmohan dissolved the legislative assembly in February. From then until the imposition of direct federal rule in July, the state was ruled by the governor under the authority of the state's own constitution.

57. Interview with the author, Srinagar, July 1993. Ex-Chief Minister Farooq Abdullah spent about three months in Srinagar in summer 1992, at all times under very heavy guard and with his movements severely restricted, in an apparent effort to test the political waters. He made it clear in an interview with Harinder Baweja at the time that he was under no illusions about his ability under existing circumstances to participate freely in elections in the valley. Harinder Baweja, "Kashmir: Normalcy Is a Pipedream," *India Today*, 31 August 1992, pp. 32–36.

58. Interview with the author, Srinagar, July 1993.

59. Interview with the author, Srinagar, July 1993.

Chapter 7

1. For discussion and documentation of these efforts, see Rosalyn Higgins, *United Nations Peacekeeping, 1946–1967, Documents and Commentary,* vol. II: *Asia* (London: Oxford University Press, 1970), pp. 313–417; K. Sarwar Hasan (ed.), *The Kashmir Question: Documents on the Foreign Relations of Pakistan* (Karachi: Pakistan Institute of International Affairs, 1966); Josef Korbel, *Danger in Kashmir* (Princeton, NJ: Princeton University Press, 2nd ed., 1966), pp. 97–197; Sisir Gupta, *Kashmir: A Study in India-Pakistan Relations* (Bombay: Asia Publishing House, 1966), pp. 110–254, 310–42; and Alastair Lamb, *Kashmir: A Disputed Legacy, 1846–1990* (Hertingfordbury, U.K.: Roxford Books, 1991), pp. 158–81.

2. See Alastair Lamb, *The Kashmir Problem* (New York: Praeger, 1966), pp. 112–34; and Rosalyn Higgins, "Findings on the Rann of Kutch," *The World Today* 24:4 (April 1968), pp. 134–36.

3. See Thomas Perry Thornton, "The Indo-Pakistani Conflict: Soviet Mediation at Tashkent, 1966," in Saadia Touval and I. William Zartman (eds.), *International Mediation in Theory and Practice* (Boulder, CO: Westview Press, 1985), pp. 141–71; and Ian Clark, "The USSR and the Tashkent Conference: A Reinterpretation Ten Years After," *Australian Journal of Politics and History* 23:2 (August 1977), pp. 207–18.

4. Thornton, "The Indo-Pakistani Conflict," p. 162.

5. Of late, Pakistan has been calling for the dispatch to Jammu and Kashmir state of a UN fact-finding mission to investigate allegations of humans rights violations there by Indian forces. "Pakistan Urges U.N. Mission to Kashmir" and "Pakistan Accuses India of Kashmir 'Reign of Terror,'" Reuters wire-service, 29 September 1993 [CompuServe Mail]. In October 1993, the government of Pakistan accepted UN Secretary-General Boutros Boutros Ghali's offer to mediate between New Delhi and Islamabad over Kashmir. "Pakistan Accepts U.N. Mediation Offer for Kashmir," United Press International, 2 October 1993 [CompuServe Mail].

6. Interview with the author, New Delhi, 8 July 1993. The letter delivered to the president of the UN Security Council by the Indian representative to the United Nations on 1 January 1948, apart from inviting UN action, also expressed India's conditional commitment to Kashmiri self-determination "by the recognized method of a plebiscite or referendum . . . under international auspices." Of course, the Indian government long ago disavowed it, but this commitment to a popular plebiscite, which we scrutinized in detail in Chapter 1, has itself been a very troublesome legal problem for India.

7. Interview with the author, Srinagar, July 1993.

8. Y. D. Gundevia, *Outside the Archives* (Hyderabad: Sangam Books, 1984), p. 248. Gundevia, at the time secretary of commonwealth relations and a participant in the talks, provides a highly detailed and illuminating account of them.

9. *Ibid.*, p. 293.

10. Retired Major General D. K. Palit, interview, New Delhi, 30 May 1990. With Gundevia, Palit prepared the maps showing the proposed modifications to the CFL for Swaran Singh's use during his private sessions with Bhutto. For Palit's revealing account of the talks, see *War in High Himalaya: The Indian Army in Crisis, 1962* (New Delhi: Lancer International, 1991), pp. 368–407.

11. Jyoti Bhusan Das Gupta, *Jammu and Kashmir* (The Hague: Martinus Nijhoff, 1968), pp. 374–75.

12. For commentary on these talks, see Jane Macartney, "Pakistan-India Talks Last Chance for Bilateral Solution," Reuters wire-service, 31 December 1993 [CompuServe Mail]; Raja Asghar, "Pakistan, India Say No Progress in Kashmir Talks," Reuters wire-service, 3 January 1994 [CompuServe Mail]; and "Indian Delegation Heads Home After Kashmir Talks Fail," United Press International, 3 January 1994 [CompuServe Mail].

13. In spring 1991, India and Pakistan reached two confidence-building agreements, one providing for advance warning to each other of troop movements, the other against violation of each other's air space.

14. An earlier version of the material in this section was published in *Indian Defence Review* (July 1991). Reprinted by permission of the publisher.

15. The first meeting of the two leaders was in November 1984 at the funeral of the assassinated Indian Prime Minister Indira Gandhi, Rajiv's mother.

16. In addition to the three agreements mentioned, the package announced on 17 December also included agreements: (1) to renew talks between the finance ministers of the two countries on trade and economic relations; (2) to resume efforts to consolidate Pakistan's draft No-War Pact and India's draft Treaty of Peace, Friendship and Cooperation; and (3) to reactivate the Joint [Indo-Pakistani] Ministerial Commission and its several subcommissions. Mohammad Ali Siddiqi, "Pakistan, India Agree Not to Attack Each Other's N-facilities," *Dawn* (Karachi), 18 December 1985; and Aslam Shaikh, "Zia Foresees Speedy Normalisation," *The Muslim* (Islamabad), 18 December 1985.

17. The discussion in this chapter on the contents of the Siachen negotiations is based mainly on author interviews and official briefings conducted during visits to the subcontinent in September–October 1989 (Pakistan), June–July 1990 (India and Pakistan), May–June 1991 (India and Pakistan), and June–July 1993 (India and Pakistan). Interviews with senior military officers and diplomats included seven Pakistanis and four Indians directly involved in the negotiations. Both governments authorized army-escorted visits by the author to the Siachen area.

18. "Cordial, Frank Talks on Siachen Issue," *Dawn* (Karachi), 13 January 1986.

19. Interview with the author, Islamabad, July 1990.

20. See Salamat Ali, "Back to the Old Refrain," *Far Eastern Economic Review,* 20 November 1986, p. 52.

21. The agreement on prohibition of attack on nuclear installations and facilities was finally signed in Islamabad on 31 December 1988 on the occasion of Rajiv Gandhi's long-postponed first visit to Pakistan. By that time, Benazir Bhutto had taken office as prime minister of Pakistan. Barbara Crossette, "Gandhi Ends 3-Day Visit to Pakistan," *The New York Times,* 1 January 1989, p. 3A. The two countries exchanged formal instruments of ratification of the agreement on 27 January 1991, by which time Bhutto had been replaced by Prime Minister Nawaz Sharif. "Pakistan, India Exchange Papers," *The Muslim,* 28 January 1991.

22. "Rajiv's Visit Not Possible Before May Next," *The Muslim,* 26 February 1986; "Rajiv Hints at Putting Off Visit to Pakistan," *Dawn,* 12 March 1986; and "Ground Work Needed for Rajiv's Visit," *Dawn,* 3 May 1986.

23. See M. Ziauddin, "Blow Hot, Blow Cold," *The Herald* (Karachi), April 1986, pp. 27–28.

24. Richard N. Haass, "South Asia: Too Late to Remove the Bomb?" *Orbis* 32:1 (Winter 1988), p. 112.

25. Ravi Rikhye, *The War That Never Was: The Story of India's Strategic Failures* (Delhi: Chanakya Publications, 1988), p. 19. For a Pakistani point of view on Brass Tacks, see Samina Yasmeen, "India and Pakistan: Why the Latest Exercise in Brinkmanship?" *Australian Journal of Politics and History* 34:1 (1988), pp. 64–71.

26. Steven R. Weisman, "India and Pakistan Reach Pact to Ease Tension Over Troops," *The New York Times*, 5 February 1987, p. 1A.

27. Interview with the author, Islamabad, July 1990.

28. Interview with the author, Islamabad, June 1990.

29. See, for example, the editorial "Outlook on Siachen," *The Times of India*, 12 May 1989. Optimism was generally guarded in the weeks prior to the fifth round, however, and skeptical reports were just as common at that time. See, for example, N. Vasuki Rao, "Breakthrough on Siachen Unlikely," *The Indian Express*, 12 June 1989.

30. The briefing, given in the presence of senior Indian army officers, was presented by the Public Relations Directorate of the Ministry of Defence.

31. This point is in reply to Pakistan's claim, discussed above in Chapter 2, that its *administrative* control over the Siachen area found international support in two respects: (1) the practice of virtually all international climbing and trekking expeditions to the Siachen area since it was opened to them in 1974 of requesting Pakistani rather than Indian authorization; and (2) the fact that most major Western atlas-makers began in the late 1970s to show the LOC reaching northeastward all the way to the Karakoram pass, thus showing the Siachen glacier entirely in Pakistani territory.

32. "Agreement to Resolve Siachen Issue," *The Muslim*, 18 June 1989; and Richard M. Weintraub, "Pakistan and India Take Steps to Defuse Long Confrontation Over Siachen Glacier," *The Washington Post*, 20 June 1989, p. A28.

33. "It is a tremendous breakthrough," a Pakistani diplomat reportedly said of the just-concluded talks. "Once the politicians signal that it won't be a flashpoint, the rest can be a protracted process. We have removed one of the major issues of recent times." Quoted by Weintraub, "Pakistan and India Take Steps to Defuse Long Confrontation Over Siachen Glacier." See also the editorial "Siachen: Reason for Hope," *The Muslim*, 19 June 1989.

34. See, for example, the editorial "Breaking the Ice Over Siachen," *The Hindustan Times* (New Delhi), 18 June 1989; and "Army Officers to Fix Positions," *The Hindu* (Madras), 18 June 1989. This last report was authored (without byline) by Manoj Joshi, probably the best informed of India's journalists on the subject of the Siachen dispute. In it, he said that India and Pakistan had "achieved a sort of breakthrough on the Siachen Glacier issue by agreeing to work toward a comprehensive settlement based on redeployment of forces. . . . The essence of the proposed settlement is that India will vacate the glacier it has been holding at an enormous cost in men and material since 1984. This is an obvious concession to Pakistan. . . . [I]t was felt that a concession should be given to the democratically elected government of Ms. Benazir Bhutto—which could claim that it has succeeded

through diplomacy what Gen. Zia had failed to achieve by force, in the wider interest of normalising Indo-Pakistani relations."

35. "It's a Long Road to Peace in Siachen," *The Hindu,* 21 June 1989.

36. According to a report circulated in the Indian press, a taped version of the airport press conference quoted the Pakistani foreign secretary as saying that the Siachen talks "had led to a significant advance `in the sense that both sides have committed themselves to an observance of the Simla Agreement and re-location of forces to positions occupied at the time of the Simla Agreement. The exact location of these positions will be worked out in detail by military authorities of the two countries.'" "Report on Singh's Statement Denied," *The Indian Express,* 23 June 1989.

37. S. K. Singh was reported to have replied to Dr. Khan's comments with the statement: "I would like to thank the Foreign Secretary, Dr. Humayun Khan, and endorse everything he has said." *Ibid.*

38. "India Denies Accord on Siachen," *The Muslim,* 20 June 1989.

39. A spokesman for India's Ministry of External Affairs reportedly suggested that the Pakistani foreign secretary "was perhaps being too precise in an area where there is a great deal of imprecision. The exact [boundary] line may be anywhere between where we are now and where we were before 1972." Quoted by Ramindar Singh, "Breaking the Ice," *India Today,* 15 July 1989.

40. "India Says No to '72 Troop Pullback Status," *The Telegraph* (Calcutta), 20 June 1989; Manoj Joshi, "It's a Long Road to Peace in Siachen," *The Hindu,* 21 June 1989; "Siachen May Be Discussed With Benazir," *The Muslim,* 24 June 1989; and Sanjoy Hazarika, "India and Pakistan Plan Pullout of Troops From Disputed Glacier," *The New York Times,* 28 June 1989, p. 2A.

41. Salim Bokhari, "Pak Confirms Siachen Agreement," *The Muslim,* 21 June 1989. See also Ghani Jafar, "Spanner in Normalisation?" *The Muslim,* 21 June 1989.

42. Interview with the author, Islamabad, July 1990.

43. Kuldip Nayar, one of India's foremost journalists, insisted that the Pakistani interpretation of the accord was accurate. The Pakistani foreign secretary, he said, was guilty only "of jumping the gun." The specific contents of the agreement, he wrote, "were to be disclosed after the elections in India. The Army commanders of the two countries . . . would have brought about the withdrawal to positions that Humayun Khan has indicated. But between now and then, New Delhi would have got time to prepare public opinion to accept such an accord in the interest of friendly relations with Pakistan." Rajiv Gandhi's hasty denial of the agreement, Nayar observed, was not proper and only confirmed Pakistani suspicion of New Delhi's intentions. "Mess-up Over Siachen," *The Tribune,* 13 July 1989.

44. Interview with the author, New Delhi, June 1990.

45. Interview with the author, June 1990.

46. "Two-day Pak, India Talks on Siachen Open," *The Muslim,* 11 July 1989; and Manoj Joshi, "Siachen Zone to Be Demilitarised," *The Hindu,* 27 June 1989.

47. Interview with the author, Rawalpindi, October 1989.

48. Interviews with the author, New Delhi, June 1990.

49. Steve Coll, "Gandhi Visit to Pakistan Signals Thaw," *The Washington Post*, 17 July 1989, p. A12.

50. According to press accounts, the joint communique released at the end of the talks on 17 July 1989 said that the Indian and Pakistani leaders had

> reviewed the discussions held on the Siachen issue at the levels of Defence Secretaries and the military authorities of Pakistan and India in June and July 1989 respectively. In this context, they approved the joint statement issued at the end of the Defence Secretaries' talks on June 17.
>
> Taking note of these discussions, the two premiers directed that the Defence Secretaries of India and Pakistan should in their future meetings work towards a comprehensive settlement in accordance with the Simla Agreement and that this settlement should be based on the re-deployment of forces to reduce the chances of conflict and avoidance of the use of force, and further directed that the military authorities should continue discussions to determine future positions on the ground to which re-deployment would take place so as to conform to the Simla Agreement and ensure durable peace in the area. . . .

"Comprehensive Settlement of Siachen Agreed Upon," *The Muslim*, 18 July 1989.

51. Raja Zulfikar, "No Quick Solutions, Say Benazir, Rajiv," *The Muslim*, 18 July 1989. Some of Gandhi's comments at the press conference seemed designed to nail shut any immediate prospects for a breakthrough in relations with Pakistan. In reply to one question, he reportedly declared that "the question of a plebiscite [in Kashmir] is out." And in reply to another, he is alleged to have said that Pakistan's nuclear installations, unlike India's, were under the direct control of the military. The first trod upon Pakistan's near-sacrosanct legal position in regard to Kashmir, the second upon the political sensitivities of Gandhi's elected civilian host.

52. *The Economist*, 22 July 1989, pp. 31–32.

53. "The Damp Squib," *The Muslim*, 19 July 1989.

54. "Glacier Talks Have Not Failed: Dixit," *The Tribune* (Chandigarh), 27 August 1989. Jyotindra Nath Dixit was at the time India's ambassador to Pakistan. Prime Minister Bhutto paid her first visit to the Siachen on 21 August—one day after the military-level talks ended. She used the occasion to reaffirm Pakistan's claim to the territory but held open the door to further negotiations. Maleeha Lodhi, "Benazir Visits Siachen, Rules Out Early Solution of Conflict," *The Muslim*, 22 August 1989; and "Additional Pressure on Delhi," *The Hindu*, 23 August 1989.

55. In the early months of 1990, according to the highly controversial account of an American writer, India and Pakistan faced one another in what he called "the most dangerous nuclear confrontation of the postwar era." Seymour M. Hersh, "On the Nuclear Edge," *The New Yorker*, 29 March 1993, pp. 56–73. For a more moderate assessment of those months, see K. Subrahmanyam's interview of retired General V. N. Sharma, Chief of Army Staff of the Indian army at the time, "The Tuesday Interview: 'It's All Bluff and Bluster,'" *The Economic Times* (New Delhi), 18 May 1993.

56. M. L. Chibber, "Siachen Solution Will Help India, Pak," *The Times of India,* 13 June 1989, and "Siachen—The Untold Story (A Personal Account)," *Indian Defence Review,* January 1990, pp. 146-52.

57. Interview, New Delhi, June 1990. By mid–1990, incidentally, Chibber had shifted his views in regard to the Siachen negotiations. Pakistan's massive interference in Kashmir, he said, had made the Siachen dispute *totally* ill-suited as a starting point for India-Pakistan negotiations. It could only be settled, he insisted, as an integral part of a broader Kashmir settlement.

58. Interview with the author, New Delhi, May 1991.

59. Manoj Joshi, "The Chill on the Siachen," *Frontline* (New Delhi), 16–29 September 1989, p. 9. See also Cecil Victor, "Siachen: To Quit or Not to Quit?" *Patriot* (New Delhi), 1 September 1989.

60. A few days following this meeting, one of the persons present, a retired army officer who had served at Siachen, requested a meeting with the author. At this meeting, he took issue with Kaul's remarks, insisting that the Siachen, while it clearly had some limited strategic value for India, had become a very costly military cul-de-sac. Indian casualties at Siachen, he said, were unacceptably high and the morale of the troops was unquestionably on the decline. Whatever the generals might say, he noted, the troops were aware of public questioning of the Siachen's military value. Siachen, he stated, had become a major burden for the Indian army.

61. W. P. S. Sidhu, "Siachen: The Forgotten War," *India Today,* 31 May 1992, p. 60. The author of this article spent two weeks on the glacier with the Indian troops.

62. *Ibid.,* p. 71. A report in an international review at about the same time claimed that Indian expenditures on Siachen came to around $1.94 million a day. On a yearly basis, it said, this came to more than 10 percent of India's total annual defense budget for fiscal year 1992–93. Rita Manchanda, "India-Pakistan: Frozen Waste," *Far Eastern Economic Review,* 26 November 1992, pp. 28–29.

63. Nawaz Sharif and his archrival Benazir Bhutto both chose to highlight the Siachen issue in their public comments in New Delhi in May 1991 on the occasion of Rajiv Gandhi's funeral. Sharif had replaced Bhutto as prime minister in 1990.

64. The Sir Creek issue is a leftover of the 1965 Rann of Kutch dispute over delimitation of the marshlands on the Sind-Gujarat border. For details, see A. G. Noorani, "Sir Creek, Wular and Siachen," *The Indian Express,* 5 August 1991.

65. For newspaper accounts of these talks, see Ashraf Hashmi, "Pakistan Blames India for Failure of Siachen Talks," *The Muslim,* 12 November 1992; and "Agreement on Siachin Eludes India, Pakistan," *India News* (Washington, D.C.) 31:21 (1–15 November 1992).

66. Interview with the author, New Delhi, 8 July 1993.

67. Interview with the author, New Delhi, 29 May 1991.

68. Interview with the author, New Delhi, July 1993. Strong opposition to the Indian army's unconditional withdrawal from Siachen is also voiced by Shiv K. Sharma, "Siachen: A Fresh Perspective," *Defence Today* (New Delhi) 1:1 (August 1993), pp. 67–74. Sharma, a retired major general, commanded the division that launched the Indian army's takeover of the Siachen in 1984.

69. Anwar Iqbal, "Pakistan Recalls Envoy Amid Tense Relations With India," United Press International wire-service, 17 August 1993 [CompuServe Mail]; and "Pakistan Says India Harassing Its Diplomats," Reuters wire-service, 17 August 1993 [CompuServe Mail].

70. Press conference, Foreign Correspondents Club (New Delhi), 23 June 1993.

71. Interview with the author, New Delhi, June 1993.

Chapter 8

1. For a recent overview of potential solutions, see Raju G. C. Thomas, "Reflections on the Kashmir Problem," in Thomas (ed.), *Perspectives on Kashmir: The Roots of Conflict in South Asia* (Boulder, CO: Westview, 1992), pp. 30-34. See also Sisir Gupta, *Kashmir: A Study in India-Pakistan Relations* (Bombay: Asia Publishing House, 1966), pp. 469–79.

2. It has been suggested, for instance, that India and Pakistan formally accept the status quo, allowing for an interim or "cooling off" period of 20 years or so before attempting to reopen negotiations over the boundary. Sumit Ganguly, "Avoiding War in Kashmir," *Foreign Affairs* 69:5 (Winter 1990–91), p. 71. Included was the recommendation that this agreement be coupled with a "no-war" pact.

3. A considerable fuss was raised in the Indian press in May 1993 over an alleged suggestion by Shimon Peres, the visiting Israeli foreign minister, that resettlement of non-Muslims in Kashmir, like the Jewish takeover of Palestinian land in the occupied territories, might be a long-term solution to the Kashmir problem. Whether Peres ever made the suggestion hasn't been established. The idea unquestionably has some support among Indian political right-wingers. In any event, the Indian government promptly declared its complete opposition to the idea. "Indian Minister Rules Out Settling Hindus in Kashmir," Reuter wire-service, 31 May 1993 [CompuServe Mail].

4. "Report Submitted by the United Nations Representative for India and Pakistan, Sir Owen Dixon, to the Security Council, 15 September 1950," in K. Sarwar Hasan (ed.), *The Kashmir Question: Documents on the Foreign Relations of Pakistan* (Karachi: Pakistan Institute of International Affairs, 1966), pp. 251–79.

5. See, for instance, Alastair Lamb, *The Kashmir Problem: A Historical Survey* (New York: Praeger, 1966), pp. 90–91.

6. Rumors circulated in summer 1992, for instance, that the Indian government was prepared to cede territory adjacent to Pakistan's Northern Areas "to secure a strategic highway linking Pakistan and China" if Pakistan would trade land adjacent to the Jammu division of the state in the south. Aziz Haniffa, "A Deal With Pakistan on Kashmir?" *India Abroad* (Washington, D.C.), 4 September 1992, p. 6.

7. See, for example, Gupta, *Kashmir: A Study in India-Pakistan Relations,* p. 478; B. G. Verghese, "Kashmir: The Fourth Option," *Defence Today* (New Delhi) 1:1 (August 1993), p. 65; and Bal Raj Madhok, *Kashmir: The Storm Center of the World* (Houston: A. Ghosh, 1992), p. 1821.

8. For generally balanced discussion of the pros and cons of secession, see Allen Buchanan, *Secession: The Morality of Political Divorce From Fort Sumter to Lithuania and Quebec* (Boulder, CO: Westview Press, 1991); and Lee C. Buchheit, *Secession: The Legitimacy of Self-Determination* (New Haven, CT: Yale University Press, 1978).

9. Reasons for avoiding the "radical surgery" of partition are given in Donald L. Horowitz, *Ethnic Groups in Conflict* (Berkeley: University of California Press, 1985), pp. 588–92.

10. Thomas, "Reflections on the Kashmir Problem, p. 32.

11. Kenichi Ohmae, "The Rise of the Region State," *Foreign Affairs* 72:2 (Spring 1993), pp. 78–87.

12. See, for example, Morton A. Halperin and David J. Scheffer, *Self-Determination in the New World Order* (Washington, D.C.: Carnegie Endowment for International Peace, 1992), especially pp. 71–93.

13. JKLF Chairman Amanullah Khan proposed in December 1993 a plan for settling the Kashmir dispute that included: (1) complete, simultaneous withdrawal of Indian and Pakistani troops and civil personnel from Kashmir; (2) reunification of the Indian- and Pakistani-controlled parts of Kashmir; (3) placement of the state under UN control for five to ten years; and (4) conduct of a plebiscite. "Jailed Separatist Urges U.N. Control for Kashmir," Reuters wire-service, 23 December 1993 [CompuServe Mail]; and "Kashmir Leader Disputes India, Pakistan Talks," United Press International wire-service, 31 December 1993 [CompuServe Mail].

14. Halperin and Scheffer, *Self-Determination in the New World Order,* p. 113.

15. Thomas, "Reflections on the Kashmir Problem," pp. 33–34.

16. V. Belokrinitsky et al., *Afghanistan & Kashmir: Report of a Joint American-Russian Study Mission* (The Asia Society & Institute of Oriental Studies, 1993), pp. 29–30. The plan proposed by this group included recognition by India of a special status for Kashmir; joint Indo-Pakistani control of both parts of Kashmir, possibly as part of a comprehensive, region-wide cooperative scheme (the "South Asia house") aimed at a regional confederation of which Kashmir would be a part. Also recommended, in spite of its seeming contradiction, was conversion of the LOC into a permanent international border.

17. Sarvepalli Gopal, *Jawaharlal Nehru: A Biography,* vol. III: 1956–1964 (Cambridge, MA: Harvard University Press, 1984), pp. 261–62.

18. Gupta, *Kashmir: A Study in India-Pakistan Relations,* pp. 476–77.

19. Raju Thomas, for instance, expressing a personal preference for a condominium-leading-to-confederation option, confesses that interest in it at least among Pakistani analysts and politicians is very slight. "Reflections on the Kashmir Problem," p. 35.

20. Ted Robert Gurr, *Minorities At Risk: A Global View of Ethnopolitical Conflicts* (Washington, D.C.: United States Institute of Peace, 1993), p. 301. Of the 11 autonomy cases studied, six were in the South Asian region. We should note here that Gurr's typology of autonomist arrangements is fivefold (confederalism, federalism, regional autonomism, regional administrative decentralization, and community autonomism), overlapping slightly this author's "modification of sovereignty" category. For additional background and case materials on the autonomy approach, see Hurst Hannum, *Autonomy, Sovereignty, and Self-Determination: The Accommodation of Conflicting Rights* (Philadelphia: University of Pennsylvania Press, 1990).

21. Jagat S. Mehta, "Resolving Kashmir in the International Context of the 1990s," in Thomas (ed.), *Perspectives on Kashmir,* pp. 388–409.

22. *Ibid.*, p. 401.

23. *Ibid.*, pp. 401–3.

24. *Ibid.*, p. 407.

25. *Ibid.*, p. 408.

26. A. G. Noorani, "Kashmir Vortex" (in 3 parts), *The Statesman* (New Delhi), 18, 19, 21 March 1992.

27. Selig S. Harrison, "Autonomy the Way Out for Kashmir Quagmire," *The Telegraph* (Calcutta), 10 March 1992. Harrison's proposal contains the familiar "soft border" component, withdrawal of armed forces under UN-supervised arrangements, and the simultaneous grant of autonomy by Pakistan to its section of Kashmir. Autonomy he defines as the surrender of authority "in all spheres except for defence, foreign affairs, communications and currency—including the right to conduct foreign aid and foreign trade dealings independently." Harrison's proposal is also spelled out in his article "South Asia and the United States: A Chance for a Fresh Start," *Current History* 91:563 (March 1992), pp. 97–105.

28. Verghese, "Kashmir: The Fourth Option," p. 65.

29. *Ibid.*, p. 66.

30. Typical of the many alarms rung in regard to these dangers are Graham E. Fuller, "The Breaking of Nations—and the Threat to Ours," *The National Interest*, no. 26 (Winter 1991/92), pp. 14–21; and Daniel Patrick Moynihan, *Pandaemonium: Ethnicity in International Politics* (New York: Oxford University Press, 1993).

31. See, for instance, Halperin and Scheffer, *Self-Determination in the New World Order*, pp. 82–93. These authors write that "the United States or other countries should not provide active support for an independence movement without first seeking to persuade the central government to take steps short of granting independence to deal with the demands. If the United States and the appropriate multilateral institution conclude that an independence movement has popular support but has not yet made the case for separation from the state, it should insist that the government blocking the independence movement live up to the criteria for the relationship between a government and its people [outlined in the book] for new states. Thus, a state resisting a separatist self-determination claim should move toward a constitutional democracy with genuinely free elections, respect for political opposition, limits on the police power of the state, and respect for individual human rights and minority rights. If, over time, a state is unable or unwilling to move in this direction, the case grows stronger for supporting a separatist self-determination movement that commits itself to creating such a government, and . . . permitting an international response if that government fails to live up to these commitments." See also Gurr, *Minorities At Risk*, pp. 292–98.

32. Gupta, *Kashmir: A Study in India-Pakistan Relations*, p. 476.

33. Ashutosh Varshney, "India, Pakistan, and Kashmir: Antinomies of Nationalism," *Asian Survey* 31:11 (November 1991), p. 1000.

34. Mehta, "Resolving Kashmir in the International Context of the 1990s," p. 403.

35. Verghese, "Kashmir: The Fourth Option," p. 65.

36. For a discussion of the use of plebiscites in settling self-determination claims, see Harold S. Johnson, *Self-Determination within the Community of Nations* (Leyden: Sijthoff, 1967), pp. 71–98. For a hostile view of the plebiscite instrument in international law, see Visuvanathan Rudrakumaran, "The 'Requirement' of Plebiscite in Territorial Rapprochement," *Houston Journal of International Law* 12:23 (1989), pp. 23–54.

37. For a recent discussion of the plebiscite option from a Kashmiri perspective, see Ghulam Nabi Fai, "The Plebiscite Solution for Kashmir: Why and How," in Thomas (ed.), *Perspectives on Kashmir,* pp. 168–74. According to Fai, the plebiscite should include the choice of independence.

38. Gidon Gottlieb, *Nation Against State: A New Approach to Ethnic Conflicts and the Decline of Sovereignty* (New York: Council on Foreign Relations Press, 1993).

39. *Ibid.,* p. 2.

40. *Ibid.,* p. x.

41. *Ibid.,* p. 36.

42. *Ibid.,* p. 39.

43. *Ibid.,* p. 93.

Chapter 9

1. Hearing, *Overview of Events in the South Asian Region,* Subcommittee on Asian and Pacific Affairs, Committee on Foreign Affairs, U.S. House of Representatives, 101st Congress, 2nd Session, 6 March 1990 (Washington, D.C.: U.S. Government Printing Office, 1990), p. 8.

2. The wording was slightly in error, since the Simla Agreement committed India and Pakistan only to meet and discuss "a final settlement of Jammu and Kashmir," not—as Pakistan would have wanted—the territorial *dispute* over Kashmir.

3. Hearing, 6 March 1990, p. 75.

4. "At the outset," said Solarz, "I should note that the U.S. is not, nor should it be, playing a major role in the substance of the dispute between India and Pakistan." *Ibid.,* p. 3.

5. Interview with the author, New Delhi, May 1991. According to some sources, there was no advance consultation about the contents of Kelly's statement with U.S. embassy personnel in either India or Pakistan.

6. Interview with the author, New Delhi, May 1991.

7. Michael Battye, "Angry India Accuses U.S. of Tilt to Pakistan," Reuters wire-service, 30 October 1993 [CompuServe Mail].

8. In one of the more thoughtful reactions, the left-leaning *Pioneer* observed editorially that Raphel's comment seemed "to have been made without taking into consideration the impact it is likely to have in moulding popular response to the strife in the Valley. . . . The instant reaction at the popular level will be to adopt not only a stridently anti-U.S. posture and thereby question the locus standi of Washington in settling the Kashmir issue,

but also lead to a demand for a hardline approach by the government in Delhi." Quoted in *ibid.* See also "U.S. Statement on Kashmir Kicks Off Political Storm," United Press International wire-service, 30 October 1993 [CompuServe Mail]; and "Indian Papers Rap U.S. Over Kashmir Remark," Reuters wire-service, 1 November 1993 [CompuServe Mail].

9. U.S. Information Service (New Delhi), Official Text: "Speech by Principal Deputy Assistant Secretary of State for South Asian Affairs, John R. Malott," India International Centre, 19 May 1993.

10. Kathy Gannon, "Pakistan," Associated Press wire-service, 9 January 1993 [CompuServe Mail].

11. Steven A. Holmes, "U.S. Says Terrorist Attacks Dropped Sharply in 1992," *The New York Times,* 1 May 1993, p. 4.

12. Official text, statement of John R. Malott, Deputy Assistant Secretary of State for South Asian Affairs, to the House Committee on Foreign Affairs, 28 April 1993; text supplied to the author by U.S. Embassy, New Delhi.

13. James A. Goldston and Patricia Gossman, "Once Paradise, Now Hell," *The Washington Post,* 25 May 1993, A19. Goldston and Gossman visited Kashmir on behalf of the human rights group Asia Watch.

14. The newest Asia Watch study of the human rights problem in Kashmir devotes fully 25 percent of its discussion of human rights *violations* in that state to those committed by militant organizations. Asia Watch and Physicians for Human Rights, *The Human Rights Crisis in Kashmir: A Pattern of Impunity* (New York: Human Rights Watch, June 1993).

15. On the first day of a major trade visit to India in mid-November 1993, Hurd was reported to have told an audience at the Indian International Centre in New Delhi that settlement of the Kashmir dispute should be seen as a political, not as a juridical, matter. "Events of 40, 50 years ago," he was quoted as saying, "are not decisive in settling it. We live in '93 and we need to look forward to a political agreement." Arguments over the 1947 Instrument of Accession, said the foreign secretary in an obvious reference to the badly received remarks on that subject only weeks earlier by the American assistant secretary, Raphel, weren't helpful. Gill Tudor, "British Minister Says Kashmir Is Political, Not Legal, Problem," Reuter wire-service, 15 November 1993 [CompuServe Mail].

16. UNMOGIP officers made a small effort on their own to enlarge the mission's mandate during the Indian army's siege of the Hazratbal mosque in Srinagar in October–November 1993. Responding to the Indian government's public announcement inviting "neutral witnesses" to observe the army siege, a number of the military observers, apparently with approval from UN headquarters in New York and in a clear departure from their mandate to police the cease-fire on the LOC, tried to approach the shrine. They were politely turned away, but their act of assertiveness did not pass unnoticed (or uncriticized) in New Delhi. Gill Tudor, "U.N. Observers Turned Away From Kashmir Siege," Reuter wire-service, 21 October 1993 [CompuServe Mail].

Chapter 10

1. Interview with the author, New Delhi, July 1993.

2. Interview with the author, Islamabad, June 1993.

3. One of Benazir Bhutto's first acts after taking over as prime minister of Pakistan for the second time was to reiterate her country's rejection of the independence option for Kashmir. Anwar Iqbal, "Pakistani Premier Rejects Option of Independent Kashmir," United Press International wire-service, 25 November 1993 [CompuServe Mail]. Bhutto was quoted as having told a group of newspaper editors in Islamabad that "the third option is a feeler floated to divide the Muslims of Kashmir, and to damage their struggle for freedom."

4. As put to the author by a very senior member of India's foreign policymaking elite, the United States, while avoiding resumption of military aid to Pakistan, should be arming India against China. This, he said, should not be worrisome to Pakistan. After all, he said, along with U.S. economic aid to India, the military cooperation would send a message to Islamabad that India and the United States were working together. That would act as a restraint on both India and Pakistan. Pakistan would know that India would not take precipitate, unilateral action against it. Interview with the author, New Delhi, July 1993.

5. Richard N. Haass, *Conflicts Unending: The United States and Regional Disputes* (New Haven, CT: Yale University Press, 1990), p. 87.

6. Interview with the author, Islamabad, June 1993.

7. Interview with the author, New Delhi, 8 July 1993.

8. The resolution adopted by UNCIP on 5 January 1949 specifies twice, in paragraphs 1 and 7(b), that the plebiscite would limit the choice of accession to either India or Pakistan. K. Sarwar Hasan (ed.), *The Kashmir Question: Documents on the Foreign Relations of Pakistan* (Karachi: Pakistan Institute of International Affairs, 1966), pp. 212–15.

INDEX

A

B

C

T

U